The Memoirs of Louis Bouyer

From Youth and Conversion to Vatican II,
the Liturgical Reform, and After

THE MEMOIRS
OF LOUIS BOUYER

From Youth and Conversion to Vatican II, the Liturgical Reform, and After

Translated and with a Preface by
John Pepino

Foreword by
Peter Kwasniewski

 Angelico Press

First published in French as
Louis Bouyer, *Mémoires*
© Les Éditions du Cerf, 2014
24, rue des Tanneries, 75013 Paris, France
First published in English by Angelico Press, 2015
English translation and Preface © John Pepino, 2015
Foreword © Peter Kwasniewski, 2015

For information, address:
Angelico Press
4709 Briar Knoll Dr.
Kettering, OH 45429
www.angelicopress.com

Pbk: 978-1-62138-142-6
Cloth: 978-1-62138-143-3

Cover design: Michael Schrauzer

CONTENTS

Foreword

Peter Kwasniewski

CONSIDERING THAT he was a highly influential theologian, a scholar of great stature, and a friend of other famous theologians in the Church of the twentieth century, it is strange how little attention has been paid in recent years to Fr. Louis Bouyer (1913–2004). Part of the problem is surely that Fr. Bouyer, although he came across as rather avant-garde in preconciliar years, ended up looking extremely conservative as he protested with increasing stridency against the depressing postconciliar auto-demolition of the Church. His honesty in assessing both the damage and the motivations—an honesty at times acerbic and always innocent of the hunger for human respect—was surely not destined to win him a favored place at the table of public opinion or a memorial from friends grateful for his criticism.

Nevertheless, at the zenith of his academic career, Fr. Bouyer was revered far and wide for a series of refined, far-reaching, ground-breaking studies, many of which had already attained the status of classics before his death—and all of which deserve to be rediscovered by a new generation. In such works as *The Meaning of the Monastic Life* (1950), *Liturgical Piety* (1955), *The Liturgical Life: A Constructive Critique of the Liturgical Movement* (1956), *Woman and Man with God: An Essay on the Place of the Virgin Mary in Christian Theology and Its Significance for Humanity* (1957), *Newman: His Life and Spirituality* (1958), *Christian Initiation* (1958), *The Meaning of Priestly Life* (1960), *Introduction to Spirituality* (1960), *Rite and Man: Natural Sacredness and Christian Liturgy* (1962), *The Liturgy Revived* (1964), *Eucharist: Theology and Spirituality of the Eucharistic Prayer* (1966), *Liturgy and Architecture* (1967), *The Church of God, Body of Christ and Temple of the Spirit* (1970), *The Eternal Son: A Theology of the Word of God and Christology* (1974), *The Invisible Father: Approaches to the Mystery of the Divinity* (1976), and *Cosmos: The World and the Glory of God* (1982), Bouyer established himself as an expert in a number of fields, with a particular gift for discerning and describing the subtle interplay of Sacred Scripture, ecclesiastical dogma, liturgical history, and ascetical-mystical theology. His is a kind of auda-

1

ciously thoughtful scholarship seldom seen since the Second Vatican Council—at once ambitious and intimate, poetic and analytical, polyphonic in sources and yet highly unified by an encompassing vision.[1] Not unexpectedly, we find the likes of Henri de Lubac, Yves Congar, Hans Urs von Balthasar, and Joseph Ratzinger avidly reading and discussing Bouyer's work throughout the middle period of the century.

While he would later distance himself from certain stances of his earlier writings (in light of the excesses of the liturgical reform, for instance, he came to regret some of his quondam critiques of the classical Roman liturgy), it could never be said that he had been irresponsible in his inquiries or impure in his purposes. There was always in Bouyer a fierce desire to get at the truth, to work at a problem from every angle and with every resource available, to take all the voices of a dense and diverse Christian tradition seriously, and to make of his mind, as well as of the age in which he lived, a worthy gift to his Lord. In this, we see part of the reason Cardinal Newman appealed so deeply and, one might say, connaturally to Bouyer. Both men had the same broad, searching, even restless intellect lifting its lamp to guide a heart of inextinguishable piety; blessedly free of self-absorbed sentimentality, both could sparkle with mordant humor. They appreciated the humble, simple things of life as much as they did the sophisticated literary ones, time with dear old friends in dear old places as much as (or more than) famous engagements in lofty arenas. Like Newman, Bouyer exemplifies an intellect baptized into Christ, permeated with evangelical charity. We see these admirable qualities of Bouyer's character, not to mention a more mischievous side, shimmering in the pages of his memoirs, as he gracefully courses over the years of his life, the many famous and not-so-famous people who walked with him or away from him, the private and public events that tested his mettle and called forth the powers of his personality.

With these virtues and accomplishments, it is no wonder Bouyer held a front-seat position in the run-up to the Second Vatican Council, participated in its preparatory committees, became a close friend of Pope Paul VI (of whom he speaks with a curious combination of affection and bewilderment), and worked in the midst of the Consilium that revised the Roman liturgy. As these pages vividly show, Bouyer grew increasingly disaffected not only with the implementation of the liturgi-

---

1. For a nearly complete bibliography of the vast output of Bouyer's pen, see Marek Chrzan, "Bibliografia di Louis Bouyer," *Rivista liturgica* 92 (2000): 533–46, and Davide Zordan, *Connaissance et mystère: l'itinéraire théologique de Louis Bouyer* (Paris: Cerf, 2008), 775–91.

cal reform but, more strikingly, with the very assumptions and processes of the reform itself. Although he was a man who skewered many types of opponents, including those he perceived (fairly or not) as theologically illiterate, change-fearing traditionalists, he came down very much on the side of Catholic tradition and very much against the mentality and project of Annibale Bugnini, whose manipulativeness and mendacity he witnessed firsthand and reports with unsparing candor in these memoirs. As Bouyer writes:

> It was . . . already quite clear that the majority of the priests who took an interest in the new [i.e., liturgical] movement came not at all to give back to the traditional liturgy all of its hidden meaning and all of its life-giving reality. They intended gradually to substitute for it another liturgy or, as the expression went, a "paraliturgy." This was to be more in conformity with the tastes and mental habits of what these nice folks called "modern man." (160)

It seems as if only now, a half-century after the Second Vatican Council, are historians and theologians possessed of the critical distance and the pre-modern/post-modern conceptual tools to develop a nuanced understanding of that epoch-making event and its ambiguous, ambivalent legacy—not merely in regard to the much-lamented dismantling of the Roman Rite, but also, and perhaps even more importantly in the long run, the semi-heretical revamping of ecumenism, the invention of an interreligious dialogue based on nominal parallels, and the embarrassingly naïve embrace of tricolored political philosophy. Thanks to the work of such authors as Romano Amerio and Roberto di Mattei and, on a popular plane, the growing traditionalist movement, an increasing number of Catholics have at last begun to move decisively beyond the days of conciliar triumphalism, the fashionable flirtation with modernity, and the promethean, neo-Pelagian exaltation of scientific progress, social reconstruction, and spiritual autonomy, all of which were manifested in a whirlwind of institutional innovation that spelled (to borrow the title of Bouyer's 1968 *cri de cœur*) the decomposition of Catholicism.

But our own contemporaries, however competent, are not enough to guide us. If we are to grasp the meaning of the history of our times and to chart a better course in decades ahead, we need to learn carefully from the past, from the *recent* past, which, in all too many minds, is still known in a cartoon version of smiling faces. The reality is far more complex and far more tragic. We need the recently published *Vatican Council Notebooks* of de Lubac, *My Journal of the Council* by Congar, and other firsthand accounts, full of enthusiasms and machinations, good ideas and bad ideas; and we need a book like Bouyer's *Memoirs*, which gives us so beautiful an account of a life expended in the service of the Bride of Christ, with a generous sharing in the Cross of her Lord. His memoirs, ranging over some of the most momentous, optimistic, volatile, and confusing decades in the history of the Church, show us how keenly aware he was of the fundamental issues, often long before others perceived them looming into the foreground. Through Bouyer's eyes and in the winding passages of his life, we can re-experience a century that is rapidly fading into the forgotten and hence becoming the unexamined. If all goes well, we will learn from others' mistakes and not embark on fool's errands. Something of Bouyer's native wit and hard-earned wisdom may even rub off on us.

In 1955, Bouyer spoke of "the temptation . . . of a false modernity, of a so-called adaptation to modern needs which actually causes the loss of true tradition as the result of an idolatry of ephemeral fashion, and as a result of the unregulated fancies of individuals."[2] Hearing this, we cannot refrain from asking ourselves: What, then, is a *true* modernity, as opposed to a false one? What differentiates an acceptable or even necessary adaptation from a "so-called adaptation"? What is "*true* tradition" and how should it regulate our fancies? In the final analysis, these are inherently philosophical and theological questions. They cannot be answered via psychology, anthropology, or sociology, nor by the consensus of any group or the spirit of any age. Unlike so many who attempted to navigate these treacherous waters without the requisite tools, Bouyer was in a position to steer a confident course. He addressed these and similar questions *as* a disciplined theologian, *as* a philosophical thinker in the best and broadest sense. Indeed, the value of the *Memoirs* goes far beyond Bouyer's life and times, for in its pages we find, again and again, passages of luminous theology that are timelessly true and, as such, absolutely pertinent to our present and to every present.

Take, for example, his discussion of church councils, the conditions of their necessity and fruitfulness, and their inherent limitations. Dismissive of hyperbolic conciliarism, Bouyer soberly assessed the parameters of "divine assistance":

> In the best-case scenario, that of a truly ecumenical council in the traditional meaning of the term, i.e. actually representative of an undivided Christendom, the most that divine assistance can ensure for the Apostles' successors is the absence of any possible error in the doctrinal definitions such assemblies venture to produce. But, short of this extreme case, any dosage of approximation, insufficiency, or simple superficiality are to be expected from even so sacrosanct an assembly. (215)

2. *Liturgical Piety* (Notre Dame, IN: University of Notre Dame Press, 1955), 40.

As a theologian who enjoys reading modern authors no less than ancient and medieval, I am accustomed to a certain amount of ponderous prose, some of it quite illuminating, and some, turgid blather. What a joy it has been to page once again through Bouyer's writings and to become familiar with this autobiographical panorama! As the reader will quickly discover, the *Memoirs* are the work of a masterful observer, a cogent analyst, a winsome writer, a sympathetic spirit. This will not surprise those who know that, in addition to his life's vocation as a theologian and a historian of spirituality, Bouyer, showing himself once again the true heir of Newman, was a high-level participant in authentic ecumenical discourse, a perceptive literary critic, and a talented writer of fiction (four novels, all under pseudonyms).

We are immensely indebted to John Pepino for an eloquent, fastidious, and eminently enjoyable translation of an author given to allusion, rich detail, and whimsical wordplay. Prodigious notes, translated and augmented by Professor Pepino, fill in the reader on the hundreds of men and women, locations, events, and publications to which the text refers. For those wishing to go more deeply into Bouyer's legacy, I highly recommend Dr. Pepino's recent articles: "Cassandra's Curse: Louis Bouyer, the Liturgical Movement, and the Post-Conciliar Reform of the Mass"[3] and "Louis Bouyer and the Pauline Reform: Great Expectations Dashed,"[4] as well as Pepino's translation of Bouyer's fascinating analysis of the Lefebvre affair, "The Catholic Church in Crisis,"[5] surely one of the most nuanced, incisive, and syntopical pieces ever written on that subject.

It took a long time for the *Memoirs* to be published in the original French, and even longer to appear in English. There have been reasons for its delay (as a P. G. Wodehouse character might say, "wheels within wheels")—among them, the fact that much of this book is an exposé of the Emperor's discomforting lack of clothes. Happily for readers of English, the delay is over, and a classic of modern Catholic writing has fallen into your hands.

---

3. *Antiphon,* vol. 18, n. 3 (2014): 254–300.
4. *Sacred Music,* vol. 141, n. 4 (Winter 2014): 8–20.
5. Published at the Rorate Caeli weblog on July 6, 2015.

Preface to the English Edition[1]

LOUIS BOUYER wrote these memoirs in the mid- to late 1980s. He was a man in his seventies by then, and, although he was to write a few more books, most of his life and the great bulk of his written production were behind him. He still had a couple of teaching engagements, notably at the Ignatius Institute that Fr. Joseph Fessio, SJ, had founded at the University of San Francisco, but spent much of his time in retirement at the Benedictine Abbey of Saint Wandrille, the very abbey where he had discovered the Catholic liturgy and where he was received into the Church half a century earlier. Here he finished composing these reflections on his life and on the events he had witnessed and in which he had participated, from his first memory (learning how to walk) to his retirement.

Louis Bouyer was born in Paris on 17 February 1913, "on the eve of that war ... that marked the end of a civilization" (17).[2] The early chapters offer a delightful portrait of Paris during World War I. Bouyer remembers the ramparts around the city, not being able to take the train to go on holiday, the taxis bringing wounded soldiers back from the front. His descriptions of his eccentric, musical (a characteristic that did not rub off on young Louis), and engaging French Protestant family, of the streets with their horse-drawn carriages and early electric tramways, are worth the read even for those coming to this book for theological reasons. One forgets how a generation that has lived into our century could have, in its own childhood, been witness to the remains of the nineteenth. Indeed, as a six-year old boy Bouyer met stage actress (and, in the 1860s, courtesan) Sarah Bernhardt, then in her eighties, who called him *Mon amour!* and kissed him on the lips (26). From a more respectful distance, he glimpsed Napoleon III's widow Empress Eugénie gravely strolling in the Tuileries (ibid.). The landscape descriptions of the Sancerre region and Bouyer's solipsistic ruminations while walking there recall Newman's "life might be a dream, or I an Angel, and all this

---

1. Much in this Preface was gleaned from Jean Duchesne's "Postface," in Louis Bouyer, *Mémoires*, ed. Jean Duchesne (Paris: Cerf, 2014), 229–232.

2. The following synopsis of the *Memoirs* is slightly adapted from the translator's review of the French edition, forthcoming in *Antiphon* 19.2 (2015).

world a deception." One puts down these chapters with the impression of a dreamy and bookish lad with an interest in drama (he would create his own world in a toy theater his father had given him) and in chemistry. It was the Alsatian grandmother of his friends in Sancerre who told him out of the blue: "You shouldn't be a professor, you should become a pastor!" to which he promptly answered: "Why didn't I think of that!"

The chapters dealing with Bouyer the young Lutheran seminarian and then pastor in Paris shed light on French Protestantism in the 1930s. He outlines sketches of his professors Oscar Cullmann, Maurice Goguel, Adolphe Lods, and Philippe de Félice—whose lectures he sometimes skipped to hear Étienne Gilson speak down the street at the *Hautes Études*. Bouyer's attraction to the liturgy caused him to frequent the Russian Orthodox *émigré* churches (he befriended Fr. Serge Bulgakov and Evgraff Kovalevsky among others) and the ecclesiastical zoo of *episcopi vagantes* to be found among and around them, not to mention an enigmatic "Monk of the Eastern Church" (66). He admired the ecumenical enterprises of such Scandinavian Lutherans as Nathen Söderblom (58), the *Faith and Order* movement to regroup all Protestant churches in some way, and the Malines conferences of Cardinal Mercier. His youthful reflection on all this led him to focus on the strong point of Protestantism: the direct relationship of the Christian with God in Christ, which relationship is nourished with meditation on the Word of God—a religion whose essence is in a total acceptance in faith of the one grace that God gives us in His Son. Yet, he soon realized that "it also was self-evident that the whole ecumenical problem was to restore these certainties to their life-giving environment: the one Church willed by Christ, established on the Apostles, and spanning the centuries in an uninterrupted tradition" (60). He even allowed himself to be convinced to receive the chrismation at the hands of "the Monk" (74)—a decision he soon understood to be absurd.

These thoughts led to Bouyer's *Spirit and Forms of Protestantism,*[3] which gives the general principles according to which one might convert to the Church of Rome. These memoirs, however, shed light on the specific circumstances that led Bouyer himself to do so. First among these was his realization that any attempt to forge a "Western Orthodox Church" (as some were doing in Paris in the 1930s) could be nothing but chimerical since orthodoxy in the West is to be found in the Roman Church. Then followed his discovery of the Western liturgy which, although as celebrated in most parishes was in need of some dusting off, left "nothing essential to be desired" as the Benedictine monks cele-

---

3. French title: *Du protestantisme à l'Église,* "From Protestantism to the Church."

brated it at Saint Wandrille (where "the Monk" recommended that he should go on retreat), which was furthered strengthened under the liturgical scholarship of Benedictine Fathers Dom Casel, Dom Marmion, Dom Vonier, and especially Dom Lambert Beauduin. Lastly, the monastic life he saw at Saint Wandrille struck him as precisely the Christian life that his Protestant seminary professors had described but of which they could not produce a concrete example. In Advent of 1939 Bouyer wrote to tell the ecclesiastical inspector of the Lutheran Church in Paris that he was withdrawing from the pastorate. He was received into the Church at Saint Wandrille on 27 December of that year (119).

Once Bouyer the Lutheran minister had joined the Church, there remained the question of what to do with him. The memoirs here again provide the answer to a question: "Why didn't he become a Benedictine himself?" Although Bouyer felt attracted to the monastic life, Dom Chambat, the prior of Saint Wandrille, had detected in Bouyer an independence of spirit that far better suited him to the Oratory, where Fathers Brillet and Ponsard, who had been waiting for precisely this, received him with open arms. Among them, as a schoolmaster at their French version of Eton in Juilly, he began work on the Easter triduum that was published as *Le Mystère pascal* in 1945.

Now a Catholic, Bouyer participated in the two movements that lay much of the groundwork for Vatican II: the liturgical movement and the ecumenical movement. He was able to explore these during his many travels and international teaching appointments, and in each he proved to be a tireless worker, but also a dry-eyed judge of both ally and opponent (he candidly expresses his enthusiasms, worries, and disappointments in the liturgical movement in the latter chapters of the *Memoirs*). It is sufficient to mention here that he intended his negative assessment of the *official* reform of the liturgy and of its Latin texts to be read only after his death.

Louis Bouyer's assessment of Catholic ecumenical efforts is no less negative. In this he proved, as in the case of the liturgy, to be faithful to his own principles throughout, and thereby incurred clerical snubs before and after the council for diametrically opposed reasons: before the Council he was suspect for having once been a Protestant; after the Council he was an embarrassment for having ceased to be one. Yet, the barbs often came from the same (unnamed) ecclesiastics (211)! For the post-conciliar period, he lamented the triumph of what he (following his friend E.L. Mascall) called "Alice in Wonderland" ecumenism, according to which "Everybody has won, and all must have prizes!" (ibid.).

On the other hand, readers will discover that the experience of Vatican II did change his thinking in one respect: his understanding of what an ecumenical council is and what it does. Although his impressions of the Second Vatican Council did not influence his book on the Church (which he wrote with still "rose-colored ink," 207),[4] he ended up limiting his estimation of an ecumenical council's effectiveness and authority to a very narrow margin. Although this disappointed the convert that was Bouyer, on this score he found solace in the company of St. Gregory Nazianzen and . . . Joseph Ratzinger.

The last two chapters published in this edition of the memoirs describe the author's later life and give a reflection on his seventy years. They are of a more literary cast: his theological efforts were still underway (his *Cosmos* was being printed) and his memoirs take a different direction. Just as he had described his friendships and conversations with T. S. Eliot and J. R. R. Tolkien in the 1940s and 1950s (178–180), in these last chapters he describes his ongoing friendship with American French-language writer Julien Green, the first non-Frenchman admitted to the *Académie française*. Green speaks highly of Bouyer in his own published diaries as "Fr. B., who is one of the most knowledgeable men I know" and "is always joyful and charming." Bouyer also had a close friendship with British author Elizabeth Goudge, whose *Green Dolphin Street* had enchanted him (234). Later he also became close friends with Cardinal Heenan, with whom he would have conversations on the state of the post-Conciliar Church. In fact, Heenan wanted Bouyer to write these conversations down and publish them. Heenan died too soon (one of Bouyer's deepest regrets, 15), but the two men's musings on this topic became Bouyer's own two favorite books (and those most hated by others): *The Decomposition of Catholicism* in 1968 and *Religieux et clercs contre Dieu* ("Religious and Clergy Against God") in 1975 (235).

Still, Bouyer had not yet said all that he had to say. He produced, between 1986 and 1994, yet another trilogy to complete the first two of his monumental theological synthesis (see 202, n. 80 in this edition), and also wrote half a dozen monographs on a variety of subjects (Saint Thomas More, Newman, icons, the legend of the Grail, "contemplative meditation," "feminine mysticism," etc.). Naturally, Bouyer does not mention these works as such, but the notes will point them out as warranted. Bouyer's health took a turn for the worse in the late 1990s. He had to give up teaching in San Francisco and, in 1998, was transferred from Saint Wandrille to the Little Sisters of the Poor on Avenue

---

4. Louis Bouyer, *The Church of God*, trans. Charles Underhill Quinn (Chicago: M. Mayer, 1982), now available again from Ignatius Press. The original French was published in 1970.

de Breteuil in Paris. He died there on 22 October 2004 at the age of ninety-one.

These memoirs would make fascinating reading from any author: the twentieth was not a boring century. What makes Louis Bouyer's memoirs eminently worthwhile is, on the one hand, that he was an uncommon man in terms of his intelligence and independence of thought, and, on the other hand, that he was in a privileged position to understand and comment on some of the most significant trends in twentieth-century Christianity, particularly the liturgy and ecumenism. Bouyer wrote extensively on both topics throughout his publishing career, but these pages offer a more personal reflection on them and may help to nuance (or sharpen!) the judgments he had emitted in his scholarly publications. Only one other of Bouyer's works of this nature exists in English: *The Decomposition of Catholicism* (1968). The other two, *Religieux et clercs contre Dieu* (1975) and *Le Métier de théologien* (1979—a lengthy interview with Georges Daix), have yet to be translated.

These memoirs also stand alone as a masterpiece of the genre. Bouyer was aware of its pitfalls and took Cardinal Heenan's humble and selective memoirs, as opposed to Rousseau's exhibitionist *Confessions*, as a model. His principle of selection was whether events or people "reveal some meaning" (15). Bouyer's principal sense seems to have been sight: his first memories are of a bright awning and an orange placed on a chair. He retains this sensory approach throughout: his lengthy descriptions of landscapes (Sancerre in France, the Lake District in England, Brittany, the city and environs of San Francisco, etc.) in many cases provide the key to his inclinations and personality. One may say that meaning came to Bouyer through sight rather than through sound.

Bouyer follows several meaningful threads throughout these memoirs, some from the very beginning, and they recur like a melody in an opera pointing both forward and backward along the plot's timeline: the centrality of the Bible in the Church and in her liturgy; the vanity of time-serving ecclesiastics of all denominations; the neglected role of the Holy Ghost; and the importance of the particularly feminine contributions of women, to name only a few. The intellectual and the personal crisscross and influence each other throughout, so that the meanings of trends, movements, and literature as Bouyer saw them come through more clearly. These memoirs will therefore prove indispensable to anyone who wishes to understand the thought of Louis Bouyer better, just as a dinner conversation with a writer may provide some keys to understanding his production. Certainly the tone here often comes close to the conversational.

A Word on Translation

We present these memoirs in English, and must therefore speak of the business of translation. Bouyer's prose is that of a highly literate and intelligent twentieth-century Frenchman. He handled French as a supple instrument to express his thought through exquisite wording and tellingly structured sentences. One is reminded of Cicero in the purity of language and elegant balance of his longer periods, while at other times the Roman historian Sallust seems to have recommended a jagged and pointedly jolting syntax. An example of the former style is this passage on Fr. Guy de Broglie, Bouyer's history professor at the *Institut catholique* in the mid-1940s:

> Après Gilson, nul n'a plus contribué à me faire apprécier exactement la force, la vastitude des vues, et cependant les limites de saint Thomas, les points diversement assurés de l'héritage augustinien et toute la complexité (voire l'ambiguïté) des traditions qui se réclament de l'un ou de l'autre en Occident.[5]

English will not brook so complex a sentence and its translation (139) breaks it up in two while seeking to retain the flavor of the original:

> After Gilson, no one has contributed more to making me appreciate with precision the strength, the breadth of view, and yet also the limitations, of Saint Thomas. This is also the case with the points of the Augustinian heritage that have been settled in varying degrees, as well as all the complexity (or even ambiguity) of the traditions that lay a claim to either him or Saint Thomas in the West.

Bouyer uses the Ciceronian period in his landscape descriptions to great effect too. In this passage, he explains how the Loire valley as seen from the village of Sancerre had the same effect on him as the Lake District had had on Wordsworth, an impression of inseparable "humanity and grandeur":

> L'élévation des collines, les vues dilatantes qu'elles proposent, alternant avec le recueillement des vallons boisés, où sources et ruisseaux abondent, mais peut-être plus encore la magie enveloppante du grand fleuve silencieux, avec la constante présence déserte de ses eaux, de ses sables et de ses frondaisons, l'une comme l'autre contribuent à cet effet.[6]

The landscape vocabulary is that of such classic French writers as Maupassant, Zola, and Balzac, but the cadence and equilibrium of the sentence draw their model from classical antiquity. Our translation is:

---

5. Ibid., 133.
6. Ibid., 45

The rise of the hills, the expanding vistas they offer, alternating with the contemplative woody hollows where sources and streams abound, and perhaps more than this the grand silent river's enshrouding magic with the constant unpopulated presence of its waters, sandbanks, and foliage all combined to produce this effect. (49)

Bouyer used his jagged style to express surprise, pique, or impatience, for instance in his discussion on the work of the prestigious International Theological Commission that Paul VI set up after the Council. Bouyer had resigned from it after a five-year tenure and writes retrospectively: "Il paraît qu'elle poursuit imperturbablement ses travaux . . . *bombycinans in vacuo!* Grand bien lui fasse!"[7] Our translation renders this "They say it continues its work unperturbed—*bombycinans in vacuo!* Much good may it do it!" (228). Bouyer here juxtaposes a colloquial expression of exasperation ("Much good may it do it!") with a learned allusion to a Latin expression he had read in an eighteenth-century controversy between a Catholic and a Protestant. This surely amounts to Sallust's vaunted *obscura brevitas*: the use of a brief epigrammatic sentence with a literary allusion. Very few twenty-first century readers will catch it unaided; certainly the editors did not!

This allusiveness, with which readers of Bouyer's work are familiar, is on every page of these memoirs. Among other factors it made explanatory notes necessary. Jean Duchesne explains them in his "Postface" to the French edition; his explanation applies to this edition too:

The biographical, bibliographical, geographical, and other explanations contained in these notes may appear excessively abundant. Some readers may not learn much from them. Yet it is doubtful whether anyone among those interested in the following pages [of endnotes] could at the same time know, for instance, who Madame Segond-Weber (19) and Batacharia Kamelashwara (178) are, when Jean Baruzi, *Saint Jean de la Croix* (85) and Michael Arthur Ramsay, *The Gospel and the Catholic Church* (105) were published, what Oscott College (106), the Sign of Toussaines (186), or even the Zodocover (211) are and where they are located, what a dolium (153, n.1) or Septuagesima (200) are.[8]

The English edition, which presents these explanations in footnotes, had to break up Duchesne's endnotes to keep them from occupying too much of any given page. Our notes also add matter which, though familiar to a French readership, is less so to an English one. This accounts for the close to one thousand notes in the pages to follow. The reader need

7. Ibid., 203.
8. Ibid., 232. The parenthetical numbers refer to the pages of the French edition.

not stop at all or even at most of them: they are there to help follow the text, not to detract from it.

As was his custom, Bouyer typed out the manuscript himself. He used two typewriters: first a manual typewriter; then, from page 37 to the last of 230 pages, an electric one. He added pencil-written corrections in two revisions, neither of which altered the substance of the text. He entrusted copies to several friends and specified that these should not be published until after his death, if, as he said, they were still deemed to be worthwhile by then. He also added, with what Duchesne calls his "gruff lucidity," that he had had fun sorting out his memories before "kicking the bucket" (*avant de "crever"*) or "going senile" ("*devenir gâteux*").[9] Photocopies (and eventually an anonymously-typed electronic version) of these memoirs have circulated privately for the ten years between Bouyer's death and the Cerf's 2014 edition, particularly among those interested in recent Church history and liturgy, and its less edifying revelations on the post-conciliar period have cropped up on the internet. Our edition simply follows the text as Jean Duchesne edited it. This translation seeks to convey Bouyer's eclectic style, which ranges from his literary landscape descriptions to his representation of Fr. Henri Carru's distinctive speech (130). At bottom, however, it seeks to stay out of the way of the intimate bond of friendship (as Bouyer says at the outset) that develops between the memorialist and his reader.

9. Ibid., 229.

Introduction

A VERY DEAR and very good friend, whose premature loss is one of my greatest regrets, Cardinal Heenan, Archbishop of Westminster, entitled his memoirs *Not the Whole Truth*.[1] He seems to me, by these very first words, to have denounced the pretense of so many memorialists since Rousseau of telling it all: as if that were possible, should one even sincerely wish so to do—which is probably never the case. Yet, as his example demonstrates, a choice made among one's memories of what seems, upon further thought, apt to reveal some meaning, first for oneself and then for a few others, is doubtless the best a memorialist can do.

Indeed, the closer I come to the end the more I feel that there is a meaning to our life: the hand of God guides us, using all things for His purposes: the failures, the disillusionments as well as, nay rather more than, the successes, the happy times—or those that strike us as such— and, which is more surprising, even our glaring faults!

And so I wish to recall in the following pages what I think has had the most meaning on final reflection, or something like it. My hope is that those who read them, especially my friends both known and unknown (for a writer, are not the latter often among the closest?), will also, perhaps more than I, derive some profit from them. I hasten to add that the diversion that these pages might provide—or such at least is my hope— is to my mind an integral part of this potential profit. It is a fact too little known, but as far as I am concerned undeniable, that Providence has a great sense of humor, and of course, the best! The terrible deficit in this regard among modern Christians (and among ecclesiastics in particular) is in my opinion what chiefly keeps them from being taken seriously—however serious they may actually be. I do not mean to provoke them, but I shall not go out of my way to spare them.

---

1. John Carmel Heenan (1905–1975) was bishop of Leeds from 1951, of Liverpool from 1957, and Archbishop of Westminster from 1963. He participated in the Council and was created Cardinal in 1963. He published his memoirs under the title *Not the Whole Truth* (London: Hodder and Stoughton, 1971). Bouyer renders this in French as: "The Truth . . . but not all of it!" (*"La vérité . . . mais pas entière!"*).

May all people of good faith who read these pages, whether or not they are Christians, sense that they are addressed to them by someone whose only ambition in writing them has been to deserve to be counted among them.

1

My Childhoods

I WAS BORN the third child of parents who were already somewhat advanced in age. My two elder siblings had already died: the first nearly at birth; the other barely two years old. Furthermore, I was born on the eve of the war of 1914, which, in common opinion, marked the end of a civilization. After these preliminaries one might think I had a difficult childhood, or at least a sad one. Nothing could be further from the truth.

Doubtless as an effect of that unconscious selection that oversees the retention of memories and also, of course, because there were good memories in abundance, my early years give me a singularly sunny impression. I can express it no better than by one of the earliest childhood memories I still have left with a precision that has saved them from so many instances of forgetfulness. Our dining-room window, in the flat where I was born at 5 rue Juliette Lamber (a stone's throw from the Place Wagram and Boulevard Péreire), is open.[1] It must be a spring or an early summer morning. I might be one year old, since I am taking my first steps. Across the street a lowered awning in orange and white stripes is dazzling with sunlight. I am on my way over to a chair placed in the same direction. An orange, itself brilliantly colored, has been placed on it to attract me to it.

According to what I have been told, my eager progress was interrupted by a memorable fall. After that, I no longer wished to make use of my legs for a while, to my family's dismay and that of Irma, my little nurse. It is quite revealing, though, that for my part I have kept no memory of that misadventure, whereas the luminous awning and the promising fruit left me with the imperishable memory of my entrance

1. The rue Juliette Lamber forms the hypotenuse of the right triangle whose other two sides are Boulevard Péreire and Boulevard Malesherbes, the right angle being at the traffic circle of Place de Wagram, in the seventeenth *arrondissement*.

into a world of happy brightness where shadows serve only to bring out the light. I can say that all of my life's struggles—and I haven't been spared them—never managed to erase that very first vision.

My mother's concern, which came out in an insistence on absolute safety that a good dose of annoyance was never to dent, Irma's kindness to me—for which, I am ashamed to say, I rewarded her, at least once, by hurling a bowl of creamy milk at her face (I always hated it, but she was under orders to have me take it in as is)—my father's generosity and dreamy idealism (the firm punishment he felt obliged in conscience to administer to me that day in no way diminished my esteem for him): all of this would have been enough to make a paradise of those early years.

That Parisian neighborhood's charm, the proximity of my young aunt and godmother Jeanne, my mother's younger sister, of her husband Uncle Francis, an expert in Oriental art who was to leave his mark on me—without realizing it, I think—and of my cousin, their daughter Jacqueline who was a little older than I: all these were naturally to confirm that impression. This is so much the case that those early years seem to have gone by as a single beautiful day like the one I have mentioned.

I was then just over a year old when we went to war: the "Great War" as it was to be called . . . before another one made it seem hand-crafted. Another of my earliest memories must go back to the very beginning, for I can see myself on our balcony in my nurse's arms as she, my mother, and I watched my father come out of a taxi (a rarity still) and call out to us: "We're not leaving: no more trains!" This could only have been in the early days of August 1914.

As it turned out we were to leave for the summer holidays a little later anyway. We went to the beach at Fouras[2] to which my paternal family's La Rochelle origins beckoned us and whose mayor was my father's cousin. To be honest, that war did not affect my childhood for a while, and doubtless too the childhood of many others whose fathers' weak constitutions kept them from being separated. We were only affected by what might seem to be droll or incongruous events: a Zeppelin overhead, or *taubes* as we called them (the first German military airplanes) flying over Paris.

The most unusual event I can remember was an endless procession of ambulance cars bringing back the victims of the Marne.[3] Otherwise,

---

2. Fouras is a maritime village in Charente-Maritime on the Atlantic shore, roughly equidistant between Nantes and Bordeaux. La Rochelle is 25 km away.

3. The battle of the Marne, 6–12 September 1914, stopped the German advance into France. There were 250,000 casualties, wounded, and missing in action.

however, for as long as we lived in that Paris neighborhood, which is to say until 1916 or 1917 if memory serves, it seems that it remained a calm little world where life ran a peaceful course and, fortunately for us, against a beautiful backdrop shaded by tall trees where the only bustle was serene and gay.

What I retain most precisely is the succession of diverse sounds there; yet they stood out on a background of silence it would seem difficult to associate with the notion of a large city today. True, we were right on its outskirts: just near the desert of fortifications where I would often go and play whenever my mother or my nurse and I did not have the leisure to spend an entire morning or afternoon at the Parc Monceau.[4] Beyond that it was very much a country suburb where the semirural disorder of mismatched buildings and small garden plots was blighted only by a few noisy and smoky industrial blocks.

But where we lived and where our aunt lived, Place Wagram or along Boulevard Péreire, the two most urban sounds—which belonged to that time's traffic—did no more than pleasantly punctuate the silence. One of these filled it without dissipating it, I should say: that of the horses going at a jog-trot on the wooden pavement. A sound one cannot imagine today: a familiar and quiet music, with a certain jollity to it, in delicious harmony with the jostling intimacy of the old hackney-carriages. One was so cozy on their large grey or blue cushions, from which one could look down upon the pageant of swaying houses, trees, and passers-by. The other of these sounds foreshadowed a civilization that was just barely emerging: the deafening clanging—though so entertaining as long as it was rare—of the electric streetcars screeching, twisting, and rattling on their tracks, with the merry dinging of their bells whenever the engineer's foot set them off.

Beyond that I only remember the shouts of the little street occupations: calls so poetic that I shall always miss them, just as I shall always miss the characters, so diverse yet alike in their charm, whose call was enough to bring us to our windows. There was above all, as far as I remember, the glasscutter, whose loud warbling reached incomparable fullness and originality. The clothes hawkers, for their part, would let out these languishing dirges that still strike me as the height of romanticism. On the other hand, nothing was more optimistic than the vigorous call of the grinders that was regularly streaked—I'm not sure why—with the clanging of emphatically-struck bells. The virtuosos in the most unexpected vocal scales doubtless remain the earthenware and

---

4. The Parc Monceau is a semi-public park a twenty-minute walk south of Bouyer's childhood address.

porcelain menders, as they were called, who on their end took a break from their invocations—which were by turns ironic or nonsensical—by splitting your ears with their comically shrill little trumpets.

I wonder what all these good people could possibly have earned. They must have delighted in their task, however, as low-income as it was, for they were all so gay and so tirelessly good humored. Generally quieter—though not always—were the chair-menders, who would set up in a nice quiet and sunny spot to repair our seats with beautiful golden straw. They always had a bundle of it between their lips and they braided it with a fascinatingly sure hand.

I have mentioned the *fortifs*[5] and Parc Monceau. They were the preserve of the merchants of *oublies*:[6] these were veritable magicians who had us twirl a sort of shiny arrow on the cover of the cylinder they carried on their back. The arrow would stop right on the variable number of these light treats to which the little *sou*[7] we had paid for the right to throw this whimsical apparatus entitled us. Sometimes it would satisfy us, and at other times it would leave us wanting.

What can I say, too, of the variety, the colorfulness if not the mystery, of the innumerable little shops, so rare in our more or less posh streets but which were crowded together on the way straight to Batignolles[8] or up Avenue Wagram towards Les Ternes?[9] Yet, that way lay the first of the department stores, Les Trois Quartiers, where I would soon grumble at seeing my mother or aunt linger forever from one counter to the next in what I felt was a crowd but was only the harmless hubbub of idle Parisian ladies.

And what about the creameries and dairies, the grocers, the fruit sellers where everything was so fresh, or, on the contrary, swelled with elaborate scents forming strange combinations: cinnamon; pepper; dried fruits and above all coffee, which was regularly roasted two or three times a week and filled a whole neighborhood with its smell! Less enticing to the nose, but even more fascinating to the eyes, were the notions dealers with their spools of infinitely graded hues, their ribbons and their lace trims in a variety one cannot imagine today—and what shall I say of the pharmacies of that time! Their windows were adorned with colossal crystal amphorae in flamboyant colors, which, gas lamps fixed behind them, would light up when evening fell.

5. Nickname for the fortifications girding Paris.
6. *Oublies* are cone-shaped waffles.
7. Sou: five centimes, the twentieth of a Franc.
8. Halfway to Montmartre, due east, from Bouyer's childhood address.
9. About the same distance, but due southwest.

Yet, when it comes to shops, the one I knew best for its hugger-mugger confusion was without contest my godfather's, the husband to a maternal aunt of mine. It took two streetcars to reach it. First, one took the double-decker from Place Péreire; its tall brown box led, if I remember correctly, to the École Militaire.[10] Then one left it to take the more imposing (though less entertaining) Compagnie des Omnibus vehicle; it had succeeded the rickety old four-horse coaches and would later hand over its green livery with yellow piping to our present-day busses. The latter would drop us off at the Mairie de Vaugirard,[11] and we had only a few steps left to reach the Rue de la Procession, where my uncle godfather's bazaar stood facing the Square Saint-Lambert.

After years of frequenting that amiable shambles I dare not say what was to be found, less yet what one couldn't have unearthed there. There were haberdashery, knick-knacks, stationery, perfumes, hardware, newspapers (especially the most popular illustrated ones)—all this in an inextricable jumble, even for my aunt, but in which all my uncle had to do in a pinch, to go straight to the desired object and to satisfy an imaginative customer's request, was to adjust his pince-nez with its black cord.

Nevertheless, all of it only had value, to his eyes, in terms of feeding his family, though this is not to say that he didn't set some pride in it. My uncle, before becoming an unsinkable storeowner, had been legitimately proud of being an artist. The repair, or, better yet, the resurrection and transfiguration of the most deplorable dolls, whether because of the mishaps that had befallen them or their mediocre construction, was his talent, if not his genius. The girlish hordes were aware of it so far abroad that very respectable little girls could sometimes be seen descending upon that still working-class neighborhood. They would come in tears, chaperoned by their posh nannies, to entrust—not without some apprehension—their nearly utterly shattered treasures to the miracle-worker surgeon whose reputation, it seems, extended even to the smart neighborhoods near the Champ de Mars. A few days later, all of these mothers in distress would recover their darling babies with an elation mingled with stupor, so creative could the reconstruction of these pathetic wrecks be.

I reckoned my godfather's high deeds at their just worth, but I must say that my interest in the smell of the warm glue he worked with was particularly equivocal. I did not know whether I liked its strong savor because it was so strange or was sickened by it on account of its lingering rotten-fish smell. My uncle and godfather (his name was Louis Dau-

---

10. On the Champ de Mars, south of the Seine.
11. In the southwestern corner of Paris, the fifteenth *arrondissement*.

phin) excelled in more than the plastic arts alone, however. He had a splendid voice of which he was harmlessly proud and would sing high opera as well as popular songs with equal flair and feeling. Where and how he had developed this talent, I couldn't say, for he had been a foundling, as one discreetly said back then. Quite a good-looking man to boot, he must have had some nobility in his obscure pedigree. With his prematurely white head of hair he looked superb in evening dress. The effect, however, was disrupted whenever he opened his mouth other than to sing. Not that he was in any way a ham (though boastful in a pleasant sort of way), but because his speech was that of a genuine Parisian *Titi*,[12] and his education, gleaned here and there, only just allowed him to read and barely to write.

I think it was his artistic tastes that caused him to end up in my mother's family. He and his wife, aunt Mélie (short for Amélie), had my grandfather living with them. He was a magnificent and inflexible old Spaniard to whom his son-in-law was bound by a delectable blend of exasperation and fondness. Indeed, this forebear, who was at the same time cordial and also prone to anger, was an exceptional musician. Son of a middle-class family of Gerona in Catalonia, he had had a falling out to the death with his people at the age of barely twenty. Having arrived in France with his father's curse as his only luggage, he joined the armed forces to earn a living and to change nationalities. His abilities allowed him to climb the rungs of the bellico-musical hierarchy so surprisingly swiftly that, despite diverse incidents due to his inborn insubordination, he was the Command Master Chief of Music of the Fleet by the time he was forty. Having settled in Toulon[13] with a sweet young Italian wife, herself also an artist though the daughter of a simple house painter, and whom he had met in Languedoc where his career began, his prestigious success at the top of his profession barely allowed him to feed the four sons and four daughters with which their union was blessed. At just the right time, a new more or less oedipal conflict—this time with the Admiral of the Levant Fleet[14]—led to his decision to give himself over to the Republican Guard's Music when it was founded.[15]

Having come up to Paris with his entire tribe, he managed to raise it by supplementing his meager pay with what he could get out of serving concurrently as First Violin and as First Clarinet at the *Opéra*, not with-

12. *Titi* is to Paris what "cockney" is to London.
13. France's principal navy port on the Mediterranean.
14. *Flotte du Levant* is the Ancien Régime term for that part of the French navy that is based in Toulon.
15. On July 14, 1880.

out having also been the conductor of the Hippodrome, the famous circus at the 1889 Expo. My kind and poor little grandmother worked herself to a premature death, but the whole family nonetheless became a nest of songbirds where everyone played just about every instrument. The sons, alas, had all been carried off in turn, hardly adults, by what was then called consumption—specifically a certain Louis, whose name and romantic library I inherited, and whom his sisters (apparently sturdier in the face of privations) all agreed in describing as a prodigy of combined kindness, intelligence, and musical talent all at once.

It was obvious that my grandfather, despite his anarchist leanings, considered that his two elder daughters had married beneath the family, all the while harboring a solid though grumbling affection at least for the one son-in-law of the two that I have mentioned (I never knew the other, or saw much of his wife, who seems to have returned early on to the ancestral type of the Piedmontese Mamma). On the other hand, this temperamental, difficult old man (with a heart of gold deep down) burst with pride for his two younger daughters; in the first place for my mother, whom brilliant studies had catapulted into a profession of governess among grand families of the PHS (Protestant High Society), including a famous British physician whose name I have forgotten. She also had served as a second mother to my godmother Jeanne, whom I have mentioned above: a marvel of youth, charm, and beauty, though she had undeniably inherited her quick temper from her father's side of the family. Not even this had kept her from attracting my Uncle Francis, who was heir to an opulent Geneva family and, as I have mentioned, an expert in Oriental art.

They have left me with the memory of a delightful couple that unfortunately died too soon, both of them carried off towards the end of the war by the same tuberculosis that had prematurely decimated my four young uncles.

My mother married in turn shortly after her younger sister—quite happily as well, though less grandly. Indeed, my father, the only son of a postal employee with roots in the Charente, had to end his studies after the *baccalauréat*[16] as his own father had died very young too. Yet, he had no trouble in finding a rather good position in one of the first electric companies in Paris. This afforded him some enjoyable experiences, as his duties included supervising (as we say today) the installation of telephones, still a novelty, among the upper crust. His tastes, though, were entirely intellectual and artistic. He read in great quantity, was quite a good draftsman and painter, and, until he married in 1908, seems to

16. High school diploma, obtained by passing comprehensive examinations.

have spent his leisure and savings on visits to the old art cities of Italy, Spain, and Central Europe.

I have already mentioned my mother's youthful British episode, which would leave her with an Anglomania she would hand on to me. For his part, my father was rather a Germanist, and it is not his fault that his influence would do no more than give me an entirely bookish introduction to German, not to mention the diverse Teutonic friends I would receive as a host—Prussian squires or Rhineland intellectuals—all of whom were distinguished by an equal Francomania that ruled out any chance of my speaking their language with them.

But I am already anticipating! These first years of my life, as one can already foresee, so long as I lived in Paris, were shared between the aristocratic visit to the Monceau plain and the somewhat plebeian excursions to Vaugirard. I appreciated, among the latter, beyond the avuncular boutique, endless strolls in the neighborhood and beyond, particularly along the riverbanks, as I trailed behind either my godfather or my grandfather.

I owe it to them to report the rare merit they both had of treating me, five or six years old at the time, exactly as though I were their contemporary, and, what is more, as an old chum trustworthy enough for them to include me in their common grousing regarding the weaker sex they pretended to look down on—though it was easy enough for me to see that they were its slaves. They would have been quite surprised, more even than flattered, if they had been told that they turned out to be far more effective teachers than their daughters, wives, or sisters-in-law considered themselves to be. Along with a sturdy independence of judgment, they handed on to me a tireless love and curiosity for old Paris and all it means in terms of its charms, be they lower-class or refined, as well as a definite taste for direct and polished speech, and an amused fondness for original characters, for those who are out of the box.

Neither my aunts nor my mother looked particularly kindly upon these forays together, but the investigations my aunt Mélie in particular tried to conduct upon me once we had come home from our harmless escapades were soon discouraged by my apparently spotty memory. This was attributed to the perpetual daydreaming in which it soon became the common opinion that I would lose myself, and which became a precious alibi to me.

The Boulevard Péreire and Place Wagram side was spiced up with less earthy pleasures, yet I was no less sensitive to them, though without any particular snobbery. I found my pretty cousin's habitual company most enjoyable. Both very elegantly dressed by our respective mothers, we would cause ecstasy among the elderly ladies who mistook us for brother and sister—which I find hard to understand, as I cannot believe that I ever could have been what is called a charming child. My cousin Jacqueline, however, was one in the highest degree—which didn't keep her from being far naughtier and more forward than I. She had won my father over the day before his wedding by telling him, at the risk of provoking a fainting spell in my future godmother, "You know, Mummy thinks you look alright and all, but it's a shame you have a drum-shaped nose!" My aunt, of course, had said "trumpet-shaped nose,"[17] but the children were raised in such a profusion of instruments that they might well get them wrong.

Among other high jinx she dragged me into, on a morning when we had each been dressed up in adorable dark green velvet outfits with broad lace collars to play exceedingly endearing roles at the wedding of a common cousin, Jacqueline talked me into finishing up by the fistful, while we were waiting to be taken along, what was left of a dish of cheese and tomato macaroni. We were caught red-handed in the midst of this operation, our accoutrements in a state it is easy to imagine. This precipitated another bout of hysterics on my poor little aunt's part. Uncle Francis, who didn't know whether to laugh or cry, was fruitlessly attempting, as usual, to calm her down. He'd blow on his pince-nez and softly say: "My dear, they're children! Forget their clothes so long as they don't cripple each other or poke an eye out." To which my aunt exclaimed in tragic accents and wringing her hands: "Ah! So that's what you men find to comfort us! Can anyone ever be as unhappy as I am?" My father butted in and, not daring to look at his brother-in-law and close friend in the eye, deflected this Italo-Spanish fury upon himself by saying: "My dear Jeanne, with a husband like yours, who could ever be happier than you?"

At this point I must admit that the southern Latin element that was dominant in my family gave everything an air of tragicomedy that was a little disconcerting to me but was even more entertaining and, in my case as in that of my exquisite cousin, contributed more than a little to the ingenious perversity that our unhappy (yet at bottom quite happy) mothers outdid each other in bewailing.

As long as I am on the topic of the theater, I should say a word regarding an advantageous relation my godmother introduced to my childhood. She lived at 5 Place Wagram and her balcony was more or less adjacent to that of Sarah Bernhardt,[18] who lived in that part of Boulevard

---

17. The French expression for a turned-up nose.

18. Sarah Bernhardt (1844–1923), the most famous stage actress of the nineteenth century (and courtesan in the 1860s).

Péreire. She cannot have failed to notice this bright young brunette who must have reminded her of her own youth. She was as prone to laughter as she was to tears, singing like a bird or pitching equally ravishing fits of wrath. The sincere cult that my little aunt devoted to the Unforgettable One[19] must have helped develop their friendship beyond mere neighborliness, and I was inevitably brought into it along with my cousin.

At this point I must admit that I am confronted with one of those episodes in which I find it difficult to disentangle what I remember and what I've been told from what my relatives' imagination or my own may have embroidered. It, nevertheless, seems that I may be able modestly to admit not only that I knew Sarah Bernhardt but also that we were on intimate terms: after all she did call me *Mon amour!*—and kissed me right on the lips! I hasten to point out that this was no more compromising for her than it was for me, seeing as she must have been over eighty at the time while I was five or six.

I remember her voice, which had an unreal richness and sweetness; it was bizarrely joined to a face whose paint would have made it frightful, were it not for her smoldering eyes, which were surprisingly youthful and gay. I must have attended one of her last recitals: between the *Phèdre* monologue[20] she delivered from a seat under ample veils or the more dazzling passage in *L'Aiglon*[21] for which she stood in a white uniform but leaning behind a table because of her wooden leg, I know not which was the more extraordinary.

I was not without a critical cast of mind already at that time, for an analogous session (by Madame Segond-Weber, if I'm not mistaken) presented a little later has only left me with the memory of a hilarity that was as irrepressible as it was indecent.

To get through the most incredible memories, or quasi-memories, of the Methuselah that I am, I also have to bring up the very distinct vision offered by a majestic old lady leaning on a gold-knobbed stick. She was all dressed up in black lace that trailed in the dust in the Jardin des Tuileries. I remember my mother or my aunt, I no longer recall which, close to ecstasy and assuring me that this was Empress Eugénie in person.[22]

---

19. One of Miss Bernhardt's nicknames, along with "the Golden Voice" (by Victor Hugo, 1802–1885, author of *Les Misérables*), "the Scandalous One," and "the Sacred Monster" (by Jean Cocteau, 1889–1963, author of *Les Enfants terribles*). She served as model for Marcel Proust's *La Berma* in *À la recherche du temps perdu* (published 1913–1927).

20. The tragedy by Jean Racine (1639–1699), produced in 1677.

21. The play by Edmond Rostand (1868–1918), produced in 1900, about the son of Napoleon Bonaparte. The role of young Napoleon II was tailor-made for Bernhardt.

22. Eugénie de Montijo (1826–1920), wife of Napoleon III (reigned 1853–1870); she would have been about ninety-four at the time.

Yet all the splendors I came into contact with as a child, I admit, did not come close to the heady sweetness of my daily walks in the pleasant streets of the Monceau neighborhood, or to the charm of their more or less old townhouses under the shade of spreading trees, or of those beautiful symmetrical houses on Place Wagram with hackneys trotting as in an Yvette Guilbert song.[23]

I especially remember my uncle Francis's Chinese exotica: the Ming vases (deemed the height of that art in those days), the sumptuous silks with their grotesque figures that managed to be so malicious and so dignified all at once, the ivories, the lacquers, the ebonies inlaid with mother-of-pearl, or the heavy bronze antiques.

There were also in our own living room a few rare pieces of the same kind; my uncle had managed to elicit my father's interest in them. Yet, like most educated Parisians of the time, who were great readers of the Goncourt brothers[24] and of the ineffable Loti[25] (whom my father had known personally in Rochefort), it must be said that he was partial to the fun of charming Japanese-style curios.

It is curious, and is perhaps due to the affectionate respect I felt towards my uncle, that I was already then more attracted to the smiling seriousness of China than to so much slightly overdone elegance.

For her part, my mother endeavored to interest me in singing and the piano, but my mediocre success distressed her. I note that although I was very early on extremely sensitive to shapes and colors, and nearly morbidly so to the scents and other smells of Paris at that time, sounds were to remain, as far as I was concerned, a simple object of vague diversion for many years to come. This was perhaps an individualist's reaction to my maternal family's musical oversaturation? I know not.

Whatever the case may be, the dappled, delicate, amusing, and enchanting dream of those early years was not to last. Concern over my health and my father's new job that took him from now-useless deluxe electricity to the production of the earliest X-ray machines led to our departure from the Plaine Monceau and to our move to the suburban hamlet of Asnières.[26] Besides an interlude in Saint-Germain, our stay there would last until a little beyond my mother's death.

23. Yvette Guilbert (1865–1944), popular café-concert singer. She was filmed singing *Le Fiacre* ("The Hackney-Carriage") in 1904.

24. Edmond (1822–1896) and Jules (1830–1870) Huot de Goncourt, famous French writers and literary critics.

25. Pierre Loti (1850–1923), famous writer of novels with exotic settings.

26. Suburb to the north-northwest of Paris.

2

Gardens, Open and Enclosed

MY EARLY CHILDHOOD years were resolutely urban, though a far cry from what the city can mean for a Parisian child today. The second part of my childhood, which the Geneva psychologists have dubbed "adult childhood,"[1] as well as my early adolescence may be described, if not as rural, then at least as having been spent in gardens.

Indeed, during the last years of the war and then the first post-war years (naturally, I'm still speaking of WWI), I feel that I spent most of my time in three successive gardens, more or less as a solitary. The first of these seems large to me, as it would to any child, but upon seeing it unchanged recently I have no doubt that it was tiny, though a confused mess of twisting alleys, trees, shrubbery, and bushes may yet contribute to such an illusion. It was located, and I believe one could still find it there, at 52 Avenue Faidherbe, in Asnières. That is to say that it was attached to one of the very last houses of that locality. Immediately beyond it lay what was called "the Plain": a plain named *Bécon les bruyères*, though I never saw any heather there.[2] It was a wide and irregular expanse, a small section of which was cultivated, the rest being left to run wild; there were trees in spots and all around it.

For me, this plain amounted to a first and wonderful discovery of nature, though it must have been passably bare! Yet the walks we took there at dusk, simply the view we had onto it from a high veranda where only a few isolated lights dotted it at night, afforded me an early experience of the world's vastness and mystery.

I now realize that this was strengthened by the strange feeling that

1. See Louis Bouyer, "Développements récents de la psychologie en Suisse," *La Vie intellectuelle* 15 (1947): 98–117.
2. This plain (the name means "Bécon in heather") is still rural and partially wooded, although there has been some construction since the railroad from Paris to Argenteuil established a station at Bécon-les-Bruyères in the nineteenth century.

two neighboring alleys gave me. The first, adjoining our house, stretched out between two tall property walls. I delighted in an imaginary exclusive property right over it for the long stretches when I was left to pedal about on a tricycle, a gift of my godfather's, I think, that did not fail to worry my mother. Nevertheless, I was allowed to use it—so long as it was only along this reserved yard. The other alley was quite different. It opened out across the way from us, between a double row of dense gardens whose reverent mystery—so opposed to the immense (in my eyes) mystery of the Plain—was closed in on a little girl who long remained inaccessible and who must have been an early incarnation of the eternal feminine for me. All I remember of her (I cannot even recall her name!) is that she had long blond hair, that she often sang in a flowing voice, and that she played ball marvelously. I later found out that she also played (quite well, I'm told) the piano. The first time I dared speak to her she informed me that she was fourteen—a mythical age to me. Alas! these successive discoveries, as likable and discreet as she may have been, seem to have been enough to use up the charm, which I then first felt and for a long time savored, of the unknown She (in the feminine, of course!).

A little beyond our house, if one turned his back on the Plain, there was another garden; this one spread out in the sunlight. It was our very own gardener's kitchen garden, into which he one day consented to allow me, to my great pride. Yet, as interesting and instructive as it was, it straightaway seemed all in all prosaic.

Farther yet in that direction lay the last and very modest buildings of the township of Asnières. A school I was later to attend closed the view from our house at a distance that seemed to me considerable. Aside from a few shopping outings, as well as others of which I shall say more soon, my entire attention seems to have been focused on our own garden in those years on Avenue Faidherbe, besides these two alleys that were so different from each other and from the Plain, be it near or far.

What was I up to there? Not much more than a little fanciful gardening, aside from my tricycle's sempiternal comings and goings. Still, I had the habitual company of a first playmate: my dog, Tobie. I exchanged endless dialogues with him in which his share, limited as it was to affectionate yapping and a whole variety of tail waggings, was nonetheless essential. Except for a swing, I must say that I found greater pleasure in games which, though transposed into the garden during the summer, were still indoor games. One was the electric train, whose enchantment was doubtless the cause of my first imaginary vocation: engineering.

Yet, another plaything was to leave a far greater mark on me forever: a splendid toy theater I got from my Uncle Francis. For years on end, as I recall, I tirelessly expanded the decors, the representations, the lighting, the incidental music: in a word, anything having anything to do with it. The day I discovered, years later, Calderón's *Great Theater of the World*,[3] the ecstasy into which its title alone would send me was the fruit of that gift, which has probably been one of the most determining elements of my entire education.

Thanks to that theater, my imagination began to draw inexhaustible grist from all that I was told, or that I was a little later on able to read. And so I would convert it into a dream-reality where, unbeknownst to me, I was living, before having even begun to live in earnest, a life whose richness surpassed all that what is called "real life" could ever give me. And, I must admit, before the curtain is definitively drawn on it, that it has not been stingy with me. It is perhaps to this blessed theater that I owe, above all, the discovery, in another title by Calderon, *La Vida es sueño*,[4] of all the meaning we shall see later on.

I have just alluded to my first reading. Although my mother started teaching me very early on, she was so alarmed at seeing that I could read at the age of barely four that she first made a well-meaning attempt at slowing down a raging famine she deemed premature. Yet, as is the case with many well-meaning pedagogical intentions, hers had an exactly opposite effect to what she had anticipated. As I was deprived of access to more or less serious books, I made do (definitively, she came to fear) with the comic books I was able to devour in peace and quiet (and for free!) at my godfather's during the interminable conferences between my mother and her sister. The result of this unfortunate propensity, which was too late detected in me, was that *Le Petit Illustré*, *Cri-cri*, *L'Épatant*, *Guignol*, and, to top it off, those two paragons of infantilo-feminine literature, *Fillette* and *La Semaine de Suzette*, became the weekly ingredients of what soon was my addiction. My poor Mamma sank into the most pathetic devastation at the particular taste I seemed to have for the amusing but villainous epic of the *Pieds-Nickelés* in *L'Épatant* and, worse yet, for the inept jokes exchanged in *Le Petit Illustré* between Carolus Bousillard the explorer, presented as the most illustrious scion of Monpied-sur-Tabouche, and his old friend the Negro king Dipaça-Samféroté.[5]

---

3. Pedro Calderón de la Barca (1600–1681), prolific playwright of the Spanish Golden Age, staged this play (*El Gran teatro del mundo*) in 1655; its theme is that every man has a role to play.

4. Calderón produced this play, *Life is a Dream*, in 1629–1635.

5. To have some idea of the level of the puns in such comics, here is an attempt at giving English equivalents: *Bousillard* = "Buster"; *Monpied-sur-Tabouche* = "Myfoot-upon-Thymouth"; *Dipaça-Samféroté* = "Nosaydat-Makemeburp."

Yet, while I was inexhaustibly chatty with my family on the subject of these merry heroes, it may interest psychologists of the now somewhat-outdated Freudian school that I kept complete silence about the endless reveries procured by the fairy tales in *La Semaine de Suzette*. These were closely monitored by Jesuit censors (as I later learned) and featured beautiful, pious, and sweet young things of the best society who would triumph, untouched and merciful, over the shady attempts of despicable oppressors. In fact, separated as I now was from my cousin Jacqueline but increasingly enclosed within a maternal world that my aunts merely expanded, it may well be the case that these reading materials and dreams happily preserved me from all the possible deviations that are said to threaten little boys who are victims to so narrowly maternalistic an education.

My mother, however, having had the candid imprudence of boasting to a friend that she knew all of my thoughts (while I naturally was feigning inattention), a scruple of conscience led me to admit these secret thoughts to her. She was visibly petrified, but unknowingly manifested her common sense and rather exceptional moral health by telling me that all this had no importance, less yet anything sinful.

It may be surprising in this regard that I have not yet said anything about my religious and moral education. What I have to reveal of it, at this point in my narrative, is that I was in the same boat as the Chinese. Many European scientists have believed that they had no religion in the strict sense, but the Chinese answer that they probably appear that way to us because their religion is so inseparable from their life that it becomes imperceptible to the outside observer. In fact, the thought of God's presence behind all things, inseparable at once from a demand for, and from a promise of, goodness and truth, went without saying in my childhood. It resided more in my mother's constant and calm demeanor, of which my father visibly but even more tacitly approved, than in any explicit lesson. I needed only to see her pray briefly, every day, with me, preparing for the prayer or prolonging it for her own purposes in a silent dialogue with the little black Bible with gilded edges that seldom left her. For a long time she gave me only a few drops of it, as of a rare and precious essence. Yet that in itself contributed in no small measure to render indisputable in my eyes not only her vision but also her practice.

Aside from this, if I'm not mistaken, my religion was for a long time made concrete only in a rather beautiful picture of the Good Shepherd on my bedroom wall. It was explained to me early on, though without any particular insistence, that it was of the Son of God, Whom He sent to be with us and to lead us back to Him.

Those last years of the war, during which the bookish phase of my education was to begin with reading, brought only two precisions. The first was of the first pious book I ever owned: a well-chosen illustrated book of biblical passages, mainly from the gospels. Its illustrations quite naturally attracted most of my attention at first and ended up eliciting more questions in me than did the text, whose pure exhaustiveness could not raise any so early. I remember in particular the effect on me of a picture of the Virgin presenting the Child to the Magi. My mother corrected the pious heresy that caused me to think, for a moment, that this Mother of the Son of God must have been divine ("lady-god,"[6] as I said in my linguistic ignorance), but she said nothing that might diminish my respect for a creature who had been brought so close to God.

This requires me to describe, to some extent, what my parents' religion was. It took me a while to recognize to what extent it was orthodox in content, yet also original in many of its forms, although they did not suspect as much themselves. I was the son of a father of old Charentais stock whose own father, as such, had retained of his ancestral Protestantism only a fierce anticlericalism. Still, my father's Breton mother had had him baptized, though without obtaining from her intransigent husband that he should go any farther down superstition's nefarious path. My mother, for her part, had made it to First Communion but no further because of her Spanish father's parallel will, himself in rebellion against all his family traditions. I should actually have ended up in a family with no religion. My grandmother had entrusted the little time she had been able to oversee her daughter's education to Catholic priests, yet these did not seem to have presented the Gospel to my mother very convincingly. She received it, late in adolescence, from those haughty middle-class Protestant families who employed her— though she did not spare them her criticisms while just as readily acknowledging the debt she owed them. Her stay in England in a Darbyite milieu,[7] that is to say in the strictest and most sectarian Evangelism, had completed her formation in a solid piety, without—which indicates the sureness of her judgment in my opinion—transmitting any of its narrow-mindedness to her. By some unknown happenstance she had come to attend, on her return to France, that Reformed parish called *de l'Étoile*, on the Avenue de la Grande Armée, where a late nineteenth-century Pastor, Eugène Bersier,[8] an excellent preacher endowed

6. *Dieuse* in Louis Bouyer's childish French.

7. John Nelson Darby (1800–1882), leading figure of the Plymouth Brethren and founder of dispensationalism.

8. Eugène Bersier (1831–1889), minister of the French Reformed Church. He worked for the unification of Protestantism.

with an exceptional liturgical sense for that time, had introduced without shouting it from the rooftops a form of worship that was nearly Catholic in substance. She had had no trouble winning my father over to it, especially since Bersier had among his successors Pastor Russier, who was to baptize me, a spiritual sort whose tact must have satisfied their equally pure tastes.

Yet, unless I am mistaken, in the last years of their stay in Paris a theoretically Protestant, but far more Evangelical-Catholic in spirit, church seems to have given them full satisfaction: the Lutheran Ascension parish, on Rue Dulong, where Pastor Schaffner was the first in Paris to dare establish a "High Church" Lutheranism whose dogmatic firmness and liturgical traditionalism of the best water went much further than even the pious and discreet Bersier.[9]

Deprived of these resources by their suburban exile, it seems to me typical of these two *naturaliter christianae* souls,[10] or I should say today "Catholic without knowing it," that they never deviated from a paradoxically Catholic Protestantism consisting in being so individualistic in their instinctive tendencies. I measure more every year the benefit this singular formation gave me: I simply owe to it the discovery, in the Gospel, not of what has been called "Catholicism" since the modern era, but simply of the true Church of Christ: Catholic not despite the Gospel, but by virtue of its pure and simple acceptance, with all that it demands. That, I think, is what simple souls and upright minds cannot fail to perceive in it unless a distorted education succeeds in masking it from them. I shall soon tell how this experience I had of my parents was later to be fleshed out by the experience—which is far more widespread than is commonly believed—of what is in fact the piety of the near-totality of those Protestants who still have one, whatever prejudices they may have against the Catholic Church ... and whatever prejudices Catholics in general have against those whom they call "our separated brethren," somewhat as we call animals "our inferior brethren." Needless to say, in opposing "Catholicism" to the Catholic Church, I mean only to oppose to the true fidelity to the tradition an anti-Protestantism that is deliberately ignorant of the Bible and suspicious of any personal religion, reducing the faith to the verbal acceptance of oft-repeated for-

9. Lutheran Pastor Auguste Schaffner, who had written his doctoral dissertation on the Protestant preacher Jean de la Placette (1629–1718), was in charge of the Ascension parish at 47 rue Dulong in the 17th *arrondissement* of Paris during the gilded age before World War I. See Bouyer, *Le Métier de théologien*, 2nd edition (Paris: Ad Solem, 2005), 21.

10. "Naturally Christian" souls. The phrase is drawn from the first great Latin Christian writer, Tertullian of Carthage (c. 155–c. 130), *Apologeticus* 17; he explains it in the appendix entitled *De Testimonio Animae* ("On the Witness of the Soul").

mulas and seeing in authority not a means, but an end—the end par excellence. We have seen since how this entirely external Catholicism, which mistakes herd mentality for faithfulness, can toss all of its baggage overboard overnight or, if it is fearful of the consequences, finds salvation only in an ultimate hardening of its emptiest shells.

But I'll close this digression to add a foundational asset I was to receive from my mother in the most sinister depths of the terrible winter of 1917. I shall always see that dark afternoon when we were attempting, she and I (she more than I, for I was then surprisingly insensitive to cold), to warm up, huddling around a meager fire made up of pseudo-coal nuts, actually balls of newspaper that had been moistened, then dried. She suddenly and without any particular preparation began to teach me to repeat by heart what she called "the prayer that Jesus taught us," the Our Father of course. Her explanations, such as they were, and although she was capable on occasion, like her entire Mediterranean family, of a loquacity that would never cease to embarrass me, were limited to the bare minimum. The simple solemnity with which she explained it to me and taught me to repeat it, however, was to assure me—better than any possible commentary—that everything was included in it, be it faith or prayer, everything that I would gradually find in it later, in fact.

I'll leave that subject at that, after pointing out that I owe to this religious formation the conviction that I would find, much later, formally expressed by Newman and justified in a way that seems to me definitive: that there can be no Christianity but a resolutely dogmatic one, but that the dogmas of Christianity transcend all the explanations that those called "the great theologians" can provide for them.[11] They have even less in common with the most diverse opinions that are the most fiercely mistaken for them by the great mass of Protestants as well as by certain Catholics, persuaded as they all are of being more and better than everyone else.

I have, for the first time, just mentioned the time when I was also beginning to realize, at least in some aspects, what I was hearing said and repeated about me and of which I had not made much sense so far: that we were at war. Yet I must also add that this discovery was for a long time

---

11. John Henry Newman (1801–1890), a specialist of the Fathers of the Church, Oxford Movement leader, and influential preacher, converted to the Catholic Church in 1845 and joined the Oratory (as Bouyer would do). He was made cardinal in 1879 and beatified in 2010. See Bouyer, *Métier*, 25–26. Bouyer wrote a couple of books on Newman: *Newman's Vision of Faith: A Theology for Times of General Apostasy* (San Francisco: Ignatius Press, 1986) and *Newman: His Life and Spirituality*, trans. J. Lewis May (San Francisco: Ignatius Press, 2011).

in my intelligence, which was apparently very alert but as yet rather unreceptive to the mentality of adults: something quite different from what they, as I would later realize, poured into that word. During those dark years, indeed, and in the winter when the mediocrity of the heating, as I have mentioned, compelled us to gather in a single room in our house, I began to undergo something of the physical rigors of war. Perhaps as an effect of my mother's evangelical asceticism, however—as far removed as she was from any sort of Manichaeism—I felt these deprivations rather as a sort of sporting exercises than as a truly onerous shortage.

My mother did not hide from me her fears of seeing my father called up "to the front," which could not mean anything specific to me. It was above all the tragic consequences that this departure would have had for us that seem magnified by her dramatic Iberian side. And so, rather than arousing my fears, these alarmist words calmed them. More than this, I was prodigiously amused by the alerts—now frequent, especially at night—that made us dress in haste to leave the house under the searchlights of the anti-aircraft batteries; above all, too, by the gymnastics my father regularly performed to put out a stubborn gaslight. After that we'd spend a while chatting with the neighbors, who were half awake and dressed in funny getups, deep in the basement of one of the buildings I have mentioned. The famous "all clear" would put an end to this, drawing us out of our holes. It was all too entertaining for me to find any tragedy in it.

Although I am hypersensitive in other respects, I must have had good nerves, or simply numb ones, to be decently saddened but not really all that disturbed by the successive deaths, at about this time, of my grandfather, of my Uncle Francis, and of my Aunt Jeanne. The hecatomb visited upon our neighbors by what was discreetly called "Spanish influenza," but which must have been a form of the plague (the only conquest our valiant *Poilus*[12] seem to have brought back from the Orient campaign), did not even manage to upset me seriously. Yet, I do remember my mother's emotion on the day when a truck loaded with coffins passed by under our windows because hearses no longer sufficed. Had not my mother herself assured me that after death life continued, incomparably better, with God, for all those who remained faithful to Him?

I must nonetheless admit that, many years later, when I suddenly realized that we might well have been hit by bombs, or even by shells from Big Bertha (which amused me when I heard its distant "boom-

---

12. *Poilus* ("The hirsute"): French nickname for WWI soldiers, who seldom could shave at the front.

boom"), I was overcome with a sudden fright which, though retrospective, was no less intense. At the time I had to feel more indulgence than sympathy for the wild joy with which my mother and our neighbors congratulated each other when the armistice bells rang. Still, later in the afternoon, I had good fun going for a walk on my father's shoulders in a sunny Paris amid an enthusiastic crowd. But I was so little disposed to getting excited over such great events, which didn't seem to affect our life much, that I was frankly surprised a little while later to see him, who was normally so much calmer than my mother, waste a perfectly good spring evening he ought to have spent in our garden with Tobie, my mother, and me to go off and contemplate, for some event anticipating the Versailles treaty, Poincaré, Clémenceau, Lloyd George, Wilson, and who knows what other great public men;[13] what he had to tell me about them left me perfectly cold. Perhaps if it had been King George and some generals, so prestigious in their uniforms![14] I absolutely could not see what these fine talkers had to offer to make the trip worthwhile. By all accounts, they had never given a thought to fighting with all the rest.

To be quite candid, "the peace," a word that seemed to me even vaguer, if possible, than "war," for a long time had as only concrete meaning the resurrection of the funfairs. I took an extreme liking to them. I was particularly attracted by the breathtaking circus parades such as Zanfretta or Rancy. In all fairness, the peace also soon afforded us a restful vacation in Saint-Germain-en-Laye, of which I regretted that it lasted only one summer.

Just as much as my theater, the world of fairground people and its dazzling concentration in circus shows have meant a lot to me. I shall say nothing about theater in general: after the great Sarah,[15] individual actors such as Gérard Philippe in *Le Prince de Hombourg*, Maria Casares, Michel Bouquet, and above all Ludmilla Pitoeff would enthuse me in turn, but too many mediocre plays would derive their only value from these actors.[16] Otherwise I would always enjoy drama far more

13. The Treaty of Versailles was signed on 28 June 1919. Raymond Poincaré (1860–1934), President of the French Republic, 1913–1920; Georges Clémenceau (1841–1929), Prime Minister, 1917–1920; David Lloyd George (1863–1945), British Prime Minister, 1916–1922; Woodrow Wilson (1856–1924), US President, 1913–1921.

14. King George V (1865–1936) succeeded to his father Edward VII in 1910 as Monarch of the United Kingdom.

15. Sarah Bernhardt, of course (see 25, n. 18).

16. Gérard Philippe (1922–1959) and Maria Casarès (1922–1996) were a well-known theatrical duo in the 1950s. *Le Prince de Hombourg* is one of the last works by Heinrich von Kleist (1777–1811). Actor Michel Bouquet was born in 1925. Ludmilla Pitoeff (1895–1951) was from a renowned Georgian theatrical family.

read straight than playacted: its (to my mind) most perfect forms, whether it be Racine or Shakespeare,[17] too often seem to me to be betrayed, if not made ridiculous, in actual representation.

I never tire of the circus, on the other hand, nor am I disappointed in it so long as it remains carefully, lovingly traditional, just as it was when it first won me over. Straightaway I shall also add that having returned to it just a few weeks ago with three lovely children, I not only rediscovered in them (it was the friendly Grüss circus) exactly the impressions I had had on the first day, but I also had no trouble reliving them. The circus, you see, lacking a text as it does, has at once the immediate and limitless poetry of an absolutely separate world in which everything belonging to the day-to-day world seems to open up in an enchanted yet familiar blooming: bodies no longer have weight or are subject to their usual limitations; animals recover a fabulous intimacy with men; and the madcap comedy is but an ironic and good-natured form of the fairyland magic with which it alternates and which it finally acclimatizes amongst us.

I should add that all that my teachers would later teach me of the superiority of character-driven comedy over situation comedy never managed to uproot from me every child's conviction: that those who hurl cream pies at each other's faces are funny in a far more relaxing, and, therefore, at bottom more satisfying way, than the more subtle forms of what is called "wit." In fact, it is quite remarkable that these latter forms usually grow stale in less than a generation.

Lastly, I shall say that the circus is, in its simplicity, the only available example of an artistic world that is of itself complete and indivisible: from the agility of the trapeze artists to the jugglers' dazzle, from the smiling grace of the equestrian performers to the lion tamers' nimble prowess, or to the trainers of superb horses or of comical performing geese, just as from the prestidigitators' bluff to the clowns' pranks, all of it produces a single family atmosphere. The smell of horse manure mingled with that of the wild animals, the spotlights, the frenzied music, and even *Monsieur Loyal*'s red or blue uniform,[18] all of it is indispensable and hangs together in a joy that cannot be matched.

But here I must stop, for I am reaching one of those chapters on which, as unexpected as it may be to my reader, I could easily become inexhaustible.

17. For Racine, see 26, n. 20. William Shakespeare (1564–1616) is as well known in France as in the English speaking world, at least in name.
18. Originally the name of a specific circus man, *Monsieur Loyal* came to designate all ringmasters.

The other unexpected gift from this peace (though I was unable to see what this peace was) was the vacation in Saint-Germain I have alluded to above. As a matter of fact, I had already spent an entire summer there with my parents and grandfather, in the very same house to boot, on Rue Henry IV, right behind the army barracks in the shade of the château, the year I was born. I naturally had no definite recollection of it, but it may be that an early vague and delightful sensation of happy leisure, of light, and of music remained and helped along the constant, dream-like happiness this next stay there was to give me.

In the first place, we lived in another garden that summer; it was the most enclosed I had ever known, behind an old-fashioned residential building. The very small house disappeared among the trees and flowering copses. Yet this enclosed garden seemed to extend, or rather to transpose itself, into the gloriously expansive garden of the château, whose large balcony dominated the entire Seine valley with Paris in the distance and was open to the sky. The forest continued it through the hazy aura of its great being which, as it seemed to me, was ever shimmering in the golden summer sun under the breeze that always blew through that high perch where we imagined we had escaped from the everyday, humdrum world.

The nearly ceaseless musical flourishes of the garrison's military band kept up and raised to its acme this strange and thrilling persuasion as they announced, or gave cadence to, the dragoons' marches and countermarches. These were joined nearly every evening by the nostalgic calls that invisible hunting horns issued to us from the forest's depths when the setting sun, as it fell upon the tall trees, seemed gradually to spread the night's soft and protective shadow.

Below the château's somewhat unreal outline, which was white and set with red bricks and had a large corbelled balcony extending the over-exquisite Henri IV-style pavilion, there was a beautiful French garden bordered by a park, then merging with the woods beyond, in a landscape that undulated softly into the distance as far as the Marly aqueduct. For me, this constituted a new universe where all was happy vacations and peaceful daydreams. It was peopled by living and fluttering, yet unspeaking, presences: those tall trees sweeping their fronds above the joyful races of chestnut horses glinting with their young black horsemen's long cavalry sabers.[19]

In the background the city, which though no less royal than Versailles was more intimate and calmer, charmed me as well with its easy ele-

---

19. The dragoons (Bouyer's "black horsemen"), as heavy cavalry, had been equipped with long straight sabers since 1882.

gance. Furthermore, there was a group of Chinese students in the ground floor of the large, happy, and peaceful house that preceded and seemed to protect our modest dwelling. God only knows how they landed there; their cordial and good-natured cheerfulness never ceased to delight me and their strange language always bewildered me in that dreamland that alone was suitable to all of these people and things, or rather to this reverie, where I had so suddenly been transported.

You can imagine how difficult it was for me to leave this sojourn to return to an apartment, as pleasant and comfortable as it was, near the Asnières train station on Rue Auguste Bailly—not to mention the school for girls, oh the horror, and for little boys, too (sic!), where I was sent that autumn. I was the only boy amid a gaggle of girls who tormented me, pestered me, pampered me, all the while making great sport of me! I'm not too sure what Ulysses must have undergone under similar circumstances,[20] but I do know, for starters, that I would never have learned a thing had I stayed more than a month in that rustling petticoat inferno; besides that, I should assuredly have caught a fierce and endemic hatred of women. Fortunately this experiment's disastrous results were not long in being noticed, as well-intentioned, though unrealistic, as it was—once again.

My mother, therefore, once more took over my education that year. The result was that I was ranked at the head of my class without any particular effort a year later when it was resolved that I should simply attend the closest local grade school—the very one whose far-off contemplation, at the end of Avenue Faidherbe, had long represented "the world" as opposed to "nature" in my eyes. There I found a young schoolmaster who was equally exquisite in culture and in manners, and, for the first time in my life, chums who were, on the contrary, solidly working-class. I was thus to enjoy an unhoped-for satisfaction for the disparate mix of refined and plebeian tastes that my early education, itself grafted on a diverse pedigree, had already established.

I did suffer at home, however, from having only façades as views. Yet, I did receive compensation in that by turning towards the right on our balcony I could look over the suburban garden plots that reached as far as the railway. On the left, meanwhile, our street stopped short on a semi-blind alley in the direction of an immense park which I knew to shelter an invisible château. Its carriage entrance never opened.

Yet, it was to open just once. It revealed to me the most fabulous sight

20. Bouyer is referring to the attentions that Odysseus had to endure and from which he had trouble escaping in Homer's *Odyssey*, first at the hands of the nymph Calypso (Book 5) and then at the hands of Nausicaa (Book 6).

of my entire boyhood. It was the funeral of this impenetrable and walled-in domain's apparently solitary master. Never before had my eyes beheld such a festival. I remember the hearse, more impressive than any carriage, with its black feathers, heavy drapes, veiled flares, and its silver stars and teardrops, but of course above all the four horses bedecked in even more grandiose and ghostly apparel. It covered their entire heads, which were plumed as well, except for their big shiny eyes. Add to this a whole crowd of sumptuous uniforms surrounding a group of women buried deep under their black crape that must have masked an unspeakable sorrow, I thought. All this within a train of towering chariots bearing heaps of flowers.

I never knew the identity of the departed man who afforded us such a parade, as the coats of arms emblazoned on the hearse were but an additional enigma to me. Yet, I must admit, what struck me the most was the master of ceremonies' funereal splendor and dignity, with his sword, a two-horned hat in hand, silk stockings, and above all his wide, satin-lined black cape. During the next few weeks my vocation as an engineer faltered for the first time: wouldn't that of funeral planner present a far rarer charm? There is no need to recount my poor mother's fright when I admitted these guilelessly ghoulish leanings to her!

This macabre festival was the conclusion, as it were, to our brief stay in Rue Auguste Bailly. We had lived there only three years when another move was to give me another garden which struck me, more even than the first two, as a place of incomparable delights.

This second Asnières garden, along with other more or less similar ones, had been carved out of the park around the Palatine Princess's château. At the time it was occupied by a Dominican-run girls' school of which, by a singular happenstance, I was to be the chaplain many years later. Its charm consisted in being completely enclosed in high walls covered in ivy and wild-grape, excepting one side where it extended beyond a light fence as far as an identical house, or rather a symmetrical one, to ours. Happily, our neighbors immediately became excellent friends: it was quite discreetly occupied by an elderly retired gentleman who smoked the pipe but whose unexpected talents as a tapestry weaver had earned him the family pet name of Penelope and his son, himself director of a musical instrument factory (not again!). Add also an old maid, born of an early marriage of "Penelope's" deceased wife, who kept house for these two bachelors and who, for her part, was one of the best-natured people I ever met. Her half-brother, a painter in his spare time and passionate about the theater, was a discreet mentor to me. His father was to provide me with a sort of honorary grandfather for as long as we were their neighbors.

But I wish to underscore that the discretion of these friends and neighbors was such that I keep the memory of that hidden garden, where I can remember the particularly abundant roses and irises, as of a place of solitude and silence first and foremost. Reclining on a chaise lounge in the garden, or in a large wicker chair inherited from my actual grandfather, on a cozy enclosed verandah, I would slake my thirst for reading at will; this satisfaction would extend into endless reveries. Our neighbors' particularly rich library, which was made available to me on the spot, completed my father's, which was now liberally open to me, at just the right time.

My father had begun to sharpen my appetite by offering my mother and me reading sessions, especially, if I remember correctly, of the *Three Musketeers*. Soon enough I could no longer contain my impatience and I devoured the end of the volume by myself. He later set me on *Twenty Years Later*, then on *The Viscount of Bragelonne* (seven volumes altogether, I believe).[21] Once that cycle had been completed, all of Dumas got it. Yet I think that I better appreciated the other cycle, which centers on Cagliostro.[22] That was the first awakening of my interest in fantasy literature. My father, who shared this interest, wasn't long in taking note of it and encouraged me in that direction, first by handing me Edgar Poe's tales in Baudelaire's translation[23]—which in turn paved the way for my initiation to the latter's poetry—as well as those by Hoffmann,[24] and also Balzac's more esoteric works.[25] From the same Edgar Poe's detective novels I moved on to Conan Doyle's series,[26] still with my father as guide. We shall soon see what an interesting effect it was to have on me.

At the same time the neighbor's library made all of Jules Verne avail-

21. Alexandre Dumas, Sr. (1802–1870) published *The Three Musketeers* in 1844, *Twenty Years Later* in 1845, and *The Viscount of Bragelonne* in 1848.

22. The Cagliostro cycle (adventures set in the eighteenth century) includes *Joseph Balsamo* (1846), *The Queen's Necklace* (1849), *Ange Pitou* (1851), *The Countess de Charny* (1853) and tangentially *The Knight of the Red House* (1846). It centers on the Italian adventurer Giuseppe Balsamo (1743–1795), Count of Cagliostro.

23. French poet Charles Baudelaire (1821–1867) greatly admired the macabre work of Edgar Allen Poe (1809–1849) and translated most of his short stories between 1856 and 1865.

24. Prussian author Ernst Theodor Amadeus Hoffmann (1776–1822) wrote many fantasy stories.

25. Honoré de Balzac (1799–1850), under the influence of Hoffmann and Swedish mystic thinker Emmanuel Swedenborg (1688–1772), included esoteric elements in some of his works.

26. Sir Arthur Conan Doyle (1859–1930), Scottish physician and writer, is the author of the Sherlock Holmes detective stories (four novels and fifty-six short stories), published between 1887 and 1930, despite his effort to "kill" Holmes in 1891.

able to me in the marvelous first edition volumes. They were made from the serials in Hetzel's *Magasin d'éducation et de récréation* with their superb engravings, which were often more evocative than the text itself.[27]

The effect of all this reading was to stimulate an intellectual orientation in me. Its first beginnings could doubtless be detected in my early childhood, but it might never have been so clearly outlined without this retreat in a place of waking dreams in which the world of books, particularly of those books, quite naturally filled out the emptiness of an enclosed garden made up of light and silence.

Two factors mightily encouraged my critical and rational tendency to analyze and reconstruct reality as well as the surreal with the most rigorous intelligence. The first was my propensity to live in a world of boundless imagination that extended the world of daily life into the discovery of its backdrop (so to speak), which, paradoxically, at least in appearance, is made up both of what lies beyond the visible world and of pure inwardness. The second factor was what Poe in particular, underscored by Conan Doyle in his complementary tendency, along with all that Jules Verne and others, such as the all-too-forgotten Jacolliot in *L'Afrique Mystérieuse*,[28] would contribute.

At first I was under the illusion (which I was to revisit, perfectly systematized, in Paul Valéry[29]) of reducing the first factor to the second one, or rather of making it equal to the second to the point that it seemed to absorb the whole. This, however, could only pave the way to the realization that the best and the most that rational intelligence can do is to recognize beyond all doubt the ultimate and irreducible superiority and anteriority of the mystery: the mystery of things themselves, which prepares us for the all-encompassing mystery of ourselves as well as of the universe—to speak like Jaspers.[30]

27. This magazine was founded in 1864 by two republican activists, Jules Hetzel and Jean Macé, for the diffusion of knowledge to a broad readership. Gustave Doré (1832–1883) collaborated as an illustrator.

28. Louis Jacolliot (1837–1890), *L'Afrique mystérieuse: illustrée de vues, scènes, types* (Paris: Librairie illustrée, 1877–1884).

29. Paul Valéry (1871–1945), French symbolist poet and philosopher, elected to the French Academy in 1925. He is claimed by adherents to constructivist epistemology, according to which scientific knowledge is the scientist's construct. Two examples, both culled from his *Monsieur Teste* (1896–1919), will give some idea of his thought: "What makes me is what I do not know about myself"; "Man, ever standing on the Cape of Thought, opening his eyes wide upon the limits either of things or of sight itself."

30. Karl Jaspers (1883–1969), German psychiatrist and philosopher, is considered to represent Christian Existentialism. See Bouyer, *Métier*, 112, 228.

But, for the time being, I wasn't there yet. The immediate effect of these readings and meditations was, as far as my incipient serious studies at the nearby Voltaire grade school were concerned, to arouse my passion for science, above all for physics and chemistry. Very soon, however, I was captivated by what was then being established as physical chemistry—actually a new "natural philosophy," as Anglo-Saxons still call it—that aims at the ultimate explanation of the universe, of all of reality, in the integral exploration and rationalization of its elementary contexture. I still have in my possession astonishing notebooks in which, when I was barely twelve, I attempted to present, on the basis of atomic theory as it was defined at the time, a kind of entirely unified global vision of all of reality. Such was my personal *Eurêka*.[31]

I was unwittingly following a sort of Pythagorean ideal. Far from implying any materialism, it brought nature itself into the mind by a kind of rational monism in which numbers and figures (seemingly circumscribed to it) made up all of reality in a coherent vision that the absolute Mind gives to Itself in our own minds, which are in every way dependent upon it.

And so I had no trouble harmonizing this vision, which was still working itself out, with the religious vision of the universe I was fed by the Protestant catechism (which was quite excellent, by the way) I was studying at the time in the little Methodist church next to the Asnières train station—the only accessible Protestant house of worship. Quite to the contrary, I could see the pursuit of my scientific ruminations spontaneously developing into a sort of Christian apologetics, or better yet, into an integral theology of which it might constitute the kernel: the ground of tangible experience spontaneously calling out to this transcendent rationalization.

All these musings were to burst, so to speak, in an implosion rather than in an explosion. This was provoked by my mother's almost sudden death.

---

31. The Greek εὕρηκα, *heurēka*, attributed to Archimedes upon discovering his principle, means "I've got it!"

3

From Paradise Lost
to Paradise Regained

MY MOTHER had always suffered from migraines, the cause of which was unknown at the time, but which modern medicine would, I think, explain as liver insufficiency. Nothing, however, had prepared us for the revelation of this liver cancer which, early in the winter of 1924, was to carry her off after barely a month of suffering.

The effect of this death on me was indescribable. The sorrow I felt does not reach the magnitude of the shock it was to produce down to the very roots of my being, and whose depth would only reveal itself later.

At the time I was able to survive only by burying myself even deeper in my reading and the speculations it fed. Two related issues also increased in those first trying months, however, which I now recognize as the warning signs of the tragic and deadly void my mother's death had precipitated. It was about to show itself in an unexpected catastrophe.

One of these issues was the reawakening of my theatrical passion. It was provoked by a performance of *Tartuffe*,[1] featuring the good actor Silvain—also from Asnières as it happens—in the leading role.[2] My new friend Jacques Ducroquet, our neighbor, had taken me to it. My first discovery of the classics at school—Molière, Racine, and Corneille, whom I had begun reading with gusto—excited my attraction. It reached such a point that I undertook the composition of an unlikely tragedy with Louis XI (I'm not too sure why; perhaps after reading

---

1. A comedy by Molière (1622–1673) first performed in 1669; its full title is *Tartuffe, or The Hypocrite*. *Tartuffe* has become the French byword for a sanctimonious hypocrite.

2. Eugène Silvain (1851–1930) was a regular member, later the secretary, of the prestigious *Comédie Française*. He held all the great roles of the French classical repertoire, including that of Tartuffe. He is also famous for his role as Bishop Pierre Cauchon in the silent film *Joan of Arc* (1928) by Danish director Carl Theodor Dreyer (1889–1968).

Quentin Durward?)[3] as subject and, at the same time, gave myself singular performances, of *The Pleaders* in particular.[4]

The other of these issues, which was subtly linked to the former, was a sudden craze (animated by the Gun Club in Jules Verne's futuristic interplanetary novels)[5] for founding clubs whose statutes I feverishly wrote up and whose presidency I generously offered to my closest schoolmates.

I think that both of these fancies, especially the second one, betrayed my increasing need as a loner for social overcompensation, accompanied with a quasi-liturgy whose elaborate rituals would allow me to participate, along with my associates, in that cosmic integration of my very existence, which my thinking alone pursued so frenetically.

All this was only a palliative, however. Indeed, up to that point my mother had been the only living being in my life with whom I lived in symbiosis. With her gone, I remained totally, absolutely alone in a world emptied of any presence besides my own.

The well-intentioned mistake that led my father to remarry, a little over a year after my mother's death, with the widowed wife of one of his best friends, surely with a view to give me a replacement mother, actually hastened an inevitable evolution. This excellent woman, as much a stranger—despite her own wishes—to my father's psychology as she was to mine, succeeded only in becoming a screen between him and me.

More and more absorbed in my reading and the writing of my *Eurêka* I have mentioned, I soon reached a veritable obsession under those conditions; it might well have turned to early dementia. Indeed, I ended up doubting that there might be consciousnesses outside of my own, and that the idea of God and of other beings in the world might be anything more than a projection of my own thought. As a consequence, I sank into that impression of stifling loneliness that can only be, to a sick conscience that nevertheless basically remains desperately normal, the only possible effect of solipsism taken seriously.

On the advice of a psychiatrist (Dr. Claude, brother of the famous chemist,[6] a hero of mine), my studies were therefore interrupted and my father asked some old friends of my mother's to take me in for a few

3. Sir Walter Scott (1771–1832), *Quentin Durward*, a novel about an archer in late fifteenth-century France.

4. *The Pleaders* is a comedy (1668) by Jean Racine (see 26, n. 20).

5. In *From the Earth to the Moon* (1865) and *Around the Moon* (1869), Jules Verne has the Baltimore Gun Club finance a flight to the moon aboard a hollow shell shot out of a massive cannon.

6. Georges Claude (1870–1960), chemist and inventor, most famous for liquefying air in 1902. He would play a leading role in Franco-German collaboration during the 1940s.

months in the little old town of Sancerre, in the Loire Valley, to which they had fled from Paris themselves some years before.[7] Nothing could have been more providential than this measure and, as a fortunate side effect, the illness that had occasioned it. Indeed, I must admit that I recognize in it a known case of the creative illness Dr. Henri Ellenberger was to observe, a few years later, as the origin of the most fruitful vocations.[8] Most of all it afforded me the chance to take to this region, more even than to the friendly welcome that awaited me there. That region will always remain something like the native land of my mind, of my soul, of my heart; in a word, of all the best that life has providentially allowed me not only to achieve but also, I think, to be.

In order to be understood on this score, I can do no better than to recall the evening of my arrival. Already at the end of that spring day, once the train had reached the Loire valley near Gien and Montargis, I had been wrested from my reading by the golden softness of that landscape, in whose harmonious lines waterways and woods surrounded peaceful and simple houses casually grouped along riverbeds and tree branches.

It was something else, though, when upon my being welcomed at the Tracy train station in the middle of the woods, I was taken off to the beach where, alone, we were to take a frugal supper in the last and softest light of that beautiful evening. Before me, on the other bank, the declining sun had not yet let the shade completely absorb the three hills where Sancerre, the first town on the north side, dominated the landscape, followed by L'Orme-Aux-Loups and La Pierre-Goupillière. Sancerre was crowned with its tower and château but was nearly entirely enfolded in its woods; L'Orme-Aux-Loups was girded with vineyards into which a quarry cut a still rose-colored crack; La Pierre-Goupillière was, again, buried under a sylvan cloak that waved into the distance as far as the great river's vicinity.

This river at my feet slid its emerald mirror between its sandbanks along leafy islands whose reflection shimmered on its water's surface, just before the peaceful houses at Saint-Thibaut under the great white viaduct linking Sancerre to the brow of the Bois-de-Charnes woods, right after the tall outline of the unfinished Saint-Satur church.

7. Sancerre is on an elevation on the left bank of the Loire, between Nevers and Gien in the Cher *département.*

8. Henri Ellenberger (1905–1993), Swiss-Canadian psychiatrist and author of *The Discovery of the Unconscious: The History and Evolution of Dynamic Psychiatry* (New York: Basic Books, 1970). Bouyer met him in Strasbourg (see 91).

To my right, the masonry piles and rhythmic curves of the suspension bridge cables spanned the river with a chain that the shrouding nightfall made more musical yet than in broad daylight.

All this was so serene and sure in its beauty that I felt a sudden peace and was won over forever. The charm only increased when we left and walked across the bridge, which bounced up and down under our footsteps in the thickening darkness. After a short walk along the sleepy burgh and another crossing (this time on the bridge over the canal between two rows of poplars) we just barely grazed Saint-Satur soon before ending up in a rural area made up of meadows and vineyards where the White Queen's path, as it is called, zigzags its way up.

It had led us, in the nearly complete night, to the ruins of Saint-Romble priory,[9] which were invaded by wild vegetation. From then began, along the park's interminable wall, the climb up the rocky footpath leading to the Porte-César esplanade, whose "lighthouse" (three powerful electric lights in a triangle formation) had long been beckoning us.

When we reached this terrace, the moment we spent there facing back towards the path we had just taken completed the enchantment. It had a view of the Loire snaking its way under the moon between its sandbanks and its woods, of bouquets of lights planted along its course by the towns and villages, of dark hillcrests overlooking it on the horizon, and, at our feet, the carpet of vineyards striped with dark hedges and light pathways as far as the ribbon-like canal stretching between its double edging of slender trees.

Far from weakening this first impression, the following days and years nurtured and perfected it. So much so that, on another beautiful summer eve with a friend quite recently, I could not again see the Sancerre hill from the road that hugs the Loire on the other side without welling up with tears.

The charm of that diverse and hilly countryside with its twists and turns, presenting as it does renewed and unexpected vistas at every moment, is certainly extraordinary in its own right. To explain the effect it had on me and on many others, I cannot do better than to say that for me it was, in a different register, an equivalent of what the English Lake District revealed itself to be for its poets, particularly for Wordsworth.[10]

---

9. An Augustinian abbey was founded there in 1034 and destroyed by the English during the Hundred Years War.

10. William Wordsworth (1770–1850), English Romantic poet. He lived in the Lake District from 1799 to his death. The other principal Lake District poets are Samuel Taylor Coleridge (1772–1834) and Robert Southey (1774–1843).

In fact, when I discovered him later, I would find as it were a pre-established harmony with what those first months' solitary acquaintance with the Sancerre region were to offer me, though in my case, too, it would never cease deepening and multiplying every year I returned there up until the second world war.

If I had to do my best to define this immediate impression, I should say that I was equally and so to speak inseparably moved by these landscapes' humanity and grandeur, especially since they are more captivating for always remaining so discreet. The rise of the hills, the expanding vistas they offer, alternating with the contemplative woody hollows where sources and streams abound, and perhaps more than this the grand silent river's enshrouding magic with the constant unpopulated presence of its waters, sandbanks, and foliage all combined to produce this effect.

Strangely, but not as unexpectedly as it might seem at first, the solipsistic obsession I have spoken of spontaneously vanished in my solitary walks all over this (to me) brand-new world. Indeed, this world both called out to human presences and immersed them, plunged them back into their source, if you will, into a presence that was limitless yet by no means vague and hazy. This presence was suggested, I thought, by the both paternal and maternal expectation of an inspired gratitude.

And so I immediately sympathized with Wordsworth in his protestations against those who accused his cosmic poetry of pantheism. In fact, in my case as in his, this life in regular contact with a landscape that is so evocative of a presence, of supernatural presences behind or within nature itself, quite naturally harmonized with a rediscovery, or simply a renewed discovery, of the most precisely evangelical kind of Christianity.

I was helped along, of course, by the reading material quite simply provided by the rather well-furnished library I found in the room set aside for me under the rooftops.

I was enthused by Adolphe Monod, the nineteenth-century preacher; more so by his *Adieux*,[11] which are a series of meditations improvised on his deathbed and taken down by his friends, than by his sermons— as excellent as those were. I am not sure that my discovery of Alexandre

11. Adolphe Monod (1802–1856), *Les Adieux d'Adolphe Monod à ses Amis et à l'Église, octobre 1855 à mars 1856* (Paris: C. Meyrueis, 1856), published posthumously. English version: *Adolphe Monod's Farewell to His Friends and to His Church*, trans. Owen Thomas (London: Banner of Truth Trust, 1962). For Bouyer's mature and sensitive analysis of these, see *The Spirit and Forms of Protestantism* (Westminster, MD: Newman Press, 1956), 36–41.

Vinet and his marvelous *Pastoral Theology* joined them that soon in my retreats in the Sancerre region, but it remains forever bound to their memory.[12]

What held perhaps even more promise of future developments would be the very simple yet excellent religious instruction that Pastor Coudirolle gave me and my hosts' children.[13] This subtle Béarn man,[14] who was finishing up his career in Sancerre, combined with a genuine countryman's wisdom and shrewdness a culture that was, even for the time, quite rare among Protestant and Catholic clergy alike. In the early years of the century, he had been a student of the great patrologist Eugène de Faye.[15] Not only had he retained his lessons, but he had assimilated them so well that he was able to excite the gang of kids we were for the writings and lives of the Fathers of the Church, particularly Tertullian, Clement, and Origen.[16] As far as I am concerned, this excellent man was to sow in me the seeds that would later germinate in both my studies and my own research.

I think it was in Adolphe Monod that I first found so clear an expression of the idea that God is love, and that this love finds its manifestation par excellence in the Cross of Christ: this, I saw with absolute clarity, is the very heart of Christianity.[17] Vinet, on the other hand, though without in any way denying this intuition, persuaded me that the broadest kind of humanism, far from contradicting it, must make it explicit: how could one love God, loving Him with His own love, the love which is He Himself, without loving as He does all that He loves?

I must also point out that, at the time, I read with an intimate satisfaction a very sensitive essay by Pastor Henri Monnier (who was later to

12. Alexandre Rudolf Vinet (1797–1847), Swiss literary critic and Reformed theologian who defended the Church's independence from political institutions; he has been called the "Protestant Pascal." Bouyer here refers to his *Théologie pastorale ou Théologie du ministère évangélique*, rendered in English as *Pastoral Theology: The Theory of a Gospel Ministry*, trans. Thomas O. Summers (Nashville, TN: Southern Methodist Pub. House, 1861).

13. Joseph Coudirolle obtained his doctorate in 1885; his dissertation was about the Protestant Academy of Orthez, which the future Henri IV (1553–1610) raised to the rank of university in 1582. Coudirolle settled in Sancerre in 1927.

14. Béarn: a region in the foothills of the Pyrenees.

15. Eugène de Faye (1860–1929), author of works on Gnosticism, Clement of Alexandria, and Origen. He taught Church History at the Sorbonne until the school of theology was closed in 1885, then at the *École Pratique des Hautes Études*.

16. St. Clement of Alexandria (c. 150–c. 215), author of the *Stromata*. Origen (c. 185–c. 254), founder of Christian biblical exegesis. For Tertullian see 34, n. 10.

17. See 49, n. 11.

be one of my most respected professors)[18] on the Redemption.[19] It convinced me that the Cross of Christ saves us as a supreme act of solidarity with us. This supposes of course, as he didn't fail to point out, that it does not save us by exempting us from suffering, but by rendering us capable of suffering fruitfully. This was to be my first tether to an ascetical view of Christianity, though I would remain far removed from it for a long time. My education up to that point as well as my deepest instincts remained and, I think, always will remain the source of a deeply rooted eudaemonism.[20] It had for many years retained the naiveté of an existence that was doubtlessly overprotected until it was rent asunder by my mother's premature and utterly unexpected death.

This is obviously what my passion for science had expressed up to that point, as well as the beguiling charm of the familiar places I have described and which the discovery of the Sancerre region only refreshed and deepened.

Yet the influence of the fervent and somewhat narrow Protestant milieu in which I was then immersed was developing, in a contradictory yet simultaneous manner, with a passing horror for Catholicism, my distance from any sort of asceticism—which I saw as a mutilation. Yet, at the same time, it also developed a Quaker style of extremism in the refusal of any intermediary, of anything but the soul's direct and personal contact with God.

I only progressively came to discover that the cosmic aspect of my discovery of God as reality, not as mere notion, itself postulated a social and incarnate worship, while there could be no victory over evil, in a sinful world and for sinful men, without painful effort—not, to be sure, sought out for its painfulness but rather for the price to pay for the purification of love itself; that is, the only source of the greatest and abiding joy. Other influences, which I shall address shortly, contributed to this as well. Then, too, what I have qualified as "Quaker"[21] would find no less

18. See 61.

19. Henri Monnier (1871–1941) taught at the Protestant School of Theology in Paris. He wrote an *Essai sur la rédemption, conférences données à l'Université d'Upsal sous le patronage de la Fondation Olaus Petri* (Neuilly: Éditions de "la Cause," 1929).

20. Eudaemonism is a system of ethics that bases moral obligation on the tendency of actions to produce happiness; it is found in Aristotle, Montaigne, Spinoza, Diderot, et al.

21. The Quakers arose as a radical branch of English Puritanism in the seventeenth century. Their name seems to derive from the admonishment to "quake before God" that their leader, George Fox (1624–1691), gave to the court that was trying him as a dissenter. Quakers reject all dogma and institution and claim that religious faith is entirely a matter of a personal relationship with God.

satisfaction in the purest mystical tradition: Saint John of the Cross in the first place; then Dionysian and Rheno-Flemish mysticism.[22]

But I am anticipating once again. Before getting there, I shall have to consolidate and expand what my first stay in the Sancerre region had so serenely and vigorously sketched out—but also correct certain aspects of it. That was the work of new books I undertook to read, of new encounters too, in the years that followed.

My father and stepmother, since she wished to lead a more active life, had decided to leave our house in Asnières to acquire a store, first on Rue du Chevaleret near the Place d'Italie, and, a few years later, on the Rue Louis Braille, not far from the Bois de Vincennes.

The first of these moves led us, my father and me, to attend the little Lutheran church, La Trinité, on the Boulevard de la Gare, where Pastor Samuel Lambert officiated. I was to become his vicar some years later. But Pastor Russier, who had baptized me, advised Pastor Louis Kreyts, of the Reformed church of Port-Royal near the Gobelins, of our new address and it was he who first contacted us.[23] The result was that our Sunday practice alternated somewhat between these two neighboring churches.

From the outset, and despite my instinctive Quakerism, I must admit that the charming little church of La Trinité, which was very discreetly Catholic in style, and its liturgical services were far more to my taste than the Port-Royal temple[24] and its "worship service" that was more wordy and tangibly less prayerful. On the other hand Pastor Kreyts, a Jewish convert and an enthusiastic self-taught man, not only was cordiality incarnate but revealed himself to be an excellent teacher of mine through the books he lent me and the explanations he gave me of them. I am indebted to him, above all, for having revealed Newman to me through Henri Bremond's book.[25] It captivated me on the spot and I never tired of rereading it, especially, I have to say already at this time,

22. "Rheno-Flemish" mysticism arose in the Middle Ages along the Rhine valley and in Flanders, first in the Béguinages (see 111, n. 40) and among Religious women: Hildegard of Bingen (c. 1099–c. 1179); Hadwijch of Antwerp (c. 1220–c. 1260); Gertrude of Helfta (c. 1256–c. 1302). Some Dominicans came to adopt it: Meister Eckhart (c. 1260–c. 1328); Henry Suso (c. 1295–c. 1366); Johannes Tauler (see 88, n. 23); and Jan Van Ruysbroeck (c. 1293–c. 1381). The theme of the soul's union with God derives from Dionysius the Aeropagite (traditionally held to be St. Paul's convert in Acts 17:34 but now often dated to the late fifth century) and is called "Dionysian"; St. John of the Cross (1542–1591) developed it in Spain.

23. Lévi Russier (born 1881) was pastor until 1948. Louis Kreyts (born 1873) was pastor until 1939.

24. In the French Reformed Church, churches are referred to as "temples."

for the choice and excellent translation of texts that make it an anthology of Newman's most exquisite passages. It was not long, however, before I realized—despite the brilliance of its style and presentation—that Newman's thought was singularly more complete and vigorous than his biographer's.

Another factor had prepared me for what was then revealed to me of the Catholic tradition along lines that were more particularly accessible to a Protestant: the friendship of three young ladies, distant cousins of my stepmother's, who did not live far from our new residence. They were profoundly religious; the conversations I had with them and, there again, the books that were lent to me, starting with Huysmans's *La Cathédrale*,[26] had already sapped my anti-Catholicism.

But its definitive debacle was brought about by a few excellent articles by the Lutheran Pastor Frank Wheatcroft,[27] who was destined to become one of my best friends and my mentor on traditional liturgy. They definitively convinced me of the inanity, and most especially of the unbiblical and unchristian character, of the anti-ritualism I had breathed in the Sancerre milieu. It had been only too well suited to my individualism and my tendency to maniacal interiorization, and was very questionably healthy for both intellect and soul.

Needless to say, during these last years of high school, first at Jean-Baptiste Say and then at Chaptal,[28] I read much else besides.

First, I need to say a word about a certain Father Moreux's general-public scientific works, which include a vigorous apologetics.[29] My curiosity had been attracted to them by the simple fact that he was the director of the observatory in Bourges, a town close to Sancerre; it had fascinated me the very first time I visited it. The somewhat facile con-

25. Henri Bremond (1865–1933), French Catholic scholar in the Modernist movement. He wrote about Newman (see 35, n. 11) and translated some of his works. See his *The Mystery of Newman*, trans. H. C. Corrance (London and Dublin: Williams and Norgate, 1907). See Bouyer, *Métier*, 25, 143.

26. Joris-Karl Huysmans (1848–1907). His 1897–98 novel *The Cathedral*, trans. Clara Bell (New York: E.P. Dutton, 1922), is a highly detailed examination of the art and architecture of the Cathedral of Chartres.

27. The Englishman Frank H. Wheatcroft, author of a dissertation on Anglican liturgy, *Essai Sur la Formation de la Liturgie Anglicane* (Montauban, 1906), was a pastor on the southern coast of France in Nice (1919–1927) before moving up to Paris.

28. Jean-Baptiste Say and Chaptal, now among the most prestigious high schools in France, are respectively in the sixteenth and eighth *arrondissement*.

29. Théophile Moreux, *Pour comprendre la philosophie* (Paris: Gaston Doin, 1926). English version: *Modern Science and the Truths Beyond: Being a Popular Outline of Philosophy in Relation to the Scientific Problems of Today*, trans. Michael Fitzsimons (London: Browne and Nolan, 1931).

cordism of these works prevented neither an exalted vision of creation
nor a good number of wise and perceptive remarks. The idea that the
world cannot be the observer's unconscious waking dream, since it
shows itself to be totally resistant to playing the will's game—an idea
that incorporates something like a summary of Maine de Biran's
thought,[30] which I would only discover much later—gave my solipsism
its death blow.[31] Above all, though, I for a long time relished Charles
Secrétan's *Philosophie de la Liberté* in the same perspective as this last
remark.[32] Although the inclination it communicated to me for Duns
Scotus's thought[33] was not to survive direct contact with his all-too-
famous subtlety, I remain deeply indebted to Secrétan's conception of
an essentially personalist universe. I am no less indebted to him for an
inclination to treat—as I would later do myself—theological research as
an analysis of the organic evolution of questions in the collective human
mind. It seems to me that, at equal distance from an abstract a priori
systematization and a spineless eclecticism, this is the only philosophical method to be truly and durably fruitful, so long as it remains
open ... at the opposite of Hegelianism and its by-products!

These diverse discoveries, however, would deploy themselves in those
years only in the wake of, and so to speak within, my initiation to Newman and, through him, to the creative formation of the Christian tradition, starting with the Fathers of the Church.

My second sojourn in Sancerre, which left no less a mark on me than
the first one did, was the next year on the return of summer. It remains
inseparable from my meditation on the *Apologia*[34] and some of the best
passages of the *Parochial and Plain Sermons*.[35] The former of these two
books was the nearly invariable companion of my walks around

30. Maine de Biran (1766–1824), French philosopher of subjective psychology and
editor of the first journal of philosophy in France.

31. According to solipsism, the thinking subject is the only reality of which one can
be sure.

32. Charles Secrétan (1815–1895), Swiss Protestant theologian and philosopher, disciple of Alexandre Vinet (see 50, n. 12). He aimed at reconciling Christianity with meta-
physical philosophy.

33. Franciscan Friar Duns Scotus (1266–1308) is termed "the Subtle Doctor" because
of his brilliant demonstrations. He elevates the role of faith and will over that of reason,
as opposed to Dominican Friar Thomas Aquinas (1225–1274) who insists on the reason-
ableness of faith.

34. John Henry Newman (see 35, n. 11) wrote the *Apologia Pro Vita Sua* in 1865–66 to
explain the reasons for his conversion.

35. These are a collection of Newman's sermons as Anglican vicar of St. Mary's, near
Oxford, between 1834 and 1843. They were first published in 1869 and can be found in
Parochial and Plain Sermons (San Francisco: Ignatius Press, 1987).

Sancerre at that time. Their horizons will always be linked, in my mind, to that reading, which I have renewed who knows how often, just as the visions of Oxford which, later on, would become just as familiar and nearly as enthralling.

Under the influence of these different studies, but of course under that of Newman first and foremost, especially of his two sermons for the Feast of Michaelmas and All Angels and on the invisible world, not to mention the good part played by my impressions of the Sancerre region, I came to elaborate in those early years the view of the world I have attempted to pin down in my *Cosmos*, which is now under press.[36]

The English poets—Wordsworth most of all—whom I was soon to discover would confirm this view and contribute to giving it all of its resonances.[37] At a speculative level, it would gain strength from my later study of the Alexandrian Fathers and even more of Gregory of Nyssa,[38] as well as of Saint Thomas Aquinas's *De Veritate*, and lastly an attentive reading of Berkeley guided by the trenchant exegesis of his last editor, A. A. Luce (with whom I would undertake a most cordial correspondence in the 1960s).[39]

Here I shall simply say that, in this view, the material, physical world cannot be separated from an invisible, essentially "intelligible," spiritual world. The material world is, so to speak, the common irradiation of this spiritual world as far as concerns the first-born spirits, the angels; from it the human mind emerges and finds within it not only its medium of communication, but also the awakening of its consciousness. This world, wherein the intelligible and the sensible form a single tapestry, is but a single thought of God. It is eternally present in Him and projected in time and simultaneously in the distinct existence of other consciousnesses.

Later on I would come to recognize it as the projection of a Wisdom

---

36. *Cosmos: Le monde et la gloire de Dieu* (Paris: Cerf, 1982), rendered into English as *Cosmos: The World and the Glory of God*, trans. Pierre de Fontnouvelle (Petersham, Mass.: St. Bede's Publications, 1988). Since it was first published late in 1982, Bouyer must have written this chapter in the same year.

37. For Wordsworth see 48, n. 10.

38. The "Alexandrian Fathers" are principally St. Clement of Alexandria and Origen (see 50, n. 16), and St. Cyril of Alexandria (c. 376–444). St. Gregory of Nyssa (c. 335–c. 395) is one of the Cappadocian Fathers, along with his brother St. Basil of Caesarea (c. 330–379) and their friend St. Gregory of Nazianzus (c. 330–390).

39. George Berkeley (1685–1753), Anglican theologian and philosopher. He was a bishop in Ireland before going to America to promote evangelism. He sought to reconcile Lockean empiricism with Christian faith. Arthur Aston Luce (1882–1977) was Fellow at Trinity College (Dublin) from 1912 to his death; he and Thomas Edmund Jessup (1896–1980) edited *The Works of George Berkeley, Bishop of Cloyne* (London: Nelson, 1964).

of creation outside of the eternal Word, animated by the divine Spirit who, at the same time, urges it to return to this filial Word to espouse it and come back up with it, in the same Spirit, to the Father, as if in an eternal Eucharist.

Newman's influence at the outset was to mean yet more to me. It elicited my admiration for his exceptional union of intellectual honesty and lucid rigor in the search for truth with a demanding sense of all of existence's religious character. But this reached its climax in the attraction, which I found irresistible, not only of the richest and most refined human culture, but also of a poetic gift that is just as rare in its purity and intensity, and which is doubtless what Bremond was best able to bring out in his book,[40] as much as it shows itself to be limited in the last analysis, or even slightly off-track in nearly all its comments.

I cannot bring this chapter on Sancerre to a close without also mentioning the importance of the personal encounters I had there. I have already brought up the attractive figure of that old Pastor who, in opening up the Fathers of the Church to me, especially the Alexandrians, had unwittingly prepared me for the best lessons to be had in Newman.

I wouldn't be much less unjust if I did not say at least a word about the excellent bonds I developed with my hosts' children, particularly with their eldest son, who was a little younger than I. With him I discovered all that long walks and games played together, with their complement of endless conversations, can give to youth who are very different from each other, but perhaps get along all the better because they complete each other, be it only in discussions without end in sight that fail to convince either one of them.

I am even less inclined to fail to mention the affection, the intense fondness that developed very early with one of my young friends' cousins. She was seven years younger than I and these feelings, at least on my part, soon turned to love.

Soon I could no longer contemplate my future life without sharing it with this Élisabeth. She was witty and gay, though no less mysterious for all that, despite the exceptionally light blue coloration of her eyes, which I have never found since. This sentiment was to contribute to the definitive formation of my personality, in equal measure, I think, through the enthusiasm and hope it would long foster and through the heart-rending disappointment in which it would end.

40. See 52–53, n. 25.

4

Initiation

THE LAST YEARS of my secondary education were again filled with an overabundant intellectual activity.

Newman, along with my discovery of the liturgy, spurred me on to develop my knowledge of English. My mother had already initiated me to it by having me regularly use the Prayer Book[1] and the English Bible, all the while attending Evensong every Sunday either at the American Pro-Cathedral on Avenue George V or at the charming little English church on the Rue Auguste Vacquerie (which has been atrociously disfigured since), St. George's.[2] To this was soon added, over and above my school studies and my personal reading, an accelerated study of Greek and Latin; my scientific orientation had until then kept me from them. I had not yet, until my second stay in Sancerre, considered a change in my vocation myself, despite my increasing immersion in theology and religious philosophy. Yet, as on many other occasions in my life, an unexpected intervention determined a capital change. This time it was giving up a career as a physicist or a chemist, even though I was still looking at it more and more from a perspective of Christian witness.

My new friends' paternal grandmother, an old Alsatian lady who was perspicacious yet deeply religious and who was much more to my liking, I must say, than their maternal grandmother's pious imperialism

1. Bouyer doubtless refers to the *Book of Common Prayer*. It was first published under Edward VI in 1549; Thomas Cranmer (1489–1556), Archbishop of Canterbury, was the editor. It contains Morning Prayer, Evening Prayer (a service combining Vespers and Compline), a Litany, the Communion Service, and various rites (baptism, marriage, etc.).

2. The American Episcopalian Cathedral of the Trinity was built in 1882–1886 on Avenue Georges V in the 8th *arrondissement* near the Champs Élysées in the neo-Gothic style. St. George's, the English Church built in 1887–1889, is not very far from the American church just mentioned, near the Place de l'Étoile in the 16th *arrondissement*. It is also neo-Gothic but was updated in the 1970s.

(as cultured as she was), had only to tell me, "It's not a professor you ought to become, it's a pastor!" for me to tell myself immediately, "Why didn't I think of that? Well, if she thinks so, she must be right!"

Protestant theological studies were serious in those days, so I had to make up for lost time. I devoted myself to it all the more willingly that Newman had sharpened my old attraction to Hellenism.

Yet the effect of going to Anglican churches would be greater than simply captivating me with the liturgy they continue to foster and initiating me both to traditional liturgy and to a more detailed and intimate meditation on the Bible in its context of prayer and adoration. By chance, one of the first times I was at the Holy Trinity Pro-Cathedral I have mentioned above, Dean Beekman (one of the best pioneers of nascent ecumenism)[3] had invited me to the Saint Serge Institute of Russian Theology, on the Rue de Crimée. This was the occasion for me to discover both the unsuspected splendor of Orthodox liturgy and the brilliant personality of Father Sergei Bulgakov, who preached in that correct yet rough-hewn English that was always to be the medium of his contacts with the West.[4]

I straightaway had the impression of seeing reappear before me the very Christianity of the Fathers, especially the Greek Fathers, that Pastor Coudirolle had so engagingly opened up to me and to which Newman had permanently won me over.

These new interests were encouraged by the ecumenical movement, which was taking off in those very years. The Protestant periodicals I read more or less regularly gave it a lot of space. In 1925, Nathan Söderblom,[5] Primate of the (Lutheran) Church of Sweden, and the *Life and Work* conference[6] from Stockholm were launching a movement of cooperation in social action among, in principle, all the Churches. They acquired my intense admiration, which was second only to that I felt for

3. Frederick W. Beekman came to France as American Military chaplain during the First World War and stayed as dean of the Cathedral until after World War II.

4. Sergei Bulgakov (1871–1944), Russian Orthodox priest and theologian, founder of the St. Sergius Orthodox Theological Institute in Paris in 1925. His speculations center on sophiology. Bouyer recounts his meetings with him in "La Personnalité et l'œuvre de Serge Boulgakoff (1871–1944)," *Nova et Vetera* 53 (1978): 135–44; see also *Métier*, 25, 174, 184, 210, 212, 218, 262.

5. Nathan Söderblom (1866–1931) preached in Paris from 1894 to 1901. He was elected Archbishop of Uppsala (and therefore Primate of Sweden) in 1914 and was awarded the Nobel Peace Prize in 1930. See *Métier*, 169.

6. This conference, held at Stockholm in 1925, was the crowning achievement of Söderblom's work along ecumenical lines. It brought together Anglicans, Protestants, and Orthodox Christians.

the second conference that met in Lausanne two years later to deal directly with the problem of the unity to be recovered in the churches' faith and institutions.[7] The American (Anglican) Bishop Brent,[8] and Gardiner, a layman,[9] had played the same role in organizing this conference and the entire Faith and Order movement as that played by Söderblom for Stockholm.

I was not unaware that despite the reticence that Pius XI had expressed in the encyclical *Mortalium Animos*[10] some Catholics, and of the highest quality too, also took an active interest in these movements, or rather in this double movement. I had read with passionate curiosity a report on the conferences at Malines centering on Cardinal Mercier in the wake of the meeting of those two exceptional personages, the Abbé Portal and Lord Halifax.[11]

All of this confirmed a sentiment that has never left me since and which I was to explain and develop in my *Spirit and Forms of Protestantism*.[12] It was completed and published after my conversion, but conceived and outlined long before it.[13] There was no question of jettisoning what I saw as the unquestionable strong points of Protestantism: a direct relationship with God through Christ involving the whole person, whence, as a universal principle, a Christianity nourished, for all its faithful, by the meditation of the divine Word, and, from that point, a religion whose essence could only consist in a total acceptance in faith of grace alone, which God gives us in His Son.

---

7. The first World Conference on Faith and Order met at Lausanne, 3–12 August 1927. This organization would merge with Life and Work (see foregoing note) in 1948 to become the World Council of Churches.

8. Charles Henry Brent (1862–1929), appointed Bishop to the Philippines in 1902 and Bishop of Western New York from 1918. He was one of the organizers of the first World Conference at Lausanne.

9. Robert Gardiner, Secretary of the Commission of the Episcopal Church USA during the 1910 World Missionary Conference in Edinburgh.

10. 6 January 1928.

11. Vincentian Father Fernand Portal (1855–1926) and Lord Halifax (1839–1934) were collaborators in ecumenical endeavors, particularly the Conversations of Malines, along with Cardinal Mercier (1851–1926), Bishop of Malines and Primate of Belgium from 1906, made Cardinal in 1907. For Mercier see D. A. Boileau, *Cardinal Mercier: A Memoir* (Leuven, 1996).

12. Louis Bouyer, *Du Protestantisme à l'Église* (Paris: Cerf, 1954). English version: *The Spirit and Forms of Protestantism*, trans. A. V. Littledale (Westminster, MD: Newman Press, 1956). The original title translates to "From Protestantism to the Church."

13. Bouyer was received into the Church on 27 December 1939; see chapter 7 below and *Métier*, 33.

Yet, as a consequence, it seemed to go without saying that the whole ecumenical question was about restoring these certainties to their vital environment: the one Church willed by Christ, founded on the Apostles, and cutting across the centuries in an uninterrupted tradition.

These sentiments, already in the years before I entered the Protestant seminary of Paris, were encouraged—within the limits of prudence—by Pastor Kreyts himself, but far more decisively by Samuel Lambert, Pastor of the Lutheran Trinity Church with whom I had finally also made contact. The latter's welcome, more reserved at first than that of his Reformed colleague, had soon become even more trusting. And so I would soon be introduced to a small circle of Lutheran pastors of the Paris area who shared the same leanings. Pastor Wheatcroft, whose articles had had such an influence on me, was to play an increasing role in this circle despite his extreme humility.

It was nevertheless on the recommendation of Pastor Kreyts, with whom I had long had regular interactions, that I was accepted as a student in theology, at the outset for the purpose, in principle, of joining the ranks of the Reformed pastorate.

The Protestant theological faculty of Paris, located on Boulevard Arago in the immediate vicinity of the seminary where the students were housed, was a mixed faculty. Those preparing for ministry, be it in the Reformed or in the Lutheran Church, received their formation from a learned assembly of theologians from both denominations; the seminary rector was taken alternately from each.[14]

I must admit that I did not undertake these studies without somewhat mixed feelings. An acrimonious polemic had just taken place in the Protestant press, which had been enough to let me know that Professor Maurice Goguel,[15] responsible for New Testament Studies, denied the Resurrection of Christ—in the name of critical science, naturally. Yet, when all is said and done, this was no less naturally with only

14. The Reformed Church of France combined the principal branches of French Protestantism in 1938 thanks to the work of Pastor Marc Boegner (1881–1970). The Evangelical Lutheran Church of France and the churches of Alsace and Lorraine (which remained under the terms of the Concordat between Napoleon I and the Holy See because they were under German occupation at the time of the separation of Church and State in France) belonged to the Protestant Federation of France (created in 1905), but formally entered into communion with the Reformed Church of France only in 1969; a process of unification was undertaken in 2007.

15. Maurice Goguel (1880–1955): New Testament professor, 1905–1953; dean, 1936–43 and 1947–50; author of *Jesus the Nazarene: Myth or History?* trans. F. Stephens (New York: Appleton, 1926). He succeeded the modernist leader Alfred Loisy (1857–1940) as director of research at the École Pratique des Hautes Études.

Hume's old sophism for an argument:[16] since miracles are a departure from the laws of nature, there can be no miracles. The pastor of the Methodist church in Asnières, which we had attended for a while for lack of any other Protestant house of worship nearby, had made great use of this polemic to urge me to join the little ultraconservative school of theology he directed. Although I respected his undeniably Christian convictions, the cliquish, if not sect-like, atmosphere of his entire entourage did not tempt me in the least.

I must say, after experiencing it, that the faculty's general level of instruction, and even its religious quality, taken as a whole, would soon appear superior to what I had expected. Even Goguel, despite his ivory-tower intellectual's unrealistic biblical criticism, would reveal himself to have deep integrity in exegesis. For example, he unhesitatingly acknowledged that Saint Paul's teaching on the Eucharist was practically what the Church has defined by the term "transubstantiation."[17] Of course he concluded, as a good "liberal" Protestant, that one could therefore not consider the Pauline corpus as a doctrinal authority. I thought the conclusion worthless, but I would remember the premise.

I have already mentioned the esteem I still hold for Henri Monnier,[18] who with great finesse taught a generally very positive Reformed dogmatic theology. His Lutheran colleague in that field, André Jundt,[19] was more eclectic, but I have met few souls with such good will, or even simply few clergymen of such goodness.

I had great admiration for Wilfred Monod's skill as a preacher.[20] He taught us pastoral theology, but it did not take me long to realize the

---

16. David Hume (1711–1776), Scottish philosopher, historian and friend of Jean-Jacques Rousseau's (1712–1778). His phenomenological empiricism inspired Immanuel Kant (1724–1804). He expressed his skepticism about miracles in his 1748 *Enquiry Concerning Human Understanding.*

17. The doctrine of Transubstantiation, according to which the consecrated Bread and Wine substantially change into the Body, Blood, Soul, and Divinity of Jesus Christ, was challenged by heresiarch Berengarius of Tours (c. 998–c. 1088). The Fourth Lateran Council (1215) taught this doctrine and St. Thomas Aquinas (see 54, n. 33) explained it (*Summa Theologiae* IIIa pars, q. 75); the council of Trent (1545–1563) confirmed it. Lutherans speak of a "sacred union" (in which the substance of bread and wine coexist with that of the Body and Blood of Christ) and Calvinists speak of His "spiritual" presence within the "species" of bread and wine during the Memorial of the Lord's Supper.

18. On Henri Monnier see 51, n. 19.

19. André Jundt (1877–1947) was professor of practical theology at the Protestant Faculty from 1907 to 1938 and actively supported Söderblom's (see 58, n. 5) ecumenical endeavors from 1908 on.

20. William Frédéric, alias Wilfred Monod (1867–1943), authored over sixty books. He worked in ecumenism early on and claimed to be a "son of the Methodist awakening,"

inconsistency of his ideas. I also gradually grew weary of his literary cast, which was excessively dazzling and romantic. I was only too inclined to favor it as a result of my uncritical reading of Huysmans, added to that of Poe and Baudelaire,[21] whom I admired just as much, I'm afraid, for their flaws as for the best that is in them. And it did not take me long (my fellow students, actually, were ahead of me in this) to detect the artificiality of his public persona, which was put together with too much care. Nevertheless, I have kept an affectionate respect for him, though tinged with some amusement, for he was a prayerful man, as is demonstrated (despite some rather fanciful aspects) in the abridged history of spirituality he published. Thanks to it, I owe him my initiation to many works and persons that few Protestant authors have treated as sympathetically as he did.

Only later would I perceive how scholarly Adolph Lods's work on the Old Testament[22] really is, despite—there again—the prejudices it inherited from nineteenth-century Germanic criticism. My excuse is that, although he was an excellent writer, he was (on account of simple shyness, I think) the dullest of lecturers.

Paradoxically, the only instructor with whom I had any epic wrangles was Philippe de Félice,[23] in whose lectures on the history of religions I was very keenly interested. Like many very short men, he was extraordinarily touchy, and unfortunately his class took place on Boulevard Arago at the very same time when, at the Hautes-Études,[24] Étienne Gilson gave the most riveting lectures on medieval philosophy![25] De Félice

---

i.e., a proponent of an open and deeply felt Christianity. He was pastor of the Protestant temple of the Oratory of the Louvre (145 rue Saint-Honoré in the first *arrondissement* of Paris) and belonged to a family of influential ministers. He was related to Adolphe Monod (see 49, n. 11), one of whose grand-daughters, his first cousin Dorina (1868–1963), he married.

21. For Huysmans, see 53, n. 26. For Edgar Allen Poe and Charles Baudelaire see 42, n. 23.

22. Adolphe Lods (1867–1948), Sorbonne lecturer of Hebrew language and literature, 1892–1905; professor, 1937–1943. See Bouyer, *Métier*, 26.

23. Philippe de Félice (1880–1964), lecturer and later professor of the History of Religions, 1920–1950; dean, 1943–1947. He published works on religious delirium and other "inferior forms of mysticism."

24. The prestigious *École Pratique des Hautes Études*, founded in 1868 as a post-graduate institution.

25. Étienne Gilson (1884–1978), Thomistic philosopher and historian of Thomism, elected to the Académie française in 1946. He taught medieval philosophy at the Sorbonne, 1921–1932, then at the Collège de France where he directed the École Pratique des Hautes Études. He would teach at the Pontifical Institute of Medieval Studies in Toronto, which he had helped found in 1929, from 1950 to 1973. See Bouyer, *Métier*, 27, 184, 206, 249.

spotted me among the few who weren't always able to resist this temptation and he never forgave me for it.

Unexpectedly, the only one of these professors to thrill me was Auguste Lecerf.[26] This was despite his orthodox Calvinism, which, basing myself on his delicious sense of humor, I suspect he took pleasure in formulating in terms perfectly chosen to scandalize good souls given over to a simply sentimental sort of Evangelicalism.

Furthermore, it was he who interested me in Saint Thomas in his ecclesiastical Latin classes, even before Étienne Gilson did so. He did it in such a way as to make a clean sweep of the vestigial Scotism I had retained from my reading of Secrétan.[27]

I don't think I have ever known a man whose intellectual rigor was so perfectly united to his cordiality—which could actually include a rather funny mischievousness. Add to this a highly religious character in the precise sense of the term, while at the same time highly human.

The seminary director, who was Goguel's brother-in-law, was a peculiar man:[28] kind, but very weak; pious, but his piety was no firmer in the faith than was his personality. At first I trusted him greatly, but the way he used me to try to win the students over to the convoluted liturgies he offered them, and then withdrew when he realized that they were attractive to no one, leaving their responsibility entirely on my shoulders, shocked me deeply and ended our personal relations. This constituted a first opportunity for me to discover, within Protestant clergy, what would be termed "Jesuitism" elsewhere; alas, it was far from the last!

As for my classmates, with whom I spent the bulk of my time in the seminary's very relaxed atmosphere, they were by and large excellent lads except for two or three generally despised Tartuffes.[29] With very few exceptions, however, the direction of their pastoral vocation did not

26. Auguste Lecerf (1872–1943) was a pastor in Normandy before being lecturer of Greek and English, 1922–1936, and professor of Reformed dogmatics, 1936–1943. His lectures at the Protestant Faculty of Paris drew increasingly large audiences; see Bouyer, *Métier*, 25–27. He wrote *An Introduction to Reformed Dogmatics* (London: Lutterworth Press, 1949), originally published in French, 1931–38. Bouyer reports a conversation with him on the topic of Catholic mysticism, at the end of which Lecerf exclaimed: "If that [St. John of the Cross's *Ascent to Mount Carmel*] is the real Catholic mysticism, it is precisely the religion for which Calvin fought all his life." See L. Bouyer, *The Spirit and Forms of Protestantism* (see 59, n. 12), 65 and id., *Métier*, 15–17.

27. See 54, nn. 32–33.

28. Gabriel Bouttier (1879–1970): director, 1928–1938. His wife, Hélève *née* Nyegaard, was the sister of Jeanne, who married Maurice Goguel in 1906.

29. Sanctimonious hypocrites, after a character in Molière's comedy by the same name; see 45, n. 1.

seem to get much in the way of their top concern: to be, as they put it, "just like other students."

Yet, I must acknowledge that there were among them some characters of an unquestionably evangelical spirit, in an altogether respectable and even admirable sense. Still, it was hard not to sense in them a degree of idealism, or even already the influence of a more or less Marxist-leaning ideology.

I soon belonged to a small group with which I felt a strong bond of fellow-feeling, even though we didn't agree on everything. Besides me it was made up, in the first place, of the son of a high-ranking magistrate in the Nord,[30] Jacques Deransart,[31] who had had a sudden conversion experience—which I always take as a very good sign. He combined this with a very free spirit and even a passably offhand way of speaking.

Jean Malbert,[32] typical of his native Clamecy[33] in his cold humor and his applied realism, and André Hardy,[34] a simple soul with a generous heart who was as cordial as he was fervent, were our two associates. I must add that Jacques Deransart belonged, though unquestionably at a lower rung, to what is called "Protestant high society," while Hardy was issued from "Protestant good society," though at a very honorable level. These distinctions provoked in me, who was clearly not native to that reservation, not much more than a vaguely amused indifference, but occasioned a few sneering movements of impatience in Malbert and his wry provincialism.

It was a vast, luminous house at the nearly rural end of the Boulevard Arago next to the Santé prison,[35] and had for its neighbors, besides that, only convents lost within enclosed parks. With a good library at our disposal and an amusing Le Corbusier chapel, the four of us spent two undeniably pleasant years between its courtyard and garden.

The first year I shared a large room with Hardy and, when he noticed that I had set aside the Anglican Prayer book and had begun reciting the Roman breviary, he suggested that we should do so together. This garnered for us, who had made no effort to hide it, a reputation as genuine eccentrics—not without pleasing us both. I must say that I was pleas-

30. The Nord is the northernmost *département* in France.

31. Jacques Deransart (1910–1985) studied with Bouyer in Paris, 1930–1931, and then in Strasbourg, 1932–1934, after which he took over the parish of Valdrôme. Throughout his pastoral assignments he remained passionately interested in ecumenism among Catholics, Evangelicals, and Pentecostals.

32. Jean Malbert was born in 1913 and made Reformed pastor in 1940.

33. Small town in Burgundy.

34. André Hardy de Vîmes (1908–2001).

35. One of the Parisian prisons, built in 1867.

antly surprised to find that such a thing seemed so natural to him. But it was soon to get far worse! We would both frequent the Benedictine Abbey on Rue de la Source in Auteuil (at the time one would never have believed it capable of turning "Progressive" someday!)[36] or, better yet, the Benedictine nuns on Rue Monsieur.[37]

Deransart looked upon these escapades with indulgent surprise, but Malbert had been the first to drag me to the Sorbonne garret where Gilson, still banished at the time, explained Saint Thomas's most delicate theses with blinding clarity.

I remember very specifically the first time I ever had a taste of the pleasure that poor de Félice hated so intensely. It was on the substantiality of the human soul, but as form of the body: that is what won me over to the Angelic Schoolman, if not to his School![38] Malbert, too, astounded me—one had to expect the most unexpected things from him, it seems—one day when we were on our way to the Sorbonne, when he told me out of the blue that Saint Thérèse of the Child Jesus was, for him, Christianity itself.

One can, on the basis of these samplings, form a judgment on the fanciful as well as serious character of our tireless discussions. A cordial sense of humor helped us get along, even when we'd been at it with the ardor of youth and stuck to our respective positions which, truth be told, were never as far from each other as they seemed to us at the time.

The institution in which we lived provided our conversation with ready-made targets, starting with the concierge, the perfect type of what is called *le mômier* in Swiss French: forever oozing piety, but fake as a plug nickel. We were particularly amused by the liberal tips he used to extract from macabre party-goers for introducing them on the sly into our garden on execution nights. Indeed, the proximity of the Paris jail

---

36. The *Abbaye bénédictine Ste Marie*, 3 Rue de la Source in Auteuil in the 16th *arrondissement* of Paris; it is part of the Solesmes congregation. It was founded in 1893 and erected as an abbey in 1925.

37. The Benedictines of the Perpetual Adoration of the Most Blessed Sacrament moved from Saint-Louis du Temple (a former Templar building Louis XVIII had given them when the monarchy was restored in France) to their convent at 20 Rue Monsieur (the *Hôtel Montesquiou*) in 1851 and stayed there until 1938. After thirteen years in Meudon, they moved to their current location in Limon in 1951, where they built a convent also called Saint-Louis du Temple. Until the nuns' departure from the rue Monsieur in 1938 their convent was a meeting place for Catholic intellectuals, including Jacques (1882–1973) and Raïssa (1883–1960) Maritain, Henri Daniel-Rops (1901–1965), Paul Claudel (1868–1955), François Mauriac (1885–1970), Julien Green (see 232, n. 4), et al.

38. The "Angelic Schoolman" is St. Thomas Aquinas (see 54, n. 33), the *doctor angelicus*.

gave us front seats to see the guillotine being set up and used. I must say that only few among the regular denizens of that pious household paid any attention to it . . . except, at the dismal climax, to douse the heads of our doorman's clients with some pot of water.

But let's return to more serious concerns.

Thanks to the Federation of Christian Students (*la Fédé*, as we used to say) in which Protestant students consorted with Russians issuing from the emigration,[39] I was soon to develop a warm discovery of Orthodoxy beyond even my Anglican- or Catholic-leaning wanderings. My more or less inseparable associates joined me in this further exploration, which the authorities appreciated even less than those that had come before. It was to be established upon two of the greatest eccentrics I was ever given to come close to.

One of them remains enshrouded in the deepest mystery, even though no one at the time or since has had a deeper influence on me. He was a monk-priest who was to become famous years later under the cover of the enigmatic signature of "a monk of the Eastern Church."[40] He was in fact a French Benedictine who had made his profession at Farnborough and had theoretically gone over to Russian Orthodoxy, but I wonder (and I suspect that he wondered all his life himself) to what religion he did, in fact, belong.

The amount of theological, or more generically ecclesiastical, information I owe him is hard to imagine, not to mention disparate knowledge in nearly every field. His culture was peerless; the attractiveness and, when needed, unctuousness of his delivery were incomparable. He conducted services with the dignity of a holy prelate despite his short stature, and sang liturgical melodies like a nightingale. But one never knew whether he was going himself to destroy in an instant, with an unexpected sidelong glance dripping with contemptuous irony, the effect he had so artfully produced.

He had a formidable dry wit heightened by his terms, which were

39. I.e., who had fled the Bolsheviks after the 1917 Communist revolution in Russia.

40. This is Father Lev Gillet (1893–1980), as Bouyer revealed in 1978, *Métier*, 23. Novice at the Benedictine abbey of Clervaux (in Luxembourg, not to be confused with the better known abbey of Clairvaux in Champagne, eastern France) in 1920, he soon entered the Benedictine Abbey of Farnborough (in Hampshire, England) where, in 1921, he met the Uniat Galician Metropolitan Andrey Sheptytsky, whom he would join in 1924 as a monk in the monastery of Uniov (in Poland at the time, now in Ukraine) where he took the name Lev (Russian for Leo). He was received into the Russian Orthodox Church by Metropolitan Eulogius in 1928, and was made rector of the Western Orthodox parish Ste-Geneviève the same year. See Élisabeth Behr-Sigel, *Lev Gillet: "Un moine de l'Église d'Orient"* (Paris: Éditions du Cerf, 1993).

nearly always well-chosen and also carefully kept in memory. He seemed to derive equal pleasure in utterly tearing down his own successes as well as those of others. Since Bergson's *Two Sources*[41] had just been published I naively asked for his opinion. He just answered that he had once seen Bergson coming out of the League of Nations, in Geneva, equipped with a brand-new umbrella. At the first few raindrops, though, he hastened not to open it but to shelter it under his overcoat! As if this weren't enough, he added that when Bergson and Capus (the songwriter)[42] were elected to the Académie française on the same day, some wag, upon hearing the news in the Mazarin Palace courtyard,[43] had said in his presence: "It's a good thing that they were elected together: they're both jokers, each in his own style, of course, but, still, they're jokers!" On those occasions when I had the misfortune of thanking him, once for his book on Judaism[44] (a real revelation to me; I am still glad of it), another time when I told him how moved I had been by his even more admirable little volume on the Jesus prayer,[45] he most scathingly crushed both Jewish mysticism and hesychasm[46] in two words. It really seemed that all he had to do was express some idea or motif to perfection for it to disgust him.

More unpleasantly, he would sometimes suddenly shift from the most cavalier talk to a surprising servility. I shall always remember a meeting

41. Henri Bergson (1859–1941), *The Two Sources of Morality and Religion*, trans. A.R. Ashley (New York: Holt, 1935), first published in French in 1932 as *Les Deux sources de la morale et de la religion* (Paris: F. Alcan, 1932).

42. Alfred Capus (1857–1922), elected to the Académie Française on 12 February 1914.

43. The Académie française was founded in 1634 under the patronage of Cardinal Richelieu (1585–1642) to watch over the purity of the French language and render it capable of the highest degree of eloquence. Nomination to it carries great prestige; its forty members are termed "the Immortals." It is housed, as part of the Institut de France, in the Palace of the Quai de Conti (in the 6th *arrondissement* of Paris), which Cardinal Mazarin (1602–1661), Richelieu's successor as First Minister of France, had commissioned.

44. Lev Gillet, *Communion in the Messiah: Studies in the Relationship between Judaism and Christianity* (London: Lutterworth, 1942). For Bouyer's views on the relationship between Judaism and Christianity, see his *The Church of God: Body of Christ and Temple of the Spirit*, trans. Charles Underhill Quinn (Chicago: M. Mayer, 1982), 522–26.

45. Id., *On the Invocation of the Name of Jesus* (London: Fellowship of St. Alban and St. Sergius, 1949).

46. Hesychasm is the practice of quiet prayer, involving posture and controlled breathing, usually centered on the Jesus prayer ("Lord Jesus Christ, Son of God, have mercy upon me [a sinner]"). When Bouyer was suffering from what was to be his last illness, he relied on this prayer in his solitary cell (and, for as long as he could do so, on reciting the Rosary with the community of the Little Sisters of the Poor that had taken him in in 1998).

when a Metropolitan of the Phanar[47] had just presented Constantinople's current approach to ecumenism, in the presence of Metropolitan Eulogius[48] of the Russian émigrés in Paris. While the former was coming to the end of his speech, the Father in question was saying to a small group of us: "As far as I'm concerned, Eulogius is an abominable rascal."

Just then someone came to tell him, on behalf of the prelate in question, whose French was not as good as that of his Hellenic confrere, that he wished to entrust him with interpreting his response. After a short whispered discussion with the aged Metropolitan, he bowed before each of the hierarchs in turn with all the forms, not of respect, but of Levantine obsequiousness, and began in his suavest tones: "My Lord: His Eminence My Lord the Metropolitan Eulogius has charged me with telling Your Eminence. . . ."

I have to say that, back in our corner, we had a hard time holding in our guffaws, but also that I felt a strong urge to drop all relations with the interpreter there and then. Yet, the attraction of his mind, if not always of his manners, was such that I never did do it, even though it did not take me long to have no doubt that he had a low estimation of me, considering me to be, I think, both a half-wit and a fanatic.

Now regarding him, as far as I am concerned, I should not wish to give the impression that I believed him to be insincere, despite this and much else besides. It's just that his sincerity, or rather his sincerities, were successive. I do not doubt for all that that he was deeply religious. I do think, however, that he was a good example of what modernism, in which he was immersed during his early formation, could do to so versatile and brilliant a mind. I am told, and I am inclined to believe it, that his last years were more solidly edifying. Actually, he seemed to perceive, if not fear, the effect he might produce, for he once told me, with a mix of honesty, cynicism, and even regret that I shall not attempt to sort out, what a common friend had thrown at his face (an eccentric if ever there was one, which may explain why he didn't hesitate to repeat his words, while not quite knowing whether or not he hoped they'd be taken seriously): "I do wonder how such a Judas as yourself hasn't hanged himself yet!"

What puzzles me the most in this astonishing man, however, is that he, who had such perfect and refined taste, could sometimes throw

47. Phanar: the district of Istanbul where the Patriarch of Constantinople has his See.

48. Metropolitan Eulogius (also Euloge) Georgievsky of Paris (1868–1946). He was established as the representative in Paris of the Patriarchate of Moscow, from which he split in 1927. The Ecumenical Patriarch of Constantinople, Photius II, received him and made him Exarch in 1931.

himself body and soul into the most perfectly grotesque adventures. True, he did generally get out of them in the nick of time—though not without leaving those he had brought along to struggle or lose themselves in them, as we shall soon see.

Yet I owe to him perhaps more than anyone too many priceless acquisitions, including my conversion, not to remain extremely grateful to him, although, had he ever known it, he would have held me in even more heartfelt contempt, I'm afraid.

My second initiator to Orthodoxy, who came to me by way of the self-styled "monk of the Eastern Church," was just as mysterious in his own way. Yet, despite his fancifulness that included a sometimes irrepressible sense of humor, his discreet yet cordial friendship remains one of my most luminous experiences. I shall always regret that his death put a premature end to it. That character, despite some strangeness, is certainly one of the most purely Christian men I have ever associated with.

Evgraff Kovalevsky was the minister's nephew and the brother of another Maxime, a musician and musicologist, as well as of the excellent Pierre, for a long time Russian lecturer at the Sorbonne.[49] Yet, whatever his two brothers' endowments, he was without contest the genius in the family, and he may well have been its saint despite the ludicrous adventure into which what Goethe would have called the "monk's" "demonism" caused him to lapse, and in the end absurdly to waste all his gifts.

He was an artist and an amateur theologian, yet was endowed with surprisingly good and deep intuitions, a mystic most certainly, and he had a charity that, though not showy, was none the less boundless. Nevertheless, he was also the most joyful perpetrator of hoaxes, without for all that ever losing the perfect aristocrat's tact and distinction.

He was as Russian as Neri[50] could be Florentine, and no one has ever seemed to me better suited to be that saint's friend and accomplice. I would gladly say that he prepared me, without being any more aware of it than I was, to become someday the latter's disciple.

Evgraff and "the monk" were involved in the latter's bizarre "French

---

49. Vladimir Ivanovich Kovalevsky (1848–1935) was Russian Privy Councillor and Deputy to the Minister of Finance, 1899–1902; his nephews, who emigrated to Paris after the 1917 revolution, were Pierre (1901–1978, writer on Russian history and spirituality), Maxime (1903–1988, liturgical chant composer in the French Orthodox Church), and Evgraff (1905–1970). Evgraff and Vladimir Lossky (see 76–77, n. 84) led the Saint Photius Confraternity for the rebirth of Orthodoxy in the West from 1925 on.

50. Saint Philip Neri (1515–94), founder of the Oratorians. See Bouyer, *Saint Philippe Neri* (see 118, n. 23 and 170, n. 46).

Orthodox Parish," designated under the incongruous title of St. Genevieve.[51] Evgraff was its jack-of-all-trades: sacristan, cantor, master of ceremonies, and buffoon in the grand style. They soon brought me into a
whirlwind of conversations, exchanges, encounters, the lot studded with
prayer services. These were sometimes conducted by "the monk," or,
better yet, at the cathedral on Rue Daru[52] or at Saint Serge's *Podvorie*[53]
on the Rue de Crimée,[54] or even sometimes in that extraordinary
church on Rue Pétel. It was a catacomb, sheltered under a garage, where
the celebrant was the seraphic Bishop Benjamin, a prodigious shooting
star of Holy Russia who had landed in Vaugirard. I shall always regret
not having had a closer acquaintance with him.

I must add that the Benedictine who lived on under a Muscovite
rason[55] was at the same time providing me with a by no means less precise initiation to the monastic tradition of the West, though punctuated
by the occasional sneer.

Huysmans had given me a taste for the Benedictines,[56] but I soon
owed my knowledge of all their resources to "the monk." Yet, I think
that it was Pastor Lambert who had already put in my hands the *Book of
Ancient Prayer* by the former abbot of Farnborough, Dom Cabrol.[57] It
was by ceaselessly reading and rereading it that I had gone over, as I have
mentioned, from the Prayer Book to the Roman Office. It was, however,
"the monk of the Eastern Church" who sent me, albeit with a smirk, to
the abbey of Auteuil,[58] and then (perhaps the greatest service he ever

51. Saint Genevieve (c. 416–502) is the patroness of Paris, where she had helped
organize resistance to Attila and the Huns in 451. She has no connection with Russian
Orthodoxy. In 1935 the first (and modest) premises of the "French Orthodox parish" was
located at 36 Rue Montagne-Sainte-Geneviève in the Latin Quarter, in the fifth
arrondissement. It moved nearby in the 1960s, to 4 Rue Saint-Victor. Its first rector was
not Lev Gillet, but Michel Belsky.

52. Saint Alexander Nevsky Russian Orthodox Cathedral, 12 Rue Daru in the eighth
arrondissement, consecrated in 1861.

53. A *podvorie* is a small monastic community centered on a church.

54. At number 93. Acquired in 1924, it had been the site of a German church abandoned in 1914.

55. The *rason* is a broad-sleeved black coat worn by monks from the time of their
novitiate and for which they are termed "Rasophores."

56. For Huysmans see 53, n. 26. His novel *L'Oblat* takes place in a Benedictine abbey.

57. Dom Fernand Cabrol (1855–1937), prior of Farnborough from 1896 and its abbot
from 1903. He founded, with Henri Leclercq, the *Dictionnaire d'archéologie chrétienne et
de liturgie*. He wrote *Le livre de la prière antique* (Paris: H. Oudin, 1900), which was
widely distributed.

58. The Abbaye Sainte Marie, 3 Rue de la Source; see 65, n. 36.

did me) recommended that I should go on retreat at the abbey of Saint-Wandrille, whose community, after a long exile, was just then rebuilding it.[59] It was also he who introduced me to the liturgical theology of Dom Odo Casel and the monks of Maria-Laach,[60] at the very time that he was my likewise efficacious guide among the equally stimulating speculations of Bulgakov and his school,[61] then going all the way back up to Florensky[62] and Solovyov.[63] It would be beyond me to tell how seriously he took all of this, so I only had a vague feeling on that score. Nevertheless, he was an ideal guide in all of these fields just as, to repeat, he would be in the labyrinth of Merkabah[64] Jewish mysticism or in the Athonite[65] visions of uncreated light.

Yet another Russian friend, on whom I shall say more later, would make the remark, which was a little unfair (though not that unfair), that he would just as well have initiated us to Methodist revivalism or to the silent prayer of the Friends . . . or even, if such had been our desire, to Zen or to Tibetan mysticism!

The fact is that one fine day he astounded me when he explained that he had entered into communication with *"Monseigneur* Winnaert,"[66]

---

59. Founded by Saint Wandrille in 649, this abbey was closed during the French revolution and reopened in 1894. After an exile in Belgium caused by the anti-clerical laws of 1901, its monks returned in 1931.

60. Odo Casel (1886–1948), Benedictine monk at the German monastery of Maria-Laach and leader in the Liturgical Movement. See his *The Mystery of Christian Worship, and Other Writings,* ed. Burkhard Neunheuser (Westminster, MD: Newman Press, 1962) and Bouyer, *Métier,* 149.

61. For Bulgakov see 58, n. 4.

62. Pavel Florensky (1882–1937), Russian Orthodox priest, theologian, philosopher, and artist. See Bouyer, *Métier,* 174, 184.

63. Vladimir Solovyov (1853–1900), Russian philosopher and poet. Unlike his friend Dostoyevsky, he considered the possibility of a reunion of the churches. See *Métier,* 16, 210, 212.

64. Merkabah: the chariot in Ezekiel 1, the interpretation of which is a feature of Jewish mysticism.

65. From Mount Athos, a center of Greek Orthodox monasticism where Saint Gregory Palamas (1296–1359) was the great theologian of uncreated light in the hesychastic tradition (see 67, n. 46). See Louis Bouyer, "Gregory Palamas and the Hesychast Prayer," in id., Jean Leclercq and François Vandenbroucke, *A History of Christian Spirituality,* 2, *The Spirituality of the Middle Ages* (New York: Seabury Press, 1982), 584–88.

66. Charles-Louis Winnaert, ordained a Catholic priest in 1905, left the Catholic Church in 1918 and established the "Evangelical Catholic Church" after receiving episcopal consecration from James Ingall Wedgwood (1883–1951) of the English Liberal Catholic Church. *Monseigneur* is the title given to bishops in France. Winnaert took on the Christian name "Irénée," launched the so-called "Orthodox Rite of the Gauls," and sought recognition first from Constantinople, then from Moscow.

one of those *episcopi vagantes*[67] whom Brandreth[68] and Anson[69] have so humorously captured, tossing about between modernism, theosophy, and simple megalomania.

To my question: "But isn't he a mountebank?" I saw him, for the first and only time, respond with a shocked, if not an offended, reaction.

But I find it difficult not to believe that it was so especially because I had expressed what he couldn't help sensing (but which he did not wish to have to acknowledge, even *in petto*).

I had already observed the poor "bishop" in ecumenical meetings of that time, where he displayed a prelate's cassock girded with a wide violet cincture. At this moment he had, in one more caper, just married and, to boot, had done so at the Protestant church of the *Oratoire* with the blessing of Wilfred Monod (I can just imagine him smiling in his beard at this).[70]

This did not seem to bother "the monk" in the least, even though he had always been, I am sure, perfectly irreprehensible in matters of chastity himself. What might excuse, or at least explain, his fancy for such a *curiosum*[71] is the fact that the aforementioned *Monseigneur* was assuredly a good man despite his queer notions and his touch of paranoia. The proof of it would be that on his deathbed he was apparently to attempt to arrange for his return to the Catholic Church's fold (he had started out as curate of Viroflay.[72]) Since it was demanded of him that he should first separate from his wife, he decided as a last resort to turn at last to the Orthodox Church of Russia, whose doors "the monk" had been fruitlessly opening to him up to that point. The latter hoped, unless I am mistaken, that once the good fellow and his motley little flock joined that fold, he would find in it, *inter muros ecclesiae*,[73] a field of action more suitable for his own experiments than what the Russian émigrés' fiercely exclusive conservatory had been.

Metropolitan Eleutherius, a holy man if ever there was one, anti-

---

67. Validly consecrated bishops who have no canonical attachment to any ecclesial body.

68. Henry R. T. Brandreth, *Episcopi Vagantes and the Anglican Church* (London: SPCK, 1947).

69. Peter F. Anson, *Bishops at Large* (London: Faber and Faber, 1964).

70. In 1930. For Wilfred Monod, see 61–62, n. 20.

71. *Curiosum* is the Dutch-Latin term for a rare or unusual item in a collection, akin to the English "curio."

72. Viroflay, a village in the *département* of the Yvelines, between Paris and Versailles.

73. "Within the walls of the Church." Bouyer wrote *inter* for *intra*.

Roman as was only fitting, and gullible to boot, was ultimately to push this "reunion" through in the Muscovite Patriarchate's name.[74] It was, for its part, rightly suspicious, and would soon realize the trick that had been played on it for the sole purpose of launching some kind of "Occidental Orthodoxy" at a more ambitious level than the monk's very humble French-speaking parish. The patriarch then did not waste time in excommunicating this pseudo-Church and suspending its dress-up costume clergy.

Good old Winnaert (may he rest in peace!) was already dead at that point, "reconciled" at the end of the day, as Eleutherius had set the same condition as the Roman Holy Office had.

In the meantime, the monk, even as he was withdrawing from the whole enterprise himself (the farce had become too much, you see), had carefully put the skids under the unfortunate Evgraff, who ended up being put in charge of the problematic church in question. To bring this about—and thereby to get rid of the aforementioned church—Metropolitan Eulogius, who was not the "rascal" the monk had described but was assuredly an old fox, had precipitously ordained him to the priesthood, pretty much willy-nilly on the ordinand's part. He had been dropped as pastor on a more or less non-existent flock, and, worse yet, was assisted by a gang of wretched derelicts for vicars. Fortunately, the war and mobilization were to tear him away from that pious shambles. He was at first a French officer, then was made prisoner and sent to a Russian prisoner-of-war camp. There, thank God, he would have an entirely admirable ministry. I would see him much later back in Paris, where he had returned after the war; he was involved in renewed tribulations in that collage—no other term will do—to which that caricature of a "Catholic Orthodox" Church managed to reclaim him. The whole thing would end up in an episcopate which, alas, was no less over the top than that of his predecessor of sad memory.[75]

Meanwhile "the monk of the Eastern Church" had played one of his signature tricks on me, too.

In my simple candor I had explained to him that my friends in the little group of Lutheran pastors who met around Frank Wheatcroft and

---

74. Moscow ended up naming Metropolitan Eleutherius to replace Metropolitan Eulogius as the latter aligned himself with Constantinople.

75. Evgraff Kovalevsky (see 69, n. 49) was consecrated bishop under the name John of Saint Denis in 1964 at the hands of Metropolitan John (1896–1966) of San Francisco (and formerly of Shanghai) of the Russian Orthodox Church Outside Russia (ROCOR), which is separated from Moscow.

Samuel Lambert[76] (and which I had now resolved to join) desired to restore within the French Lutheran Church the fullness of ministry inherited from the Apostles, just as many "High Church" Anglicans had tried for themselves.[77] Couldn't one substitute regularly consecrated bishops for the "Ecclesiastical Inspectors," who amounted only to a shadow of the episcopate, and thus reconstitute unquestionably apostolic orders in that Church?[78] Could we, I therefore asked him, expect anything of the kind from a rapprochement with the Orthodox Church?

Without compromising himself in any overly precise affirmation, "the monk" soon told me that, in such a perspective, the first thing to do would be for us to receive—supposing our baptism was valid—the sacrament of confirmation or, as it is called in the Orient, of chrismation. This could be done, he told me, on the sole condition that we should confess the Orthodox faith. Nothing, in theory, could be easier, since there was no doubt that we all held that faith, the faith of the Ecumenical Councils. If such should be my desire, he said, he asked for nothing better than to introduce me into the communion of the formerly undivided Church in this manner.

I admit that I had never supposed that such a thing was so easily possible and so immediately feasible. Yet, I had the feeling that such a procedure could not be absolutely regular. What ambiguous position would it put me in? Still, my initiator seemed so free of any concern in this regard and showed himself to be so discreetly persuasive that I gave in.

An insufficient experience had not yet taught me to mistrust my first inclination—not because it is good, as Talleyrand so cynically said,[79] but because in my case it would suddenly show itself to be bad in many other circumstances too. All of my life, in fact, the people I took into my friendship right off the bat have as a general rule betrayed it, while my

76. Samuel Lambert, Pastor at La Trinité Lutheran church since 1906. For Wheatcroft, see 53, n. 27.

77. Three currents developed in nineteenth-century Anglicanism: the High Church, which insists on the hierarchy and rites inherited from Roman Catholicism; the Low Church, which is less highbrow and closer to Evangelicalism; and the Broad Church, which is more liberal and less dogmatic.

78. The Lutheran Church of France does not have bishops, unlike other European Lutheran Churches; it elects "Ecclesiastical Inspectors" as provided for in the 1802 Concordat.

79. Charles Maurice de Talleyrand-Périgord (1754–1838) had been a bishop before the French revolution and became minister under the Directorate, Napoleon I, and (after the restoration of French monarchy) Louis XVIII; he was noted for his competence and cynicism. His actual words are: "Don't trust your first inclination—it is always a generous one."

most solid friends are nearly invariably those of whom I had at first been wary on account of some trifle or simple misunderstanding.

In a word, I put up no resistance and, after a discreet ceremony one fine morning in an Orthodox chapel in Saint-Cloud in which "the monk" then had his lair, I found myself shriven, absolved, confirmed and a communicant—all, certainly, under all the conditions of perfect validity, as Catholic canonists say. This was supposing, of course, that my baptism was valid (of which I was no longer quite sure and which would occasion increasing, and surely well-founded, doubts when I realized how negligently that rite was practiced then, and now more than ever, in the Reformed Church where I had received it). As far as licitness was concerned, it was of course best not to bring it up. After this I found myself in a peculiar frame of mind, back at the seminary.

Whatever my hopes were at the time—and although today I am as sure as ever that non-Catholics in good faith receive sacramental grace subjectively, even when they receive the sacraments at the hands of an invalidly ordained minister, despite the objective invalidity of the actual celebration—I was moved by the thought of communicating now in the Body and Blood of Christ in actual reality, and thus of participating in the oblation of His sacrifice by those delegated by Him to do so, i.e., His priests, and moreover of being able to confess my sins and receive unquestionable absolution for them. But there was something in the quickness and secrecy of it all that bothered me. And, more importantly, I keenly felt the meaninglessness of living not within the Church from which one receives such graces, but within and at the service of another Church which, for the time being, at best tolerated neighborly relations with it.

Although I never had an actual falling-out with "the monk" and never ceased receiving from his hand—though with decreasing frequency—sacraments I could believe to be valid, what ought to have consecrated our cooperation only inaugurated an increasing distance. I don't think I am being too hard on "the monk of the Eastern Church" when I say that, in this precipitation and these too-cleverly unresolved ambiguities, he had abandoned any serious hope, if indeed he ever entertained it, of involving me in his projects, which were by their very nature always destined to remain in the same hazy "Occidental Orthodoxy." Another orthodox priest, also a former Catholic, to whom I mentioned the problem a little later plainly told me that the hybrid position in which "the monk" had put me was not only irregular, but absurd. I was all the more aware of it that my progress in the knowledge of Latin Catholicism convinced me more and more that, if a "Western Orthodoxy" should exist, it was there and nowhere else.

Thanks to youthful inconsistency—and although this preoccupied me more and more towards the end of my stay in Paris—it did not keep me from finding profound joy in all my discoveries, or rather quite simply in the discovery I was making of the most traditional faith and life of faith. I now realized that they are the portion equally of Catholicism and of Orthodoxy. Still, I did notice that both of them had the same need of being energetically dusted off, even though the dust, or even the grime, had not accumulated in exactly the same spots. Still, it was there, and only there, that the authentic Church was to be found, even if I could see that there were on either side somewhat palsied, or even atrophied, organs, although I was not always clear on what was lacking here or there.

Despite these reservations, Casel's doctrine of liturgical mystery, at its core and independently from dubious historico-philosophical justifications, satisfied me more and more with its unquestionably traditional content.[80] Yet, the Catholic liturgy, as I was beginning to see it brought back to life among the Benedictines, seemed to me to leave nothing essential to be desired. Moreover, the piety their monasteries seemed to foster achieved that Biblical religion that the Protestants had always taught me, but had never really brought me to see as a completely and constantly lived-out reality.

My first stay at Saint-Wandrille was decisive in this respect.[81] My reading, at the same time, of the best books by Dom Marmion[82] (and later by Dom Vonier)[83] finished the job of convincing me, despite the layers of manualistic Thomism that Dom Thibaut (Marmion's editor) felt obliged to stack between his slices of Saint Paul—seeing as the Apostle to the Gentiles might, without this sandwiching, have too Protestant an effect upon run-of-the-mill "good Catholics."

Above all, I must admit that it was Orthodox theology's continuity (and not just its contiguity) with spirituality, as I discovered it in Vladimir Lossky[84] as well as in Sergei Bulgakov and his disciples, as well as what I was discovering at the same time about the more humble Bene-

---

80. For Casel see 71, n. 60.

81. For the Abbey of Saint Wandrille, see 71, n. 59.

82. Blessed Columba Marmion, OSB (1858–1923), Abbot of Maredsous. His secretary, Dom Raymond Thibaut, gathered his oral teachings in four books: *Christ, the Life of the Soul* (London and Edinburgh: Sands & Co., 1925); *Christ in His Mysteries* (1931); *Christ, the Ideal of the Monk* (St. Louis, MO: B.Herder, 1926); *Christ, the Ideal of the Priest* (1952).

83. Anschaire Vonier, OSB (1876–1938), Abbot of Buckfast, best known for *The Human Soul and Its Relations with Other Spirits* (St. Louis, MO: B. Herder, 1925).

dictine theology, that revealed to me that the tradition of the Fathers, which had brought Newman into the Church, was dead neither in the East nor in the West, and was everywhere only waiting to live again.

I have just mentioned Vladimir Lossky for the first time: Evgraff put me in touch with him the very first time I ever came to Meudon (that Russian colony!) in the house where the Kovalevskys lived at the time.[85] It was in a dead end, a long garden really, grafted onto the peaceful Rue de la République, a stone's throw from that other friendly house to which, years later, I would often return to see Pierre Leyris and his English wife.[86]

Lossky will always remain one of the most solid minds it has ever been granted me to come near to; he had a profound religion, made up of a fierce, but very intelligent, fidelity to tradition, whose true riches he helped more than anyone to bring back to light.

This didn't make him any less favorable to Bulgakov's brilliant speculations, to be sure, or more generally to the whole riot of idealist metaphysics that the Slavophiles, somewhat unexpectedly, have inextricably mixed with their exclusive exaltation of the most typically Russian Orthodoxy, and which Solovyov's disciples would pursue on a larger scale. But he was also a great gentleman and had an excellent heart. Much later, on the eve of his death, he would tell me regarding Bulgakov, against whom he had struggled so long: "Father Sergei's solutions are inadmissible, but one has to grant that he posed the real questions!"

From that point, although I already did appreciate the worth and central importance, within the Christian East's spiritual theology, of that tradition whose first master was Saint Symeon and whose first lucid defender was Gregory Palamas, and which makes of "uncreated grace" and "divine energies" the very substance of God's communication with

84. Vladimir Lossky (1903–1958), Russian Orthodox theologian and collaborator with Evgraff Kovalevsky in the Saint Photius Confraternity, which sought to convert the West to Orthodox Christianity. This was precisely what Irénée Winnaert (see 71, n. 66) was hoping for; Vladimir Lossky laid the intellectual foundations for such an enterprise.

85. Meudon is to the southwest of Paris. Many Russians who had fled from the Bolshevik revolution settled there in the 1920s and build the church of the Resurrection. The Jesuits moved Saint-Georges, their boarding school for émigré boys, to Meudon in 1946; it also housed the Slavic libraries they had gathered since the nineteenth century. Once the school closed in 1970, Saint-Georges became a center for Russian studies and closed in 2002.

86. Pierre Leyris (1907–2001), perhaps the most respected translator of English-language literature, notably of Shakespeare, into French. Bouyer wrote the preface to this translation of twelve of Newman's sermons: John Henry Newman, *Douze sermons sur le Christ*, trans. Pierre Leyris (Paris: Seuil, 1995).

men in Christ,[87] I was well aware on the other hand of the ill-exorcized gnosticism there was in Bulgakov's and his group's synthesis. I still persisted in thinking that his vision of Divine Wisdom as an eternal model, in God's thought, of that Spouse that creation must ultimately become once it is entirely reunited with His Son, reconciled with Him and exalted in Him towards the Father in the Spirit, was entirely biblical and traditional in its first principles.

Indeed, the evocation of it seemed to me to be so to speak the crowning of that vision of the world that Newman had helped me to attain. In fact, I already knew that he had pointed out, among the Fathers, especially Saint Athanasius and Saint Augustine,[88] that created Wisdom, which is inseparable from the uncreated Wisdom that is the Word Himself, can alone express the eternal vocation of the created universe.

I never sensed this better or more successfully than during an ecumenical week of the *Fédé* in its *Oiseau Bleu*[89] property on the outskirts of the Fontainebleau forest. There, Bulgakov showed himself to be the unquestionable genius that he was—an intellectual genius above all, to be sure, but whose intellectualism was shot through with the most unquestionably Christian, if not Christic, religion. I would realize this even better, if that is even possible, a few years later, in the little monastery of Sainte-Geneviève-des-Bois.[90] I saw him there after the exhausting operation he had undergone for his cancer of the larynx; as a celebrant he was imploring the descent of the Holy Ghost with a fervor and a simplicity that directly called to mind the Prophet Elias, even more than the figure of Moses, whose Michelangelo-esque reproduction he seemed to be physically.

Yet, the other Eucharistic celebrations I attended soon after the Oiseau Bleu session, at Saint-Wandrille (in the austere seventeenth-

87. On St. Gregory Palamas, see 71, n. 65. Saint Symeon the New Theologian (949–1022), monk of Constantinople, had contributed to the tradition of hesychasm before him.

88. Saint Athanasius (c. 295–373), Bishop of Alexandria, was the primary defender of orthodoxy against Arianism. He also wrote the biography of Saint Antony of the Desert (c. 252–c. 356), founder of Christian monasticism. Saint Augustine (354–430), bishop of Hippo, is considered to be the greatest Latin Father of the Church.

89. "Blue Bird."

90. The château of the Cossonnerie at Sainte-Geneviève-des-Bois (about sixteen miles south of Paris) had been taking in Russian refugees since 1927. The church of Our Lady of the Assumption was built there in the fifteenth-century Novgorod style in 1939. Among others, Metropolitan Eulogius (see 68, n. 48) is buried there. The château became a retreat house and the local municipal cemetery turned into a Russian cemetery, notably with the tombs of Fr. Sergius Bulgakov (see 58, n. 4), dancer Rudolf Nureyev (1938–1993), film director André Tarkovsky (1932–1986), et al.

century chapter room, which then functioned as a church), seemed to me clearly to achieve, in a form whose sobriety was all Roman but whose beauty was in no way inferior, the same "descent of heaven on earth" that Orthodoxy, revealed as such, made visible. Immersed as I was at the time in my discovery of Casel's theology of the mysteries, I saw in all this, be it under the shimmering mantle of the Orient or under the translucent veil of the West, the accomplishment of Hellenic humanity's own hazy expectation as proclaimed by the Christian Alexandrians to whom Newman had led me: the ultimate meaning of death and of love rendering death fruitful, of which the Eleusinian mysteries, above all, seemed to be something like a premonitory glimpse.[91] This was truly, I thought, the conjunction of the fullness of time and the fullness of divinity communicating itself in Christ for the human and cosmic fulfillment of his own plenitude, as Saint Paul had announced in his Epistle to the Ephesians.[92]

At about the same time I was acquiring a more intimate knowledge of Anglicanism. Indeed, thanks to Wheatcroft—who was himself very much steeped in his British roots—I had been involved in the translation work required for the French publication of Canon Moreton's review: *Œcumenica*.[93] By way of thanking me for my collaboration, Moreton had invited me to a first stay with him in the enclosure of Hereford Cathedral, where he had just been installed.[94]

Only years later would I read Trollope's amusing accounts of English

91. In the ancient Greek and Roman world the mysteries of Eleusis (a town near Athens) granted access to a sort of "salvation" by degrees of initiation in a dialectic of death and resurrection.

92. Eph 1:3, 9–10.

Blessed be the God and Father of our Lord Jesus Christ. . . . That he might make known unto us the mystery of his will, according to his good pleasure, which he hath purposed in him, [i]n the dispensation of the fullness of times, to re-establish all things in Christ, that are in heaven and on earth, in him.

93. Harold Moreton (1889–1966), Canon of the Anglican Cathedral of Hereford, was the editor-in-chief of the bilingual *Œcumenica: Revue de synthèse théologique trimestrielle*, published in London and Paris since 1934 by the Society for the Promotion of Christian Knowledge. Its subtitle changed to *Revue de l'anglicanisme et des questions œcuméniques* in 1938. Publication was suspended during World War II. Bouyer collaborated with this review, first as a translator, then with two articles: "L'Église luthérienne et l'œcuménisme," *Œcumenica* 4.4 (1938) and "Le culte des saints dans le protestantisme," ibid., 5.4 (1939).

94. Hereford is on the English side of the border with Wales. Its Anglican cathedral, which for the most part dates to the twelfth century and is therefore in the Romanesque style, has cloisters on its flanks. It possesses a map of the world (with Jerusalem at its center) dating to the time when it was built as well as an original copy of the *Magna Carta*.

cathedral towns.[95] Still, this stay allowed me to get to know a perfect model of such a town just before it would be unthinkable to find one intact. It was all there: the cathedral resting on the edge of its enclosure as in a vast garden, with its quadrangle bordered by the deanery and the canons' houses, the episcopal palace hard by along the Wye River. The hours passed by in a peace marked by the rhythm of bell-ringing and the alternation of the long sung office with piously learned chatter. I had such conversations with Canon Lilley, who was filled with his memories of Loisy and Tyrrell,[96] and with Canon Bannister, a musicologist and medievalist but above all a delightful humanist whose already advanced softening of the brain was restoring him to childhood without yet making him ridiculous.[97] I also met with Canon Warner, who was so perfect a Latinist that he could say his office only in Jerome's, if not in Virgil's, language while the choir chanted Coverdale's sublime English in harmonies by Merbecke or Byrd (a real Bembo in reverse!)[98]—not to mention the Bishop (Lisle Carr),[99] who seemed to come straight out of the eighteenth century, like a Whig prelate *redivivus*.[100]

On a couple of occasions I went to the neighboring parochial church for Sunday "Mass." It was one of those parodies of modern Catholicism that are, to be sure, full of the best intentions, but which make one think irresistibly of the old patch of clothing sewn onto the new—or the other way around!

95. For Trollope's novels on Cathedral towns, see 172, n. 58.

96. Alfred Leslie Lilley (1860–1948) was friendly to the Modernists. Alfred Loisy (1857–1940) and George Tyrrell (1861–1909), a convert to Catholicism and a Jesuit who was suspended in 1906, were among the best known proponents of Modernism, the notion that dogmas can evolve substantially.

97. Arthur Thomas Bannister (1861–1936) was also the historian of the diocese of Hereford.

98. Canon Warner died in 1944. St. Jerome (c. 347–420) translated the Bible from Greek and Hebrew into fifth-century Latin (the Vulgate version), which is less classical than the Latin of the first-century BC Roman poet Virgil, author of the *Aeneid*, the *Eclogues*, and the *Georgics*, all part of the regular curriculum in British schools at the time. Myles Coverdale (c. 1488–1568) is known for his unabridged translation of the Bible into English. John Merbecke (c. 1510–c. 1585) was a theologian and composer in the Church of England. William Byrd (1540–1623) set the Anglican service to music (although he was attached to Rome himself). At the same time Cardinal Pietro Bembo (1470–1547) promoted the more ornate and profane style of the madrigal—which Byrd was also able to use.

99. Charles Lisle Carr (1871–1942), bishop of Coventry from 1922 and 107th Bishop of Hereford since 1931.

100. "Whig" is the term applied to classical Liberals in England. The Latin adjective *redivivus* here means "brought back to life."

It is only among the Scandinavian Lutherans or those in northern Germany—or, of course, transplanted in America (thanks to Prussian-style persecution at the hands of Protestant "liberalism")—that this is no artificial resurgence but a simple survival. There, all the Catholic ceremonial and decor, even in their Baroque form, do not produce this self-conscious effect.

I cannot, however, conclude these reminiscences of my early years of formation to the ministry and leave it to be understood that I was exclusively occupied with theology, spirituality, and ecumenism. Certainly these objects of study, with the charm of novelty, reduced the time left for more secular reading, at least in appearance. Yet, it was at this time (thanks to a suggestion on the part of Madame Bouttier,[101] our seminary rector's wife) that I launched into the correspondence between Alain Fournier and Jacques Rivière.[102] Thence I went on to a first taste of Claudel,[103] from whom I passed over to Péguy[104]—with more reticence, however—although Claudel himself left me, and still leaves me, somewhat dissatisfied. I would also come to Gide,[105] and Charles du Bos too;[106] the latter would satisfy me more and more in the following years, despite a few moments of amused impatience.

But all of this would only prepare one of the encounters that most influenced the entire course of my thinking: that with the English poets,

101. Hélène Bouttier, *née* Nyegaard, married Gabriel Bouttier (1879–1970), director of the Seminary of the Protestant Faculty of Paris from 1928 to 1938, in 1920.

102. Jacques Rivière (1886–1925) and Alain-Fournier (Henri Alban-Fournier, 1886–1914), literary men, kept up a daily correspondence later published as *Correspondance de Jacques Rivière et Alain Fournier: 1905–1914* (Paris: Gallimard, 1926).

103. Paul Claudel (1868–1955), Catholic dramatist, member of the Académie française from 1946.

104. Charles Péguy (1873–1914), poet and essayist. Baptized at birth, he delayed his commitment to Catholicism until 1907–1908 because his strongly atheistic wife refused to have their civil marriage regularized by the Church as Jacques Maritain, who converted at about the same time, had been urging Péguy to do. His socialism, too, made him suspicious of conformist Catholics. His writings have been influential among many of the faithful.

105. André Gide (1865–1951), symbolist writer, recipient of the 1947 Nobel Prize for literature. He rejected his childhood Protestantism in part, but his output is shot through with the uncertainties and demands of a moral life.

106. Charles du Bos (1882–1939), French writer and literary critic who converted to Catholicism in 1927. He sought to love and understand the works he reviewed rather than to discuss their strengths and weaknesses. As a polyglot and voracious reader, he introduced classic and contemporary English, German, and Russian literature to the French readership. He and Paul Claudel (see 65, n. 37) were the standard-bearers of the literary French converts of their time, the "Gilded Age."

Shelley and Wordsworth first, then Coleridge and Keats, and finally Hopkins and Eliot.[107] These, however, were to remain in reserve, so to speak, until the time when I left Paris for a four-year stint in Strasbourg.

107. Percy Bysshe Shelley (1792–1822), William Wordsworth (1817–1850), Samuel Taylor Coleridge (1772–1834), and John Keats (1795-1821) all belong to the second generation of English Romantic poets, along with their friend George Gordon, Lord Byron (1788–1824) in whom Bouyer found little interest. Gerard Manley Hopkins, SJ (1844–1889), was converted thanks to Newman and joined the Jesuits; his poetry allied the Christian faith to universal myths in innovative verse forms. The poetry of Thomas Stearns Eliot (1888–1965) moved from denouncing the absurdity of the modern world in the wake of World War I to celebrating penance and the Redemption; he is best known for his poem "The Waste Land" (1922) and his play on Thomas à Beckett, *Murder in the Cathedral* (1935). He received the Nobel Prize in Literature in 1948. Bouyer and Eliot would become friends; see at 178–79. For Bouyer's thinking on these and other poets' significance, see his *Cosmos* (see 55, n. 36), 161–79 and his posthumous work *Religio poetae* (Saulges: Ad Solem, forthcoming). Bouyer's friend Jean Duchesne reports that Bouyer found peace in hearing Wordsworth and Keats recited to him during his last and lengthy illness.

5

Retreat on the Rhine

AS DIVERSE as it was, our little group of four took part in this departure together, right in the middle of our studies preparing for the baccalaureate in theology (actually more like the Catholic licentiate). I was its initiator only to the extent that the idea occurred to me first. It was to be accepted easily and nearly immediately by my three friends.

Indeed, we all felt that we had got out of the Parisian college all that it had to offer us. Furthermore, though perhaps for more or less different reasons, all four of us had the justified feeling that we had made ourselves, individually and collectively, *personae non gratae*: collectively in our agreement in a vigorous independence of mind; individually, Hardy and Malbert no less than I, by the various nuances of our "Catholic" sympathies, and Deransart even more perhaps by his expressions of a simple Protestant orthodoxy. It had become intolerable to most of our professors' theoretical liberalism by the very fact that it emanated from an intelligence that was no less critical or less free than that on which they prided themselves.

As for our dear old director in particular,[1] though he was rather fond of us *in petto*, he had the cold sweats at our mere appearance at chapel, all the while considering our absence to be a challenge to what ought to have been his moral authority.

All in all I think our masters would at least have been disappointed if French Protestantism might have to go without our services. Several of them, however, would doubtless rather have had others besides themselves bear the responsibility of introducing such oddballs into its clergy.

Furthermore all four of us, if I am not mistaken, held scholarships

---

1. Gabriel Bouttier; see 63, n. 28.

from our respective churches. In Strasbourg, where the theology schools depended on the State, the scholarships did, too.[2]

The result of these various considerations (and others, too, perhaps) was that rather than any objection being raised against our project, everything possible was done to advance it. We were, therefore, rather warmly recommended both to the dean of the faculty of Strasbourg, Henri Strohl,[3] and to the Canon of Saint Thomas's church, who had held the title of "ephor"[4] since the sixteenth century, since he was in charge of the seminary next to the church by the same name.[5] Our transfer went through without the shadow of any trouble.

None of the four of us, it ought to be said, had any idea of what we might find there, by the way. Yet, the very novelty must have been enough for our youth. We were not to be disappointed.

More than this: a certain number of our new masters awaited us, perhaps, as they would have said themselves, *mit gemischten Gefühlen*.[6] We soon noted, however, that the apprehension of a good number of our Alsatian classmates was of an entirely different order.

One has to take into account the ambiguous relations between Alsace and what its inhabitants called by the humorous moniker of "the interior." These good people anxiously wondered whether we, far from being indomitable individualists, hadn't been sent to Strasbourg by suspicious Parisian ecclesiastical and university authorities to report back to them on the loyalty of these long-lost brethren. I must say that when we realized this supposition, it seemed so over the top to us, as Flaubert would have said,[7] that it sent us into a laughter worthy of Rabelais.[8] Deransart, whose insolent courtesy had not taken long to get noticed, and who had gone out of his way to lend credibility to this hilarious ver-

2. Alsace and Moselle became German in 1871. The 1802 Concordat passed between Napoleon I and the Holy See, therefore, was not affected by its repudiation by the French Republic in 1905, and the Protestant and Catholic schools of theology remained part of the State universities. This has remained the case even after the return of those regions to France in 1918 and to this day.

3. Henri Strohl (1874–1959), lecturer, then professor of Church History, 1919–1945; dean, 1929–1939. He specialized in Luther and promoted ecumenism.

4. In ancient Sparta the Ephors were the five members of the elected council who advised the King. Their title was taken over to indicate holders of some administrative responsibility in Protestantism. At this time this was Antonin Causse, regarding whom see 94, n. 59.

5. The church building, considered to be the cathedral of Protestantism in Alsace, was begun in 1196. It went over to Lutheranism in 1524.

6. German for "with mixed feelings." Alsace, whose capital is Strasbourg, had been under German administration from 1870 to 1918; its people speak a Germanic dialect to this day.

sion of our exodus, did all in his power to make it last as long as possible. Nevertheless, I don't think it was meant to last. As much as we had the reputation of being a bunch of hard-headed misfits in Paris, we had no trouble passing for a syndicate of anarchists in the Lower-Rhine atmosphere, not to mention in Strasbourg.

We immediately distanced ourselves from our classmates and from our masters, who were falling over themselves to express their tricolored[9] feelings with sufficient emotion. Soon we, to the contrary, fell in with some of those most suspected of independence, if not of harboring more or less pro-German leanings. This brought the above-mentioned impression to its acme.

In fact, one of the reasons for which Strasbourg had attracted us had been the opportunity (or the illusion of the opportunity) of finding easier access to German culture, with which none of us was really familiar. On the other hand, we were soon given to understand that a good number of Alsatians who claimed to be the most French at heart—starting with Dean Strohl—had protested diametrically opposed sentiments back when the Kaiser reigned over both sides of the Rhine. As a result, the term *Boche*,[10] which Deransart least hesitated to employ, was never employed by the rest of us but for Alsatians of that sort. This clinched our adoption by those who did not belong to that clique, and spared us acquaintances that were as dubious as they might have been burdensome.

Before leaving Paris, however, we had, thanks to Deransart, a vision of the world that was leaving us much more than we were leaving it, though we did not know it at the time. I mean to speak of that magical Colonial Exposition, which had sprung from Liautey's genius alone.[11] Deransart was the most worldly of all of us; I don't think the other three of us had had a single worldly entertainment for two years. It was he who dragged us to it on a beautiful spring evening. All of us were to return to it many times by the end of the school year. We had no inkling,

---

7. Gustave Flaubert's (1821–1880) word for "over the top" in French is *hénaurme*, a humorously emphatic spelling of *énorme*. He coined it in an October 1857 letter to his friend Jules Duplan (died 1870).

8. François Rabelais (1483/94–1553), French humanist, creator of the larger-than-life character Gargantua.

9. Meaning patriotic French, after the Tricolor (French flag).

10. French for "Kraut." Frenchmen of the interior sometimes use it derogatively to refer to Alsatians, whose accent and cuisine strike them as Germanic.

11. Marshall Louis-Hubert Lyautey (1854–1934), French officer and empire builder in Indochina, Madagascar, Algeria, and especially Morocco. He was promoted Marshall during World War I and organized this exposition in 1931.

we did not for an instant suspect, that this vision of an enchanted world that Western, and especially French, civilization had taken to its bosom as the symbol of its supremacy and perfection was also its swan song. All of this would be torn away from us within a few years. Even after a final, but ever so dubious, victory, we would be left with doubt instead of the calm possession of an as-yet still unshakable tradition. These dreamlike images themselves, like that of Angkor Wat[12] shimmering in the calm summer night, would be handed over to a fallacious liberation and collapse into the demented horror of the Khmer Rouges![13]

I can still remember the sudden foreboding I felt at about the same time when I read a newspaper article as I sat on a bench near the observatory. It portended, in the Nazism whose victory was barely perceptible, the little cloud on the horizon that is the harbinger of a storm to come, or rather of the flood into which our lives, so safe until then, would collapse. It is symbolic that on the same bench, a mere few years before, I had read with disbelief the news of the Briand-Kellogg pact signed the night before.[14] Through it all the nations of the civilized world solemnly—definitively, as was underscored!—renounced recourse to war.

The following summer vacation, during which Deransart joined me in Sancerre for the first time, was for me something like another, more personal, version of dusk in an evening still naively bedecked with the colors of dawn.

Along with another of my friends' cousins who was notably older than I—an excellent musician of whom I may say that she initiated me to Chopin and especially to Schumann—I went on many a walk across the Sancerre region. Élisabeth, I thought more than ever, was its very soul. Sometime later, though, Deransart, whose Douai family were friends with Élisabeth's parents, revealed to me that her mother did not look kindly at all on the relationship she and I had slowly developed. My attentions, he told me, were considered to be the ruin of her education. In fact, I don't think I am wrong in saying that with his discretion, which, as I already knew, was matched by his verbal insolence, he was

---

12. The great Hindu temple in Cambodia, which had been a French protectorate since 1863. It was built over several centuries, from the ninth to the fourteenth.

13. The Khmers Rouges were a Communist group that ruled Cambodia, 1975–1979. Their revolutionary policies resulted in the death of about 1,700,000 people.

14. This pact was signed on August 27, 1928. It was a solemn commitment to abandon war as means to settle international disagreements. The signatories were the French Minister of Foreign Affairs, Aristide Briand (1862–1932), and his American counterpart Frank Billings Kellogg (1856–1937). Sixty-three governments ratified it, which did not prevent World War II, but it did form part of the prosecution's case against Nazi leaders at the Nuremberg trials (1945–1946).

trying to communicate to me that "someone" thought that my transparent hope of someday marrying a girl from so elevated a milieu was
ridiculous. This, once I understood it, would amuse rather than hurt
me, I have to say: the "someone" was obviously Élisabeth's mother. I
knew perfectly well that her opinion of me was precisely what her own
mother-in-law had always held of her! This state of affairs convinced me
to break off all contact with Élisabeth until she should reach an age that
the English would call "marriageable." But this did not blunt my hopes
at all. Such is the candid confidence of youth in itself and in life!

These were my dispositions when I took the fast train to Strasbourg
for the first time with my classmates one evening in early November.
This train was to become an old friend as time went by.

I was immediately smitten with the half-familiar, half-anarchic atmosphere the town then had, especially the Saint Thomas quarter, where
we were to live. In the shade of the tall Romanesque, or more precisely
Ottonian, church,[15] the seminary's Second Empire buildings and the
Oberkonsistorium were reflected in the Ill River between the poplars.[16]
These buildings prolonged the Canons' beautiful eighteenth-century
houses, which in turn seamlessly succeeded to the picturesque (and, in
its cutthroat way, medieval) "Little France." The ineffable President
Albert Lebrun,[17] with sobs in his throat, had recently hailed the name as
a witness to Strasbourg's unswerving loyalty to France. The poor man
hadn't been warned that the name simply designates the neighborhood
that used to be set aside for . . . victims of the "French disease"![18]

The river's other bank, across from this little Lutheran Vatican, was
by-and-large Catholic, conventual even, and church bells were to be
heard nearly without ceasing. Lucie Berger Middle School (a green-
house in which select maidens, generally of clerical descent, matured as
lettuces in a bell jar) was the only exception, if it can be called such, for
it was without a doubt, in its own way, what Saint Athanasius would
have called a "parthenon."[19]

For those, like me, whose windows did not give out on that side but

---

15. Ottonian architecture, named for Holy Roman Emperor Otto the Great (936–
975), tends to be decentralized.

16. The *Oberkonsistorium* (literally "Supreme consistory") is one of the administrative units of European Lutheranism. The Ill River runs through Strasbourg.

17. Albert Lebrun (1871–1950): President of France, 1932–1940.

18. I.e., syphilis.

19. The term παρθενών (parthenōn) in classical Greek refers to the unmarried
women's and girls' quarters (and to the temple of Athena in Athens). Saint Athanasius
was the first to use the word to describe a convent, specifically that to which Saint Antony of the Desert committed his sister before he became a hermit, *Life of Saint Antony*, 3.

towards the east, the sight of the old brown-shingled roofs rising sharply to the sky among their numberless little dormers served as jewel box for the cathedral's high façade. Its one spire shot out like a rocket, "that raised finger that writes in the sky," as the Russian poet Tyutchev wrote.[20] It was a doubly astonishing vision: for its sandstone was not the same hue two days, or even two hours, in a row, and it would pass from the spring mornings' blazing rose to the crimson gold of summer evenings, which a simple fog turned to purple, and rain to indigo.

The neighboring spire, made over-ornate by a pompous Kaiser Wilhelm-era reconstruction, rose in its shadow, so to speak. It was that of the Neue Kirche (bizarrely rendered in French as *Temple neuf*),[21] where I would later give the examination sermon which, in the Church of the Augsburg Confession, confers the *venia concionandi*,[22] a necessary prelude to ordination. I already knew that it housed the tomb of Johannes Tauler.[23]

In Strasbourg, as in England for Anglicanism, all the older churches belonged to the Church that had gone over to the Reform. The cathedral itself was no exception and remained, in theory, the property of the Protestant canons whom Louis XV[24] had simply compelled to rent it, for a yearly sum of one Franc (which was punctually remitted), to their Catholic confreres.[25]

In my state of mind at the time, I shared the hopes of my little group of Parisian friends with a notably wider group of Alsatian pastors. Our hopes were in another church, which was the (unforgettable, I have to say) incarnation of High-Church Lutheranism. This was certainly only what Luther would have wanted in his religious heart of hearts, but the intemperance of his Ockhamist logic,[26] even more than the truculence of his anti-Gallic passion, had dashed all hope of this very early on. I am

---

Louis Bouyer knew this work well; see his *La Vie de saint Antoine. Essai sur la spiritualité du monachisme primitif*, Figures Monastiques (Saint Wandrille: Fontanelle, 1950), and his thesis for the licentiate in Protestant theology, *L'Incarnation et l'Église Corps du Christ dans la théologie de saint Athanase* (Paris: Cerf, 1943).

20. Fyodor Tyutchev (1803–1873), Russian poet, worked for the Russian office in Munich from 1822, where he met the German poet Heinrich Heine (1797–1856). He is known for his anthropomorphisms.

21. "New Temple."

22. Latin for "license to preach."

23. Johannes Tauler (1300–1361), Alsatian theologian and mystic, student of Meister Eckhart. See *Métier*, 30.

24. Louis XV (1710–1774), King of France from 1715.

25. In fact, the cathedral was restored to the Catholic cult in 1681, under Louis XIV.

26. William of Ockham (c. 1288–1348), nominalist philosopher.

of course thinking of the Saint-Pierre-le-Jeune church, which was consecrated by the Alsatian Pope Saint Leo IX[27] and restored (only too generously) by Pastor Horning[28] during the Romantic period. It was in its Baroque sanctuary, whose graceful grey and gold woodwork harmonize so well with the flamboyant red stone arcades framing its high stain glass windows, that I would celebrate the beautiful traditional Lutheran Liturgy of the Eucharist for the first few times. I celebrated it for my future students over at the gymnasium, the venerable college that succeeded, in the same place and without transition, to the Dominican Convent in which Eckhart had taught[29] and Tauler had lived. To this day I keep a reproduction of Baldung Grien's *Descent from the Cross*,[30] facing which I officiated so often, above my desk in Paris along with a few photographs of the altar and baptistery of this church, which has remained the dearest of all to me. When a friend gave me as a present an engraving of Neman's church in Oxford, Saint Mary the Virgin, I naturally put it up next to that picture.[31]

The best I owe to my stay in Strasbourg is my acquaintance with the "Evangelical Catholicity" of the Lutherans of this stripe, which is indistinguishable from my own first approaches to the great mystical tradition through the Rhineland men I have just mentioned.

These two discoveries are bound together not only by the mingling of the most eloquent memories of each tradition, which is more inevitable in Strasbourg than anywhere else, but also by the indisputable continuity from one to the other. After all, Luther had started out as the cordial editor of *Theologia Deutsch*,[32] perhaps one of the best popularizations of Rhineland mysticism. Furthermore, Alsatian Lutherans have never stopped paying attention to this school, and though sometimes critical of it, they have never been altogether averse to it. Auguste Jundt,[33] father of the André Jundt whose student I once was,[34] has devoted a scholarly

27. Leo IX (1002–1054), Pope from 1049. The church became Protestant in 1524.

28. Frédérick Théodore Horning (1809–1882), leader of the Lutheran confessional renewal, was Pastor of Saint-Pierre-le-Jeune from 1845 to his death.

29. Meister Eckhart (1260–1327), German theologian, philosopher and mystic.

30. Baldung Grien (1484/5–1545), German painter and citizen of Strasbourg from 1509. The painting dates to c. 1516.

31. Bouyer doubtless put these pictures side by side because each one had been its respective pastor's (Newman's and Bouyer's) last Protestant house of worship.

32. Luther published this anonymous mystical treatise (a work of Eckhart's?) twice, in 1516 and 1518. He ranked it after the Bible and Saint Augustine only.

33. Auguste Jundt (1848–1890), author of books on the medieval lay mystical group called the "Friends of God."

34. André Jundt (1877–1947), professor of Lutheran Dogmatics at the Protestant Faculty of Paris from 1920 and biographer of Luther.

study to the singular problem raised by the "Friend of God from the Oberland,"[35] and one of the professors I was to find in Strasbourg, Robert Will,[36] took a direct interest in Tauler.

My introduction to mysticism, however, had already taken place in Paris by reading Baruzi's *Saint John of the Cross*.[37] Still, despite the indisputable beauties of this masterful analysis, I had been bothered by the constant intrusion of a philosophy that was external to its object. I could tell that it tried in vain to reclaim it for itself. I must also add that after my reading of Huysmans[38] and an initial contact with the learned and absurd tome of Father Poulain on *The Graces of Prayer*[39]—both of which are pretty entirely absorbed in a visionary type of mysticism— this first contact with what has been called *Wesenmystik*,[40] the mysticism of the essence, baffled me. In reading Tauler, to begin with, in Father Théry's translation and commentaries,[41] I would become persuaded that here was, if anywhere, the only mysticism worthy of the name. It is the grace-filled entry into the mystery par excellence, the mystery of the interior life of the God of love, the one and transcendent God of the Gospel.

I had undertaken this last reading at Couhé-Vérac, in the Poitou,[42] towards the end of the last vacations during my stay with Pastor Valentin de Bachst. He had just finished up his theological studies in Paris, after which he had accepted this parish.

He was an émigré Russian officer with a remote German ancestry. His own attraction to Orthodoxy had drawn me to him. His personality was passionate but exceptional in integrity and generosity; his restrained

---

35. Fictional character who looms large in medieval German mystic literature.

36. Robert Will (1869–1959), Lutheran theologian, professor of practical theology in Strasbourg, 1919–1937.

37. Jean Baruzi (1881–1953), professor at the Sorbonne, then at the Collège de France from 1933, author of *Saint Jean de la Croix et le problème de l'expérience mystique* (Paris: F. Alcan, 1924).

38. For Huysmans see 53, n. 26.

39. Auguste Poulain, *Des grâces d'oraison: traité de théologie mystique* (Paris: V. Retaux, 1901). English version: *The Graces of Interior Prayer (Des Grâces d'Oraison)*, trans. L. C. Smith (London: Kegan Paul, 1910).

40. *Wesenmystik* is a medieval mysticism of the Low Countries according to which the human essence, because it has an affinity with the divine essence, can be absorbed into it.

41. Gabriel Théry, *Sermons de Tauler: traduction sur les plus anciens manuscrits allemands* (Paris: Éditions de la Vie Spirituelle, Librairie Desclée, 1927). For Tauler see 88, n. 23.

42. Poitou is the name of the region around Poitiers, on the French Atlantic seaboard.

violence was tempered by an excellent sense of humor. It soon attached me to him.

His sister Émilie, who had already gone over to Orthodoxy, and his brother-in-law Henri Ellenberger, who was just then finishing up his medical studies, also became friends of mine. We were to share the results of our research in the years to follow.

Meanwhile I kept up my original reading of the great Western texts on mysticism, particularly of their principal source, Pseudo-Dionysius. I discovered the most valuable explanations of their object in Father Joseph Maréchal's studies on *The Psychology of Mystics*.[43] As far as I am concerned they are still the best works on the matter. Their title, however, indicates their limitation, which is a point of view in which psychology is predominant, although their author was far too perceptive always to stick to it.

At the same time I undertook the study of the Greek Fathers, for which I had had a priceless initiation in Father de Régnon's volumes: *Études de théologie positive sur le dogme de la Trinité*.[44] It would not take me long to realize that truly traditional theology and traditional mysticism go hand in hand. This is what would be confirmed for me a few years later in the perceptive sketches by Dom Anselme Stolz, who alas died too soon: his *Théologie de la Mystique*, followed by his equally remarkable *Ascèse chrétienne*.[45]

It is significant that the first modern theologian to have anticipated his conclusions was also the greatest thinker in Lutheranism: Johann Gerhard.[46] Finding sources for Luther's theology, especially his Eucharistic piety, in Greek Patristics in the seventeenth century, he was the first to see that the *unio mystica* must first, before being the object of experiences of a living faith, be the ontological reality that the sacraments, most eminently Communion, bring to this faith as its very content.

Paul Gerhardt was the witness par excellence of fidelity to the Catholic sacramental and spiritual tradition of this "old Lutheranism," as it is called.[47] As a hymn writer, he made it an inspiration to Johann Sebastian

---

43. *Studies in the Psychology of the Mystics* (New York, 1964).

44. Théodore de Régnon, *Études de théologie positive sur le dogme de la Trinité* (Paris: V. Retaux et fils, 1892).

45. Anselme Stolz (1900–1942), author of a book on the theology of mysticism, *Théologie de la Mystique* (Chevetogne: Éd. des Bénédictines d'Amay, 1939), and of another on Christian asceticism, *L'Ascèse chrétienne* (Chevetogne: Éd. des Bénédictines d'Amay, 1948), the latter based on lectures he gave in 1939.

46. Johann Gerhard (1582–1637).

47. Paul Gerhardt (1607–1676), Lutheran hymn writer. See L. Bouyer, *The Spirit and Forms of Protestantism* (see 59, n. 12), 27–28.

Bach. Despite persecution from the "Reformed" Prussians, and doubtless under the stimulation of Johann Arndt's *True Christianity*[48] (its author himself so Catholic that he would be read by Catholics and Russian Orthodox alike, as well as by all sorts of Protestants), this rich vein, I think, would find its most pure mystical expression in those poems by Gerhardt Tersteegen (though he was "Reformed" himself!)[49] that can only be compared to those by Saint John of the Cross. Wilhelm Löhe[50] was to bring this tradition back to light at the very moment when Newman went from Anglicanism over to Catholicism. Prussian imperialism and the entire rationalist- and pantheist-leaning *Aufklärung* movement had nearly snuffed it out. Alsace, with Pastor Horning (whom I have mentioned above), inherited it, and Pastor Louis Meyer[51] brought its seed to Paris. It was above all Pastor Ihme, however, author of the best collection of traditional Lutheran music, who implanted it in the Rhine valley.[52] Prussian persecution, inspired by Schleiermacher,[53] the father of so-called "liberalism," transplanted it from East Prussia to the United States, where it now seems to have found its most lively home.

Ihme's grandson, who was a student at the Saint Thomas Stift[54] at the same time we were there, was its most faithful heir, along with his cousins the Guerrier.[55] He was one of the best personalities my Protestant theology days caused me to meet. He, more than anyone, helped me to appreciate that tradition's vitality.

I daresay that in all of Protestantism there is nowhere else that ecumenism such as I have outlined it above is more likely to yield tangible results—far more, I'm afraid, than can be hoped for Anglicanism, which is divided beyond repair and is prisoner to too many confusions and artificial transplants.

48. Johann Arndt (1555–1621), Lutheran theologian, published this work in 1609.

49. Gerhardt Tersteegen (1697–1769), German Reformed writer. See L. Bouyer, *Spirit and Forms*, 28–30.

50. Johann Konrad Wilhelm Löhe (1808–1872), Lutheran pastor, founding sponsor of the Missouri Synod.

51. Louis Meyer (1809–1867), Lutheran pastor from 1837. See L. Bouyer, *Spirit and Forms*, 41–43, and "Une grande figure du luthéranisme français: le pasteur Louis Meyer," *La Vie intellectuelle* 64 (1939): 166–89.

52. Friedrich August Ihme (1834–1915), editor for 38 years of the *Evangelisch-Lutherischer Friedensbote aus Elsass Lothringen* and author of an organ hymn book, *Halleluja*.

53. Friedrich Daniel Ernst Schleiermacher (1768–1834), German theologian and philosopher who sought to reconcile Protestantism and the Enlightenment.

54. Student center in Strasbourg since 1544. Originally the German term *Stift* meant "convent."

55. Fritz Guerrier, a Lutheran church bell designer, and Christian Guerrier, organist.

Although he did not issue from this milieu as such, one of my Strasbourg masters, Oscar Cullmann, exhibited an entirely similar spirit.[56] I am most grateful to him for it. I can say that his classes totally renewed my understanding of the New Testament and finished convincing me that it is impossible to isolate its study from that of the patristic tradition. I was immediately smitten by his class on the Epistle to the Romans; perhaps even more so by the lecture notes of another class he had given the year before on the Gospel of John. The books he published since then on the sacraments and the tradition from which that Gospel arose, to mention only those, as remarkable as they are, cannot give a good idea of the wealth of his oral teaching.

I slowly came to know this great master and discovered his spirit of total consecration in the service of the faith of the Gospel. He had chosen to remain celibate for it. Above all, he bore the most painful and drawn-out illnesses with admirable Christian courage and dealt with his students with a discreet and smiling charity. I am inclined to think that if a scholar can also be a saint, and, if indeed there are saints in Protestantism, he was for me the most direct witness of it.

Sometime later my other master, Auguste Lecerf,[57] who was so different in appearance yet so similar in many respects, came to Strasbourg for a conference. I rejoiced at seeing those two men of God, who were so faithful and so real, recognize and appreciate each other.

I have already mentioned Robert Will, a muddled intellect but a tenacious workhorse. His enormous theoretical synthesis on worship, *Le Culte*,[58] though it encompasses any number of interesting observations, remains unreadable. I should know: I proof-read it; I cannot complain since this excellent man paid me a very decent salary for that thankless task. The poor man was saddled with a wife who must have been very beautiful once, but whose stupidity, alas, had never waned. She made him as sad as rocks, but he put up with her with the patience of the angels.

Another excellent man, though one couldn't tell at first blush because he had Ernest Renan's poisonous yet suave manner, was Anto-

---

56. Oscar Cullmann (1902–1999), New Testament and Church History professor, 1930–1938; he then took a position at the University of Basel, where he taught until 1972. His academic activity focused on historical and theological research and ecumenism. He would be a Protestant observer at Vatican II. See Louis Bouyer, "L'Œuvre exégétique d'Oscar Cullmann et le problème eschatologique," *La Vie intellectuelle* 16.3 (1948): 22–24.

57. See 63, n. 26.

58. Robert Will, *Le culte: étude d'histoire et de philosophie religieuses.* Vol. 1: *Le Caractère religieux du culte*; vol. 2: *Les formes du culte*; vol. 3: *Les éléments sociaux du culte* (Strasbourg: Istra, 1925–).

nin Causse.[59] Although he didn't harbor the shadow of a doubt regarding our radically divergent orientations, his paternal solicitude for me would be even more constant. He was the "ephor" I mentioned above and, as such, one of the most reverenced dignitaries in the Chapter of Saint Thomas. He delighted in quoting the more-than-irreverent poem about the institution whose author (a student, naturally) proclaimed, among other things: "Antonin was not the chapter, but to see him was to see the chapter!"

I should point out, while I am on the topic, that the Chapter, which was a survival of the medieval Chapter founded by the Holy Roman Emperor and had made it through the Reformation, had long since given up singing the Divine Office, even though it continued to wear a sumptuous costume. Of all the French Chapters, however, it was the only one to have retained its landholdings despite the Revolution. This was because Kalb, the jurisconsult who went on to be the principal author of the Napoleonic code, guaranteed that he had long since laicized them. This was nearly true in the sense that aside from their modest yet comfortable benefice (and their beautiful houses along the Ill), these "learned, discreet, and venerable personages" paid their revenues over to scholarships and other university foundations. I should be the last to complain on this score, for in the years when I was preparing my superior examinations I was endowed with a benefice which, though minor, was absolutely *sine cura*,[60] thanks to the benevolence of Will and Causse. I never even thought the thing possible! I also proofread, for a particularly liberal remuneration, Causse's drafts. I have to say that this allowed me to appreciate, besides his culture and French, which was refined as well as occasionally mischievous, his exceptionally deep views on the application of the comparative history of religions to the study of the Old Testament.

His essay on the *Poor of Israel*,[61] although he himself, in the modesty of his scrupulous rigor, made little account of it, was the first to bring out one of the elements of the piety in the last psalms that already foreshadows the spirit of the Beatitudes. As for his great work *Du Clan à la Communauté religieuse*, whose elaboration I can say that I followed very

---

59. Antonin Causse (1877–1947), Professor of Old Testament and the history of religions, 1919–1945. His work on Israel parallels Max Weber's with its sociological approach, and is synthesized in his *Du groupe ethnique à la communauté religieuse* (Paris: F. Alcan, 1937).

60. Entailing no responsibility.

61. *Les Pauvres d'Israël* (Strasbourg: Librairie Istra, 1922).

closely, it still seems to me to be the best that has been written on the evolution of the People of God to the Church of Christ.

I shall add that this pseudo-skeptic was also perpetually ill. He overcame his state, superficially at least, by being the first to mock the shabby, gelatinous-Buddha appearance caused by his maladies. In this regard, I'll mention in passing that back in the days when he occupied the Old Testament chair there was in Strasbourg an international conference of specialists in that field. He was absent because of one of his illness's recurring episodes. All these augurs therefore examined amongst themselves who might be considered for the apparently imminent succession. As Cullmann himself—who had outlived them all—was to point out to me twenty years later, all these charitable confreres were already in their graves while Causse still occupied his chair as well as his stall, so to speak... and, naturally, still at death's door in appearance!

After these two amiable figures I should mention Charles Hauter, the religious philosopher.[62] He was a man of dizzying brilliance and the author of a short work titled *Le problème sociologique du protestantisme*,[63] a masterpiece of clarity. Besides this, he was an incurable sloth. What stimulating conversation, though!—and a good fellow deep down, under his German ogre appearance.

The only incident in my university years in Strasbourg happened during my final examination for the theology baccalaureate. The dogmatic theology professor,[64] being as he was a typical example of those "liberals" who, though claiming to be such, reckon that freedom of thought belongs to them alone, refused to grade my paper on the historical development of the notion of orthodoxy in the Church. According to worthy judges like William Seston,[65] I had given an irreproachable scientific presentation of the question. I had, however, allowed my lack of esteem for the interpretation that my master had given us of data he only knew second-hand, as was only too obvious, to show through.

This compelled me to take the examination over again, not without having vehemently protested against this procedure. Apparently, only

62. Charles Hauter (1888–1981), lecturer and then professor of the philosophy of religion, 1919–1941; professor of dogmatics, 1941–1961.

63. *Le problème sociologique du protestantisme* (Strasbourg: Istra, 1923). He actually did publish other books besides this.

64. Fernand Louis Auguste Ménégoz (1873–1944). His principal work, *Le problème de la prière: principe d'une révision de la méthode théologique* (Strasbourg: Istra, 1925), brought the influence of Karl Barth into France.

65. William Seston, instructor in Ancient History, 1929–1936.

Dean Strohl had been naive enough to support his confrere on the council. He declared that he had, for his part, understood close to nothing in my history paper because I quoted from memory—in Greek, of course—ancient council texts without bothering to translate them. The other professors had been unanimous in judging this personal vendetta very severely. My second paper got me (I dare not say deserved) an exceptional grade even though I took no trouble this time around.

After this, I stayed in Strasbourg for another two years. I taught at the famous gymnasium I have mentioned and, once ordained, I was one of its chaplains. I wrote my theses at the same time. For the baccalaureate I wrote *Newman et le christianisme alexandrin*. I never published it except for one chapter, which Yves Simon's *Revue de Philosophie* accepted on the unexpected recommendation of the *Revue des Deux Mondes*.[66] The latter had politely declined it for being too technical (I am blushing more deeply at the thought than that grand old lady ever did!).

I should have defended my licentiate thesis after taking its final examinations, but I had no opportunity to do so since I became Catholic in the meantime. It would be published years later by the Éditions du Cerf under the title *L'Église Corps du Christ dans la théologie de Saint Athanase*.[67]

These last years in Strasbourg (last for the time being, as we shall see) were not spent in the old Saint-Thomas quarter Stift. I spent them in the modern part of town, beyond the so-called false city walls, in the pleasant Protestant student house on Rue Finkmat. It bore the peculiar name of *Le Cercle évangélique*. Among other fellow boarders there I had Albert Garaudy and Thomas Merton.[68]

Albert Garaudy then handled his financial survival not by giving private lessons or by proofreading, as I did, but by resoling his friends' and acquaintances' shoes. I can positively declare, by reason of my personal experience, that his work in this field was unfailingly sturdy. Thomas Merton, too, was a guest in that house in the same years, but in those days he was so discreet and so shy that I cannot have exchanged three words with him. Once we had both become Catholic we never met again, but we did have a most cordial correspondence. In this *Cercle* we had spent some time with one of the faculty professors I have not men-

66. "Newman et le platonisme de l'âme anglaise," *Revue de Philosophie* 45 (1936): 285–305.

67. Louis Bouyer, *L'Incarnation et l'Église Corps du Christ dans la théologie de saint Athanase*, "Unam Sanctam" Collection, 11 (Paris: Cerf, 1943).

68. Thomas Merton (1915–1968), the famous Trappist monk. He would spend his Christmas holidays in Strasbourg starting in 1930, when he was a pupil at Oakham School in England.

tioned yet: Jean Héring.[69] He held the chair of New Testament and had his rooms in that house too. In his autobiography, Merton has drawn a charming portrait of the man, but it doesn't fully do justice to how colorful he was.[70] I don't think anyone will mind if I add a few strokes.

I have mentioned a few eccentrics, but the term, if applied to Héring, would be too weak; the more informal "nut" [*phénomène*] alone will do.

Although he couldn't compare with Cullmann, his knowledge was solid. He authored an excellent volume, *Le Royaume de Dieu et sa venue dans le Nouveau Testament*,[71] and a far from negligible commentary on the first Epistle to the Corinthians. This, however, was only the professional side of his life, and I do not believe he would be shocked in the least when I say that this was the side to which he attached the least importance. Not that this kept him from giving me some excellent advice, such as carefully plowing through the great book by the Anglican A. E. J. Rawlinson, *The New Testament Doctrine of the Christ*, and a volume of essays the same author edited on the Trinity and the incarnation in the theology of the early centuries.[72] Yet, I think that he was more interested, besides his magnificent Persian stamp collection, in astrology and demonology. How much he actually believed in them and the extent to which they amused him is beyond my ken, and I am inclined to believe that he didn't know himself. What is for sure is that his little knickknacks, underscored by his Mephistopheles goatee and his squeaking falsetto voice, gave him prodigious pleasure. With that he was certainly indulgence and kindness personified.

I was ordained pastor by Ecclesiastical Inspector Boury in Paris, at Trinity church, during my next-to-last year in Strasbourg.[73] It was from

---

69. Jean Héring (1890–1966) taught New Testament, 1926–1937 and 1945–1956; he taught moral theology 1938–1945. He had been a student of Edmund Husserl (1859–1938), the father of phenomenology, and stayed in touch with his fellow students, among them Adolf Reinach (1883–1917), Edith Stein (1891–1942), St. Teresa Benedicta of the Cross), and Alexandre Koyré (1892–1964).

70. Merton's portrait is in fact quite brief and may be reproduced here. Thomas Merton, *Seven Storey Mountain* (New York: Harcourt, Brace and Co., 1948), 84:

"Professor Hering was a kind and pleasant man with a red beard and one of the few Protestants I have ever met who struck one as being at all holy: that is, he possessed a certain profound interior peace, which he probably got from his contact with the Fathers of the Church, for he was a teacher of theology."

71. "The Kingdom of God and Its Advent in the New Testament," Héring's 1937 doctoral thesis. It was republished at Neuchatel: Delachaux & Niestlé, 1959.

72. A. E. J. Rawlinson, *The New Testament Doctrine of the Christ: The Bampton Lectures for 1926* (London: Longmans, Green, 1926); id. ed., *Essays on the Trinity and the Incarnation* (London: Longmans, Green, 1933).

73. In 1936.

that point that I started celebrating the Eucharistic services I have mentioned on the altar in the Chancel of Saint-Peter-the-Younger, for my Lutheran gymnasium students. I shall simply say that along with these celebrations, my experience teaching both "Religion" and classical studies in those years has left me with one of the best memories of my life. I believe I acquired, according to the headmaster, my pupils' interest and friendly trust. In any event, I drew from it the lasting assurance that this type of ministry was what I was made for. A small book, *Venez, car tout est prêt* (three letters to a catechumen preparing for his First Communion),[74] is the fruit of it; it is the first and, I believe, one of my best publications.

The next year, Pastor Lambert asked me to become his vicar at Trinity parish. I could not refuse him, and this afforded me three more years in Paris, which would also be the last of my life as a Protestant.

I cannot, however, leave off Strasbourg without reminiscing about two places in Alsace, even though their full import was only revealed to me later.

The first I have in mind is Mont Sainte-Odile[75] and all that this ancient monastic place, with its frescoes inspired by Herrad of Landsberg's *Hortus deliciarum*,[76] represents. The ancient fervor survives there in the pilgrimages of one Alsatian town after the other taking its turn for perpetual prayers before the Blessed Sacrament alongside the touching miracle-worker virgin. Its access is in my mind inseparable from the long hilly walk along three castles in ruins, around the sacred mountain, and through its pine tree forest. Once there, one discovers all at once the view onto the immense Rhine valley stretching out to the peerless spire's outline.

The semi-pagan pilgrimage at Sessenheim is entirely different. A veritable Goethean *tempietto*, in a perfect, and perfectly Germanic or rather Weimarian, taste, awaits you next to the old church and rectory that can no longer be separated from the famous interrupted idyll ... interrupted, that is, except for her whose faithfulness to memory would never fade.[77]

---

74. The title of this book means "Come, for all is ready." It was published in Strasbourg at the Librairie Évangélique in 1936 and has been republished in 2012 by Ad Solem, with a preface by Grégory Sotari.

75. A convent in the Lower Rhine, originally founded about 700.

76. An illustrated Christian encyclopedia dating from the twelfth century. It was made under the supervision of Abbess Herrad, daughter of the Lord of Landsberg nearby.

77. While studying law at Strasbourg in 1770–1771, Goethe had a brief but intense idyll with eighteen-year-old Frédérique Brion, daughter of the Pastor of Sessenheim. She never married.

I knew the last great-grandniece of Frédérique. She was as exquisite as her ancestress, but a stupid car accident sent her to her death as she was leaving the Conservatory. Her brother, last bearer of the Brion name, had been my classmate; he, too, was to die, by falling off a horse at the Poitiers riding-school.

Yet it is Saint-Thomas's rectory, on Rue Salzmann, that most vividly evokes Goethe to me: I have never been able to go up its staircase to visit old Pastor Héring without some emotion. I always pictured myself running into the elegant figure of Herder,[78] wrapped in his *Predigermantel.*[79]

The astoundingly clumsy French "revenge" consisted in a bewildering sandstone monolith claiming to glorify Pasteur.[80] It had been set up in the Strasbourg university quad, facing the other, exquisite, monument to Goethe, which is still there. . . . I cannot forget Ihme telling me, as we stood between the two: "Tell me: where is barbarity, and where civilization?"[81] I shall not repeat what Hauter himself jeered at it: only Albert Lebrun, in his innocence, could have been able to use it! For me, though, the memory of Goethe in Strasbourg dwells in his great-grandson, whom I had met in Paris: Pastor von Goethe, one of the first and most courageous artisans of Franco-German reconciliation. Actually, he would end up being received into the Church and becoming the very first married pastor to be ordained a priest.[82] When I reflect on that unexpected passage in *Dichtung und Wahrheit* about the beauty of the sevenfold Catholic sacramental system,[83] I cannot believe that *M'sieur Goeth',* as Napoleon used to say,[84] would have blamed the last descendant in his bloodline for either.

78. Johann Gottfried von Herder (1744–1803), philosopher and literary critic. Goethe met him at Strasbourg in 1770.

79. Preaching robe.

80. Louis Pasteur (1822–1895), the French chemist and biologist, was one of the French Third Republic's great scientific heroes (despite his devout Catholicism).

81. French anti-German rhetoric often dwells on the alleged barbarity of German culture.

82. It is difficult to determine who this is, as Goethe had only one son, August (1789–1830), whose own children all died childless.

83. The full title of Goethe's autobiography is *Aus meinem Leben: Dichtung und Wahrheit*; it covers the years 1811–1833. Its seventh chapter gives a positive evaluation of the Catholic Church's seven sacraments (Baptism, Confirmation, Eucharist, Confession, Holy Orders, Marriage, and Extreme Unction).

84. Emperor Napoleon I claimed to admire Goethe, whom he met on 2 October 1808 after the French victory over Prussia at Iéna.

6

Pendent Opera Interrupta[1]

AND SO, from the autumn of 1936 to that of 1939, I was a vicar in Paris, in that small Lutheran parish of the Trinity I have already mentioned, on the Boulevard de la Gare, very near to the Place d'Italie. I was at first vicar for Pastor Samuel Lambert, whose age and worsening health compelled him to more and more frequent stays in Switzerland.

For the first two years I lived at the vicarage in a vast apartment, particularly a living room transformed into an office where I had access (the one time in my life) to an immense desk on which I could pile up papers and books nearly without limit.

I should note that already in Strasbourg I had composed, in addition to my thesis on Newman and Alexandrian Christianity, my first novel, *La Fontaine scellée*.[2] It was so transparent regarding my friendships in Sancerre that I do not regret having destroyed it after a few fruitless efforts at finding a publisher for it.

The hours of leisure that my Parisian ministry afforded me allowed me to work at what was to have been my second dissertation in Protestant theology. Dean Strohl, however, had the hypocrisy of mailing it back to me during the "Munich affair,"[3] under the false pretense that he could not keep it during the current insecurity: in actual fact, of course, it was because he did not care for its content.

Father Congar, of whom I shall speak again soon, would later accept it as one of the first volumes of his *Unam Sanctam* series: *The Church: Body of Christ in the Theology of Saint Athanasius*.[4] I should point out by

---

1. Virgil (see 80, n. 98), *Aeneid* 4.88, which Dryden translates as "The works . . . interrupted lie."
2. "The Sealed Fountain."
3. For Dean Strohl, see 84, n. 3. The "Munich affair" refers to 30 September 1938, the day France and the United Kingdom abandoned Czechoslovakia to Hitler.
4. *L'Incarnation et l'Église Corps du Christ dans la théologie de saint Athanase*, Unam Sanctam 11 (Paris: Cerf, 1943). For Fr. Congar, see 106, n. 20.

way of parenthesis that my *censor deputatus* on this first occasion, Father Jules Lebreton, SJ (who was to be one of my masters a few years later), did not himself accept it without protest. From then on it was clear that my humble thinking on the history of dogma, in which Protestant theologians could sniff Catholicism, had the complementary effect on those of the other side: those experts passed the judgment that it *redolet haeresim.*[5] The most humorous aspect of it all is that, although the orientation of my few ideas hasn't much changed since then, I should generally receive about the same encouragement from so-called "post"- as from the most indisputably "pre"-conciliar theologians!

Enough said. For the time being let us return to my experience of those years in Paris. It would convince me that thinking and writing books, whether strictly theological or also literary works depicting the quest for essential truths in its vital element, were to constitute one of the great axes of my life. But it would also convince me that my vocation was to pursue these within a Church ministry. Barring this, as I would be more and more convinced, theology—all theological reflection, in fact—loses contact with what gives it its meaning. Then it can either vanish into fruitless abstractions or degenerate into an almost entirely verbal pastime. Conversely, I should say, ministry, or simply religious life, equally risks falling into unreality if its pursuit lies outside of the total humanism that is inseparable from serious belief in a creator God—a God incarnated in His own creation to boot.

I have to say that ministry in that little parish lent itself admirably, and for me providentially, to pursuing my research. Yet, as long as I contemplated spending my life in Protestant Church ministry, I never ceased hoping that I might carry it out in the countryside rather than in the city. My experience in Sancerre had convinced me that only there would I be able to combine recollection, without which I could not really live a Christian life, and intellectual work or a pastoral task accomplished with diligence.

This is what led me to propose myself in 1938 for the little parish of Montécheroux, in the town of Montbéliard.[6] I was particularly attracted to it by the memory of Pastor Jacques-Emmanuel Paur, whose enduring fame is due both to his mysticism and to his culture.[7] I was supposed to

5. A *censor deputatus* is literally the "deputy censor" who is entrusted with verifying that a work submitted to his examination is free of anything that *redolet haeresim,* i.e. "smells of heresy." For Jesuit Father Jules Lebreton, see 137, n. 51.

6. In the *département* of Doubs, on the border between France and Switzerland.

7. Jacques-Emmanuel Paur (1820–1905), Lutheran Pastor of Montécheroux from 1845 until his death. His Pentecost Monday fêtes, complete with church choir competitions, endure to this day.

get my nomination there from the local Church authorities, but the hateful counterpropaganda that the incumbent whom I was to succeed unleashed against me in the last weeks before his retirement compelled me to give it up. I therefore had to take up one last year of ministry in Paris, this time as vicar to Pastor Waltz, who replaced Pastor Lambert while keeping his Saint-Marcel parish (on Rue Pierre Nicole).[8] But I am once again anticipating the future; I must go further back into the past for this misadventure to be understood.

I don't mean to say that I had no opportunity to perform acts that might lend themselves to polemic at Trinité. Even before I set foot there, Pastor Lambert had turned it into a discreet, but very successful, home for the faith and piety I have dubbed "evangelical Catholicism," in line with a Lutheranism maintained and revivified in faithfulness to a tradition I have already described. There I enjoyed a profound satisfaction in celebrating a beautiful Eucharistic liturgy in the very simple little pseudo-Gothic oratory. I also enjoyed regularly preaching there before a modest but receptive audience; those sermons were doubtless the least pretentious I have ever written, but I think they were the best I ever did in that genre, probably for that very reason. The baptisms, the weddings, the frequent but not too numerous funerals, and above all perhaps the catechism busied me in an equally satisfying way.

Visits to parishioners, especially to the sick, tested a certain shyness in me, or rather the awkwardness of one who is an intellectual among people who are not, or not much. But there I would find abundant compensation in the discovery of humanity in its boundless diversity and in the surprising sameness of its needs, of its aspirations, and of its widespread weaknesses, along with its unsuspected grandeur.

Two events in this ministry have left me with an unforgettable impression.

The first was at the very beginning of my ministry. It was the last communion I was to bring to an old woman who had a truly evangelical piety. The way in which I saw her die in a radiant serenity a few moments after I gave her the *viaticum* as she answered the prayers herself will be, for the rest of my life, a memory of lasting benefit.

My other memory is more humiliating, but no less profitable. A deaconess[9] originally from my parish had asked me to call on her elderly

8. Jean-Maurice Waltz (1902–1986) was president of the Paris Consistory of the Union of Lutheran Churches. Saint-Marcel Parish is at 24 rue Pierre-Nicole in the fifth *arrondissement*, close to Port-Royal and not too far from the Place d'Italie.

9. A Lutheran community of "deaconesses" had been founded in Paris in 1841. These women were devoted to caring for the poor and abandoned and running a hospital.

and sick mother. I admit that this person, whom I knew so little, struck me (as did her daughter, in fact) as somewhat off-putting. Not imagining for a minute that there was any urgency, I delayed my visit longer than I ought. Upon learning that the good woman was dead—unexpectedly, as far as I was concerned—I bitterly repented of my negligence. At least I came away with the resolve never again to postpone fulfilling such a duty, as unappealing or even as little urgent as it might seem. Since then, both when I was still a pastor and as a priest, I have done my utmost always to honor that resolution; I don't think there are many that have a higher claim upon all those who have accepted this kind of responsibility.

I derived inestimable encouragement for my various endeavors in a weekly meeting I hosted at my parish because of its relatively central position. Every Monday, a few Lutheran pastors in the region of Paris would gather there with a view to the publication of a little weekly, *Le Témoignage*.[10] Thanks to Pastor Lambert, this publication maintained a rather high quality; above all it openly expressed the tendencies I have described as being my own. As traditional as they were within a certain kind of Lutheranism, they were far from pleasing everybody, especially among pastors of the Parisian parishes of that denomination—not to mention the Reformed churches, which were twice as numerous at least in the capital.

The religious, intellectual, and simply human quality of the confreres I thus met week in and week out was an exceptional opportunity. In the main, however, their friendship was far from inciting me to prudence; on the contrary, it excited what others were already calling my Catholic-leaning tendencies, and this in a greater measure than they realized themselves. Distressing incidents occurred, such as that I have already mentioned regarding the Montchéroux parish. As a sort of reaction these would cause me to ask myself the same question with increasing frequency: Could I—should I?—remain always in that Lutheran Church where it had seemed to me possible to remain a Protestant while reclaiming the best of the truly authentic Catholic tradition?

Yet, it was only at the end of those three years, on the eve of World War II, that the question presented itself with real urgency.

Up to that point, what stimulated me most in those Monday meetings was the prospect of making a reality, in this French Protestant minority Church, of the entirely positive ecumenism that had won me over.

---

10. *Le Témoignage, journal de l'Eglise de la Confession d'Augsbourg*, a French Lutheran weekly, then twice-monthly publication, published 1865–1940.

I have already spoken of Pastor Lambert and Pastor Wheatcroft.[11] Closer to me in age was Pastor Waltz, whom I have only named but whose intrepid faith and invincibly good mood were exactly the comfort I needed. Closer to me in age, too, was Pastor Gueutal, a typical Montbéliard man, though his apparent aloofness did not conceal a solid and clear mind combined with an unshakable fidelity.[12]

Our group was less regularly joined by Pastor Étienne Meyer,[13] who would later succeed to M. Bouttier at the helm of the Paris seminary. He was in sympathy with our leanings but sometimes alarmed by their uninhibited expression; he, for his part, was a frank and solid believer.

My Catholic and Orthodox contacts, however, continued to develop apace. Since the parish of "monk of the Eastern Church"[14] was in need of a venue, I had no trouble arranging for a large meeting room to be made available for it in the vicarage where I lived. Besides, as a result of a visit to the Priory of Amay,[15] I received at my house Dom Clement Lialine[16] and, in turn, Dom Olivier Rousseau,[17] who one day ended up bringing along Dom Lambert Beauduin,[18] the extraordinary and very friendly founder of that ecumenical Benedictine monastery. For the time being, his acts of audacity had garnered for him an exile in the southern French monastery of En Calcat and then, as a commuted sen-

11. Pastor Lambert is mentioned in chapter 3 above. For Wheatcroft, see 53, n. 27.

12. This is most likely Franck Gueutal (1904–1983), pastor at Montécheroux at the time.

13. Etienne Meyer (1895–1982) was pastor at the Saint-Pierre Lutheran parish on rue Manin in the nineteenth *arrondissement* of Paris.

14. For the "monk of the Eastern Church," see 66, n. 40.

15. In 1925 Dom Lambert Beauduin established a Benedictine community at Amay, in Belgium, in response to Pius XI's call for work in bringing the Orthodox back into communion with the Roman Church. It became a hub of ecumenism. It moved to Chevetogne in 1939, and was raised to being an Abbey in 1990.

16. Father Clément Lialine, OSB (1901–1958), Russian émigré and convert to Catholicism. As a monk at Amay (then Chevetogne) he directed the ecumenical journal *Irenikon*, 1934–1950. See Michel van Parijs, "Dom Clément Lialine, théologien de l'unité chrétienne," *Irenikon* 76 (2003): 240–69. Bouyer was to dedicate to him a book on monasticism: L. Bouyer, *Le Sens de la vie monastique* (Turnhout: Brepols, 1950), rendered into English as *The Meaning of the Monastic Life*, trans. Kathleen Pond (London: Burnes and Oates, 1955), v: "To Dom Clement Lialine, to whom he owes not only the notion and term 'eschatological' humanism, but the idea which has prompted this book, the author dedicates it as a respectful token of fraternal friendship, gratitude and esteem."

17. Olivier Rousseau, OSB (1898–1984), monk of Amay/Chevetogne.

18. Lambert Beauduin, OSB (1874–1960), pioneer of the liturgical movement. Bouyer was indebted to his thinking in the liturgy and wrote his biography: *Dom Lambert Beauduin. Un homme d'Église* (Paris: Casterman, 1964). See also *Métier*, 40–41, 66, 210–11, and 298.

tence, the chaplaincy of a convent of Oblates of Saint Françoise Romaine in Cormeille-en-Parisis.[19]

Our first meeting, as I have said elsewhere, had been most comical. He had not quite fully been informed as to who I was, and started out calling me "Doctor." Then, after his confrere and disciple had discreetly set him straight, he never would stop calling me "Pastor," as in an André Gide novel.

Likewise Father Congar, whom I had already known when I was in seminary in Paris during his initial search for Protestant contacts and whom I had visited since then at the old Saulchoir in Belgium, seldom failed to meet me whenever he was staying in Paris.[20]

During the last year I spent in Paris, I naturally gave my apartment over to Waltz. I also had had the other empty rooms in the rectory allocated to my friend Malbert, who had since become the pastor of the Free Church on rue Madame and had just married a charming Scottish girl—who was even more Catholic-leaning than he.[21] A big room right above the sacristy was turned into my new living quarters and office. It presented the advantage of looking out onto a little street that was far more peaceful than the noisy Boulevard de la Gare, where, several times a year, a funfair supplied me with the equivocal pleasure of facing a strongman's cabin. I must admit, however, that his spiel was a great diversion, involving as it did the inevitable appearance of an accomplice, usually dressed up as a soldier, who showed up three or four times a night to be effortlessly knocked down by the professional champion.

19. En Calcat is a Benedictine abbey founded in 1890, 70 km west of Toulouse. The Oblates of Saint Françoise Romaine was established in Cormeille-en-Parisis (roughly sixteen miles northwest of Paris) in 1924; they moved to Bec-Hellouin (southwest of Rouen in Normandy) in 1949. Saint Françoise Romaine (1384–1440) was the foundress of the Oblates of Saint Benedict.

20. Fr. Yves-Marie Congar, OP (1904–1995), is known especially for his theological work on the Church; he would play an important role at Vatican II and was made cardinal in 1994. He and Bouyer first met in 1932, as Congar recorded in his diary, *Journal d'un théologien (1946–1956)*, ed. Étienne Fouilloux (Paris: Cerf, 2001), 26–27. Le Saulchoir is the name of the old abbey near Tournai in Belgium where the French Dominicans settled after their expulsion in 1904. They returned to France in 1939, first near Évry (southeast of France), and in 1971 they moved to the Saint-Jacques convent in the 13th *arrondissement* of Paris.

21. This "Free church" was part of the *Union des Églises évangéliques libres* formed in 1849 as a merger of Reformed and independent communities during a religious revival centered in Geneva. This particular congregation is at 58 rue Madame (in the sixth *arrondissement*) and is usually called *l'église du Luxembourg*. It is reasonably close to the thirteenth *arrondissement*.

As a rule my father, now a widower for the second time, would come round to have supper with me. Then, unless I had a meeting, I would work on one of my books, particularly on a commentary on the Gospel of Saint John intended for the faithful; it relied heavily on Cullmann's lectures.[22] After this, to help induce sleep, I would often go on a long nocturnal walk, going as far as the Austerlitz bridge along the Boulevard de l'Hôpital, then along the quays as far as Place Saint-Michel, and coming back up the boulevard where I would often run into the little train from Arpajon bringing a load of vegetables to the Halles.[23]

Among my diverse activities, I had a very distinct feeling of living in a middle state between my university studies and the life that was to be mine later on. I did not yet picture it in any other setting than in the Lutheran Church of France, even though my ability to stay within it for very long without bursting or suffocating (or without life being made intolerable for me) was already highly doubtful for many outside observers.

I was already drawing up an outline of the book that was later to become *The Spirit and Forms of Protestantism*.[24] In it I had intended to offer the program for an ecumenism that might prepare for a reconciliation of all that seemed—and still seems—to me to have durable and even essential value in the positive principles of the Reformation with the Catholic tradition, and ultimately a possible reintegration into the Church founded upon the Apostles.

I first found comfort for this approach and hope thanks to a long trip in Scandinavia, through Denmark, Sweden, and part of Norway. Wheatcroft, in 1937, had arranged for the Lutheran church of Paris to send me there with a view to tighten its bonds with these mother churches of Lutheranism.[25]

My conversations with such churchmen as Archbishop Brilioth of

22. Louis Bouyer, *Le Quatrième Évangile. Introduction à l'évangile de Jean, traduction et commentaire* (Paris: Éd. Je Sers, 1938); 2nd edition (Paris: Casterman Maredsous, 1955). English version: *The Fourth Gospel*, trans. Patrick Byrne (Westminster, Md., Newman Press, 1964).

23. This route, which roughly corresponds to the perimeter of the Latin Quarter on the Left Bank, amounts to about two hours' walking. The "little train" operated from 1911 to 1936. It would leave Arpajon (twenty-five miles south of Paris) at night, go down the Boulevard Saint-Michel, and unload fresh produce in the central Parisian market of Les Halles, which at the time were across the Seine from their present location (since 1969) in Rungis.

24. For this book see 59, n. 12.

25. The Scandinavian Lutheran churches can be termed "mothers" to the extent that they were among the first national churches and thus provided a stable reference within Lutheranism.

Uppsala,[26] Primate of Sweden and son-in-law of the famous Söderblom (but whom he outstripped in traditionalism), and even more so with the holy, learned, and delightful bishop of Strängnäs, Gustaf Aulén,[27] seemed already to make a reality of my most ambitious dreams.

What then can we say about the "ecclesiastical awakening" launched by Gunnar Rosendal, Kontraktprost (i.e., rural dean) of Osby, whose guest I was for a few days? Although they did not go as far down that path, even other Scandinavian prelates, such as Bishop Fuglsang Damgaard of Copenhagen, commentator on Kierkegaard,[28] and Bishop Berggraff (who was to cut so magnificent a figure during the German occupation), convinced me that the success of such a movement would find little to no opposition in broad sections of Lutheranism.

I returned home after three months. I wish to dwell on a fairy-tale week I spent on the island of Kollandsö, in the middle of Lake Vänern.[29] I was in the parish of my congenial friend Nils Tofft, whom I had met in Paris, and whom I had had no trouble dragging along to Saint-Wandrille.[30] Rising up close to his church was the funeral chapel of the La Gardie family,[31] which gave his inspiration to Ralph Mortimer James in his best fantasy novel, *Count Magnus*.[32] Even so, I can report that the incredible stories the villagers told me on site go beyond even his imagination.

The return trip took me through northern Germany. This afforded me a too-short but unforgettable view of old Hamburg before its destruction. At last coming through Holland (which I was to visit in earnest only years later) I boarded a ship at Hook of Holland.[33] A new

---

26. Yngve Brilioth (1891–1959), Archbishop of Uppsala, 1950–1958, had married the daughter of Nathan Söderblom (see 58, n. 5).

27. Gustaf Aulén (1879–1977), Bishop of Strängnäs, 1933–1952. He is best known for his *Christus Victor: An Historical Study of the Three Main Types of the Idea of the Atonement* (London: Society for Promoting Christian Knowledge, 1930). Louis Bouyer wrote the preface for the second French edition, *Le Triomphe du Christ*, trans. G. Hoffmann-Sigel (Paris: Aubier, éditions Montaigne, 1970).

28. Bouyer doubtless had read H. Fuglsang-Damgaard (1890–1979), *Pascal et Kierkegaard* (Strasbourg: Je Sers, 1930).

29. Lake Vänern is the biggest freshwater lake in Sweden, in the southwest, near Göteborg.

30. This pastor is most likely Nils Oskar Tofft (1898–1986); a number of Swedish pastors had come to Paris for their theological studies. For Saint Wandrille, see 71, n. 59.

31. This family moved from France to Sweden in the seventeenth century, where it prospered and achieved the rank of Count.

32. First published in R.M. James, *Ghost Stories of an Antiquary* (London: Edward Arnold, 1919).

33. Hook of Holland (*Hoek van Holland* in Dutch) is a port near Rotterdam; a regular ferry line links it to Harwich in England.

stay in Hereford awaited me in England, with Canon Moreton.[34] I met him at the entrance of Christ Church; he provided me with my first initiation to Oxford, where his son was reading at Pembroke at the time.[35]

This journey had allowed me to make direct contact in Sweden with the famous theologian in Lund, Anders Nygren, the author of the controversial book *Eros and Agape*.[36] It is a work of genius, to be sure, although over the top in parts. At Uppsala I had also paid a visit to the pioneer of that excellent school of New Testament criticism, the Norwegian Anton Friedrichsen,[37] who was soon to be succeeded by Harald Riesenfeld[38]—himself a student on Boulevard Arago at the time of my ordination and, today, also a Catholic.

Shortly thereafter, but after I was back in Paris, Moreton arranged for my first encounter with an Anglican thinker of exceptional quality: Arthur Michael Ramsey, future archbishop of Canterbury. His just-published book, *The Gospel and the Catholic Church*,[39] was so marvelously in the same lines as my own "positive principles" that it brought an unhoped-for confirmation to all my deepest convictions.

I hoped, or rather was absolutely convinced, that I would be able to carry on in this attempt at recatholicizing Protestantism not only while remaining faithful to the primary and fundamental insight of the Reformation, but in fact by becoming even more faithful to it in the very

---

34. For Canon Moreton and Hereford, see 79, nn. 93–94.

35. Christ Church College was founded at Oxford 1525–1532 and houses the town's Cathedral; Pembroke, another college there, was founded in 1624.

36. Anders Nygren (1890–1978), bishop of Lund from 1948 and along with Aulén (see 108, n. 27) one of the leaders of the "Lund School," which put Scandinavian theology on the map in the twentieth century. He is also known for his *Agape and Eros* (New York: MacMillan, 1937–1939), in which he contrasts Eros (desire) with Agape (selfless love).

37. Anton Friedrichsen (1888–1953), biblical scholar in the Lund School (see foregoing note), was a critic of the exegetical system of Rudolf Bultmann (1884–1976) and others who sought to "demythologize" the Gospel narratives.

38. Harald Riesenfeld (1913–2008), professor at the University of Uppsala and president of the *Studiorum Novi Testamenti Societas* 1968–1969. See Bouyer, *Métier*, 177 and 184, for the links between Riesenfeld, Friedrichsen (see foregoing note), and the Norwegian exegete Sigmund Mowinckel (1884–1965). The Lutheran State Church of Sweden began to split in the 1950s over such issues as women's ordination; this led some "Conservatives" to join the Catholic Church, including Riesenfeld.

39. *The Gospel and the Catholic Church* (London: Longmans, Green, 1936). Arthur Michael Ramsey (1904–1988) was successively Canon of Durham (1940–1950), Regius Professor of Divinity at Cambridge and Fellow of Magdalene College (1950–1952), Bishop of Durham (1952–1956), Archbishop of York (1956–1961), and hundredth Archbishop of Canterbury (1961–1974). He was educated at Cambridge and, although he had been raised as a Non-Conformist, became an Anglo-Catholic and joined the High Church. He promoted ecumenism throughout his career.

attempt. I should add that this hope, or conviction, was nurtured by the ideal of a married clerical life, the only kind of existence for which I thought I was fit at the time. In this respect, I have already mentioned what maternal opposition I had more than sensed against any possible union between Élisabeth and me. Yet, I kept confident in my ability to win out, believing that I was assured of the concerned party's affection and thinking, not without motive, that her father himself in no way shared her mother's negative feelings towards me.

In the days before the summer of 1938, as Élisabeth was nearing her 18th birthday, I went down to her family's residence, that is, to Douai. I did not do so without communicating my intentions to a pastor in the area, a mutual friend, whose warm encouragement increased my hope.

An afternoon of quiet conversation with her—I had left her still a child and now met her again as a young woman—convinced me, perhaps too easily, that we had a better understanding than ever.

That very evening I presented my request to her father. His reaction, which was surely sincere, was more than agreeable. He declared to me without hesitation that he had told his wife that very morning that I had surely come for this purpose, and he was no less hesitant in assuring me that he was favorable to it.

We were, by a mutual agreement, to resume our conversation with Élisabeth's mother on the morrow, towards the end of morning. From her very first words I could tell that she had not budged an inch in her hostility, especially since her first words (evidently she was unaware of what her husband had told me the night before) were a brazen lie. Indeed she said: "My husband and I could never have imagined that you were going to make this request."

Finally, without having seen Élisabeth again, I returned to Paris with a promise (if that is what it was) that we would discuss the matter again, and that I would be able to reveal my hope to her whom it concerned at the end of the school year, once she had completed her eighteenth year.

It must have taken a lot a presumption and singular naiveté on my part for me to leave still—and more than ever—confident.

In fact, as I should have expected, early in the summer I received from her father himself an obviously awkward and chagrined note telling me that she was far too young for me to propose to her. I realized that I had been played. I was furious and wrote directly to Élisabeth, who was then at a girl-guide camp. The panicked answer she gave me confirmed that she had been turned against me and that there was nothing left for me to hope for from her.

Over twenty years later I would see her again at her request, and she would bitterly complain that I had not waited and insisted.

After all this she had remained ten years without agreeing to marry. I met her husband, and I immediately felt a great liking for him. He was manifestly more attractive and richer than I, and his rigid Protestantism certainly made him more acceptable than I had ever been. It was clear, however, that the union was not a success, despite the two charming little boys who were born to it. I endeavored, with unfeigned sincerity, to persuade Élisabeth, for whom I kept an affection that was all the more devoted that it was now disinterested, to show herself a better wife to her husband and mother to her children than she was doing, rather than being an extension of her mother's little girl—which it had obviously been obtained from her that she remain.

It was doubtless too late for this advice to be put into practice. The marriage was soon broken . . . and I too had to break off relations with my poor friend who had called me to her rescue and who, as was all too obvious, was now pursuing the dream that she had been unable or unwilling to share in good time and which she had thereby forced me to abandon.

I never regretted the lack of patience she passionately blamed me for. It was obvious that if her mother had managed to ruin a relatively late union that had everything to please her, she would have done worse yet to a union that was so precocious and which she abhorred.

As for me, I had so intensely and exclusively concentrated upon Élisabeth all that there was in me in terms of a capacity for attachment that giving her up plainly meant giving up marriage.

At about the same time, other and far more serious oppositions than those I had encountered in Montécheroux assured me that I would only ever be considered as a *persona non grata* there, even though they emanated from the very church where I was ordained.

I soon decided to spend a year of studies at Oxford to obtain a doctorate, which would also allow me to think over what I ought to do.

The events of autumn 1939 were to knock that project down.

But before I get to that, I wish to tell what the last days of the peace were for me. We took advantage of my father's vacation and began with a few days' excursion in Belgium, more precisely through Flanders, above all Ghent and Bruges. I would especially remember our visit to the Béguinage in Bruges, along with that to Old Saint John's Hospital.[40]

---

40. Bruges is about nine miles from the North Sea and was once a thriving seaport. Béguinages are small medieval Flemish communities of devout women established around a church; they led a quasi-monastic life, though without vows. Saint John's Hospital dates from between the twelfth and fifteenth centuries.

Little did I know at the time that, shortly after the war, I would stay there as Canon Hoornaert's guest to preach a retreat to nuns.[41]

There was nothing like this place to affirm with such gentleness and force "the peace [...] which surpasseth all understanding,"[42] in the face of the Armageddon that a dechristianized civilization had brought upon itself. In Ghent van Eyck's *Mystical Lamb*,[43] in Bruges Michelangelo's *Virgin and Child*,[44] and above all the prayerful beauty of the Béguine convent and of its Minnewater,[45] so familiar yet where another world seems to show through from under our own, will forever in my mind remain inseparable from the peace that was preserved—or found—in the midst of the rising chaos. Never again would I think about Rheno-Flemish mysticism, with which I had just had a first contact through Wautier d'Ayguillers's uneven but perceptive book on Ruysbroeck the Admirable,[46] without imagining that I was hearing the bells of Bruges or seeing the washed-out northern skies reflected in its green waters.

To the last fair days before this new war I must attach another excursion we took together shortly before, to Chartres, on a quest for all that had captivated Huysmans there.[47] My father came back with a pencil sketch of the Cathedral, which I still have in my possession.

We had expected that after these two escapades we would calmly spend the rest of our holidays in Sancerre. We were able to stay there only a few days, however, since the declaration of war suddenly brought us back to Paris,[48] after one last day's walk among the hills with Élisabeth and all our friends.

With the war, however, and all that one could expect of it, I could absolutely not see myself resuming my ministry in Paris, even though I was exempt from service because of my health, which at the time was

41. Canon Rodolphe Hoornaert (1886–1969) reopened the Béguinage of Bruges in the early years of the twentieth century with a women's religious community following the Benedictine rule: the Daughters of the Church.

42. Philippians 4:7: "the peace of God, which surpasseth all understanding."

43. Jan van Eyck (c. 1390–1440) painted this polyptych (a two-dimensional work on several hinged panels) in 1432. It is kept in the cathedral of Saint Bavo of Ghent (the capital of Belgian Flanders, about 50 miles from the coast).

44. Michelangelo (1475–1564) sculpted this Virgin and Child between 1501 and 1504. It is kept in the church of Our Lady (*Notre-Dame*) in Bruges.

45. The *Minnewater* near the béguinage is a lake in the middle of the park. A legend of lost love attaches to the place.

46. John Van Ruysbroeck (1293–1381), foremost Flemish mystic. See Alfred Wautier d'Aygalliers, *Ruysbroeck the Admirable*, trans. Fred Rothwell (London: J.M. Dent & Sons, 1925).

47. For Huysmans and his novel on the Chartres cathedral, see 53, n. 26.

48. On 3 September 1939.

rather mediocre. This was because of the atmosphere of suspicion that was beginning to surround me there. I made some requests to be sent to the Protestant military chaplaincy, but I could immediately see that they were even less disposed to take me over there.

It was at this point that I began seriously wondering, as most Protestants of my acquaintance, friend and foe alike, seemed to think, whether my place might not indeed be in the Catholic Church rather than in any Protestant Church. But I needed a period of calm to let all this mature. At a loss for what I should do, I went to Father Brillet,[49] superior general of the French Oratory, whom I had met at the *École Normale Supérieure*[50] where he was the chaplain, and where I had been invited by the *Tala*[51] group for a discussion on salvation by faith. There I had presented the Protestant view of the problem, alongside Father Guy de Broglie who gave the Catholic position.[52] I had been struck by his openness and depth. Little did I know I would soon be his student and then assistant!

So I explained my situation to Father Brillet and asked him whether he could get me some useful, preferably charitable, occupation in this time of war, to think things over. He told me that an auxiliary field hospital was being set up at the *Collège de Juilly*,[53] where there would doubtless be some way of putting me to use, while I would find peace and quiet, an excellent library, and priests with whom I might talk over my troubles.

The superior of Juilly, Father Philippe Ponsard, an old humanist from the Bourbonnais region, had an imposing frame but was a refined man.[54] He was very welcoming towards me in his Paris office. He told me that the hospital in question, like so many others in what was

---

49. Fr. Gaston Brillet (1878–1967), chaplain at the *École Normale Supérieure* (see n. 51), 1929–1944, and Superior General of the Oratory of France, 1929–1939; for a biography see *Oratoriana* 13 (1967): "Le Très Révérend Père Gaston Brillet."

50. The prestigious state institution that trains teachers and researchers.

51. The period term *Tala* is short for *ceux qui vont* à la *messe*, "the Massgoers." It was used for students who, though enrolled in the secular *École Normale Supérieure*, the prestigious and exclusive college intended to train members of the French intellectual élite, nevertheless attended Mass on Sundays and were thus somewhat suspect.

52. Guy De Broglie, SJ (1889–1983), Theology Professor at the *Institut catholique de Paris*, would later write the preface to Bouyer's *The Spirit and Forms of Protestantism* (see 59, n. 12).

53. In the town of Juilly, about twenty-five miles northeast of Paris, the Oratorians founded a boarding school in 1638 to educate the sons of noble families, on the model of Eton in England. Before then it had been an Abbey of Canons Regular dating to the twelfth century. It closed in July 2012.

54. Fr. Philippe Ponsard (1876–1958) received Bouyer either at the Massillon school (see 133, n. 31) or at the rectory of Saint Eustache (see 123, n. 52).

already being dubbed "the phony war," rather seemed to house a plethora of idle personnel with a total absence of wounded soldiers. On the other hand, however, what had been kept up of the school had been gutted by the principal teachers' departure for the war. Could I not take over the tenth grade in French, Latin, and Greek? Now this was beyond expectation and more or less matched my duties back at the Strasbourg Gymnasium.

The autumn term was approaching.[55] A few days later, I celebrated yet another funeral at Noisy-le-Sec as replacement for Gueutal,[56] who had been called up. It was my last Protestant service. I had been granted an official leave of absence for a year by the Lutheran authorities for the year of further studies at Oxford I had anticipated, and so I left for Juilly, my only luggage consisting of my personal effects and my already numerous books.

55. In 1939.
56. Saint Marc's Lutheran parish is in Noisy-le-Sec (four miles northeast of Paris). For Pastor Gueutal, see 105, n. 12.

7

Laqueus contritus est...[1]

AFTER ALL that had just happened to me plus the war, I was understandably in a state close to nervous exhaustion. My arrival at Juilly, the few days of freedom I had been granted before the term began, and the beginning of term itself were a veritable resurrection for me. The very beautiful autumn played its part too, for it allowed me to become familiar with the school in one of those moments when its still-intact beauty was at its height.

In the first place, of course, there was the charm of this park, whose parallel alleys were lined with tall beautiful trees along the rump and sides of a long and low hill, at the foot of which there ran a stream: the Swallow's Brook, itself bordered with one last alley along the large pond teeming with carp more or less a hundred years old. Gigantic linden trees, planted in the seventeenth century, closed off the view at the end of this pond. On its other bank, plane trees that nearly matched them in majesty led to the old farm.

The school's buildings, with their three big yards (for the older boys, the middle boys, and the younger boys), were nestled within a maze of seventeenth and eighteenth-century structures and led to the pond. The main courtyard separated them from the park and adjoined the building where the Oratorians and the other teachers lived. This last courtyard was a rose garden off which a twin flight of steps led, under an enormous wisteria growing on a Louis XV grating, down to the French garden whose central alley led to an eighteenth-century statue of Saint Geneviève up against the edge of the park.

The patroness of Paris was indeed also this place's patroness. The chapel—alas!—was redone at the end of the nineteenth century and there subsisted only a few remains of the fifteenth century, of the Renaissance, and of the classical period. In front of it, adjoining the

---

1. Ps 124:7a: "the snare was broken."

courtyard, was a fountain dominated by another statue of the same saint in the most exquisite fifteenth-century style. It called to mind the healing miracles she had performed here with the water that had sprung up at her request.[2]

At a short distance, among the flowerbeds, there was a charming Louis XVI theater. It was soon to be just as familiar to me as the classrooms, the library, and the chapel.

All of this, taken as a whole, was grand, very much in an Old France sort of way, yet in a happy and calm atmosphere, with something of the Nerval-style fairyland that juts out from nearby Valois into duller Goële as far as those sleepy villages that are (or were) Juilly, Montgé, Thieux, or Nantouillet.[3] From the longest alley, which ended at an imposing Roman *dolium*,[4] one could make out in this last village the Renaissance château of Louis XII's chancellor, du Prat.[5]

Oratorian portraits of Condren (buried in the chapel), Bérulle (who was later brought back to it), Thomassin, Morin, Duguet, Malebranche and many others[6] had invaded the staircases with their magnificent wrought-iron bannisters, the long halls, the bedrooms with Louis XIV

---

2. Legend has it that Saint Genevieve (see 70, n. 51) went through the woods at Juilly and caused a fountain to bubble up so that Saint Céline might drink. Saint Céline was a noblewoman of Meaux who wished to follow Saint Genevieve and has sometimes been identified as the mother of Saint Remigius (c. 437–533), who as bishop of Rheims baptized King Clovis c. 496. This fountain's water was then reputed to have miraculous healing properties.

3. The Valois region is about thirty-seven miles northeast of Paris, towards Soissons; the Goële is just to its south. Gérard de Nerval (a.k.a. Gérard Labrunie, 1808–1855) was a romantic author and precursor of surrealism; his masterpiece is a novella entitled *Sylvie: Souvenirs du Valois*.

4. A very capacious earthenware container, shaped like a squat amphora. It served to contain wine, oil, provisions, or even the remains of the dead.

5. Antoine du Prat (1463–1535), Chancellor of France from 1515. In point of fact, he was appointed Chancellor by Louis XII's successor, Francis I. As a widower he was ordained a priest and ultimately would be a bishop and cardinal. He built this château c. 1525.

6. These men are all famous Oratorians. Charles de Condren (1588–1641) was Bérulle's successor at the head of the French Oratory in 1629 and founded the school at Juilly in 1639. Pierre de Bérulle (1575–1629) had founded the Oratory of France in 1611; he is considered to be the initiator of the French school of spirituality. Louis Thomassin (1619–1695) led a return to the Fathers of the Church. Jean Morin (1591–1659), a former Calvinist, converted to Catholicism and developed biblical studies. The Augustinian leanings of Jacques-Joseph Duguet (1649–1733) brought him close to Jansenism. Nicolas Malebranche (1638–1715) was a devoted follower of René Descartes (1596–1650) and had many disciples and critics of his own among the Philosophes around the turn of the eighteenth century.

or Louis XV woodwork among beautiful furniture that had not yet been stolen or destroyed.

The library's riches were even more imposing, including immense antiphonaries and other manuscripts or incunabula from the abbey of Canons Regular.[7] These had been the Oratorians' predecessors, whom Louis XIII had installed there under Condren as superior general to found a "royal academy." It was explicitly destined to be the equivalent of Eton for the French nobility. This was attested to by the royal arms everywhere joined to the Oratorian crest's crown of thorns. The old registers, kept since the school's foundation, justified so many celebrities' busts, from Villars[8] to General de Sonis,[9] from Cardinal de Joyeuse[10] to Bishop de Mérode,[11] and from Montesquieu[12] to Louis de Bonald,[13] all of whom had had a turn there in their youth.

As though this weren't enough, a glorious refectory with particularly royal woodwork attested, by the number engraved on it, that Louis XV himself had inaugurated it. It displayed amusing paintings of the buildings and gardens at that time.

To put a finishing touch to all these memories, a spacious guestroom let one know, in a pompous inscription, that Bossuet[14] and Napoleon[15] (at different times, obviously) had slept there! It still had Directory-

---

7. An antiphonary is a (generally large) book containing liturgical chant. An incunabulum is a book printed in the infancy of the printing press, i.e., before 1500.

8. Barthélémy de Villars (1653–1734) saved Louis XIV's kingdom at Friedlingen in 1702, where the troops acclaimed him Marshall—which title the king ratified. He would do the same at Denain ten years later.

9. General Louis-Gaston de Sonis (1825–1887), former pupil whose bravery in fighting the Prussians on the Loire while commanding the Papal Zouaves cost him a leg on 2 December 1870.

10. Cardinal François de Joyeuse (1562–1615) was actually Abbot of the Juilly, 1613–1615, twenty-two years before Fr. Condren took it over from the Augustinian Canons Regular to found the Oratorian school there in 1637.

11. Xavier de Mérode (1820–1874), former pupil at Juilly who left a military career for the priesthood. He reformed the prisons of the Papal States and convinced Pius IX to form the Papal Zouaves. He was consecrated titular Archbishop of Melitene in 1866 and died in Pius IX's arms a few months before he was to be made cardinal.

12. Charles de Montesquieu (1689–1755), political philosopher, author of *The Spirit of the Laws* (1748), was a pupil at Juilly, 1700–1705.

13. Louis de Bonald (1754–1840), monarchist and ultramontane philosopher, inducted into the Académie française in 1816.

14. Jacques-Bénigne Bossuet (1627–1704), the "Eagle of Meaux," the town whose bishop he was; one of the great literary figures in France under Louis XIV. He is best known for his Funeral Orations.

15. Napoleon Bonaparte (1769–1821), Emperor of France 1804–1815.

period furniture[16] that the latter had donated for his brother Jérôme[17] and, to boot, the manuscript of one of the former's funeral orations.

Finally, it was a matter of common knowledge that Lamennais,[18] before retreating to La Chesnaie, had been his friend the Abbé de Salinis's[19] host for a time. It was also known that Sainte-Beuve[20] (also a native from Valois, where his family name remains common) had also visited him often, not to mention Maurice de Guérin,[21] who was to stay there a little later, perhaps even teaching for a while.

Lastly, not even La Fontaine failed to spend a novitiate there—not exactly an edifying one, believe me, according to local tradition (his brother, however, did persevere).[22]

All this blended together both classical and the most romantic reminiscences in a dreamy atmosphere where beautiful trees, bountiful flowers, and reflecting ponds kept up an air of gaiety for the old stones in anticipation for all those youthful voices and presences.

At night, especially with the wartime blackout, everything became absolutely fantastical, particularly when the autumn winds groaned in the high chimneys. They would draw from the tempest-driven trees that song that is eerier than even the clamors of the sea.

In the room where I set up my books on the awaiting shelves, I immersed myself in the school's history, and also in that of Saint Philip Neri,[23] founder of the Oratory, between my readings in Montaigne and Ronsard as preparation for class[24]—not to mention Saint-Beuve's

---

16. The Directory (*Directoire*) was the French form of government 1795–1799. The furniture of this period is classicizing.

17. Jérôme Bonaparte (1784–1860), Napoleon's youngest brother, went to school at Juilly. He would be King of Westphalia in modern-day Germany, 1807–1813.

18. Hugues-Félicité Robert de Lamennais (1782–1854), precursor of Liberal Catholicism, Social Catholicism and Christian Democracy. He retired to his property in Brittany, La Chesnaie, after the Bonapartist coup d'État on December 2, 1851.

19. The Abbé Antoine de Solinis (1798–1861) had helped restore Juilly in 1828 and was its principal in the 1830s. He had been a supporter of Lamennais.

20. Charles-Augustin Sainte-Beuve (1804–1869), French literary critic and author, often visited Lamennais at Juilly.

21. Georges Maurice de Guérin (1810–1839), French poet, whom Lamennais dissuaded from becoming a priest.

22. Jean de La Fontaine (1621–1695), French fabulist. He entered the Oratory with his younger brother in 1641, there to remain only eighteen months.

23. Philip Neri (1515–1594) founded the Oratory in Rome in 1575. See Bouyer, *Saint Philippe Neri* (see 118, n. 23 and 170, n. 46).

24. The works of Michel de Montaigne (1533–1592) and of Pierre de Ronsard (1524–1585) were part of the program in the class of *seconde* (sophomore year, year eleven in the UK), which Louis Bouyer was to teach that autumn.

Volupté, a first edition of which I soon discovered in the library.[25] He had doubtless brought it there himself.

I can still remember that on that first evening the Superior forgot to come and fetch me for supper, as he had promised to do. I preferred to go without, as I doubted whether I would be able to find my way in the immense building as it was still more or less empty and entirely plunged into darkness.

On the morrow, however, I was introduced to a young priest of the Oratory, Joseph de Tinguy,[26] whose friendliness, humor and distinction—not to mention a far from mediocre poetic talent—were an excellent initiation for me to the somewhat unreal life we were to lead in this Sleeping Beauty castle until the next year's "exodus."

Actually, our life in those first few months of the war rather called to our minds the semi-fairytale film *Les Disparus de Saint-Agil*.[27]

I only had a few pupils. By and large they were well-intentioned and easily interested. It turned out to be a sort of renewal of my happy first experience teaching in Strasbourg, plus the charm of that common yet very open life in this beautiful location that seemed to have been preserved by some miracle.

Quite naturally, I relaxed and as Christmas was approaching I came to write to the Ecclesiastical Inspector of the Lutheran Church of Paris to let him know that I was giving up the ministry, as I no longer felt at home. This happened without any kind of proselytism on the part of the Fathers, believe me. Had there been any, it would doubtless have simply delayed everything.

It was at the Benedictine abbey of Saint Wandrille, which had welcomed me on more than one occasion, that I was received into the Church by Abbot Dom Louis Pierdait[28] on December 27, 1939.

Indeed, I can say that it was here that Benedictine life had convinced me that the Catholic Church, despite the possible shortcomings of many of her representatives—starting with some of the most eminent

25. Charles Augustin Sainte-Beuve, *Volupté* (Paris: Garnier, 1834). English version: *Volupté: The Sensual Man*, trans. Marilyn Gaddis Rose (Albany: State University of New York Press, 1995).

26. Joseph de Tinguy (1907–2005) was ordained a priest of the Oratory in 1933. He would publish poetry starting in 1976.

27. This 1938 film by Christian-Jacque, based on the Pierre Véry (1900–1960) novel by the same name, recounts mysterious goings-on in a boys' boarding school located near Meaux—just like Juilly.

28. Jean-Louis Pierdait (1857–1942), Coadjutor at Saint-Wandrille (see 71, n. 59), 1920–1923; Abbot 1923–1942.

(as Saint Paul says: "if any man think himself to be something,")[29]—was nevertheless the survival of the one Church founded by Christ upon the Apostles. I had been helped along by the cheerful as well as both cordial and discreet hospitality of the guest master: Dom Paul Cosse,[30] a native of the Landes region. I was also helped by the theological knowledge and undeniable spiritual depth of the prior, Dom Lucien Chambat.[31]

I admit that by then I had more or less convinced myself that Benedictine monasticism was, at the end of the day, what I was destined to. I should have liked to pursue a pedagogical task there, as its monasteries have often devoted themselves to such enterprises. Yet the Congregation of Solesmes never wished to do so, for it feared it might end up entirely submerging itself in it.

Still, my admiration for Newman had already garnered my favor towards the Oratorians. Furthermore, the way the Juilly Oratorians welcomed me, so friendly and so generous, could only sharpen that impression. It did not take me long to realize that Father Brillet in particular had set his sights on me, as the expression goes. I did not absolutely exclude this other path, although I was more attracted to Juilly and its possibilities than to what I could already perceive of that congregation in general and its general state in France at the time. Indeed I soon discerned in it the weakness of a spiritual tradition that was rather celebrated than deeply lived, as well as the weakness of an intellectual tradition whose liberalism, though less inconsistent than that found in Protestantism generally, was yet neither very solid nor very deep as a whole. I was both amused and annoyed at the fuss that was made over me because I was coming over from Protestantism, but also at the surprise—I could already feel it—that having such a past I could take the essentials of the Catholic tradition so seriously.

The more I became familiar with this new milieu, the more I was struck by the fact that its best elements in the generation before mine, such as Father Brillet, seem never to have recovered from the brutal repression of modernism. Sheltered under a half-skin-deep, half-sincere conformism akin to a kind of family loyalty, they had concocted their own little religion within Catholicism, by blending with a kind of moral stoicism an "evangelism" in which the fervent love of Christ was able to overcome a certain vagueness of belief thanks only to a healthy dose of

29. Galatians 6:3: "For if any man think himself to be something, whereas he is nothing, he deceiveth himself."

30. Paul Cosse, 1870–1950.

31. Lucien Chambat, 1893–1967. A prior is a monk chosen by the abbot to assist him or lead a new foundation, termed a priory.

emotionalism. The debt of all of this to Gratry[32] and to Perreyve[33] didn't much attract me, I have to admit.

Happily Bérulle and Condren[34] were much in honor, though little read. Newman inspired pride although he was only ever approached though Bremond,[35] and Saint Philip was well loved, which reassured me the most, perhaps, that the Oratory of France was not simply, as a scoffing critic had said, "a grand name with a grand past." One could at least hope to revive the Philippian, Bérullian, and Newmanian tradition there some day.

For the time being, it was clear that there was no pressure to take a decision until summer.

The "exodus," for me, happened in two stages. First, when everything fell apart, I was sent to Lower Normandy,[36] at the Count de Kergorlay's Château de Canisy.[37] He had taken in the examination classes of the Parisian schools and was now doing the same for a few students of Juilly or Saint-Martin de Pontoise,[38] whom their parents thus hoped to keep safe from the war.

None of this lasted more than a month, but it enabled me to make the acquaintance of Father Leblond, whose friendship as well as his reserve, his good taste as well as his unassuming courage, immediately won over my trust.[39] I shall say nothing of Father Lenoble except that besides being an excellent historian of philosophy he was also quite a small fellow.[40]

---

32. August-Joseph-Alphonse Gratry (1805–1872), priest who had been instrumental in restoring the Oratory in France in the 1850s and 60s. He emphasized the role of experience over reason in knowing God. He influenced a younger Oratorian, Lucien Laberthonnière (1860–1932), who was condemned for modernism in 1907.

33. Henri Perreyve (1831–1865) helped Gratry restore the Oratorians. He was involved in liberal Catholicism with Montalembert and others.

34. For Bérulle and Condren, see 116, n. 6.

35. For Bremond see 52–53, n. 25.

36. By "Lower Normandy," Bouyer means in substance the *département* of La Manche (in modern terms it would also include Calvados and Orne).

37. A spacious château in the *département* of La Manche between Saint-Lô and Coutances, dating to the seventeenth century for the most part but incorporating parts from the Middle Ages and Renaissance. Its owner at the time was Count Thibault de Kergorlay (1879–1952).

38. Another Oratorian-run school, founded in 1929.

39. Marc Leblond (1894–1964) would later be the bursar at the Oratorian residence in Auteuil (sixteenth *arrondissement*), Villa Montmorency, where Louis Bouyer was to reside (see 133, n. 32 and chapters eight, nine, and fourteen).

40. Robert Lenoble (1902–1959, ordained 1925) had ambitions of bringing to life the thought of Gratry (see n. 32), but was above all a good specialist on Fr. Marin Mersenne (1588–1648), a scientist, mathematician, and philosopher.

I also renewed my acquaintance with the Cotentin region where my parents and I had spent our holidays during the other war.[41] It had left me with a fond memory that was then revived and was to prepare the long stay I made there later.

This stage came to an end with a pilgrimage to Mont-Saint-Michel, the first chance I'd had to go there. It excited my imagination, which this extraordinary place had long since captured, to the highest degree. My intention was to take the train that evening back from Granville to Paris, where I was to take my exams for the licentiate in letters on the morrow.

From the Mont Saint-Michel, however, we had seen black smoke billowing over the horizon. We had been told that this was the Rouen oil refinery burning and that there would be no trains that evening.

The next day, or a couple of days later, we took off for the south in two cars with Father Leblond, taking along the last pupils whom their parents had been unable to fetch. I shall not attempt to describe the unbelievable crush in which we were soon trapped. In a village on the Loire banks—I don't remember which—we stopped for a few days until a reserve officer in the medical service took me aboard his truck to go farther yet. I had got it into my head to reach the monastery of En Calcat,[42] which I knew to have a small school attached. I thought I might perhaps find the kind of life I desired there.

In point of fact, after a few days spent in a small village across Montségur where I was a cordial curé's houseguest, I arrived there on a crammed coach belonging to a line that was still operational—God knows how! But my request for hospitality at the monastery, which was overpopulated to be sure, was met by a *nolle prosequi* whose selfish indifference felled my vague hopes in one swoop. I did, however, enjoy a very humane and attentive hospitality among the nuns of Dourgne.[43] I was to meet the widow and daughter of Charles du Bos in their hostel;[44] this meeting was all the more providential that reading his *Journal* and a few of his *Approximations* had been one of my most recent delights.

That is where I first heard of the Armistice. I would soon find out that

41. Louis Bouyer does not mention these holidays anywhere in these *Memoirs*.
42. For En Calcat, see 106, n. 19. The trip would cover roughly 400 miles, or 650 km, due south.
43. This Benedictine convent, dedicated to Saint Scholastica, is near the masculine monastery of En-Calcat and was founded at the same time.
44. For Charles du Bos, see 81, n. 106. He had died just one year earlier. His *Journal* was published in nine volumes in 1946–1961; the seven volumes of his *Approximations* had been published in 1922–1937.

Dom Clément Lialine[45] and Dom Lambert Beauduin[46] had recently come as guests of the neighboring monastery. And so thanks to them I spent a few weeks of talks and walks between the two abbeys; these allowed me to get through those disastrous days without too much discouragement in a summer whose beauty nothing quite managed to make one forget.

After this, one of them went off to try to reach Cormeille-en-Parisis and its chaplaincy[47] while the other began his quest for a more demanding monasticism in a southern Charterhouse. Through their intervention I met up with Father Feuillen Mercenier,[48] another monk of Amay,[49] at the Minor Seminary of Ardouane, where I stayed as a guest of the Vincentians for about a month.[50]

It was in this solitude, which the presence of this excellent religious and kind old man made pleasant both by his erudition in matters Oriental and by his good nature, that I was to undertake a project I had long entertained: a theological and spiritual commentary on the Easter Triduum. A book ultimately came out of it,[51] which garnered me a sudden and double-edged popularity from which I have not fully escaped to this day.

As summer was ending, the opportunity of returning to Paris to see my father again finally presented itself. I arrived there after a few days' layover in Montpellier.

Juilly, as I was to find out from Father Brillet (whom I saw again at Saint-Eustache),[52] though partly occupied by German troops, was not

45. For Dom Lialine, see 105, n. 16.

46. For Dom Beauduin, see 105, nn. 15 and 18.

47. This was Dom Beauduin, whom the Olivetan nuns of Sainte-Françoise-Romaine in Cormeille-en-Parisis (see 106, n. 19), in response to his advertisement in the Catholic weekly *La Croix*, took on as their chaplain. This assignment, twenty minutes from Paris by train, allowed him to pursue his research at the Bibliothèque Nationale. See Jacques Mortiau and Raymond Loonbeek, *Dom Lambert Beauduin, visionnaire et précurseur (1873–1960): Un moine au cœur libre* (Paris: Cerf, 2005), 198.

48. Dom Feuillien Mercenier (1885–1965), specialist in Byzantine liturgy.

49. For Amay see 105, n. 15.

50. Ardouane is a hamlet in the Haut-Languedoc (Provence), between Toulouse and Montpellier. The Vincentians, the order founded by Saint Vincent de Paul (1581–1660) and which has since devoted itself to education and priestly formation, had run this minor seminary since 1905.

51. *Le Mystère pascal: "paschale sacramentum," méditation sur la liturgie des trois derniers jours de la Semaine Sainte* (Paris: Cerf, 1945). It underwent several editions.

52. The parish of Saint-Eustache, in the first *arrondissement* of Paris, has been entrusted to the Oratorians since 1922. The church was built in 1532–1637 and has a neo-classical eighteenth-century façade.

much more uncomfortable than the French so-called hospital there had been; it was going to carry on at half speed all the same. I was expected there with, it seemed, some impatience.

And so I resumed my position there, took up my preparations for the licentiate comprehensive examination that I intended to take the next time it was scheduled, and resumed teaching the sophomore class.[53] This time I would encounter the friendship of another Oratorian, who was quite different from Father de Tinguy: Father Robert Tardiveau,[54] a poet as well, but in a very different style. His work was vaguely Ronsard-like with a philosophy all his own—very Touraine,[55] if not Rabelaisian, and perfectly irreverent. I have never known a more impenitent author of puns and spoonerisms. He'd calmly drop them amid the billows issuing from his cigarette holder, between a biretta perpetually screwed onto his head and his Assyrian beard.

No less entertaining and delectable would be the camaraderie, rather than an actual friendship, of a young professor, a layman at the time, Guy Villette,[56] a Carnute himself as he used to say—from Chartres, if you prefer—who had a deadpan sense of humor and was an excellent philologist to boot.

And so life went on after all, following the same pleasant routine in the dreamy setting that Juilly had not stopped being despite all of the catastrophes, national and otherwise. My father had lost his position because of the war. Having read, these last years, more or less all the books I was reading myself, he had been converted before me and received into the Church by Father Brillet. He soon joined me at Juilly, where he was to act as chief of domestic personnel.

Meanwhile, back at Saint-Wandrille for the Easter holidays, I had opened my heart to Dom Chambat[57] and told him my desire to enter the novitiate there. But, although I have never doubted that he harbored friendship and esteem for me, he perceived that I would never be won over to his somewhat rigid Thomism, and it was he who persuaded me rather to yield to the promptings of Father Brillet and Father Ponsard and enter the Oratory.

53. *Seconde.* In the UK, the Upper Fifth.
54. Robert Tardiveau (1899–1950, ordained 1922) joined the Oratorians in 1931 and published books of poetry, 1926–1943.
55. Inhabitants of the Touraine region have the reputation of being laid-back and of having a wry sense of humor.
56. Guy Villette (1917–1991), who was ordained later, is known for his works on the Chartres cathedral and on toponymy (the study of place-names).
57. For Dom Lucien Chambat see 120, n. 31.

I have already mentioned that I have always paid more attention to the views that people I considered to be of sound judgment held about me than to those I might entertain about myself. I therefore gave in without much resistance.

I should only add that, many years later, after I had disclosed to Dom Gabriel Gontard[58]—novice master at the time but soon to be abbot, and whom I have always considered as a Peter the Venerable *redivivus*[59]—how his prior had deftly side-tracked me, the holy religious exploded with fury! Fortunately, Dom Chambat himself was no longer of this world!

In fact, I have the impression that my religious vocation went the way of my unsuccessful loves: what others have interpreted as deplorable misunderstandings I take to have been providential. Not that I ever ceased to love, in memory, poor Élisabeth, who didn't allow me to help her love another man any more than she wanted my affection when it was offered; nor that I ever stopped admiring the Benedictine tradition. It is rather because later events convinced me that I had at last arrived where God awaited me, albeit by unexpected paths.

In the first place, as far as concerns my entry into the Oratory, in compensation for some disappointment it allowed me to pursue studies at the *Institut catholique de Paris* at a time when its theology department was excellent. It was to be an invaluable benefit to me, although the university career into which these studies were to launch me, once again against my will, was itself but a mixed blessing.

Be this future as it might, and I in no way foresaw it at the time, I would leave Juilly once again by the end of this other school year in the autumn of 1941 to begin an Oratorian novitiate. Many years would pass before I returned there. This novitiate would then be followed by a few years back in Paris.

---

58. Dom Gabriel Gontard (1892–1986) was Abbot of Saint-Wandrille, 1943–1962.

59. Peter the Venerable (c. 1092–1156), friend of Peter Abelard (1079–1142) and Heloise (c. 1100–1164), was the ninth and last Abbot of Cluny, site of the renewal and development of Western monasticism in the tenth and eleventh centuries. He also maintained a relationship with St. Bernard of Clairvaux, leader of the starker Cistercian reform. For the meaning of *redivivus*, see 80, n. 100.

8

...*et nos liberati sumus*[1]

I SHALL SPEAK as little as possible of my novitiate, for, although it was not positively painful, it was, in many respects, the most assuredly absurd year of all my existence. It was also, if this is any compensation, the most thoroughly hilarious year I have ever known!

The Oratorian novitiate and scholasticate were housed in an appalling building.[2] It had been donated to the congregation by Bishop Roland-Gosselin, bishop of Versailles at the time,[3] when the Oratorians had returned from their exile in Freiburg in Switzerland—an exile that had left a very pleasant memory to those Fathers who had lived through it.[4] This house, however, truly was the deadly white elephant gift:[5] it was terribly costly and of as little rational use as possible. Its windows, as Cardinal Baudrillart[6] used to say, allowed one to see only the sky (particularly him: a real half-pint!). The generosity of Bishop Courcoux, who once was Superior General and then bishop of Orleans, endowed it with a chapel.[7] It rather looked like a bathroom and didn't do much to improve the place.

---

1. Ps 124:7b: "... and we escaped." These words complete the quotation begun as the title of chapter seven above.

2. Villa Béthanie, Montsoult, in the Val d'Oise *département* just north of Paris, where the Oratorians moved after World War I.

3. Benjamin-Octave Roland-Gosselin (1870–1952), Bishop of Versailles, 1931–1952, after being auxiliary bishop in Paris.

4. Because the French House of Representatives had refused to recognize them on 18 March 1903, a small group of Oratorians left for Freiburg in Switzerland. The rest joined diocesan clergy in France.

5. According to some Asian traditions, the rare white elephant is a burdensome gift, expensive to care for and hard to get rid of.

6. Alfred Baudrillart (1859–1942), created cardinal in 1935.

7. Jules-Marie-Victor Courcoux (1870–1951) joined the Oratorians in 1910, became their superior general in 1919, and was named bishop of Orleans in 1926. He was the priest who gave instruction to the young Jewish boy Aron Lustiger (1926–2007) and baptized

The location, on the other hand, was enchanting. It was on top of the Montsoult hill with a view extending over the L'Isle-Adam forest as far as the distant château d'Ecouen.[8]

But the glory (and the ruin!) of this house was its superior, who also functioned as novice master: Father Henri Carru. He was from the Nivernais region[9] and had a delightful accent.[10] He was wily and naïve, basically a good man, though endowed with the phenomenal—and perfectly unselfconscious—egotism that seems characteristic of certain ecclesiastics. The novitiate's rules were conceived along the lines of Stoicism dressed up in supposedly evangelical sentimentality, as I have mentioned above; it is attributable to Father Brillet.[11] When a character [Father Carru] so unsuited to such a task applied these rules, they became pure farce. If our little group of about ten novices hadn't made up our minds to laugh it off, the farce would have been sinister. Happily, Father Carru was, all by himself, an inexhaustible source of comedy.

In fact, the rules had only one ascetical merit, if one may so call it: they removed all possibility of getting any real work done, intellectually or otherwise, let alone leading a life of prayer and recollection. Indeed, it seemed to aim only at curbing initiative by breaking up activities to such a point that doing anything in earnest was out of the question, including the cleaning of that unlikely edifice. As for me, I may say that that year ultimately destroyed all of the somewhat regular habits, be they in piety or in work, it had taken me a long time to acquire. I'm afraid I have not been able to restore them completely since.

The only hour in which we had any peace and quiet, as dear old Carru had candidly warned us, was that of morning meditation. Unfortunately, what with a war on during which we didn't get to eat much

---

him under the name Jean-Marie in 1940. Bishop Courcoux did his best to protect the Lustiger family and sent Jean-Marie to the minor seminary in Conflans so that he might take his *baccalauréat* (high school finishing examination) there. Before being ordained to the priesthood in 1954, Aron Jean-Marie Lustiger attended the Seminary attached to the *Institut catholique* and took classes from Bouyer. He would succeed to Courcoux as bishop of Orléans in 1979, and then became Archbishop of Paris (1981) and Cardinal (1983).

8. Montsoult is roughly 13 miles north of Paris. The L'Isle-Adam forest is to the northwest and Écouen is to the southwest.

9. Nivernais is in Burgundy. Henri Carru (1901–1961) authored a few monographs on the history of the French Oratory.

10. This accent involves suppressing certain vowels and, more characteristically, trilling the "r" as in Italian.

11. For Fr. Brillet see 113, n. 49.

more than potatoes and rutabagas, it was usually spent in a state of semi-sleep.

For his part, Father Carru would abruptly emerge from meditation upon hearing, above his head, Father Guny (an excellent Church History professor) getting up to pee in his chamber pot.[12] Indeed, the partitions in that singular dwelling seemed to be made of paper—the only point it had in common with the exquisite Japanese houses, aside from the absolute lack of comfort. He would then fall on his knees while reciting the *Sub tuum*.[13] After that, we went over to the chapel for Mass.

Generally speaking and in keeping with a tradition taken over from the Sulpicians,[14] there seems to have be an attempt to perform in common, from the point of view of piety, all that is personal by nature, while on the other hand relegating to "the particular" just about everything that ought to have been public. There was, to be fair, some remnant of reciting the Divine Office.[15] But it was limited to Prime, Terce, and Sext, said straight through after the insubstantial café au lait that came after Mass. None, Vespers, and Compline, likewise, served as the lean midday meal's digestive. On the other hand, before morning meditation, we were treated to a long and insipid "morning prayer." Similarly, we never went to bed without an equally discouraging "evening prayer."

Out of the question were Matins and Lauds—the principal part of the Divine Office! There I was, who had been saying them for years, even while still a Protestant, and I had to give them up!

Besides all of this, except for highly pointless manual work, time was spent listening to talks (or pretending to listen to them). The above-named Father Guny gave some on the history of the Congregation and Father Rotureau gave a few on its spirituality (in fact these were often terribly far-fetched psychological disquisitions meted out in a drone fit to freeze whatever interest was actually in them).[16] In addition to this, once a week there would be some "ferverino" by Father Brillet, who

12. André Guny (1914–2011) was a professor at Montsoult, 1940–1954, and then at the Francheville seminary, 1955–1975, in the *département* of Bouches-du-Rhône.

13. *Sub tuum praesidium*, the Latin version of the "We fly to thy patronage" prayer, a Greek copy of which has been found in Egypt on a mid-third century papyrus.

14. The Society of Saint-Sulpice was founded in 1645 by Jean-Jacques Olier (1608–1657, then pastor of Saint-Sulpice parish). It is dedicated to forming the clergy and its priests often run seminaries.

15. The Divine Office is composed of Matins (in the middle of the night), Lauds at sunrise, then Prime (after Lauds), terce (at nine a.m.), sext (at noon), none (at three p.m.), Vespers before supper and Compline before retiring.

16. Gaston Rotureau (1911–1996) is best known for his 1944 edition of Bérulle's *Opuscules de piété*, published at Aubier. For Bérulle, see 116, n. 6.

would come from Paris especially for the purpose. [17] In these ferverini Bérulle or the Gospel were transmuted into a dazzling, yet somewhat alarming, combination of ultra-subtle psychology and dizzying metaphysics in which I didn't see much more than supercharged rhetoric. Aside from these, everything we were given was mere verbiage.

"Good Father Carru," as we agreed to call him, was the only source, or rather the usual conduit, of spiritual instruction.

Under the rubric of "General Spirituality," the poor man would water down for us old notes taken down from Father Brillet without understanding much of them himself. These were supposed to deal in turn with man, the Christian, the priest, and the Oratorian. Sharp tongues added an extra paragraph on "the Canon" ever since he began wearing the Versailles chapter's mozzetta.[18] In fact, however, his wordy patter generally did not allow him to deal with half of the syllabus within the twelve-month. All of this was so worthless that there could be no question of putting up with it without laughing him to scorn. Thank God little anecdotes of his own lent themselves to it, as did his commentaries that were spiced up with his Nièvre accent and, on top of that, an ineffable lisp!

I don't believe I have ever witnessed such fits of collective laughter anywhere else. All he had to do was announce: "P'raps ya think? Well, no way! Like me, see, why…" for us to start unbuttoning our stiff collars, only too sure of what was to follow.

His innocence was so angelic that he would occasionally fall into obscenity without even realizing it. In this respect I remember an unforgettable commentary on the parable of the sower, which he cut short when he saw us all doubled over with laughter, only to say: "I wonder what you find funny in all o' this! There really ain't aught to laugh about!" After which, obviously, the hilarity was such that the class, on that day, had to end early.

I shall confine myself to a paragraph, which I quote literally, of the most memorable of his homilies (as they are called these days). It was given early in Lent, on the topic of mortification.

"Mortification, right, I'll tell yer what it's all about. It's right easy: say I wanna mortify meself, right: say I'm a mite gluttonous: say I'm fond o' dainty dishes!" [God knows he was fond of them, poor devil, and at a time when one could only dream of them!] "Well, if I wanted to mortify meself, right: jest supposin' it's what I'm doin': I'd tell Sister Berchmans

---

17. A "ferverino" (plural "ferverini") is a sermon exhorting to religious fervor and to moral uprightness with arguments aiming at sentiment more than reason.

18. The mozzetta is an elbow-length cape worn by certain ecclesiastics, such as Canons.

[the cook and, beyond that, the superior's unimpeachable Sunamite[19]], I'd tell 'er: Right, look here: dainty dishes, yer can't fix any no more! Yer can't no more for a spell!"

I do not know how I made it (you get used to anything, even in the Gulag, they say, even to the most nonsensical regulations). I do not know, I say, during that crazy year, how I nevertheless succeeded in rereading a few essential works, such as Father de Régnon's *Études de théologie positive sur le dogme de la Trinité,*[20] Masure's *The Christian Sacrifice,*[21] Anglican Bishop Rawlinson's *The New Testament Doctrine of the Christ,*[22] and even began to crystallize in writing a few rough outlines of future theological works.

We would, at long last, leave this protracted joke bound together by a sense of camaraderie which, for most of us, was to last a lifetime. Yet, I had had a first look into the inconceivable negligence with which the Catholic Church, already at this time, could "prepare" for their religious life those who had, or seemed to have, some vocation.

After all this the years I would spend at the *Institut catholique* in pursuit of my new theological studies—at a time when its faculty was still rather exceptional—easily struck me as nearly incredible in quality by contrast.

After my novitiate, once I had been permanently admitted to the Oratory, I went to spend a vacation at Saint-Wandrille. There I once again immersed myself in the liturgy, which I had singularly missed that year except for a few solemn masses that were pompous rather than alive and prayerful. I must say, however, that the curé of Montsoult, Father Morin,[23] himself an Oratorian (an old Vendôme classmate of Tardiveau's)[24] had somehow obtained for us to come to his church on certain days, particularly for the Easter Triduum. He was an exception in believing in the liturgy, loving it, and practicing it for what it is. Not much of it

19. Sunam (or Shunem) is the Palestinian village where Abishag came from. She was the servant whom David did not marry because of his advanced age (1 Kings 1:2–4).

20. Théodore de Régnon, *Études de théologie positive sur le dogme de la Trinité* (Paris: Victor Retaux, 1898).

21. Eugène Masure, *The Christian Sacrifice*, trans. Illtyd Trethowan (New York: P.J. Kenedy, 1943).

22. A.E.G. Rawlinson, *The New Testament Doctrine of the Christ* (London: Longmans, 1926).

23. Gaston Morin (1903–1963) published several missals. Louis Bouyer wrote the preface for one of them, *Missel quotidien vespéral: Extraits du rituel et du bréviaire* (Limoges: Droguet et Ardant, 1956). A lecture he gave in 1944 contributed to the foundation of the Centre de Pastorale Liturgique (see 157–60).

24. For Robert Tardiveau, see 124, n. 54.

remains in the Holy Church, as I had long suspected, except for a handful of Benedictines and the rare faithful they have been able to influence.

We very soon recognized each other and became friends. Add to this that he was a simple and good man, sensitive and imaginative, a bit of a confabulator, but not for all that bereft of humor. He would turn out to be a touchingly understanding and unfailingly faithful confrere towards me to the very end.

All this made me feel encouraged to pursue, and nearly complete, the Easter Meditation I have mentioned,[25] during those days at Saint-Wandrille.

Yet I didn't think it would ever find a publisher. Indeed, a novel, whose manuscript Gabriel Marcel[26] had read sympathetically and passed on to the publisher Aubier, had just come out: *Alceste*, attributed to a certain (or rather uncertain!) Jean Thovenot, whom it was not at all difficult to recognize as my alter ego.[27] Father Marcel Lacroix, to whom I shall return,[28] had read its proofs and given his Oratorian go-ahead, though not without telling me, half in earnest half in jest: "Obviously some of us will wonder whether you might not someday describe us as you have the Protestants!" This hardly made me foresee any strong sympathies for my possible future output among my confreres! It was an attempt at grasping what is good and what is not so good—not to mention the worst—of either side of Western Christianity. All people saw in it, however, was criticism. Furthermore, and perhaps more significantly in this supposedly "enlightened" Catholic milieu, what was detected in it above all was criticism of certain "leading lights." Others admired these lights all the more unreservedly that they burned with the desire to have them for themselves without, however, going so far as to risk burning their fingers on them.

It will soon be seen that I was not so very much mistaken in supposing that this work, however exclusively positive *The Paschal Mystery* would end up being,[29] would most likely not meet with much more

---

25. I.e., his *Mystère pascal*; see 123, n. 51.

26. Gabriel Marcel (1889–1973), French Christian existentialist and playwright.

27. Jean Thovenot (a.k.a. Louis Bouyer), *Alceste* (Paris: Aubier-Montaigne, 1941). Louis Bouyer would write three more novels under various pseudonyms: Guy Chardin, *Les Eaux-Belles* (Paris: Desclée de Brouwer, 1959); L. Lambert, *Prélude à l'Apocalypse* (Limoges: Critérion, 1982); P. Catella, *Les Hespérides* (Paris: SOS, 1985).

28. For Marcel Lacroix see 153, n. 26.

29. *Le Mystère pascal (Paschale sacramentum): Méditation sur la liturgie des trois derniers jours de la Semaine Sainte*, Lex Orandi 4 (Paris: Cerf, 1945). English version: *The Paschal Mystery: Meditations on the Last Three Days of Holy Week*, trans. Mary Benoit (Chicago: Henry Regnery, 1950).

sympathy among my new confreres than had my *divertissement* before the Ark.[30]

But it had not got to that point yet. For the time being, the only issue was for me to begin my studies in Catholic theology.

Father Brillet told me that in my case the Congregation's council had decided not to keep me at Montsoult for the theological *cursus* but to send me to the *Institut catholique*.

The reason given was that a pontifical theological degree would silence any suspicion my Protestant past might arouse. As plausible as this was, I don't think I was wrong in sensing that the principal desire was to avoid prolonging the presence at Montsoult of a mind that was considered to be critical—critical, of course, of the postmodernist theology and piety I have more than alluded to above.

It was first decided that I should settle at the École Massillon, vis-à-vis the Île Saint-Louis,[31] as school monitor of the older pupils, all the while keeping up my studies. After a week's time, the absolute incompatibility of the two schedules this entailed was so obvious that another arrangement had to be made. This was to send me to the little residence the Oratory had recently acquired in Auteuil, the neighborhood that had been so familiar to me as a child. It was a house in the peaceful and nearly rural Villa Montmorency![32]

This had been an unexpected bequest from an old general, an alumnus of our schools, who thoughtfully filled it with quite beautiful religious art for the purpose. For my part, I feel singularly obliged to him before God, although I only ever knew him through a mediocre portrait!

I must add that by an incredible good fortune, its bursarship, and therefore its set-up, had been entrusted to a man with so sure a taste as Father Leblond.[33]

The superior there was an old priest who was prodigiously knowledgeable but also exquisitely kind under his rough Auvergnat exterior:

---

30. Meaning his novel, *Alceste*. This dance before the ark refers to 2 Samuel [II Kings] 6:16: "Saul's daughter Michal looked down through the window and saw King David leaping and dancing before the LORD, and she despised him in her heart." Michal's punishment for her contempt was barrenness.

31. The Oratorians opened the Jean-Baptiste Massillon school in 1877 at 2 Quai des Célestins on the right bank of the Seine at the level of the Île Saint-Louis.

32. Villa Montmorency is an exclusive gated community of about a hundred large houses with tree-lined gardens in the posh 16th *arrondissement*. Victor Hugo (see 26, n. 19), Sarah Bernhardt (25, n. 18), Henri Bergson (67, n. 41), and André Gide (81, n. 105) among others all lived there, as do a number of celebrities today.

33. For Fr. Marc Leblond, see 121, n. 39.

Father Rouziès, the librarian at the *Institut catholique*.[34] Besides the two
of them, I was its only boarder for a whole year, in addition to a fourth
priest, an old classmate of Rouziès's but in a completely different style:
Father Lefauqueur.[35] He was an upper-middle-class Granville man,[36] a
renowned preacher and confessor, but above all a man of refined culture
and urbanity—which didn't keep him from occasionally talking straight
with a raciness that was quite pleasing, too.

This singular but most agreeable trio greeted me with formal, though
kind, circumspection at first. Thanks (I think), however, to Father Leblond, who must have prepared the terrain with diplomacy (a virtue that
was no stranger to him), this welcome blossomed into the most cordial
rapport in less than a week. This was so much the case that my two
older confreres pitched quite a fit when, the next year, Father Brillet
transferred me to Saint-Eustache.[37] I think that this reaction, though it
honored their feelings towards me, was sharpened by the prospect of
seeing old Father Falaize come to take my spot;[38] he had a reputation
for his difficult personality, although we were, he and I, to find each
other again in Auteuil a few years later and become an excellent pair of
friends.

As for Father Brillet's decision in itself, though I regretted it at the
time myself, I must say that I can see how entirely wise it was. It would
have been dangerous for a young ecclesiastic's future to spend his entire
formation period in an Oratory that at the time could pass for a pious
Sybaris.[39]

Indeed, not only were the denizens of this dwelling rather outstand-
ing in culture and affability, but the house itself was, I must confess, a
little palace—especially in those days. Two old domestic servants,
Joseph and Marie, had been inherited from the testator; their devotion
as well as their manners were from a former age. Although the ameni-

34. Urbain Rouziès (1872–1956) was one of the main editors of the classic *Dictionnaire d'histoire et de géographie ecclésiastiques* (Paris: Letouzey et Ané, 1912–) begun
by Oratorian priest and future cardinal Alfred-Henri-Marie Baudrillart (1959–1942). As
of this writing it has reached the entry "Lentolo."

35. Alfred Lefauqueur (1875–1954) was ordained a priest in 1902 and joined the Oratorians in 1909.

36. Granville is a coastal town on the English Channel in the Manche *département* of
Lower Normandy. It had a little over 10,000 inhabitants in the 1940s.

37. The grand 17th-century church in the middle of Paris, in the first *arrondissement*.
Louis XIV was baptized there; it is known for its organ.

38. Gabriel Falaize (1893–1956) was ordained for the Rheims diocese in 1920 and
joined the Oratorians in 1926.

39. Sybaris was a southern Italian holiday resort for ancient Romans and was known
for its luxurious refinement.

ties were no more than those of an old house that had never been modernized, the tapestries, paintings, beautiful antique furniture, not to mention the library, rather called to mind a nest of half-aesthete, half-devout humanists than any normal type of clerical residence.

Father Leblond's good taste, which was only too perfect, had put a last touch to it by transforming the ground floor drawing-room into a chapel. It came pretty close to resembling a boudoir.

I was about to forget that after a few days I was joined in this Oratorian heaven by a fifth boarder, the best man ever, but whose superb naiveté was equaled only by his unintentional drollery. This was Father Léon Dandin, a preacher as well, and so eloquent![40] But upon his return from his apostolic rounds he became the absolutely defenseless (and in fact, three-quarters of the time, perfectly unaware) target of Father Lefauqueur's sarcastic remarks and of old medical school student Father Leblond's jokes as well as of Father Rouziès's massive humor. All I did was to add my own laughter to all of this, since the victim of so much teasing, which by the way was absolutely without malice, was such a good sport and had such a kind heart.

I should specify that this last boarder had managed to seek refuge in this deluxe Oratory. He had fled from a house of preachers we had in Boulogne where he had been subject for an entire year to a former Superior of Juilly, Father—or rather now Monsignor—Sabatier, a remarkable philosopher and, deep down, a very good man, but endowed with a pedantry and a solemnity that beggar belief.[41] There, Dandin had left behind as that astounding megalomaniac's last surviving subject my Juilly commensal, Father de Tinguy.[42] You can be sure that his incredibly sharp wit and aristocratic nonchalance were exactly what was called for to nail shut the Monsignor's trap.

One last detail concerning my new friend: good Father Dandin was so enormous that he had to give up serving as chaplain for the Helpers on Rue Michel-Ange after getting stuck in one of their house's hallways during a procession.[43] The sisters had been able to wrench him from his sad fate only by tearing to shreds the sacred vestments with which they had so imprudently decked him.

40. Léon Dandin (1903–1952) gave up the academic career his anticlerical family had intended for him and entered the Oratorian noviciate in 1929.

41. Désiré Sabatier (1877–1948) had been the superior at Juilly, 1919–1929, then became the Oratory's representative to the Holy See and was made monsignor.

42. For Joseph de Tinguy, see 119, n. 26.

43. The convent is at 27–33 Rue Michel-Ange.

Like all the houses at the Villa, ours was nestled in a very pleasant garden, where there even was a cherry tree next to Father Leblond's apartment. In the spring, he had trouble fending off the Parisian blackbirds and sparrows from its cherries.

At Juilly, I had known a grandiose oasis of peace in the midst of the "phony war"; in Auteuil I found a tiny but, if possible, even more perfectly serene home just as the war had turned into a nightmare.

It was only half an hour away by Metro from the *Institut catholique*, but right next to the still-intact Bois de Boulogne. I was able to go for endless walks, alone or accompanied by Leblond or Dandin.

My stay for a whole year in that Oratorian house, where everything was in such pleasant contrast to my novitiate, made a positive contribution to my studies' fruitfulness. Yet, I am indebted above all to the quality of the instruction I received at the *Institut catholique*. Still, I must point out that the Oratorian course in theology at the Montsoult "house of Institution" was certainly very fruitful thanks to the fathers who taught there. In practice it escaped from "good Father Carru," who perforce focused on his novices. Nevertheless, neither in the solidity of their theology nor in scientific level could these masters have compared themselves to those who then taught on Rue Vaugirard.[44]

The weakest point might have been the New Testament, had we only had the titular professor of that chair. This was the mediocre Alphonse Tricot, who was kept busier by his function as vice-rector—and by his increasingly compromised commitment to what in those years was called "collaboration."[45] Monsieur Osty's teaching,[46] however, although in theory it was limited to Greek New Testament philology, more than

44. I.e., the *Institut catholique*, which is at the corner of the Rue d'Assas and the Rue Vaugirard. It had been built in the seventeenth century as a Carmelite monastery; many priests were massacred there in 1792. An institute of ecclesiastical higher education was set up there in 1845, and the *Institut catholique* was erected there in 1875 to teach nonreligious subjects. Ten years later, the department of theology of the Sorbonne was suppressed and was taken in there, which necessitated more building in a neo-Gothic style.

45. Canon Alphonse Tricot (1881–1971), a priest from the Poitiers diocese, resigned from the *Institut catholique* in 1947. He and M. Robert edited the *Guide to the Bible: An Introduction to the Study of Holy Scripture*, trans. Edward P. Arbez and Martin R.P. McGuire (New York: Society of St. John the Evangelist, 1951–55). Louis Bouyer here means collaboration with the occupying Germans.

46. Émile Osty (1887–1981) is known for his faithful translations of Scripture, culminating in a collaborative effort with his colleague and Sulpician confrere Father Joseph Trinquet (1919–2001), *La Bible* (Paris: Seuil, 1973). Sulpicians are styled *Monsieur* in French; the congregation's initials are PSS in French but SS in the USA. Monsieur Jean-Jacques Olier founded this congregation of priests in Paris at the church of Saint-Sulpice (whence it derives its name) in 1641. Its principal task is priestly formation and education.

compensated for that lacuna. Although he was a peerless specialist in his own field, he was always spilling over into exegesis with equal mastery. Add to this that he was an exquisite humanist and, to crown it all, he had an incredible verve. As one of my fellow students used to say, after an hour's worth of sound, yet also dizzyingly brilliant, analyses in which unbridled asides came fast and furious, one wondered whether he wasn't going to end his show like Grock,[47] the famous clown, by climbing onto the piano and sliding down its lid. We'd leave his lectures prodigiously enriched by his knowledge and broadened by his culture, neither of which did any harm to our edification despite his wit, which was worthy of an Anatole France![48]

His Sulpician confrere, Monsieur Robert,[49] was his whipping boy, which didn't impede their friendship. He gave us an introduction to the Old Testament in a totally different style, but with a rigorous scholarship that was not without profound theological views.

Ancient Church History was, at the time I came to *La Catho*,[50] still taught by old Father Jules Lebreton, SJ.[51] He taught it with a distinction all his own, a critical sense that was on par with his learning, and views that were often profound though perhaps a little short on global perspective.

One could not make the same criticism of the titular professor of both chairs of medieval and modern history, Canon Arquillière (not yet "Monsignorized" at the time). Indeed, he had become famous for theories that his colleagues thought a little too bold, such as his thesis on political Augustinianism.[52] Yet under a falsely sleepy exterior he

47. Charles-Adrien Wettach, alias Grock (1880–1959), Swiss musical clown and polyglot, whom Bouyer, given his delight in the stage and the circus (see chapter three above), doubtless appreciated.

48. Anatole France (1844–1924), notable French novelist and poet, Nobel laureate and member of the Académie française. His wit was ironic and skeptical. His entire œuvre was put on the Index in 1922.

49. André Robert (1883–1955) collaborated with his Sulpician confrere André Feuillet (1909–1998) in editing the *Introduction to the New Testament* and *Introduction to the Old Testament*, trans. Patrick W. Skehan et al. (New York: Desclée, 1965, 1968), which replaced the *Initiation à la Bible* he had edited with Alphonse Tricot (see 136, n. 45).

50. *La Catho* is the nickname for *Institut catholique*.

51. Jules Lebreton (1873–1956), renowned scholar on the history of Trinitarian doctrine, available in English: *History of the Dogma of the Trinity* (New York: Benziger, 1939).

52. See Henri-Xavier Arquillière (1883–1956), *L'augustinisme politique: essai sur la formation des théories politiques du Moyen Âge* (Paris: Vrin, 1933). He maintained that it is unfair to attribute to Saint Augustine theories on the subordination of the State to the Church. For a rebuttal, see Henri de Lubac, "Augustinisme politique?" in id., *Théologies d'occasion* (Paris: Desclée de Brouwer, 1984), 255–308.

had a lively wit and handled historical criticism with more than virtuosity.

This didn't keep us from teasing him for his overwrought style, which didn't fool even him, and especially for his crafty and disingenuous knack for transitions, not to mention for suspense. You just had to hear him whisper in his thin voice at the end of a class: "Finally, my dear gentlemen, was Alexander VI, or was he not, the father of the Roman Infante to whom his daughter, Lucrezia Borgia, gave birth? . . . That, gentlemen, is what we shall see next week!"[53]

In no less a clerical style, but with the same upper bourgeoisie manner of Norman law nobility, our canon law professor, Monsignor Andrieu-Guitrancourt,[54] was just as delightful in his own way. He was in the greatest possible contrast to the Upper-Loire peasant that Arquillière remained under his academic robe as well as under his monsignorial cassock. Harboring no illusion about the interest that most of the budding theologians listening to him had in the most arduous juridical problems, he put little effort into preparing his classes. Yet, he was admirably adroit at making us realize that law and legalism are two distinct realities and, on occasion, at letting us know in terms whose politeness matched their insolence exactly what he thought, and why, of the current governance of the Church by "Our Lords, the Bishops." He never failed to call them that—especially just after ridiculing one of them beyond all appeal.

But it was the doctrinal teaching we received that was incomparable. Up until the end of the hostilities, which were marked by his tragic end in the Vercors resistance where he had gone to assist those on the point of death, I should not say that Father de Montcheuil, SJ, was the most brilliant in the field, for his elocution was often awkward. His thought always remained luminous, even when it didn't manage to be convincing.[55] On the other hand, he had an infectious sense of tradition, of its continuity, of its inexhaustible fruitfulness in the face of problems whose depths he never hesitated to plumb or to turn on all their facets. His was a teaching made up both of deep fidelity and of unfailing intel-

53. The Spaniard Rodrigo Borgia (1431–1503) was pope under the name Alexander VI from 1492. He remains notorious for corruption and incontinence, two of his children having been fathered while he was still cardinal: Cesar (1475–1507), who was the model for Machiavelli's The Prince (published in 1513), and Lucrezia (1480–1519). The alleged incestuous relationship between the latter and her father has been a matter of comment, but remains unproven.

54. Pierre Andrieu-Guitrancourt (1901–1984), author of Introduction sommaire à l'étude du droit en général et du droit canonique contemporain en particulier (Paris: Sirey, 1963). He also studied Norman history.

lectual honesty; it garnered for him our esteem as well as our respectful affection.

Yet his confrere Father Guy de Broglie left most of us, I think, an even more ineffable impression. At the age of 94 as I am writing these lines,[56] he remains more or less the same as forty years ago: slender to the point of seeming fragile, but endowed with an undiminished intellectual vigor that is equally powerful in analysis and in synthesis, and with a breadth and depth of views the like of which I don't think I have ever met. No man, I can say, will have been so effective a master for me. Add to this an exquisite charity, though by no means exclusive of a formidable mischievousness. He was ever ready to understand and to help, but impossible to lead astray with faulty logic, although he was always attentive to all sides of a question, however complex it might be.

After Gilson,[57] no one has contributed more to making me appreciate with precision the strength, the breadth of view, and yet also the limitations, of Saint Thomas. This is also the case with the points of the Augustinian heritage that have been settled in varying degrees, as well as all the complexity (or even ambiguity) of the traditions that lay a claim to either him or Saint Thomas in the West.

Furthermore, his feel for scripture and Patristics, in their main lines at least, was such that I have not met its like among any other systematic thinker; likewise his implacable perspicacity that left no false solution stand, however brilliant it might seem, be it about the modal supernatural or the mediocre knowledge of one or another of his Jesuit confreres, or Bañez's *entitas fluens*.[58] In the most courteous but also, on occasion, the most scathing of terms, nonsense was detected, brought to light, and irrevocably exploded.

The purest of religious sentiments animated his entire thought, which was so alert, so inexorably lucid, that a class of his on faith or on

---

55. Yves de Montcheuil, SJ (1900–1944), professor at the Institut since 1936. He helped found the Resistance-oriented *Cahiers du Témoignage chrétien* in 1942. The Germans shot him in Grenoble during the night of 10–11 August 1944. See David Grumett, "Yves de Montcheuil: Action, Justice and the Kingdom in Spiritual Resistance to Nazism," *Theological Studies* 68.3 (2007): 618–41.

56. Guy de Broglie, SJ (see 113, n. 52), born on 3 February 1889, died at the age of 94 on 13 May 1983. Bouyer wrote these lines, therefore, between de Broglie's ninety-fourth birthday and his death the same year, i.e. between 3 February and 13 May 1983.

57. For Étienne Gilson see 62, n. 25.

58. Domingo Bañez, OP (1528–1604), Spanish Thomist theologian; spiritual director and confessor of St. Teresa of Ávila (1515–1582). He was involved in a polemic about free will and divine grace with the Jesuit Luís de Molina (1535–1600). His concept of *entitas fluens* ("fluid entity") has long been the object of skepticism.

grace was equal or easily superior in its effect on all of us to the most pious considerations of so many other men.

I am obliged to him more than to anyone for having repudiated from the Church none of Protestantism's intuitions or most authentic values. On the contrary, he incited me, encouraged me, despite all possible mis-understandings, to develop them to the bitter end. The preface he kindly wrote for my book *The Spirits and Forms of Protestantism* is but one testimony among others of all that I owe him, as much as or even more, if it is possible, in my interior life than in my theological thought.[59]

It was also he who convinced me of the inanity that some people, including not the least of the Neo-Scholastic theologians, put into their efforts to get rid of all that scripture reveals regarding our relationships with the divine persons, as though these were mere "appropriations." His *De gratia* is strikingly clear as well as deep on this point.[60]

Father de Montcheuil and Father de Broglie, although they were con-freres in the holy Company, were not for that reason always in agreement. Since they were both equally well-bred, neither would ever have dreamed of mentioning the other by name to oppose him. But when Father de Broglie would get joyfully excited about those people "who don't believe in original sin," or when Father de Montcheuil would joke about "the metaphysicians," we didn't have the slightest doubt as to whom either was aiming at.

This didn't keep Father de Broglie from giving Father de Montcheuil the most sober, yet most moving, eulogy I have ever heard one priest give another once we had learned of his death under the circumstances I have evoked above.

Father de Montcheuil's position was taken over by Father Paul Henry, a Belgian Jesuit famous for his flawless critical edition of Plotinus.[61] His classes, as might be expected from so distinguished a scholar, were models of presentation of what is called today "positive theology," meaning the evolution of theological doctrines. But in the way he would draw conclusions from these superb analyses and tie them together, he was in the company of the great positive-theology masters in the seven-teenth-century meaning of the term, i.e., a theology that speculates only to bring out all of tradition's implications within its own trajectory.

59. G. de Broglie, "Letter to the Author," in Louis Bouyer, *The Spirit and Forms of Protestantism* (see 59, n. 12), vii–xi.

60. G. de Broglie, *[Tractatus] De Gratia* (Paris: *Institut catholique de Paris*, 1932–33).

61. Paul Henry and Hans-Rudolf Schwyzer eds., *Plotini Opera*, 3 vols. (Oxford: Clarendon Press, 1964–1982). Born in 1906, Fr. Henry would die in 1984. Henry had made a name for himself at the age of 28 with his *Plotin et l'Occident* (Louvain, 1934).

That superb intelligence was, alas, to come to a pathetic end. The last time I saw him, he was clinging to a lamppost on the Rue d'Assas with a book bag hanging from his shoulder. From among the books emerged the neck of a bottle of whiskey, in which he was soon to drown.

Now to come back to the venerable Father Lebreton: he was to end up in a mild sort of senility, though he managed to keep all his dignity by some grace from above. One of the earliest warning signs of that eminent mind's unraveling had been that we could get away with making up our papers for his class from a simple patchwork of his own books. Towards the end, in fact, he just read out loud his learned works by way of lecture. And, when he half-recognized his own prose in our papers, he would note in the margin: "Beautiful thought, well expressed"!

His position was taken over by the bubbly, ever-hopping about, imprecise but always evocative Father Jean Daniélou.[62] He was journalism personified, a superior journalism, though. He was incapable of teaching anyone to work, for sure, but he gave one the desire to do so thanks to his unquestionable knack for detecting every interesting goldmine. Only one couldn't count on him too much to go very far with any precision.

At the time he started teaching, I was myself ready finally to end these university studies—without in the least suspecting that by the next trimester I would become his colleague. Anyone who had predicted this to me wouldn't have pleased me at all. I had loved—I still loved—and I wished to resume opening adolescent minds to intellectual activity as soon as possible. Nevertheless, I still preferred to mature, slowly and entirely within myself, this wealth of thoughts, which were inseparable from the spirituality that these admirable classes had allowed me better than ever to plumb in the Christian tradition. I should simply have liked to deepen and develop this treasure, both for my priesthood and for my own interior life.

Therefore, after the period of interior decantation my novitiate had been despite its exterior indigence, these new Parisian years were most constructive, more even than they were enriching. Guided as I was by excellent masters, I had been able to start giving shape to my spiritual

---

62. Jean Daniélou, SJ (1905–1974), was appointed to the *Institut catholique* in 1943. He had founded the French patristic series *Sources chrétiennes* in 1941, with his confreres Henri de Lubac, Claude Mondésert (1906–1990), and Victor Fontoynont (1880–1958). This series now numbers over 500 volumes; see É. Fouilloux, *La Collection "Sources chrétiennes": Éditer les Pères de l'Église au XXe siècle* (Paris: Cerf, 1995), 77. He was also student chaplain, a *peritus* (theological expert) at Vatican II, and elevated cardinal in 1969.

life as well as to my culture. Their classes and the conversations I had been able to have with them had doubtless contributed much to this. Perhaps just as important in this were the closely directed assignments they gave or suggested to me along with the reflective readings or re-readings these entailed. To tell the truth, I was so delighted by the topics proposed for our written assignments that I went into more than one of them in greater depth than was expected of me, just for the pleasure of it. Never for one instant did I think that these outlines, once well-developed, would inspire in certain of our teachers the idea of calling me to become their colleague without any further delay. I am here thinking in particular of the first sketches I made for Father Lebreton or Father Henry on Gnosticism[63] or on the Mystery cults.[64] I am also thinking of those Monsignor Arquillière suggested to me on the Renaissance and its connection with Christian renewal, and also on Romanticism and the rediscovery of Catholic tradition. Lastly, and perhaps above all, I am thinking of what Father de Broglie had asked of me, especially on the subject of the unified complexity of the act of faith, or on the insertion of divine grace into our nature.

In all of this, as much as in the very personal reflections begun at Montsoult, lay the seed of most of my future works.

Now to return to my own meditations: in those years they were nearly all devoted to the synthesis of a total Christian humanism and asceticism. Later, they would extend and, I think, gain a necessary greater precision in my works on spirituality, particularly monastic spirituality in its great Benedictine line, although also in its more eremitical or more strictly ascetical extrapolations, be they Palestinian or Byzantine in the East, Cistercian[65] or Carthusian[66] in the West.[67]

I have already mentioned that this phase of my life was to end at

---

63. Gnosticism was the first heresy to confront the early Church. It was based on the notion that salvation depends on the knowledge (γνῶσις, *gnōsis*) of hidden truths. It involved Manichaean dualism according to which the material world, including the human body, is under the dominion of evil. St. Irenaeus of Lyons (c. 130–202) wrote his lengthy *Adversus haereses* (*Against the Heresies*) against it. Bouyer would later endeavor to show that there is a legitimate gnosis, namely the scripture-based knowledge of God, in *Gnôsis: La Connaissance de Dieu dans l'Écriture* (Paris: Cerf, 1988).

64. Mystery cults were a subset of ancient pagan religion into which one was initiated in a series of arcane steps.

65. Cistercian monasticism began in the eleventh century at Cîteaux (in Burgundy) as a renewal of monastic life. St. Bernard (c. 1091–1154) would amplify this renewal as a monk at Cîteaux and then at his own foundation of Clairvaux (in Champagne—not to be confused with the Benedictine Abbey of Clervaux in Luxemburg) where he was the abbot. The Cistercian order underwent a reform in the seventeenth century, notably at the Abbey of La Trappe, which gave its name to the Trappist monks.

Saint-Eustache, that magnificent church entrusted to the Oratory after the Great War. We came close to using it as it deserved, in the years I was there and those that followed, with the Church music renewed by Father Émile Martin[68] and with Father Désiré Bouley's preaching.[69]

Despite a good start already between the two wars, when Bishop Courcoux was its pastor, the liturgical quality of the services there would never be what it should have become, except in a few vague attempts that went nowhere.

Towards the end of the war I was, at least, the guest of a varied and pleasant community. I enjoyed the contrast between this church's majesty, which probably is the most admirable product of the transition from Gothic to the Renaissance in France, and the still intact and picturesque popular aspect that the old Les Halles district presented.

At Father Brillet's request the nuncio, Valerio Valeri,[70] obtained from Rome that I might be ordained as soon as my third year of studies. It was at Juilly, on Father de Condren's very tomb,[71] that I received the priesthood from the hands of the Bishop of Meaux[72] on the Feast of the Annunciation in 1944, which fell on Passion Saturday that year.[73]

66. The German monk Saint Bruno established the Carthusian order in the Chartreuse Mountains north of Grenoble. Carthusian monks pray, meditate, and live in separate dwellings; they come together for certain religious services and recreation.

67. Louis Bouyer was prolific on monasticism: *La Vie de saint Antoine: Essai sur la spiritualité du monachisme primitif* (Saint-Wandrille: Fontanelle, 1950); id., *Le Sens de la vie monastique* (Turnhout: Brepols, 1950), in English *The Meaning of the Monastic Life*, trans. Kathleen Pond (London: Burns and Oates, 1955); id., *La Spiritualité de Cîteaux* (Paris: Flammarion, 1955), in English *The Cistercian Heritage*, trans. Elizabeth A. Livingstone (Westminster, MD: Newman Press, 1958); id., *Introduction à la vie spirituelle: Précis de théologie ascétique et mystique* (Tournai: Desclée, 1960), in English *Introduction to Spirituality*, trans. Mary Perkins Ryan (New York: Desclée, 1961); id., *Histoire de la spiritualité chrétienne*, 3 vols. (Paris: Aubier Montaigne, 1961-1965), in English *A History of Christian Spirituality*, trans. Mary Perkins Ryan (New York: Seabury Press, 1982).

68. Father Émile Martin (1914–1989), Oratorian priest, one of the great twentieth-century composers of religious music. He directed the *Société des chanteurs de Saint-Eustache* from 1946.

69. Father Désiré Bouley (1900–1993) was renowned for his preaching. In 1949 he gave the funeral oration for transfer of the remains of poet Max Jacob (1876–1944), a convert from Judaism who died during the Holocaust.

70. Valerio Valeri (1883–1963), Apostolic Nuncio (the pope's representative) to France, 1936–1944.

71. For Fr. de Condren, see 116, n. 6.

72. Georges-Louis-Camille Debray (1892–1961), Bishop of Meaux, 1942–1961.

73. On 25 March 1944. The next day was Palm Sunday. Bouyer was the first Oratorian to prostrate himself on Condren's tomb during his ordination Mass. Fr. Émile Martin (see n. 68) composed and directed a much-remarked-upon cantata for the occasion.

As a result of unexpected and unhoped-for circumstances, my meditation on the Triduum was to be published soon thereafter by the title that Father Roguet, OP,[74] suggested: *The Paschal Mystery*.[75]

I can say that it expresses, as best as I could find in myself to do so, all the positive liberation my adherence to the one Church had meant to me, despite my wretched novitiate. By this I mean being able to enter fully and without hindrance into the reality of Catholic tradition.

I still wished, however, to preserve the best of my Protestant formation, or even to push its demands to their logical conclusion. My faithfulness to it would become stronger a very short time later in my other book: *The Spirit and Forms of Protestantism*.[76] This one, however, would be completed only once I was back in Juilly for, as I then hoped, the rest of my life.

Yet I was under no illusion about the understanding that this double orientation might encounter, even among the best-disposed among my confreres.

At about this time an old Saint-Eustache father, a former dragoon[77] who had kept a rather unecclesiastical frankness, told me: "It's obvious you're a convert: you're far too interested in the Bible and the liturgy! Real Catholics [he meant by that those who had had only to be born to be so], real Catholics don't attach such importance to them!"

How right dear Father Lamblin was, and how I thank him for having kept me from any chimeric hope on that score![78]

Yet, I shall say that this lack of understanding, like the ridiculous organization and running of my novitiate, did not trouble me in the least. They appeared to me in a perspective I have already noted as quite conscious long before my conversion. I mean to say that these observations themselves could only bring to completion the liberation that my conversion constituted. For I am more and more convinced that one has not truly adhered to the Church in her catholicity so long as he mistakes her for what a mere portion of the people of God, which is the Church, may express, and *a fortiori* achieve, in a particular time and place. All one can ask of this portion is not actually and deliberately to separate

---

See Jacques de Givry, *Juilly: 1177–1977: Huit siècles d'histoire* (Mayenne, France: Floch, 1978), quoted in Bouyer, *Métier*, 29, n. 1.

74. For Fr. Roguet see 154, n. 27.

75. See 123, n. 51.

76. See 59, n. 12.

77. Light cavalry trooper.

78. Jules Lamblin (1870–1958) had been a military chaplain with the dragoons during WWI, as well as with the French air force and units from the USA, Madagascar, and other places.

itself, to cut itself off, from the *Una Sancta*,[79] i.e., from the faith structure and the organic, sacramental common life in the Body of Christ.
But it is the duty of one and all, starting with "those who seem to be
something in it,"[80](!) to work with all their might at connecting themselves to it and to connect it to the fullness and purity of the tradition
entrusted once and for all to the Apostles and to their successors.
Whether they do this well or poorly is their business, but it will also be
the primary object of God's judgment on one and all.

79. *Una sancta*: the "One, Holy," Catholic, and Apostolic Church mentioned in the
Nicene Creed.
80. Cf. Gal 6:3: "For if any man think himself to be some thing, whereas he is nothing, he deceiveth himself."

9

Return to Juilly

A Liturgical Movement is Launched

BACK AT JUILLY, a little over a year after my ordination to the priest-hood on its founder's tomb, as I have said, I could feel that I was finally reaching a safe harbor. In addition to my extra doctoral year, at my superiors' request I had to agree to substitute for Father de Broglie (who had suggested the arrangement to me) for the fifth-year seminar in the very same doctoral program I had just finished. He was required to teach one semester per year at the Gregorian University in Rome.[1] I consider this to be the most flattering proposition that was ever made to me. Nevertheless, I fully expected that this would only be temporary. Furthermore, the agreement had been that so long as I would perform this task (amounting to a single day in Paris per week) I would also reside at Juilly and keep the sophomore year I had taught the humani-ties to with such pleasure, and which I had taken up again upon my sec-ond return.

Actually, this double responsibility, with the continual to-and-fro and scattered professional duties it entailed, soon proved to be more bur-densome and harder to pursue in a balanced manner than I had first imagined. Add to this writing my doctoral dissertation.[2] At Dom Chambat's[3] excellent suggestion, its subject was dogmatic, as a sequel to the first study I had made of Saint Athanasius. It was an analysis of the themes in his *Vita Antonii*, one of the first theoretical documents on monastic life.[4]

---

1. Guy de Broglie began teaching at the Gregorian in 1947.
2. This dissertation is his *Vie de Saint Antoine* (see n. 4).
3. For Dom Chambat see 120, n. 31.
4. Louis Bouyer, *La Vie de Saint Antoine. Essai sur la spiritualité du monachisme primitif* (Saint-Wandrille: Fontanelle, 1950).

Yet, other responsibilities were added to these at Juilly: the school chapel ceremonies, running the library, not to forget the at least twice-yearly theatrical representations by the students I soon was asked to oversee and then to direct.

Once I add that my school teaching entailed grading about forty French essays or textual analyses per week, as many exercises to and from Latin, plus another good ten to fifteen of the same in Greek depending on the year, you will have no trouble understanding that I had to spend nearly my entire summer holidays on my dissertation. Likewise, I soon came close to despairing, once I had finished it, of ever being able to undertake the future theological enterprise I had already conceived during my novitiate year—barring a change in my obligations. But, for the time being, this was unforeseeable.

Thinking back on those days now, I myself find it difficult to understand how, considering my mediocre constitution, I was able to bear such a task for years on end.

Yet, it would be inaccurate to see these toilsome years as a real burden on me. Quite the contrary: everything I was doing enthralled me. Never had Juilly and the possibilities it offered of going so far beyond its achievements up to that point, such as I perceived them to be, seemed so attractive to me.

This was encouraged by the interest, and even the friendliness, that both my Juilly pupils and my Parisian students manifested for me. And I must say that I was perhaps even more stimulated and supported by two new friendships this return to Juilly soon had given me.

I have voiced some criticism about the then-current reality of the Oratory, which I had perceived to be rather inferior to its professed ideal. Be that as it may, it brings me to say that I was (and still am) far from regretting my admission there in the first place and my definitive incorporation after the three years of probation. My long-held suspicions regarding clerical circles generally—and what I had already verified for myself—easily convinced me that, in spite of its weaknesses, the Oratory of France of the time, aside from a few mediocrities who were nevertheless not scandalous, numbered a rather honorable proportion of seriously religious priests endowed with a culture that was easily superior to that of the clergy on average. Here there was the veneration of Saint Philip Neri, that man of prayer, that ardent evangelist, who was for all that not only an affable humanist but was also endowed with quite an exceptional sense of humor. I attribute to this the fact that, at least at the Oratory as in so few clerical or religious communities, I have always found an atmosphere of both true and simple Christian charity and also of freedom. This was usually different from laxity, yet always included good cheer in joyful and healthy contrast to the grotesque pomposity of a certain kind of preconciliar clergy or, in the same measure, to the "self-importance matched only by the unimportance" of so many of its present-day successors, as one of my confreres says.

This general atmosphere, as will become clear, became even more pleasant to me thanks to the two new friendships I have mentioned, although they were as different to each other as one could possibly imagine.

I formed the first of these with a priest from the diocese of Clermont-Ferrand. He was never to belong to the Oratory canonically, but he possessed its spirit to a greater degree than did most of its members. I had just settled in for the second time when I met him. He had come for a few days' retreat upon his return from a German prison camp in what was still then called Koenigsberg.[5] He was there to prepare himself for his priestly ordination, which had been delayed by the war. Before the war he had been a student at *La Catho* (he had left a particularly brilliant impression at the Séminaire des Carmes,[6] though not entirely in conformity with the Sulpician ideal that was supposed to reign there under the aegis of Monsieur Baufine).[7] He would soon be Prefect of Studies at Juilly, a colleague, and then my successor at the Faculty of Theology and, at the time of his premature death, its dean. I am speaking of Louis Cognet, who is deservedly known for his studies on Port-Royal.[8] He would later publish one of the two volumes on seventeenth-century and modern spirituality,[9] which he intended to contribute to the *History of Spirituality* I would launch a few years later.[10]

I need not give the full description he would deserve, for sound judges have effortlessly recognized him as Father Louis de Hauranne in

5. Former capital of the Kingdom of Prussia, now part of Russia under the name Kaliningrad.

6. This was the seminary attached to the *Institut catholique* (*La Catho*), housed in a former Carmelite monastery.

7. André Baufine, Sulpician (1893–1980), Superior of the Séminaire des Carmes, 1936–1945.

8. Louis Cognet (1917–1970), specialist on Jansenism; see for example his *Le Jansénisme*, Que sais-je? 960 (Paris: PUF, 1961). He held the chair of the history of Christian spirituality at the *Institut catholique* from June 1962, and was elected dean of the Institut on 21 April 1969, a year before his death.

9. Louis Cognet, *Histoire de la spiritualité chrétienne: La spiritualité moderne*, vol. 1, *L'essor: 1500–1650* (Paris: Aubier, 1966). See next note.

10. Louis Bouyer, et al., *Histoire de la spiritualité chrétienne* (see 187, n. 15). Indeed, this *History* follows spirituality as far as the middle ages (volume 2), then to deal only with Eastern Orthodox and Protestant spirituality (volume 3).

another of those novels I have already mentioned in passing.[11] I was to publish it years later, although I must specify that no one encouraged me to begin it and pursue it more than did Cognet. This friendship is the only one I have come across within the Catholic clergy that I might compare to that which had joined me to Deransart, Hardy, and Malbert at a younger age in the Protestant milieu. For this reason, I shall take some time to dwell on it.

When I learned of Cognet's death, I may say that I suddenly stopped being young.[12] I shall add that I just felt definitely sunk into old age by the very recent passing of the man I shall mention next with no less affection, Father Pierre Joseph,[13] even though I never had as much in common with him as I did with the Abbé Cognet.

Cognet was a good typical Auvergne man, husky, but in the muscular sense, with a thick black head of hair always styled in a strict crew cut and a nose like Blaise Pascal's. Though extremely near-sighted, he still had a piercing gaze. The usual extreme softness of his voice and expression did not exclude terrible fits of rage, though it was hard to tell what part was played by genuine passion, and what part was deliberately put on. He was full of humor on occasion, sarcastic without malice, limitlessly generous, and withal an indefatigable worker. I have only ever known him to have one failing, particularly unexpected in so great a mind: a childlike vanity as is found only, it would seem, among ecclesiastics.[14] Not only was his knowledge incredible in its variety and precision, but his culture was as vast as it was keen.

11. Bouyer here refers to one of his pseudonymous novels: Louis Lambert (after a hero in a novel by Balzac by the same name), *Prelude à l'Apocalypse ou les derniers chevaliers du Graal* (Limoges: Critérion, 1982). The narrator, "Fr. Antonin Ollivier," is Louis Bouyer; Louis Cognet is clearly represented in the character of "Fr. De Hauranne" (7–8): "His former-athlete-turned-fat girth was cinched in a well-cut cassock, which was divided by a fringed cincture. His face, reminiscent of Pascal, jutted out because of his near-sightedness . . . his nose was magnificently Roman." The two priests smoke the pipe together while savoring excellent teas as Fr. De Hauranne knits woolens for Lilou, the obese dog he takes for rides in the sidecar of his spluttering motorcycle. The pseudonym Bouyer picked for Fr. Cognet is the (long-forgotten) surname of a decisive figure in Jansenism and close friend of Bishop Cornelius Jansen (1581–1643): Jean Duvergier de Hauranne (1581–1643), titular Abbot of Saint-Cyran-en-Brenne.

12. Cognet died on July 20, 1970; Bouyer was fifty-seven.

13. Fr. Pierre Joseph (1911–1983), ordained a priest for the diocese of Orléans in 1937; joined the Oratory the same year.

14. Cognet was so fond of smelling good that Julien Green (Bouyer and Cognet's common friend; see 232, n. 4) compared him to an otter coming out of a lake of Eau de Cologne. See J. Green's journal for 30 March 1975, *La Bouteille à la mer, 1972–1976* (Paris: Plon, 1976), 331–32.

We would generally end our evenings together around a cup of tea. Never have I got so much out of friendly conversations. They ran the gamut from the pleasant to the severe.

When I had to leave Juilly, I realized that my greatest loss would be the unreserved friendship between two men who were equals in age and outlook. It was as trusting as it was faithful, however different our personal histories were.

Entirely different was Father Joseph's personality, except that he too was cut like Hercules and was kindness incarnate. He was not an intellectual, but was quite intelligent: he had that intelligence of the heart that nothing can match or replace. Add to this the same gift of humor, although in this Orleans man it took a particularly delightful working-class form. Children adored him and he had a most healthy and tonifying influence on them.

I think it would have been difficult to find two more different types of man and of priest, yet, nearly from the very outset, there was a perfect rapport between the two of us. As we took turns as vice-principal and as head teacher of the sophomore and junior years, I believe I can say that the Juilly high school division, which normally gives boarding school administrators the cold sweats, never knew any true crisis (perhaps only the odd incident) in all the time that we were there together. It left to the children who went through it as well as to us a literally enchanted memory. Philippe Noiret today is probably the most deservedly well-known among French actors.[15] I had cast him in the role of Lamendin in Jules Romains's *Donogoo Tonka*.[16] It was such a success that, with the help of Marcel Jouhandeau, whom I had called upon as reinforcement (his wife happened to be a cousin of Cognet's),[17] I had no difficulty in convincing his parents—upper-middle-class people who were horrified at the prospect—to allow him to follow his inclinations. This same Noiret has

15. Philippe Noiret (1930–2006), noted French screen actor known to English-speaking audiences for his role as Pablo Neruda in *Il Postino* ("The Postman") and as Alfredo in *Cinema Paradiso*. He never missed a chance to mention that he owed his career to the priest who taught him literature in the *seconde* class at Juilly.

16. Jules Romains, *Donogoo Tonka or the Miracles of Science: A Cinematographic Tale*, trans. Brian Emerson (New York: Princeton Architectural Press, 2009). Its plot involves a crook who claims to have founded in a remote part of Brazil the city that an unfortunate cartographer had made up on a map.

17. Marcel Jouhandeau (1888–1979), French writer most famous for chronicling his back-and-forth between strict Catholic asceticism and exuberant homosexuality (not to mention anti-semitism). His wife, Élisabeth, a.k.a. Élise or Caryathis née Toulemont (1888–1971), a dancer, married him in 1929 in hopes of reforming him. The couple was famous for its epic quarrels. See Jacques Danon, *Entretiens avec Elise et Marcel Jouhandeau* (Paris: Belfond, 1966).

recently given the most convincing testimony one could give to the matter in a televised interview.

I should add that with Father Joseph directing the schola and myself in charge of the liturgy served by the more experienced altar boys, we effortlessly produced the unhoped-for result of having nearly all the seniors either among the servers or in the choir. In former years, it had been a real chore to impose any regularity at services on the examination classes![18]

Better yet, it was soon they who insisted on coming back to school to participate, in the middle of Spring break, in the liturgy of the Paschal Triduum, which was as thorough as in a Cathedral or Abbey. With few exceptions, of course, our confreres, who under these conditions could not afford to skip these services, bore us a murderous grudge for it.

The best of it was a fearsome letter from the bishop of Meaux[19] condemning us without naming us because we had dared to celebrate the Paschal Vigil during the night of Easter. In those days it was celebrated furtively, if at all, on the morning of Holy Saturday. His misfortune was that this letter of our good shepherd's was published at the very moment that Pope Pius XII (under the influence of Father Vagaggini)[20] produced, from his end, just as flamboyant an encyclical[21]—to reestablish the normal usage we had had the audacity of being the first to restore after the monks of Maria-Laach.[22]

Yet, it would not be long before I perceived that at Juilly itself this liturgical and biblical orientation of mine, against which an old confrere had wisely forewarned me,[23] was enough to make me *persona non grata* with the new superior, Father de Givry,[24] just as with the bishop.

18. The Junior and Senior classes, who had to undergo parts of the *baccalauréat* examination at the end of the school year.

19. Georges-Louis-Camille Debray (1892–1961), Bishop of Meaux, 1942–1961.

20. Dom Cipriano Vagaggini (1909–1999) was a religious of the Camaldolese branch of the Benedictines that Saint Romuald founded in Tuscany in the eleventh century. He was to play a great role in the elaboration of the Vatican II Decree on the liturgy *Sacrosanctum Concilium* and in the reform of the Mass after the council; see 219, n. 78.

21. Actually this was a Decree from the Sacred Congregation of Rites, "*Dominicae Resurrectionis Vigilia*," *Acta Sedis Apostolicae* 43 (1951): 128–29, dated 9 February 1951. It was made public later the same year, which dates these events to Easter of 1951, on 25 March. It was Bouyer's seventh anniversary as a priest.

22. The Benedictine abbey of Maria Laach in Germany had been the flagship of the liturgical movement in the 1920s and 1930s under the guidance of Dom Odo Casel (1886–1948). Unbeknownst to Bouyer, Fr. Doncœur, SJ, had had this audacity already in 1945; see 158, n. 47.

23. Father Lamblin; see 144.

It was becoming clearer and clearer that this turn my religious teaching was taking, as well as the whole thrust I was trying, along with Father Joseph, to give to the students' Christian formation, not to mention Father Cognet again, was encountering nearly all of my confreres' disapproval beside the hostility on the part of the authorities.

I was slow to realize this. But, upon returning from a retreat I had preached to the monks of La Pierre-qui-vire,[25] I discovered that the Middle School Vice-Principal (I had had to switch to the Middle School because of changes in my obligations at the Insitut catholique) had taken advantage of my absence to compel my now fifth-grade pupils to return the bibles I had had them purchase for my religion class. He had done this with the superior's encouragement. After that I could not long refuse to face the facts.

I asked for Father Lacroix's counsel.[26] He was one of my oldest confreres and had always shown me his kindness, though without sparing me his criticisms on occasion. With his full encouragement, I alleged the increasing pull of my Parisian duties (in the meantime I had been appointed professor of both Spirituality and Modern Church History) to ask for a second transfer to the Villa Montmorency. At the time it was undergoing renewal to become a center for preachers and lecturers.

The obvious relief with which my Juilly confreres accepted this solution (except Cognet and Joseph) gave me the full measure of the illusions I had once again been harboring. But I must admit that giving up Juilly and all that I loved there, all that I hoped to see live again there, certainly has been one of the most painful experiences of my life.

My career at Juilly had been ruined by my interest in the liturgy, a

24. Jacques de Givry (1912–2008) was superior of Juilly, 1946–1954; see Bouyer, *Métier*, 41. Givry wrote the history of the institution, *Juilly, 1177-1977: huit siècles d'histoire* (Mayenne: Imprimerie Floch, 1976, 1978).

25. A Benedictine abbey founded in 1850 by the Subiaco congregation—as were En-Calcat (see 106, n. 19), Landévennec (see 201, n. 76) and Farnborough in England (see 66, n. 40). The French congregation includes the abbeys of Solesmes (restored and expanded by Dom Prosper Guéranger, 1805–1875, who promoted its principles), Fontgombault, Ganagobie, Kergonan, Ligugé, Randol, Saint Wandrille (see 71, n. 59), Wisques, and that on rue de la Source in Paris (see 65, n. 36). The Abbey of Bec-Hellouin, which dates to the eleventh century, belongs to the monastic family of Mount Olivet (the Olivetans), which was founded in Italy in the fourteenth century. There are about twenty Benedictine congregations throughout the world; they were confederated in the Benedictine Confederation in 1893.

26. Marcel Lacroix (1891–1977), friend of Father Brillet (see 113, n. 49) and philosophy professor, was from 1931 to 1955 the principal of the Rocroy-Saint-Léon school in the tenth *arrondissement* of Paris. It had been founded in 1871 and staffed by Oratorians from 1903.

deplorable interest (to the mind of "real Catholics," as Father Lamblin said), and, worse yet, in the Bible! Likewise, it would give me other equivocal experiences farther afield.

In the last years of my preparation for the priesthood, two French Dominicans, Father Roguet and Father Duployé, had an idea that was particularly unexpected on the part of men of their order. These were quite different men, but they complemented each other well. They intended to found what would be called the Center for Pastoral Liturgy.[27] They were to be unceremoniously dispossessed of it by the post-conciliar episcopacy when their enterprise fell to the hands of a blissfully incompetent bishop.[28] He was assisted in this by a veritable freebooter[29] who at the outset saw it principally as a potential cash cow; it would now be termed *Centre National de Pastorale Liturgique*.[30]

---

27. *Centre de Pastorale Liturgique* ("Center for Pastoral Liturgy," usually referred to as the "CPL"), founded 20 May 1943 at the Éditions de Cerf. Those present at the founding meeting were Dom Lambert Beauduin, OSB, presiding (see 105, n. 18); Fr. A.M. Roguet, OP, Fr. Lejeunie, OP, and Dom Debar (monk from Ligugé) as stenographers; Fr. Duployé. Forty people were there altogether. See P. Duployé, *Les Origines du Centre de Pastorale Liturgique, 1943-1949* (Mulhouse: Salvator, 1968), 281–88. For Fr. Roguet's role in the CPL and the reform of the Roman liturgy, see A.-G. Martimort, "Le Père Aimon-Marie Roguet (1906–1991)," *La Maison-Dieu* 187 (1991): 97–136. Georges-Aimé Martimort, who happened to be in Paris to find a dissertation director at the Sorbonne, was invited at the last minute; see Duployé *Les Origines*, 286 and R. Cabie, "L'Œuvre liturgique de Mgr Georges-Aimé Martimort," *La Maison-Dieu* 222 (2000): 100, n. 17.

28. In July–September of 1965. This bishop was René Boudon (1910–1994), Bishop of Mende, 1957–1983, president of the French episcopal commission on liturgy and pastoral sacramental affairs, 1964–1971, in whose name he oversaw the transformation of the CPL into the *Centre National de Pastorale Liturgique* (CNPL) in 1965; see P.-M. Gy, "Monseigneur R. Boudon et la réforme liturgique," *La Maison-Dieu* 199 (1994): 9–11. Martimort had recommended such a merger to the president of the commission on the liturgy, then Bishop J.M. Martin of Rouen, in 1962. His principal reason was that the CPL needed the authority to curb the anarchy and abuses he believed might result from the reform of the liturgy and the extension of the use of the vernacular; see the extract of his report on the matter in A.-G. Martimort, "Du Centre de Pastorale Liturgique à la Constitution liturgique de Vatican II," *La Maison-Dieu* 157 (1984): 15–31, at 27–31.

29. This was Father Jacques Cellier (1922–1999), named first director for the CNPL on 11 February 1965, a post he would hold until July 1973. See L. Mougeot, "Le Père Jacques Cellier (21 janvier 1922–10 janvier 1999)," *La Maison-Dieu* 223 (2000): 113–17. He is also responsible, among other things, for the new rite of baptism, in collaboration with Father Louis Ligier, SJ. See A. Bugnini, "The XIth Plenary Session of the *Consilium* of the Liturgy," *Osservatore Romano*, English weekly edition (31 October 1968): 6. He was appointed as a member of the *Consilium* on 16 March 1966, ibid., 946. The original CNPL team included Fathers Pierre-Marie Gy and Hum. The terms "freebooter" and "cash cow" are explained in Bouyer's 1978 *cri de coeur*, "L'Église catholique en crise," *Commentaire* 1 (1978): 21, the publication of which pleased him to no end, according to

The original idea had been to undertake a liturgical movement in France that would be something other than just so-called "Gothic" chasubles[31] and the application of Solesmes's famous rhythmic signs to Gregorian chant.[32] It was very much inspired by the example of Dom Lambert Beauduin along these lines in Belgium a generation earlier.[33] At his recommendation, they soon contacted me (still only a deacon at the time!).[34] I wrote them a letter on the subject, in which I developed what I thought should be the goals and principles of this movement.[35] To my misfortune, and perhaps theirs too (!), they were enthused by it.

Better yet, the manuscript of my meditation on the liturgy of the last three days of Holy Week was immediately earmarked by Duployé to be

his friend Jean Duchesne. The CNPL would refuse to distribute the French bishops' official new French missals through bookstores that carried the original Latin versions, presumably to prevent priests from checking the French against the official Latin texts. The one bookstore that dared to brave the ultimatum made a brisk business selling the authentic Latin texts, for a far greater number of priests than expected wanted to see the renewed liturgy at its source.

30. For the first twenty years of the CNPL, see Henri Denis, "La Pastorale sacramentelle en France depuis 25 ans," *La Maison-Dieu* 157 (1984): 111–59. Its founders set out their program during its first congress, held at Versailles in 1965: J. Cellier, "Les Pasteurs devant la réforme de la messe," *La Maison-Dieu* 84 (1965): 5–22; R. Boudon, "Programme d'une pastorale liturgique," ibid., 166–79. Besides Bishop Boudon as president and Fr. Jacques Cellier as director, the *Centre National de Pastorale Liturgique* had Dominican Father Gy as subdirector and A.-G. Martimort and P. Roguet as advisers; see "Notitiae," *Ephemerides Liturgicae* 79 (1965): 166.

31. Gothic chasubles, which are broader and more flowing than the narrower, stiffer "fiddleback" chasubles, were the hallmark of priests aligned with the liturgical movement in the 1940s and 1950s. They achieved near-universality after Vatican II.

32. These signs, a result of scholarship on Gregorian chant at Solesmes, indicate the supposed length of the notes.

33. For Beauduin, see 105, nn. 15 and 18. For his influence on the CPL, see. A.-G. Martimort, "Dom Lambert Beauduin et le Centre de Pastorale Liturgique," *La Maison-Dieu* 62 (1960): 10–16.

34. Beauduin had been introduced to Bouyer while the latter was still a Lutheran pastor; see 105–06. Frs. Roguet and Duployé met Bouyer on the evening of 6 October 1943 to discuss liturgy. Bouyer had a bad cold that prevented him from saying everything he had meant to.

35. Bouyer wrote this letter at Saint-Eustache on 8 October 1943 to supplement what he had been able to say at the meeting two days before. Its original French version is reproduced verbatim in Pie Duployé, *Les Origines du Centre de pastorale liturgique* (see 154, n. 27), 289–97; English version, "Letter to Father Duployé," *Communio* 16.2 (1989): 283–91. Duployé considered this letter to be the "charter of our foundation" (ibid., 288). Its contents were further developed and presented at a meeting early in the CPL's foundation. The text of that presentation, with minor modifications, is available: L. Bouyer, "Quelques principes historiques de l'évolution liturgique," *La Maison-Dieu* 10 (1947): 47–85.

one of the first volumes of the *Lex Orandi* collection he was launching at the Éditions du Cerf. It was Father Roguet who proposed its title: "Pascal Mystery." Everyone today imagines it was a current expression among the Fathers of the Church and the Middle Ages. In fact, however, as I pointed out to no effect, while Christian Latin does have *Paschale sacramentum*, it does not have *myterium paschale*; furthermore, there has never been an equivalent formula in Greek. Today I derive bitter satisfaction from this mistake, for it is so symbolic of the misunderstandings that would never cease disfiguring, and finally paralyzing, the intended movement.[36] On the other hand, this book was to afford me the unshakable reputation of being mildly mad—about those very "Gothic" chasubles, rhythmic signs, and other trifles that have never interested me in the least!

I should also add, by the way, that those who are not fooled by that reputation and who think of me as a liturgist as they define the term see me in a different light. Those people, particularly but not only among the disciples of Archbishop Lefebvre,[37] see me as among the first men responsible for the pathetic shambles that are adorned today with the name "new liturgy." As a matter of fact, I was among the first to rise up against them—perfectly in vain, of course!

The CPL ultimately gave birth to the CNPL in an entirely "ecclesial," as they say nowadays, caesarian section. The latter organization would produce in every point the exact opposite of all that its poor progenitors had initially intended. The whole business is so deplorable that I have no desire to dwell on it, but I do have to go over its more eventful moments.

This, however, requires that I start by going back to my relationship

36. The term ended up being the title of Paul VI's Apostolic Letter "*Mysterii Paschalis*" (14 February 1969) approving the new universal norms of the liturgical year and the new General Roman Calendar; *Notitiae* 5 (1969): 159–162.

37. Marcel Lefebvre (1905–1991), Bishop (then Archbishop) of Dakar, Senegal, 1947–1962; Apostolic Delegate for French Africa, 1948–1959; Bishop of Tulle, France, 1962; Superior General of the Holy Ghost Fathers, 1962–1968. He is famous for resisting the new orientations within the Church after Vatican II. He established a seminary in 1969 to provide traditional formation to those young men who desired it, and moved it to Ecône, Switzerland in 1971. In 1970 he founded the International Priestly Society of Saint Pius X, which the Bishop of Fribourg established *ad experimentum* for a period of six years. After six years, the next bishop of Fribourg dissolved the society, but Lefebvre pursued his work of preserving preconciliar liturgy and theology regardless and was suspended. Ultimately, the rift between Lefebvre and the Church culminated in his consecrating four bishops without mandate in 1988, an act Pope John Paul II called schismatic. For Bouyer's analysis of the causes of the Lefebvre affair, see "L'Église catholique en crise," *Commentaire* 1 (1978): 17–26; English version http://rorate-caeli.blogspot.com/2015/07/the-catholic-church-in-crisis-1978.html#more.

with Dom Lambert Beauduin. Upon meeting him, I had, of course, been attracted by his bonhomie, his mischievousness, and above all by his superior intelligence, his kindness, and his cordiality. I still think he was one of the twentieth century's greatest religious figures because of his broad and generally correct views, be they in theology, in monasticism, in liturgy, or in what has ended up being called ecumenism. Ecumenism, however, no longer has much in common with what he was one of the first Catholics to understand by that term.

Yet, this exceptional openness, in a man so personally solid and sound, came at a price. He had this *a priori* trust in all those whom his generosity and broadmindedness had attracted to him. To a large extent, this trustfulness explains, even if only secondarily, many of his difficulties and many of the deviations in the enterprises and movements that he launched. Now the founders of the CPL declared themselves his disciples at the outset and solicited his advice and support with unfeigned sincerity, especially Duployé.[38] Nevertheless, I must say that it didn't take him long to sniff out what would rapidly lead that new movement to near total ruin.

It took me longer to see things clearly. Yet, from the word "go," I would realize that its chances for success were slim. Indeed, the initial members seemed to be far from agreement amongst themselves. Furthermore, and above all, they came to it with hopes and projects that were quite different not only from Dom Lambert Beauduin's, but also from Father Roguet's and Father Duployé's. In their initial generous enthusiasm towards me, these two would have liked me to define the goals and spirit of the liturgical pastoral movement that was envisioned. I made the objection that I was a recent convert, not even a priest yet. The best I could get was for my excellent confrere I have mentioned, Father Gaston Morin,[39] to produce and give this programmatic presentation while I collaborated in putting it together. After this first meeting[40] it later became a little booklet entitled *For a Pasto-*

38. Duployé met Dom Lambert Beauduin in 1942 in the Parisian suburb of Chatou. Yves Congar (see 106, n. 20) had told Duployé before the war: "If you decide to work in the field of liturgy, don't forget Dom Beauduin." Duployé, *Les Origines*, 33–34.

39. See 131, n. 23.

40. It took place at Vanves on 26–28 January 1944. Its papers were published as *Études de pastorale liturgique* (Paris: Cerf, 1944). It opened with a 1930 ethnographical film by White Father Francis Aupiais (1877–1945), who promoted a great role for local custom in religious expression: *Les cérémonies fétichistes et les danses sacrées des nègres du Dahomey* ("Fetishist Ceremonies and Sacred Dance Among the Natives of Dahomey"); see Duployé, *Les Origines*, 288.

ral Liturgical Movement.[41] He and I had long been in agreement in all things. Although I did assist him in putting it together, therefore, there is nothing in this text that hadn't been his long before I came to it.

From the very beginning of the discussion that followed his presentation, however, the ambiguities that would later impair the movement came to a head.[42] Father Morin, more even than I, admired Pius Parsch[43] and his outline of a liturgy that is inseparable from the initiation to the Bible as a spiritual and also doctrinal book.[44]

This immediately provoked the following reaction from Father Michonneau:[45] "It's all well and good to have to initiate our people to the liturgy, but, if we also have to initiate them to the Bible, what's next?"[46]

As soon as he had uttered these revealing, though certainly not malicious, words, Father Doncœur[47] seized the occasion to explain, with

41. G. Morin, *Pour un mouvement liturgique pastoral* (Lyon: Éditions de l'abeille, 1944). It is also found in *Études de pastorale liturgique* (Paris: Cerf, 1944), 13–52.

42. Bouyer contributed an appendix consisting of "precisions on the meaning and role of the liturgy" that helps to shed some light on "certain oppositions (which remained cordial) that had emerged at Vanves," according to an eyewitness: Robert Flacelière, review of the *Études de pastorale liturgique*, in *Revue d'histoire de l'Église de France* 32 (1946): 143–6. For the text of these precisions see Bouyer, "Quelques mises au point sur le sens et le rôle de la Liturgie," in *Études de pastorale*, 379–89.

43. Pius Parsch (1884–1954), Canon Regular at the Abbey of Klosterneuburg near Vienna, Austria. At the time he led the German *Bibel und Liturgie* movement. He promoted a deeper understanding of Scripture and a greater participation of the faithful in the liturgy. See his *The Liturgy of the Mass* (Herder, 1940) and *The Church's Year of Grace* (Liturgical Press, 1953).

44. Morin developed the theme of the Bible in the liturgy especially in "Pour un movement," *Études de pastorale*, 13–25. Among other statements, he said, "Whether we rejoice in it or deplore it, the liturgy is, therefore, biblical. To claim to make anyone understand it without initiating him into the Bible is a contradiction in terms" (19).

45. Georges Michonneau (1899–1983), priest of the *Mission de France* and pastor of Sacré Cœur de Colombes in the suburbs of Paris. It was held up as model by the then-Archbishop of Paris, Cardinal Suhard, and later by Archbishop Cushing of Boston. His contribution to the liturgical movement was his "paraliturgies"; for a critical analysis of these see A.-G. Martimort, "Une expérience des paraliturgies: 'Fêtes missionnaires et populaires' du Sacré-Cœur de Colombes," *La Maison-Dieu* 3 (1945): 164–70. For Michonneau's own account of his experiences, see *Revolution in a City Parish*, with a foreword by Archbishop Cushing (Westminster, MD: Newman Press, 1950). Bouyer speaks of the danger in these paraliturgies in his *Liturgical Piety* (see 165, n. 14), 67–68.

46. Michonneau's actual words as recorded are: "[After four years] we still have to explain the very essence of the Mass to them again. So if we have to add the Bible now!" ("Il faut encore leur expliquer l'essentiel même de la messe. Alors, s'il faut maintenant que nous ajoutions la Bible!"), *Études de pastorale*, 75.

47. Paul Doncœur, SJ (1880–1961). He was deeply committed to the French Catholic scouting movement in the 1920s and 1930s. He was among the first to celebrate the Paschal

obvious delight and in highly mellifluous terms, that this detail of Father Morin's presentation was clearly due to his collaborator's Protestant background. There was, therefore, no need to trouble with it any further.[48]

The immediate reaction on the part of Father Roguet and Duployé, as sincere as it was, could hardly build a consensus among the clergy in attendance.

Furthermore, a few representatives of Solesmes (including its prior) haughtily declared that what we wanted to do might be quite good and all in the popular genre, perhaps even necessary.[49] But it had nothing to do with what they considered to be liturgy, and they could only offer us a neutrality which was clearly rather indifferent than benevolent.

I remember meeting with them as a small group after the session had ended. I begged them not to abandon the movement like this. My entreaties met with a supreme disdain that hurt me just as much as the Jesuit sarcasms had.

I was too young for this false start to discourage me. I must admit, however, that I already had a feeling that my new Dominican friends' beautiful project, if it turned out to progress at all, would do so only with great difficulty along the path they had imagined.

Yet, the issue seemed too serious for me not to keep on fighting for it both against those opposed to any liturgical renewal and against the early enthusiasts. The latter group did not intend a renewed or revivified traditional Catholic liturgy, but rather some radical mutation of its very nature.

Dom Lambert Beauduin, to repeat myself, who was usually so optimistic, was far less so than I from that point on.[50] He soon told me: "Thankfully, at the time of the Reformation, no one in the Catholic Church wanted to change anything to the liturgy! It was understood so

---

vigil in the evening, in 1945; see H. Beylard, "Paul Doncœur," in *Dictionnaire du Monde Religieux dans la France Contemporaine*, vol. 1 *Les Jésuites*, by Yves Marie Hilaire, et al. (Paris: Beauchesne, 1985), 95–96. For his contributions to the liturgical movement, see P. Duployé, "L'œuvre liturgique du P. Doncœur (1940–1945)," *La Maison-Dieu* 3 (1945): 25–37 and id., *Les Origines*, 335–45.

48. This intervention is not recorded in the meeting's published papers.

49. No intervention on the part of Solesmes monks is recorded. On the other hand, some of the monks of its foundation at Ligugé, whose prior at the time was Dom Basset, are recorded as making substantially this objection; *Études de pastorale*, 76.

50. Martimort reports Beauduin's critical attitude towards "pastoral counterfeits, alibis, and unrealistic attitudes" as well as "paralogisms of slogans and the dangers of

little and so badly that there would be nothing left of it. I'm afraid," he added, "that we haven't made as much progress in this regard as our good Dominicans thought!" God knows he was right!

It was hard to maintain doubts on this score later on. When I had presented a paper on the Word of God of biblical and gospel revelation and sacramental efficacy,[51] Father (future Cardinal) Daniélou declared categorically that these two realities had nothing in common.[52] The Word was merely a matter of teaching, while the sacramental reality was an essentially different divine intervention. He added that my tendency to put them together was not only sheer Protestantism, but (and I quote him verbatim) actually the most unacceptable feature of Bultmann's teaching.[53]

Father Roguet then protested with a courage for which I am profoundly obliged to him. He maintained that all I had said could be vindicated with authentically Thomistic teaching. It was nevertheless clear that Daniélou had expressed what the manuals usually called "the common doctrine."

It was, therefore, already quite clear that the majority of the priests who took an interest in the new movement came not at all to give back to the traditional liturgy all of its hidden meaning and all of its life-giving reality. They intended gradually to substitute for it another liturgy or, as the expression went, a "paraliturgy."[54] This was to be more in con-

partial attitudes"; A.-G. Martimort, "Dom Lambert Beauduin et le Centre de pastorale liturgique," *La Maison-Dieu* 62 (1960): 10–16. See also L. Bouyer, *Dom Lambert Beauduin, un homme d'Église* (Paris: Casterman, 1964), 178–79: "the hasty infatuation with 'paraliturgies' that had so quickly moved from introductory liturgies to the pretension of being a liturgy of the future, a future which itself was all too easily at odds with the traditional past, meant nothing good to him."

51. This would have been at the 1957 Strasbourg congress. For Bouyer's contribution, see his "La Parole de Dieu vit dans la liturgie," in *Parole de Dieu et liturgie, III Congrès National du CPL*, Lex Orandi 25 (Paris: Cerf, 1958): 105–26. English version: "The Word of God Lives in the Liturgy," *The Liturgy and the Word of God* (Collegeville: The Liturgical Press, 1959), 53–66.

52. For Daniélou see 141, n. 62. For the "existence, homogeneousness, and coherence of the same intellectual world" among the editors of this series and the CPL, see Duployé, *Les Origines du Centre de Pastorale Liturgique* (see 154, n. 27), 46. Daniélou wrote a book on the topic: *The Bible and the Liturgy*, Liturgical Studies 3 (Notre Dame: University of Notre Dame Press, 1956).

53. Rudolf Bultmann (1884–1976), Lutheran theologian, father of the project of demythologizing the New Testament.

54. The term "paraliturgy" was first used at the CPL's founding meeting on 20 May 1943; see Duployé, *Origines*, 287 where he calls them "'pseudo' liturgies." In addition to Michonneau and Martimort (see 159, n. 50), see J.T., "Liturgie et paraliturgies de la Quinzaine Paschale," *La Maison-Dieu* 19 (1950): 87–113.

formity with the tastes and mental habits of what these nice folks called "modern man," who actually stood in for a *homo clericalis* more or less cut off from his roots long before what was to be termed "openness to the world" was set in opposition to conversion to the Gospel.

Where all of this was to end up was made perfectly clear to me by a CPL lecture presented by a Dominican who, at the time, headed up the "Économie et humanism" group (since then he has been defrocked and gone over to Marxism).[55] It foreshadowed only too well what Bernanos would later call the confusion of apostolate with apostasy. When I saw even a serious liturgist like Martimort declare that he was convinced by this speech, I simply withdrew from the movement without a saying a word. I had expected of it the exact opposite of what it would soon, more and more decidedly, produce.

A little later on Martimort insistently asked me not to abandon what had, in the meantime, become his business.[56] By then he seemed to have realized the at least potential danger, and I think he wished me to counterbalance it somewhat. Yet, he did not wish to run afoul of the other side, either. And so, after inviting me to speak once again (at the movement's Strasbourg congress this time),[57] he introduced me in terms that not only minimized but in fact ridiculed in advance whatever I might say against the distortions that were already more than just mere threats.[58] I got the message loud and clear. I did contribute to the *Lex*

55. This was Henri Desroche, OP (1914–1994), of the Lyons province. He left the Dominicans and *Économie et humanisme* in 1951. See É. Poulat and C. Ravelet eds., *Henri Desroche, un passeur de frontières* (Paris: L'Harmattan, 1997). Already his book *Signification du Marxisme* (Paris: Éditions ouvrières, 1949) had caused alarm, as Congar (see 106, n. 20) reported in his diary on 17 August 1950; see his *Journal*, 164. *Économie et humanisme*, founded during World War II to foster economic development in keeping with the Church's social doctrine, incurred suspicions of compromising with Marxism, especially in liberation theology. The organization ended in 2007.

56. Martimort joined Roguet and Duployé as co-director of the CPL in 1946; see R. Cabié, "L'Œuvre liturgique de Mgr Aimé-Georges Martimort (1911–2000)," *La Maison-Dieu* 223 (2000): 100. Duployé left his position as co-director in November 1947, and informed Martimort of his decision to quit the CPL altogether on 6 January 1949; see Duployé, *Les Origines*, 320.

57. 24–28 July 1957, on the Bible and the liturgy. The collected papers translated into English are in *The Liturgy and the Word of God* (Collegeville: Liturgical Press, 1959).

58. Bouyer's contribution was "The Word of God Lives in the Liturgy," in *The Liturgy*, 53–66. It is indeed a scathing critique of the trends of the time, at one time imagining a twenty-first century liturgist deriding the fads of the 1950s, including "favorite liturgical playthings of those days long ago: the altar *versus populum*, the 'podium,' etc. . . . conventional phrases then current: 'Mystical body,' Catholic Action, 'helping the worker,' 'presence in the world,' 'responsibility of the laity,' a 'Gelineau psalm' (always one of the most popular two or three)," "The Word," 58. He also warned against

Orandi collection a few last volumes that they were willing to accept.[59] These were simple translations of works written for the American public, to which a new intervention (more providential than any other) on the part of Dom Lambert Beauduin had allowed me to speak, as I shall explain in due time.[60] Besides that, I had nothing more to do with the CPL. As for the CNPL, no need to say any more here!

---

exaggerated ultramontanism, 65: "After all (said an Englishman in a recent article), the supreme authority of the Church is not bound by anything and could freely give us an entirely new liturgy, answering to today's needs, without any further concern for the past." Daniélou's own contribution was "The Sacraments and the History of Salvation," 21–32.

59. These last contributions were *La Vie de la liturgie. Une critique constructive du mouvement liturgique* Lex Orandi 20 (Paris: Cerf, 1960), an abridged French version of *Liturgical Piety* (see 165, n. 14); *Le Rit et l'homme: Sacralité naturelle et liturgie* Lex Orandi 32 (Paris: Cerf, 1962), the French version of *Rite and Man: Natural Sacredness and Christian Liturgy* (South Bend: University of Notre Press, 1963).

60. These circumstances are explained in chapter thirteen below. Bouyer wrote several books in English for the American public that stemmed from his teaching in the USA: *Liturgy and Architecture* in 1968 (see 165, n. 19); *The Liturgy Revived* (South Bend: University of Notre Dame Press, 1964); and, after these *Memoirs* had been completed, *Newman's Vision of Faith* in 1986 (see 35, n. 11).

10

Between Two Continents

HAVING LEFT JUILLY, I once again found myself in the Villa Montmorency where I had spent such a pleasant year. The staff had changed, however, except for Father Leblond.[1] Father Rouziès and Father Lefauqueur had retired, the former back in Auvergne and the latter in his native Contentin.[2] Dear Father Dandin had died prematurely.[3] Father Rotureau, whom I had known as a professor at Montsoult, had just been named its superior.[4] He succeeded to Father Sanson, a famous preacher, but suddenly fallen into deep senility.[5] Father Morin, too, had been called to Villa Montmorency after a few years spent as pastor of the Oratory's parish in Juan-les-Pins.[6] Fathers Pabot, Brossard, Dupland and Masurel lived there too, as "Preachers."[7] This meant, as I soon discovered, that they restricted their activity to Lent, Advent, and a few occasional retreats or sermons. They relied on Morin, Rotureau, and me to work more strenuously to help the house get on. Father Falaize still lived there and was to succeed to Father Leblond as bursar, even though he

1. For Fr. Leblond, see 121, n. 39.
2. For Fr. Rouziès and Fr. Lefauqueur, see 134, nn. 34 and 35.
3. For Fr. Dandin, see 135, n. 40.
4. For Fr. Rotureau, see 129, n. 16.
5. Fr. Pierre Sanson (1885–1945) had preached the Lenten retreat at Notre Dame Cathedral in Paris from 1925 to 1927; Laberthonnière, still proscribed for Modernism (see 121, n. 32), had written them for him.
6. For Fr. Morin, see 131, n. 23.
7. Fr. Joseph Pabot (1905–1991), ordained in 1931, was in Auteuil, 1954–1961. Fr. Gontran Brossard (1909–2000), ordained in 1937, came to Montmorency in 1946 after being at the Oratorian-run parish in Juan-les-Pins (on the Côte d'Azur). Fr. Dupland (1920–2003) also lived at Juan-les-Pins, where he became friends with jazz musician Sidney Bechet (1897–1959). Fr. Gilles Masurel (born in 1921) joined the Oratory in 1941, was ordained in 1948, and left the congregation in 1957.

was in very poor health and was a neighboring girls' school chaplain.[8] Father de Tinguy, too, had been assigned there, but the unrelenting and stupid hatred Father Rotureau (a Christian Democrat if ever there was one) harbored against him soon forced him to move out. Happily, the excellent and amusing Father Aulagner, who was the women students' chaplain, replaced him.[9]

Except for the casual manner in which six or seven of the ten men in that motley community soon managed to live off the work of others, the atmosphere wasn't positively unpleasant. The intellectual level (and the manners!), however, was no longer what I had known and appreciated. For my part, I had to accept a good number of preaching and retreat assignments, and multiply my publications and lectures, not to mention my teaching at La Catho, to contribute to the common subsistence. Nevertheless, I cannot say that the years I spent back in that house were unpleasant.

At Msgr. Arquillère's insistence, I had agreed to take over his Church History Since the Renaissance class. This was in addition to replacing Msgr. Combes in the Chair of Spirituality and directing the Institute whose center it soon became.[10] Add to this my collaboration with the Liturgy Institute at its foundation.[11] I named Dom Bernard Botte[12] to it as director since I had been tapped for that post, too. I was certainly not out of work.

8. For Fr. Falaize, see 134, n. 38.

9. For Fr. de Tinguy, see 119, n. 26. Fr. Antoine Aulagner (1912–1996) was for a long time (1937–1952) assigned to Saint-Martin de Pontoise (see 121, n. 38); then he was chaplain for young ladies near the Villa Montmorency (see 133, n. 32), perhaps at Notre-Dame des Oiseaux (10 rue Michel-Ange, see 135, n. 43) since the "neighboring girls' school" where Fr. Falaize was chaplain, 1939–1955, was the Institut Maintenon at number 72 of the same street.

10. For Msgr. André Combes (1899–1969), see Bouyer, Métier, 51. Combes was also professor at the Lateran University in Rome and researcher in France at the prestigious Centre National de Recherche Scientifique. The title of the chair in which Bouyer succeeded him is "Of the History and Theology of Spirituality." For Bouyer's understanding of what spirituality is, see the preface to his History of Christian Spirituality (see 143, n. 67), 1, The Spirituality of the New Testament and the Fathers, vii–xi.

11. The Institut Supérieur de Liturgie was founded in 1956 under the aegis of Joseph-Marie Martin, Archbishop of Rouen and president of the French Episcopal Conference of Pastoral Care and Liturgy. Its founders were Mont César Abbey and the CPL. It was attached to the School of Theology of the Institut catholique, in Paris. See P. Jounel, P. De Clerck, and P.-M. Gy, "L'Institut supérieur de Liturgie de Paris (1956–1981)," La Maison-Dieu 149 (1982): 7–25. Botte directed it for eight years; see P.-M. Gy, "Dom Bernard Botte (1893–1980)," La Maison-Dieu 141 (1980): 168. Gy was his co-director before assuming complete directorship.

On top of all this I also had to add alternating classes: The Oriental Churches and Liturgy and Christian Archaeology.

In addition to my Parisian courses, Dom Lambert Beauduin had also recommended me to Fr. Michael Mathis, as I have indicated above.[13] He was in many respects the American equivalent of Beauduin in terms of scholarship and the promotion of a liturgical movement in the United States. He was also a former missionary to India and an excellent biblicist. He had founded summer liturgy courses at the University of Notre Dame in Indiana. He led these with a fervor and a sprightliness to match his scholarship. All of this was capped with a Midwesterner's candor combined with shrewdness, good humor and, simply, goodness.

He had called upon me already in 1952 to give a general introduction to the liturgy. He was so delighted by it that he published it, tacking onto it the title of *Liturgical Piety*.[14]

This had been inspired by Beauduin's famous booklet, *La Piété de l'Église*.[15]

It was such a bestseller that the Éditions du Cerf wanted its translation into French (*La Vie de la Liturgie*).[16] In the same vein I came to publish *Rite and Man* (*Le Rite et l'Homme*),[17] *Eucharist* (*Eucharistie*),[18] and, lastly, *Liturgy and Architecture*.[19] This last volume had a twofold privilege: the best archaeologists and specialists on the question greeted it as the first work on the topic not to be fanciful—and the brand-new CNPL

12. Dom Bernard Botte (1893–1980) was a Benedictine monk of Mont-César in Louvain (Belgium); he joined the CPL in 1948. For Dom Bernard Botte's work see P.-M. Gy, "L'Œuvre liturgique de Dom Bernard Botte," *La Maison-Dieu* 114 (1973): 141–46 and id., "Dom Bernard Botte (1893–1980)," *La Maison-Dieu* 141 (1980): 167–69.

13. Michael A. Mathis, CSC (1885–1960). He began summer conferences on the liturgy at Notre Dame in 1947 and launched the summer graduate program in 1948. He was converted to the liturgy in 1936 upon reading Pius Parsch, *The Church's Year of Grace*, trans. Daniel Francis Coogan, Jr. and Rudolph Kraus (Collegeville, MN: Liturgical Press, 1953–1959), originally published in 1931 at Klosterneuburg.

14. Louis Bouyer, *Liturgical Piety* (Notre Dame, IN: Notre Dame University Press, 1954).

15. Lambert Beauduin, *La Piété de l'Église, Principes et faits* (Louvain: Maredsous, 1914), the first of his works on the liturgy, rendered in English as *Liturgy: the Life of the Church*, trans. Virgil George Michael (Collegeville, MN: Liturgical Press, 1926).

16. Id., *La Vie de la Liturgie: une critique constructive du mouvement liturgique* (Paris: Cerf, 1956).

17. Id., *Rite and Man: Natural Sacredness and Christian Liturgy* (Notre Dame: Notre Dame University Press, 1963).

18. Id., *Eucharist: Theology and Spirituality of the Eucharistic Prayer* (Notre Dame: Notre Dame University Press, 1968).

19. Id., *Liturgy and Architecture* (Notre Dame: Notre Dame University Press, 1967).

nearly immediately issued a fatwa pillorying its French version for "deviating from the general line" (as they say in the Communist Party!).[20]

This entirely unexpected opening in the United States first gave me a series of Midwestern summers that weren't particularly restful. They were intensely interesting, however. I was to acquire a number of excellent friends besides Father Mathis. I shall first name one of my first American students, a young and highly distinguished priest who would turn out to be a remarkable scholar: John Quinn.[21] He was in turn professor at Notre Dame, then at the (high-quality) seminary of Mount Saint Mary (Maryland) and lastly at Saint Joseph's seminary in Dunwoodie, for the Archdiocese of New York.[22] To him I shall add the delightful and frail C.A. Bouman, from the University of Nijmegen, a specialist in Oriental languages.[23] There was also a southern German who summed up in my eyes the impeccable scholarship, patriarchal wisdom, and robust sense of humor that can make the Catholics of that region so winsome: Karl Anton Chroust.[24] I should add that this famous jurist who was soon to go over to Yale was passionate about the history of philosophy. Putting to good use his fabulous knowledge of Syriac and Arabic, he was to publish a biography of Aristotle. It

20. This fatwa (or *oukase* as Bouyer calls it) came in the form of a review by S. Goossens, *La Mason-Dieu* 95 (1968): 172–75. Half of this review (174–75) is devoted to Bouyer's "secret discomfort" (*un secret malaise*) and "fear of the altar facing the people" (*peur de l'autel face au peuple*) that "seems to fetter his freedom of judgment" (*semble enchaîner la liberté de son jugement*). The reviewer is disappointed that Bouyer did not, "in our age of audio-visual civilization, frankly admit that a worthily performed celebration facing the people favors the active participation of the faithful" (*Pourquoi, à notre époque de civilisation audio-visuelle, ne pas admettre franchement qu'une célébration face au peuple, dignement accomplie, favorise la participation active des fidèles?*).

21. John Richard Quinn (1921–), author of *God's People at Mass: A Guide to Understanding the Missal* (New York: Benziger Brothers, 1964).

22. Mount Saint Mary's University was founded in Emmitsburg, Maryland, at the very beginning of the nineteenth century by a French priest, John DuBois (1764–1842), who later became bishop of New York. It houses a seminary that the Sulpicians helped to found. The seminary of Saint Joseph in Dunwoodie, a neighborhood of Yonkers, New York, was opened in 1896 to form priests for the Diocese of New York and originally entrusted to the Sulpicians (see 129, n. 14).

23. Cornelius Adrianus Bouman (1925–2008) was a specialist in such rites as the crowning and anointing of kings and episcopal blessings; he coauthored with Bouyer *Prières de la liturgie, des Pères de l'Église, des auteurs spirituels: De la vie liturgique à la prière personnelle* (Tournai-Paris: Desclée de Bouwer, 1962).

24. Anton-Hermann Chroust (1907–1982) taught at Notre Dame, 1945–1972, then taught at the prestigious Yale law school. His juridical works include the multi-volume *The Rise of the Legal Profession in America* (Norman: University of Oklahoma Press, 1965–).

breathed new life into the subject because it relied on decisive sources not used seriously before him.[25]

Through Quinn I would become friends with Myles M. Bourke, who was already then (excellent!) New Testament professor at the above-mentioned New York seminary. Since then he was appointed "pastor," as they say in the USA, of Corpus Christi parish, a stone's throw from Broadway; he has turned it into a center of liturgical life.[26]

My American activity was only to increase in the years to follow. It had been prepared and made possible by my developing relationship with England years before. I have already said how it began while I was still a Protestant. It is now time to tell what it had become since my conversion, that is, since the war when it occurred.

I should specify that my mother initiated me. She herself had been indelibly struck by a relatively short stint in that country. Her Guernsey friend, Mademoiselle de Garis, prolonged that influence for a long time.[27] I have mentioned how my early stays with Canon Moreton confirmed this orientation, which frequent visits to the Anglican churches of Paris had maintained.[28]

Yet, it was the trip I took to England and then to Scotland right after the war that was the true starting point of my familiarity with British religious circles, be they Catholic or Anglican. This was right after the congress organized at Beaumont College, Old Windsor, in 1945, for the centenary of Newman's conversion.[29] What came next constituted a

---

25. A.H. Chroust, *Aristotle: New Light on His Life and Some of His Lost Works* (Notre Dame, IN: University of Notre Dame Press, 1973).

26. Msgr. Myles Bourke (1917–2004), professor of sacred scripture at St. Joseph's Seminary, Dunwoodie, NY, 1947–1966, and pastor of Corpus Christi in Manhattan, 1966–1992. Along with biblical scholar Raymond E. Brown, Bouyer was one of his closest friends. Bouyer would often come to New York for Holy Week at Corpus Christi for the "rather sumptuous yet austere liturgies" Msgr. Bourke celebrated. See Frank Oveis, "Remembering Fr. Myles Bourke, Scholar and Pastor," *National Catholic Reporter* (Dec. 17, 2004). Bouyer specifies the meaning of the term "pastor" in the USA because the equivalent term in Anglicanism is "vicar" and his assistant is called "curate"—the French term *curé* meaning "pastor" in the American sense!

27. Guernsey is the westernmost Anglo-Norman isle and the second largest after Jersey. The Garis family is among the oldest on the island, with records going back to the thirteenth century.

28. For Canon Moreton see 79, n. 93; for the Anglican churches in Paris, 57, n. 2.

29. Newman's conversion occurred on 9 October 1845. Beaumont College in Old Windsor in Berkshire (west of London, just south of Oxfordshire) was at the time a Jesuit boarding school (opened in 1861 and closed in 1967) housed in a manor house built in 1790 on an estate established on the banks of the Thames during the Middle Ages. Bouyer describes his "Newmanian pilgrimage" in "Un Pélerinage newmanien," *La Vie spirituelle* 73 (1945): 418–28.

decisive stage in this initiation: a first stay at Oxford with the Blackfriar Dominicans[30] between two stays with the Oratorians (first in London, then in Birmingham)[31] as well as a stay at Oscott,[32] the seminary that Wiseman developed and where its vice-rector, Msgr. Davis, welcomed me.[33] I must also immediately add the beginning of my Benedictine relations: first with Prinknash, the Catholic monastery that issued from the conversion of the Anglican monks of Caldey,[34] and especially with Downside Abbey,[35] the great center of the English Benedictine congregation.

The following years would regularly bring me back across the Channel, first to work on my *Newman: His Life and Spirituality*.[36] Omer Englebert, he too pushed by Dom Lambert Beauduin, had asked me for it for a collection he directed at Albin Michel. In fact, it was published at the Éditions du Cerf,[37] since Englebert had meanwhile left for South America and Albin Michel lost interest in his collection.

This book was the first to make abundant use of Newman's unpublished materials, starting with his Journal. It was the occasion as well as the fruit of the growth of one of my best English friendships, with

30. "Blackfriars" is the term used in Britain since the thirteenth century for the Dominicans because of the black cloak they wear over their white habits. Their foundation at Oxford dates to 1221 and it was closed down during the schism in the sixteenth century. It was founded again in 1921 and was incorporated into the University in 1994.

31. The present-day Birmingham Oratory was built at the turn of the twentieth century next to the school building that Newman (see 35, n. 11) had founded in 1852.

32. Oscott College is the seminary of the Archdiocese of Birmingham. It was opened in 1794 and expanded in 1838 after the emancipation of Roman Catholics in England and Wales.

33. Bishop Wiseman (1802–1865) invited John Newman and other converts from the Church of England to Oscott, whose president he then was, in 1845. Wiseman went on to be the first Catholic Cardinal Archbishop of Westminster in 1850 when the Catholic hierarchy was reestablished in Great Britain. He also wrote *Fabiola or The Church of the Catacombs* in 1854. Newman was not to get on as well with Wiseman's successor, Cardinal Henry Manning (1808–1892), a less intellectual and more social man, although he had hailed his conversion in 1851. Msgr. Henry Francis Davis (1903–1986) taught at Oscott and was among the first promoters of the beatification of Newman. He was named vice-postulator when the cause was introduced in 1958.

34. Ælred Carlyle (1874–1955) founded a community of Anglican monks in 1895, which settled on Caldey Island in South Wales in 1906. He and his monks went over to the Catholic Church in 1913, and moved to Prinknash (pronounced "Prinnish") in Gloucestershire in 1928. The original abbey dates to 1096.

35. The English Benedictines of Douai (in Flanders), where they had been since the 1605, moved to Downside in Somerset in 1795 to escape the French Revolution.

36. *Newman: His Life and Spirituality* (London: Burns & Oates, 1958).

37. *Newman: Sa vie, sa spiritualité* (Paris: Cerf, 1952).

Father Henry Tristram of the Birmingham Oratory.[38] He was a man of immense culture (I don't think I have met a Hellenist to match him), of a kindness equaled only by his wit. One may say that he had dedicated his entire life to the memory of Newman. The books on Newman that could never have been written without his tireless inspiration are innumerable—not to mention those published under other names but whose principal author was, in fact, he. For his part, he had written an analysis of Newman's life and thought that was so well researched and so sweeping that its enormous size made it impossible to finish and especially to publish, as he was the first to realize. Yet, he made this work available to me with a selflessness I have never found elsewhere among researchers. The best of my own book is attributable to his research or to our endless conversations.

After all this, I shall confine myself to saying that this book attracted only contemptuous reviews in the French Catholic press. Among its Catholic reviews in England, it provoked fury, except for one understanding and courageous article by the future Cardinal Heenan, who at the time was archbishop of Liverpool. It was the starting point for a friendship between the two of us, of which I shall say more later.[39]

And what an extraordinary (and delightful) house the Birmingham Oratory was in those days! Nothing in it seemed to have been touched since Newman's death (not even the dust, as malicious gossip had it). Better yet, one of the most splendid eccentrics I have ever known survived there: Father Denys Florence Sheil.[40] He had been a schoolboy at the school when Newman directed it. He had been a novice in the house before Newman was made cardinal, with the result that while he never would have permitted himself to say "Newman," but at the same time had never quite got used to saying "Cardinal Newman," he always spoke of "Doctor Newman." Above all, as is the case with all great old men, his memory for the distant past was the more faithful. Every so often towards the end of his life (he died just a few days short of one hundred) he had to be reminded that Newman no longer was in rooms next to his but had been in a tomb of Rednal cemetery, the Oratorian country residence, since 1890.[41]

---

38. Louis Bouyer edited, annotated, and prefaced the French translation of Newman's *Autobiographical Writings*, ed. Henry Tristram (London-New York: Sheed and Ward, 1957).

39. For John Carmel Heenan see 15, n. 1 and chapters twelve and thirteen below.

40. Denis Florence Sheil (1865–1962) was born in Dublin and came to the Birmingham Oratory as a pupil in 1875. After his ordination in 1889 he was the last novice to have been received by Newman.

41. Rednal is a dozen miles south of downtown Birmingham.

I couldn't dream of evoking many other "characters," in the English sense of the word, that were housed at Edgbaston.[42] I spent many weeks, if not months, there in the very room where Newman had died and among his very furniture, with leisure to handle his papers. These were more or less exactly as he had left them.

I was also a frequent guest at the London Oratory, in its beautiful Brompton house—although I prefer the smaller, but more simply beautiful, Birmingham church. It wasn't much less archaic in its customs, but its tone was perhaps less intellectual, although more fully (and how aristocratically!) English. I have kept some firm friendships there, beginning with Father Michael Napier, its longtime superior.[43] He is now the Visitor General of all the Oratories of Saint Philip Neri, which has enabled me to meet him as far as on the Pacific Rim.

To return to Birmingham. I was introduced there by Father Geoffrey Wamsley, whom I had met in Old Windsor.[44] He had been vice-principal at Cuddesdon, the Anglican theological college near Oxford; he too had recently converted. He succeeded Father Dessain as superior, who went on to edit Newman's immense correspondence.[45] I must also mention the charming (and he, too, an eccentric!) Father Michael Day, who many years later published a very elegant translation of the little book Saint Philip Neri had inspired me to write.[46] He called it, with my warm approval, *The Roman Socrates*.[47]

Through Fr. Tristram I would meet another convert: Dom Illtyd Trethowan.[48] He has remained one of my best friends across the English

---

42. Edgbaston is the name of the Birmingham district where Newman's Oratory is located.

43. Michael Napier (1929–1996), provost of the Birmingham Oratory, 1969–1981. He converted to Catholicism in October 1952.

44. Geoffrey Speight Wamsley (1909–1977) was ordained to the Anglican ministry in 1934. For Old Windsor, where he lived after his conversion in 1941 and before he entered the Birmingham Oratory, see 167, n. 29.

45. Charles Stephen Dessain (1907–1976) wrote *The Mind of Cardinal Newman* (London: Catholic Truth Society, 1974). Bouyer here refers to John H. Newman, *Letters and Diaries: Edited at the Birmingham Oratory with Notes and an Introduction by Charles Stephen Dessain* (London: T. Nelson, 1961–).

46. L. Bouyer, *Saint Philippe Néri* (Paris: Albin Michel, 1948).

47. L. Bouyer, *The Roman Socrates: A Portrait of St. Philip Neri*, trans. Michael Day (Westminster, MD: Newman Press, 1958). The second French edition matched this English title: *Saint Philippe Néri: Un Socrate romain* (Paris: Éditions SOS., 1979).

48. Dom Illtyd Trethowan (1907–1993). He converted in 1929 and entered Downside Abbey in 1932, after a brief stint as schoolmaster at the London Oratory and then Ampleforth. He was Sub-prior, 1958–1991. He was to translate Bouyer's *The Christian Mystery: From Pagan Myth to Christian Mysticism* (Edinburgh: T.&T. Clark, 1989).

Channel and is the current Sub-prior of Downside. He is doubtless the most remarkable religious philosopher in the English-speaking world today.

I also went to Prinknash, where Dom Wilfrid Upson was still the abbot during my first stay there.[49] He had been among the first companions of Dom Ælred Carlyle, the erratic founder of Caldey.[50] This is where I became friends with the delightful Bede Griffiths.[51] This makes me particularly deplore that his enthusiasm for Indian spirituality, which had always worried me, has since caused him to go off into an insipid and unacceptable syncretism.

All these high places of British Catholicism were exceptionally open in those postwar years, 1945–1950. Yet, I must say that Downside is the one that won over and still retains my preference. I love it all: the beautiful, vast, hilly, and varied garden; the playgrounds all around it; the very beautiful square tower which, jutting out of the monastic and school buildings, looms over it. This tower is doubtless the best product of English Neo-Gothic. The church, regarding which sculptor Eric Gill said that it was "an honest piece of engineering," is just as well built.[52] I confess that I am particularly fond of its Lady Chapel, one of Sir Ninian Comper's masterpieces.[53] Yet, Peter Anson has described its style, which blends a very personal Baroque with a pseudo-Jacobean[54] and a fanciful flamboyant gothic style, as a "deluxe chocolate shop"![55]

But, most of all, I appreciate its integration with the monastery. It calls to mind our old Maurists, at the school, which for me evokes my dream of a synthesis between Juilly and Saint-Wandrille. And, of course, what is very dear to me is the friendship of those monks, who unite the tradition of a very interior monasticism with the intellectual rigor of Cambridge.

49. Dom Wilfrid Upson (1880–1963) was Abbot of Prinknash, 1938–1963.

50. See 168, n. 34.

51. Bede Griffiths (1906–1993) converted to Catholicism in 1931 and entered Prinknash in 1932. He went to India in 1955 and in 1958 helped found a Syriac-Rite monastery near Kerala. In 1968 he joined the Catholic Shantivanam Ashram, where Catholic liturgy and spirituality draw on Hinduism. He was known there as Swami Dayananda, "Bliss of Compassion."

52. Eric Gill (1882–1940) was a graphic designer, architect, and sculptor whom Catholicism had fascinated—as did a monumental eroticism.

53. Sir John Ninian Comper (1864–1960), Scottish architect and last "master" of British neo-gothic architecture.

54. The Jacobean era (1603–1625) is that during which James I reigned in England.

55. Peter Anson (1889–1975) was a monk at Caldey, 1910–1924, after which he returned to the lay state and became a renowned marine artist. He also wrote a book on *episcopi vagantes*; see 72, n. 69.

And then also, Downside, in the heart of Somerset, is surrounded by that western English countryside that is so beautiful. It has archaic and charming villages and churches, and, over those landscapes, along with the Glastonbury Tor nearly always on the horizon, hovers the magic of Arthurian legends and the Quest for the Grail.[56]

I can only add my memories of Anglicanism to those of these Catholic shrines and to the memories from which they are inseparable for me. After all, are not the English Benedictines, and to a certain extent the Oratorians, the only Catholics of England to have neither shunned nor lost contact with the Church of England?

I have already mentioned the charm of Hereford as it was when I first saw it.[57] At the time the most endearing and entertaining aspects of Trollope's ecclesiastical novels still survived nearly intact in its close and its denizens.[58] And what can I say about Durham? It has a colossal and fantastic cathedral perched on an enormous rock with the river round about it.[59] I do not know which enchanted me more: the times spent with Michael Ramsey when he was a canon there and later the bishop,[60] or, long before that, those spent with Greenslade, since then Regius professor of Church History at Oxford.[61] What, too, can one say of that

---

56. The Glastonbury Tor is a hill in Somerset (in southwestern England) where a monastery was founded in the early eighth century on what was at the time an elevation in the middle of a lagoon. All that is left of the monastery is a fourteenth-century tower at the top of the hill. According to legend, this is the site of Avalon, which houses the tombs of King Arthur, Queen Guinevere, and Sir Gawain. Camelot, the royal castle of the Knights of the Round Table and of the heroes of the Quest for the Holy Grail, is located nearby on the heights of Cadbury. These places in Somerset and the legends of the Arthurian cycle are an important facet of Bouyer's thought and imagination; see especially *Les Lieux magiques de la légende du Graal: De Brocéliande en Avalon* (Paris: Œil, 1986).

57. For Hereford and its cathedral see 79, n. 94.

58. Bouyer is here referring to the six novels in the Barsetshire Chronicles by Victorian writer Anthony Trollope (1815–1882). These portray the lives of clergy and gentry in the fictional cathedral town of Barchester.

59. Durham (in the northwest of England) has a twelfth-century Norman cathedral with an adjacent castle that rise above a rocky peak around which the Wear River flows. Saint Cuthbert (seventh-century missionary to the region) and Saint Bede the Venerable (c. 672–735, the monk-scholar who was proclaimed Doctor of the Church in 1899) are buried in the Galilee chapel, which is also the Lady chapel.

60. For Michael Ramsey, see 109, n. 39.

61. Stanley Lawrence Greenslade (1905–1977), author of *Early Latin Theology: Selections from Tertullian, Cyprian, Ambrose, and Jerome* (London: Westminster Press, 1956) and editor of *The Cambridge History of the Bible*, vol. 3, *The West, From the Reformation to the Present Day* (Cambridge: Cambridge University Press, 1963). He was Regius professor of Church History, 1959–1972, and Dean of Christ Church at Oxford.

tomb with its unscathed relics of Venerable Bede, which always has flowers in the Galilee chapel overhanging the abyss?

And what shall I say of Oxford, most particularly of Christ Church, Tom Quad, the Meadow surrounded by the Cherwell, and the Merton and Magdalen towers on the horizon?[62] I stayed there as a guest first of Frank Leslie Cross,[63] at the prior house, which is inseparable from the starting-place of *Alice's Adventures in Wonderland*.[64] I later was Demant's[65] guest in the other beautiful house, where Elizabeth Goudge had spent her youth and written her first stories; she was to become one of my best friends.[66] Another friendship that I developed over the years, with the theologian Eric Mascall,[67] was born there, and I cannot separate its memory from the evenings we would begin in the grand dining hall and continue in the senior common room.

I was received no less frequently at Brasenose,[68] on the other side of the street, by Robert Shackleton, the Montesquieu historian I had hosted at Juilly when he was writing his dissertation.[69] Later on I followed him into the especially august—and above all quiet!—enclosure

---

62. Tom Quad, also the Great Quadrangle, is the largest quad at Oxford (264' x 261'). The Meadow is a broad grassy triangle encompassed by Christ Church, the Thames, and one of its tributaries, the Cherwell. Merton and Magdalen are two more colleges at Oxford, founded in 1264 and 1458 respectively.

63. Frank Leslie Cross (1900–1968), Lady Margaret Professor of Divinity and Canon of Christ Church from 1944. He was the first editor of the *Oxford Dictionary of the Christian Church* (London: Oxford University Press, 1957).

64. Written by Oxford Don Charles Lutwidge Dodgson (a.k.a. Lewis Carroll, 1832–1888); the rabbit hole in the novel was inspired by the stairs behind the main hall of Christ Church. Alice Liddell (1852–1934) was the daughter of its dean, Henry George Liddell (1811–1898), coauthor with Robert Scott of the classic *Greek-English Lexicon* (Oxford: Clarendon Press, 1843 with many reprints and editions).

65. Vigo Auguste Demant (1893–1983), theologian and social commentator, Canon of Christ Church and Regius Professor of Moral and Pastoral Theology, author of *Religion and the Decline of Capitalism* (London: Faber and Faber, 1952).

66. Elizabeth Goudge (1900–1984), British novelist. Her father had been Regius Professor of Divinity at Oxford, 1923–1939. While living with her father at Oxford she wrote first *Island Magic* (London: Duckworth, 1934), *The Middle Window* (London: Duckworth, 1935), *A City of Bells* (London: Duckworth, 1936), and some short stories for the *Strand* magazine. For her friendship with Bouyer see chapter 13 below.

67. Eric Lionel Mascall (1905–1993), Anglo-Catholic priest and Thomistic theologian. After Oxford he taught at King's College in London, then served at the Cathedral of Truro in Wales. For a photo and biographical essay, see H.P. Owen, "Eric Lionel Mascall, 1905–1993," *Proceedings of the British Academy* 84 (1994): 409–18.

68. Brasenose is a college at Oxford, founded in 1509.

69. Robert Shackleton (1919–1986) taught French at Oxford; his best-known contribution is his *Montesquieu: A Critical Biography* (London: Oxford University Press, 1961).

of All Souls.[70] This college is privileged above all others by the fact that its fellows are dispensed from any teaching—since they are the only residents there. I had already been introduced to the place thanks to the friendship of E. O. James, the historian of Ancient Near Eastern religions (and an excellent Anglican priest),[71] and then by the rather unconventional but very penetrating historian of comparative mysticism, R.C. Zaehner.[72]

As tempting as it is, I would never come to the end of it if I went on to speak of Worcester, then Chichester.[73] Kemp welcomed me to both of these cathedrals, as dean of the former and, in time, as bishop of the latter.[74] He was the great maintainer of the most traditional Anglo-Catholicism, which was threatened by the ultra-modernism of the American "Episcopalians" with their priestesses and now their bishopesses![75]

I shall only mention York Minster.[76] Today it lies in ruin because of a fire occurring a few days after a near-total agnostic was consecrated bishop of Durham there.[77] I stayed there as a guest of Dean Milner-

70. All Souls, an Oxford college founded in 1438.

71. Edwin Oliver James (1888–1972), prolific writer of broad-readership books on the topic. His most famous book is perhaps *The Ancient Gods: The History and Diffusion of Religion in the Ancient Near East and the Eastern Mediterranean* (New York: Putnam, 1960).

72. Robert Charles Zaehner (1913–1974). As a MI6 intelligence officer he had had a daring record on the Iran-USSR border and had trained anti-Soviet guerillas in Malta among other feats before converting to the Catholic faith. He maintained the distinction of mystical experiences among different religions.

73. Worcester (in England near the Welsh border) has an eclectic cathedral, in styles ranging from massive Norman to the typically English perpendicular Gothic. Chichester Cathedral in West Sussex (south of London) also combines several styles and is characterized by double aisles and a detached bell tower.

74. Eric Waldram Kemp (1915–2009), Dean of Worcester, 1969–74; Bishop of Chichester, 1974–2001. He never licensed a woman priest in his diocese.

75. Bouyer coins a French term for women bishops: *évêchesses*. Women were first ordained Episcopal priests on 19 July 1974, though without endorsement from the General Convention, which then regularized them in 1976. Barbara C. Harris (born 1930) was the first woman to be consecrated a bishop of the Episcopal communion, on 11 February 1989 as suffragan for the diocese of Massachusetts. These lines, therefore, were written after that date.

76. York Minster (an older form of "monastery") is the Gothic cathedral of York, in the northeast of England. It ranks as the second episcopal See of England after Canterbury.

77. Bouyer is here referring to the fire caused by lightning on 9 July 1984, three days after it was the venue for the consecration of David Edward Jenkins (1925–), Bishop of Durham, 1984–1994. See David E. Jenkins, *The Calling of a Cuckoo: Not Quite an Autobiography* (London: Continuum, 2002), 62–92.

White,[78] who would certainly have had a fainting spell if he had been able to foresee such a scandal and such a ruin! For his part, he was nearly a caricature, a living type of Andrewes[79] or Cosin[80] as a prelate. He was a veritable "period piece," even more reminiscent of *John Inglesant*[81] than of *Barchester Towers*![82]

I still enjoy recalling the Society of the Sacred Mission house where the excellent Father A.G. Hebert ended his days before it became empty and then disappeared.[83] He was original, but so profound, in his biblical and liturgical studies.[84] Yet, my favorite memory of the old *clerus anglicanus stupor mundi*[85] still remains the admirable priest that was Henry Balmforth, author of doubtless the best book ever written on the universal priesthood and the ministerial priesthood.[86] I visited him first in the fantasy setting of Ely and then in pleasant Exeter, which is home to the sweet fairyland of western England to a greater degree even than Wells.[87]

---

78. Eric Milner-White (1884–1963), Dean of York Minster, 1941–1963. During his deanship he replaced many of the Minster's stained glass windows.

79. Lancelot Andrewes (1555–1626), Bishop of Chichester, Ely, and Winchester during the reign of Elizabeth I and James I. He oversaw the translation of the Authorized ("King James") Version of the Bible. He is a type of the learned High Church cleric of the period.

80. John Cosin (1594–1672), ritualist Bishop of Durham from 1660.

81. Character in Joseph H. Shorthouse's 1881 novel by the same name, set in the mid-seventeenth century. It chronicles the adventures of an Anglican involved in the ecclesiastical and political turmoil of his day.

82. *Barchester Towers* is one of Trollope's Barsetshire Chronicles; see 172, n. 58.

83. This Society was founded in 1893 by Herbert Kelly as a quasi-monastic society with a missionary apostolate. It was housed in Kelham Hall, a masterpiece of Victorian Gothic architecture, from 1903. From its peak membership in the early 1960s, numbers dwindled to the point that Kelham was closed in 1972. Arthur Gabriel Hebert (1886–1963) had been a proponent of an Anglican Liturgical Movement and had many contacts with both Catholic and Protestant liturgists on the continent.

84. See Albert G. Hebert, *The Christ of Faith and the Jesus of History* (London: SCM Press, 1962); id., *The Authority of the Old Testament* (London: Faber and Faber, 1947); and id, *Liturgy and Society: The Function of the Church in the Modern World* (London: Faber and Faber, 1935).

85. This expression, meaning "Anglican clergy, the wonder of the world," was used to describe the Anglican delegation at the Synod of Dort (1618–1619), convened to settle the dispute between strict Calvinists and Arminians. The first application of this expression had been to Frederick II Hohenstaufen (1194–1250), Holy Roman Emperor from 1215 to his death.

86. Henry Balmforth, *The Royal Priesthood* (London: The Church Union Church Literature Association, 1956) and id., *Christian Priesthood* (London: SPCK, 1963).

87. Ely, 15 miles north of Cambridge in eastern England, has a medieval cathedral (built between the eleventh and fourteenth centuries) known for its enormous octagonal tower. Wells, in Somerset just north of Exeter, also has a beautiful cathedral that is

I will finish these recollections with the Royal Chapel of Windsor.[88] Vidler, that great eccentric, extended his affable hospitality to me there when he belonged to its chapter.[89] My stays there were often as profitable as they were enjoyable, in a setting where one lives a waking dream of medieval chivalry.

I can only go from England to Scotland—without, to be sure, the slightest temptation to mistake one for the other![90]

My first stay in that country immediately followed the Newman conference in the south of the United Kingdom at the end of the war. The Secours Catholique, which at the time was still entirely French but would soon go international,[91] had asked me to make a first contact with the British episcopate. My first advance north for this purpose led me first to Glasgow. There I was a guest in a (most Irish, in fact) rectory at the end of the interminable Dumbarton Road; that is, in what was at the time a shipbuilding area whose workers all came over from the neighboring island. A little later, in France, I made the (delightful) acquaintance of the writer Bruce Marshall. I am in a position to verify that the parish he described in *All Glorious Within* is exactly that where I was a spoiled guest for a few days![92] I was taken to the only football match I have ever laid eyes on, and I shall add only that the next day's (Irish Catholic) local paper sported the following headline: "The

---

remarkable (among other features) for its monumental façade, which is wider than it is tall.

88. Windsor has been the English monarchs' West London residence since the eleventh century. The royal chapel, built about 1500, is as big as a cathedral (though with neither towers nor bells) and is the seat of the prestigious Order of the Garter that King Edward III created in 1348 during the Hundred Years War.

89. Alexander Roper Vidler (1899–1991), liberal Anglican theologian and Dean of King's College. He had been Canon of Exeter since the late 1930s and was active in apologetics and ecumenism. He was influential in the conversion of Malcolm Muggeridge (1903–1990), the English journalist and writer, who notoriously went from Communism and agnosticism to Anglicanism in 1969 and Catholicism in 1982 and brought Mother Teresa to the attention of the West.

90. To most Frenchmen, little distinguishes the countries of Great Britain.

91. French Catholic charity, founded in September 1946 by Fr. (later Msgr.) Jean Rhodain (1900–1977). It was to coalesce with other charities as Caritas Internationalis from 1980 on.

92. Bruce Marshall (1899–1987), a Scot, converted to the Catholic faith in 1917. He served in both world wars; he lost a leg a few days before the armistice in 1918 and was a liaison officer with the French resistance during the German occupation. *All Glorious Within* (London: Constable & Co., 1944) is one of his many novels and chronicles the life of a Catholic priest in Scotland in the 1930s. The title is from Ps 45:13 (KJV): "The king's daughter is all glorious within: her clothing is of wrought gold." The king's daughter represents the Church.

Immaculate Conception has knocked down Saint Joseph!" Need I point out that these were two parish teams?

My visit to the archbishop[93] convinced me that there were Scots in the Catholic Church of Scotland after all. Just as I began saying "Having visited the English bishops, I am contacting the Scottish ones, starting with Your Grace. ..." this prelate interrupted me straightaway to tell me, with the most unfeigned satisfaction: "Father, I am pleased to hear that although you hail from the continent, you do not mistake us for Englishmen! You see, when we Scots are taken for Englishmen, we have the same reaction as you French might have if you were called 'Krauts'!"

Despite this cordial reception, it was above all Edinburgh that enchanted me with its dreamlike, otherworldly atmosphere!

I have also described that house on George Square in a novel mentioned above in connection with Father Cognet.[94] I stayed there as a guest, not of Raffalovich who had died and bequeathed it to the Dominicans,[95] but of Father Hugh Pope. He was a biblical scholar, which didn't make him any less colorful in his own way.[96] He hosted me in that beautiful Georgian residence at the very top of the town, very near to the Rock and its castle.[97] None of the beautiful old Regency furniture or of the Chinese antiques had been touched yet.[98] Later on, I came to know Father Anthony Ross there.[99] He regaled me with splendid ghost stories, including that of the ghost dog, which had happened to him and which I have retold in my *Tales for Maÿlis*.[100]

Yet, it was with neither of them that I went on the excursion to Loch

---

93. Donald Alphonsus Campbell (1894–1963), Archbishop of Glasgow from 1945.

94. For Fr. Cognet and the "novel mentioned above," see 150, n. 11.

95. Marc-André Raffalovich (1864–1934), journalist, poet, and essayist best known for his works on homosexuality. He converted to Catholicism in 1896, become a Dominican tertiary and later moved to Edinburgh. There he helped fund St. Peter's Church where his lifelong friend Fr. John Gray was the rector. Raffalovich's own house was next door.

96. Hugh Pope (1869–1946), known for his *The Catholic Student's Aids to the Study of the Bible*, 3 vols. (London: Burns, Oates, Washbourne, 1922–26).

97. Edinburgh in Scotland is dominated by a volcanic promontory, the Rock, atop which sits an impressive castle that has been destroyed and rebuilt several times since the high Middle Ages.

98. Regency style corresponds with the British victory over Napoleon, Romanticism, and Dandyism. From 1811 to 1820, the Prince of Wales (1762–1830; he would rule in his own name as George IV) ruled Britain instead of his father, George III, who had been declared unable to rule.

99. Fr. Antony Ross, OP (1917–1993), elected rector of the University of Edinburgh in 1979.

100. These are in Prospero Catella (Louis Bouyer), *Les Hespérides* (Paris: SOS., 1985).

Kathrine, Loch Lomond, and the Trossachs. That was with the ever-cordial Father McGuckin. It took us through Stirling and Calendar house. I recall it in the above-named novel.

This was my first encounter with Scotland's lakes and mountains. I would renew it in another tour that brought me to Inverness and Fort Augustus, without forgetting Loch Ness and its monster, as seen in the *Tales* mentioned above.[101]

Lastly, much more recently I was given a most unexpected invitation to the Department of Theology at the University of Glasgow (Calvinist if ever there was one!) to give the Alexander Robertson Lecture.[102] This allowed me to discover Glasgow under extensive renovation as well as the unforgettable Island of Iona[103] and the brand-new community that restored, and even reanimated, its ruins.[104]

But as much as I should gladly immerse myself in these recollections, I have to cut them short. Yet, I cannot bring myself to put an end to these British reminiscences (which I had only brought up by way of preface to what has to be called my "Americanization") without a word on two of my most prized friendships. Their memory will forever remain bound to what the French all too easily consider to be "perfidious Albion."[105]

In the first place there is my friendship with T. S. Eliot,[106] whom I met during the meetings that led to the foundation of the review *Dieu vivant*,[107] and later saw again in his quiet office on Russell Square.[108]

I can remember one conversation among others about some Frenchmen's (and Americans') strange enthusiasms for what Americans call "fakes" in English literature.[109] I can still see Eliot, sparkling with good-

101. I.e., Bouyer's *Hespérides*; see the foregoing note.

102. The Church of Scotland has been Calvinistic since the sixteenth century. For the Alexander Robertson lecture, see 196, n. 58.

103. Iona is a small island to the northwest of Scotland. It served as a base for the Irish monks who evangelized the area from the sixth century on. The abbey there was a monastic landmark until the dissolutions of the monasteries at the time of the break with Rome.

104. In 1938 Church of Scotland Minister George MacLeod brought a group of clergymen and workingmen to restore the medieval Iona abbey. The idea was to close the gap between clergy and the working class; it has since undertaken ecumenical activities.

105. "Albion" was a Roman term for Britain due to the white (in Latin *albus*) cliffs of Dover, on the English Channel. Bossuet had first used the expression *perfide Albion* in a religious sense to speak of England's adoption of Protestantism, and the French have used it since whenever they have felt betrayed (or bested) by Great Britain, for instance in the case of Joan of Arc, Napoleon, the 1898 Fashoda incident, Dunkirk in 1940, the British scuttling of the French fleet in Toulon in 1942, etc.

106. For Thomas Stearns Eliot see 82, n. 107.

natured mischievousness and speaking in French, which he possessed as well as his own language.[110] He told me, regarding Charles Morgan and his *Fountain* and *Sparkenbroke*,[111] over whom our critics, from Edmond Jaloux[112] to Charles du Bos,[113] had gone deliriously wild: "He's a writer for scullery-maids!"[114]

I would enter into an even greater intimacy with John Ronald Reuel Tolkien, the prodigious philologist, though he was far more famous for the stunning fantasy of *The Lord of the Rings*.[115] I was certainly the first one in France to discover its three volumes, thanks to my London confrere Father Patrick Bushell,[116] and to publish an article on them in

107. *Dieu Vivant* was a religious and philosophical journal, published 1945–1955 under the leadership of layman Marcel Moré (1887–1969). It promoted "eschatological Christianity," i.e., a life modelled on that promised the elect at the end of time. It attracted some prestigious (or soon-to-be prestigious) contributors, not all of whom were Catholic or even Christian: beside T. S. Eliot and Louis Bouyer, there were Catholic theologians Jean Daniélou (see 141, n. 62), Henri de Lubac (see 185, n. 8), the German Romano Guardini (1885–1968) and the Swiss Hans Urs von Balthasar (see 226–27, n. 113); philosophers Gabriel Marcel (see 132, n. 26), Maurice de Gandillac (1906–2006), Henri Gouyer (1898–1994), Jean Hippolyte (1907–1971), and Brice Parain (1897–1971); Russian Orthodox Vladimir Lossky (see 76–77, n. 84); Jewish thinker Martin Buber (1878–1965); specialist in Islam Louis Massignon (1883–1962); and writers Paul Claudel (see 65, n. 37) and Graham Greene (1904–1991).

108. Russell Square is a small rectangular square near the University and the British Museum.

109. "Fake" here means a low-quality imitation.

110. Eliot had studied under Bergson at the Sorbonne, 1910–1911.

111. Charles Langbridge Morgan (1894–1958), British novelist and playwright. Bouyer here refers to his *The Fountain* (London: Macmillan, 1932) and *Sparkenbroke* (London: Macmillan, 1936). Morgan received the prestigious *Légion d'Honneur* (highest award for merit) in 1936 and was elected to the *Institut de France* (the French organization that groups the five academies of which the Académie française is the best known) in 1949. He has a better reputation in France than in Great Britain to this day.

112. Edmond Jaloux (1878–1949), French literary critic whose critiques were thoughtful and well-informed.

113. For Charles du Bos see 81, n. 106.

114. I.e., of romance novels.

115. John Ronald Reuel Tolkien (1892–1973); see Bouyer *Métier*, 114, 116, 260, 268. His lifelong interest was in the importance of Old English in the study of modern literature; he taught at Merton College, Oxford (see 173, n. 62). The *Lord of the Rings* trilogy was published in 1954–1955. Tolkien had converted to Catholicism as a young man and remained faithful to the Birmingham Oratory. He had helped C. S. Lewis in his conversion and regretted that Lewis had chosen Anglicanism over the Catholic Church. For the friendship between Bouyer and Tolkien, see Michaël Devaux, "Louis Bouyer et J.R.R. Tolkien: une amitié d'écrivains," *Cahiers d'études tolkiniennes* 2 (2003): 85–146.

116. Fr. Patrick Bushell (1912–), ordained in 1951, was an Oratorian, 1944–1961.

Robert Amadou's review, *La Tour Saint-Jacques*.[117] This exquisite old man's good nature, knowledge, and very simple yet very profound poetic and Christian view on life could only be truly appreciated in an informal tête-a-tête, however.

Our best conversation was doubtless that which filled a beautiful autumn afternoon in his Headington study, on the heights overlooking Oxford. This study, by the way, was located in what had been a garage and was the true model of one of his "Hobbit" holes! As for our interview's inexhaustible subject, it was provided by our reading together a collective book by grave university scholars from across the pond, who were totally fooled by the farcical answers Tolkien had given to these Pre-Adamites' questionnaire![118] I don't think I have ever seen the pseudo-scholarship of so many modern studies of that ilk go down in flames so magnificently, and I don't mean only American ones!

Once I finally come to recount my discovery of America, for which I have been laying the groundwork with this interlude about our neighbors across the Channel, I shall get around to another literary friendship (and much more than that). The reasons for this delay will become apparent. This is the friendship I shared with a third English writer, Elizabeth Goudge, whose first best-seller I had discovered much earlier: *Green Dolphin Country*.[119]

Need I tell the difference between England and Scotland, on the one hand, and that dreary northern Indiana plain? The little town of South Bend, which is indeed on a bend of the Saint Joseph River, developed around Notre Dame University. This university was founded there, as if by happenstance, by a few fathers of the French congregation known as the Holy Cross.[120] They had been kicked out of their native Le Mans by the French Revolution.[121]

The wooded campus around its two lakes, however, is charming and, once again, not only was Father Mathis's Summer School of Liturgical Studies captivating, but his personal welcome was peerless. After I had

117. Louis Bouyer, "Le Seigneur des Anneaux, une nouvelle épopée?" *La Tour Saint-Jacques* 13–4 (1958). Bouyer would return to Tolkien's fantasy world in his *Les Lieux magiques de la légende du Graal: de Brocéliande en Avalon* (Paris: OEIL, 1986).

118. "Pre-Adamites" are a hypothetical people created before Adam, and inferior to his descendants. Their existence was popular in the USA as a prop to theories of racial inequality. Bouyer here applies the reputed innocence of the pre-Adamites to the US scholars' naïveté and befuddlement at Tolkien's whimsical answers.

119. Elizabeth Goudge, *Green Dolphin Country* (London: Hodder and Stoughton, 1944), published in the USA as *Green Dolphin Street* (New York: Coward-McCann, 1944); see 173, n. 66. Bouyer dedicated his book on women in the Church to her: *Woman in the Church*, trans. Marilyn Teichert (San Francisco: Ignatius Press, 1979).

come there several times, I was supposed to be approached for a more comprehensive teaching post as part of an attempted renewal of the Theology department owing to the Council. Unfortunately, this attempt was aborted after a catastrophic death and a stupid nomination. Already Father Mathis's own death[122] had prepared the very ruin of the particular institution he had founded, however brilliant and solid this foundation had been. The accidental death of the young father, also very brilliant and very solid, who ought to have been the soul of a broader renewal, meant a generalized debacle.

These circumstances meant that I only ever taught one winter semester in that theology department. This allowed me to discover what winter can be like in the Midwest: snowplows everywhere at first dawn to clear all the streets of several feet of snow; but on the other hand the north wind (since there is no intervening height between you and the North Pole) all day! Still, that is where I wrote the bulk of my study on Eucharistic prayer[123] thanks to the incomparable resources of the Medieval Studies Institute, in the skyscraper that houses the library. It was founded by the librarian himself, Astrik Gabriel.[124] He was a great scholar, had no serious competition as a historian of the oldest universities, and was always very solicitous of me. I do have to acknowledge, however, that this (ultra-Francophile) Hungarian Premonstratensian harbored a barely disguised contempt for the *hoi polloi*. This caused the

120. Father Édouard (or Edward) Sorin, CSC (1814–1893), founded Notre Dame on 15 January 1844, having taken possession of the 524 acres 26 November 1842. Until the mid-twentieth century Notre Dame was known especially for its Catholicism and its American football team. Theodore Hesburgh (1917–2015) was its president for thirty-five years (1952–1987) and took Notre Dame in new directions both financially and academically, for instance by establishing coeducation of the sexes. Under his presidency, Notre Dame also became an agent for the mainstreaming of the Catholic community in the USA.

121. The Congregation of the Holy Cross was founded by Father Basile Moreau (1799–1873) in 1837. This congregation is essentially devoted to evangelization through education. It sent Father Sorin to Indiana at the invitation of the Bishop of Vincennes (Indiana), Célestine Guynemer de la Hailandière, for the purpose of founding a college.

122. In 1960; see 165, n. 13.

123. Louis Bouyer, *Eucharistie: Théologie et spiritualité de la prière eucharistique* (Tournai: Desclée, 1966). English version: *Eucharist: Theology and Spirituality of the Eucharistic Prayer*, trans. Charles Underhill Quinn (Notre Dame: University of Notre Dame Press, 1968).

124. Astrik L. Gabriel (1907–2005), with support from Étienne Gilson (see 62, n. 25) and Jacques Maritain (see 65, n. 37), founded the reputed Medieval Studies Institute at Notre Dame in 1946. The Premonstratensian order was founded in the twelfth century by St. Norbert of Xanten, a protégé of St. Bernard of Clairvaux. Its members, variously called Premonstratensians or Norbertines, follow the Rule of St. Augustine.

excellent Father Mathis to grumble about what he called "the monstrous pretension of that Premonstratensian"!

Once Father Mathis was no longer there, I stopped even coming back for the summer liturgy sessions. They were degenerating nearly as fast as our CPL that had been unceremoniously changed into the CNPL.[125] On the other hand, I had received many an American invitation. But, in order to understand how I came to accept these, I need to go over what had happened to me in the meantime on this side of the Atlantic.

---

125. For the transformation of the CPL into the CNPL (*Centre National de Pastorale Liturgique*), see 154–55, n. 30.

11

From Strasbourg to Normandy, Brittany and Around the World

AT THE END of the summer of 1960, even though nothing had been taken away either from my activity at the *Institut catholique* or from the times spent at Notre Dame, Indiana, a new task was entrusted to me. It would entail going back to Alsace, in Strasbourg. I had foreseen nothing of the sort, but I could tell right away that I would find it more profitable than burdensome. Father Tourde,[1] now superior general of the French Oratory, had just accepted on our behalf to run the International University Seminary of Strasbourg. The Vincentians' incompetence had convinced both the bishop and the Theology Department not to leave it in their hands any longer.[2]

I was spending some vacation time in the solitude of Biville, in northwest Cottentin.[3] That is where he came to ask me whether I could dedicate at least some of my time to that seminary without resigning from the *Institut catholique*. I accepted without hesitation, despite the added complications and the increased fatigue this would, of course, entail for me.[4]

Indeed, it had everything going for it. Ever since I had regretfully left Juilly, as I have sufficiently intimated, I suffered at having only a very limited priestly ministry, even despite the great interest of my university teaching in both Paris and America. Other priests with a theological

---

1. Fr. Édouard Tourde (1908–2003) joined the Oratorians in 1926, was ordained in 1934, and held the following positions: Superior at Saint Martin de Pointoise, 1950–1958 (see 121, n. 38); pastor of Saint Eustache, 1958–1970 (see 123, n. 52); superior general of the French Oratory, 1959–1969. He retired to the Villa Montmorency (see 133, n. 32).

2. For the Vincentians see 123, n. 50.

3. In Normandy.

4. Bouyer worked at the International seminary until 1963.

vocation, on the contrary, are glad to be able to dedicate all their time to study and teaching. I have never shared this way of looking at things. And I believe I can say that the more or less raving-mad fancies that circulated after the Council as so many products of some kind of new theology, and which did nothing but sow chaos and get in the way of renewal, are the typical fruits of these armchair theologians. They relegate ministry to those whom they consider to be clerical plebeians who cannot hold a candle to them. On the contrary, revealed truth is revealed to us only to lead us to salvation and lead others to it as well. This is obviously what Saint Thomas thought on the topic, as did the Fathers of the Church. So it seems to me that as soon as it is turned into a simple matter of cogitation and discussion, one no longer knows what one is saying, because one has begun no longer to know what one is talking about.

Now in the years after my Juilly ministry I did try to supplement my duties as a professor and my own studies by preaching in a series of large Parisian parishes, or by conducting retreats in seminaries and religious houses. But this remained exceptional and didn't strike me as being the same as a pastoral charge, especially one of formation with a well-defined group on a day-by-day basis, not just on the run. I therefore greeted the proposal that was made to me, not only cordially, but with the conviction that it was providential.

In the first place, at Strasbourg I renewed my acquaintance with the superior, Father Joseph Bouley.[5] I had known him as a student at Montsoult during my novitiate.[6] He was astute and learned; I got along with him perfectly. The little Oratorian community around us was pleasant, and it certainly was more hard-working in those days than that over at Villa Montmorency. More especially, I had the privilege of meeting, among these confreres, the Oratorian of whom I may say that he was the best friend I ever found in the Congregation. He was also a model priest, truly a holy priest, and what a charming, fascinating personality! I mean to speak of Father Vincent Ou Tsien Tsang.[7] He was a Chinese mathematician who converted in Lyons, where he had come to finish his studies, thanks to Father (now Cardinal) de Lubac.[8]

De Lubac had directed him to the Oratory, as well as his compatriot and friend François Houang Ka Tchen.[9] He told them, with some

    5. Fr. Joseph Bouley (1918–2002) was the superior of the Strasbourg seminary, 1960–1974, then pastor of Saint Eustache (see 123, n. 52) until 1983.

    6. For Montsoult, see 127, n. 2.

    7. For Fr. Vincent Ou Tsieng Tsang (or Tchen-Yang, 1916–1972), see *Le Legs spiritual de Vincent Ou, recueilli par François Houang* (Paris: Belles-Lettres, 1973).

humor: "If you become Jesuits, you will no longer be Chinese; at the Oratory, you'll be able to stay Chinese!"[10]

In fact, Father Ou was the son of a Mandarin of the highest rank. He was still alive and had been minister of rites for the last emperor. When his son announced his conversion to him, he had written back: "You have dishonored all our ancestors!" Yet, he was reconciled to his son when, for his ordination, my confrere had a commemorative picture printed on which the aforementioned ancestors were displayed in honorable place.

When he had a headache, he would extract square roots in his head to relax, and his great diversion was to discover the mathematical rules in different games of chance. Besides his mental ability, Father Ou was the most delightful of men. He was extremely refined in feeling and manner, in combination with a priceless sense of humor. He had become the most spiritually charitable Christian and one of the most human as well as religious priests I have ever known. He was an ideal companion and collaborator for our work, which was to prepare for the priesthood a collection of students of all races and multiple languages and cultures. Well-versed like none other in the Chinese classics, while having also become quite a good theologian, he was preparing a work on the Confucian social ideal, particularly the different human relations, as a propaedeutic to charity. His premature death from leukemia, which he accepted with perfect equanimity, unfortunately did not allow him to publish it. Nevertheless, we were able to gather together some of his

8. Fr. Henri de Lubac, SJ (1896–1991); see Bouyer, *Métier*, 202. He was named professor of theology at the Catholic Faculty of Lyon in 1929, where he became interested in the Fathers of the Church; there he founded, with J. Daniélou, the Patristic series *Sources Chrétiennes* in 1941. He also wrote on medieval exegesis, ecclesiology, Buddhism, atheism, etc. His work on human nature and the supernatural led to difficulties with Jesuit authorities in the wake of Pius XII's 1950 Encyclical *Humani generis* warning against a "new theology." Lubac was an active participant at Vatican II and become friends with Karol Wojtyla, who as Pope John Paul II made him Cardinal on 2 February 1983. Father de Lubac invoked his advanced age against the usual title of bishop associated with the cardinalate. Bouyer took great care of him in his old age and would obtain for him to be invited to the abbey of Saint Wandrille over the summer (see chapters seven and fourteen as well as 71, n. 59).

9. Fr. François Houang Ka Tchen (1911–1992) was influenced by French philosopher Jean Wahl (1888–1974) and, in collaboration with Pierre Leyris (see 77, n. 86), translated a treatise of Lao Tzu, the Chinese proponent of Taoism sometime in the sixth to fourth century BC.

10. The Superior General of the Oratory of France, Fr. Gaston Brillet (see 113, n. 49), had brought François Houang and Vincent Ou into the Oratory, just as he did Bouyer. See Étienne Fouilloux, *Une Église en quête de liberté* (Paris: Desclée, 1998), 105.

homilies and lectures into a very beautiful little book. Still, the simple memory of his personality, in which friendship and piety were but one, surpasses all that can be said of him.

The seminary, which was in the *Orangerie* neighborhood near the Rhine and Marne canal, gave the impression of being out in the countryside, or close to it, even though it was very close to the University.[11] Indeed it was set among giant cherry trees that buried us in their silver petals every spring. When one left it one might find oneself on the riverbank within minutes and walk along it, or take an endless walk in the forest beyond it to the north.

I thus found an atmosphere that was not too different from that I had so loved at Juilly. There I also found an ideal peace for the pursuit of my personal endeavors between confessions, spiritual direction and meetings with students. I did have to go to and from Paris once or twice a week. But in the then-exceptional comfort of the grand express train *L'Européen*, that in itself afforded me four or five hours of perfect peace and quiet in which to read with no risk of interruption by a visit or a telephone call.[12]

When I would come back in the middle of the night from my classes at the *Institut catholique*, I found silence and peace and, before succumbing to sleep, heard no sound but the piping call of the electric engines crossing the Kehl Bridge.[13] And, on the morrow, I had at hand the neighboring large park, on the Ill riverbanks. The *Dôme*,[14] as they say in Strasbourg, dominates the view from afar. I was able both to prepare my research and to relax from it by taking a slow walk in this most inspiring, and most relaxing, of settings.

Meanwhile, I had in the preceding years undertaken and finished putting together the first volume of the *History of Christian Spirituality* in which Dom Jean Leclercq and Dom François Vandenbroucke took part along with Father Cognet.[15] I had done so at the invitation of publisher Fernand Aubier, who had become my friend since he had accepted my novel (*Alceste*).[16] This volume, on the New Testament and the Fathers, was sold out nearly immediately. I was to put it back on the drawing board and rework it at leisure for a second edition, and then

---

11. The *Orangerie* is to the northwest of the historic district of Strasbourg. The nineteenth-century canal linking the Marne to the Rhine goes from Vitry-le-François to Strasbourg, a distance of over 190 miles.

12. *L'Européen*, the predecessor of the modern ultra-fast *TGV*, began service in 1957 and at first had only first-class cars.

13. This railroad bridge connects Strasbourg to the German town of Kehl.

14. That is, the 142-meter (466-foot)-tall cathedral. Cathedrals are termed "domes" in Italy, Germany, and eastern Europe generally—including in Strasbourg.

add a third volume on Orthodox, as well as Protestant and Anglican, spirituality plus a copious appendix on Byzantine spirituality to complete the medieval volume by the two Benedictines.

Add to this my *Introduction to Spirituality*,[17] which the publisher Desclée had commissioned, as well as the final composition of my works on theology and on the spirituality of the liturgy. Lastly, as if all this weren't enough, since the Seminary's budget was hard to balance because of the inelegant condition in which it had been handed over to us, I launched a series of religious dictionaries. My confreres generously promised their assistance, but in fact it never materialized except for a few—excellent—articles by Father Birollet for the first volume, on theology, so I put an end to this other enterprise.[18]

And then there was my participation in the preparatory work at the preconciliar Commission for Universities, now that John XXIII was the reigning pontiff.[19] The new nuncio, Bertoli, who had succeeded Ron-

---

15. Louis Bouyer, *Histoire de la spiritualité chrétienne*, 3 vols. (Paris: Aubier Montaigne, 1961–1965), published in English as *A History of Christian Spirituality*, trans. Mary Perkins Ryan et al. (New York: Seabury Press, 1982). The first volume, *The Spirituality of the New Testament and the Fathers* (originally published in 1961) was all Bouyer's, as was volume 3, *Orthodox Spirituality and Protestant and Anglican Spirituality* (first published in 1965). For volume 2, *The Spirituality of the Middle Ages*, he collaborated with two Benedictines: Dom Jean Leclercq (1911–1993), of the Abbey of Clervaux in Luxemburg, and Dom François Vandenbrouke (1912–1971) of the abbey of Mont-César near Louvain in Belgium. A second and enlarged French edition was published in 1966 containing the first part of what was to be a fourth volume with the title *La Spiritualité modern*; it deals with Western spirituality from 1500 to 1650 and is the work of Fr. Louis Cognet (see 149, n. 8). Les Éditions du Cerf republished this second edition in 2011.

16. Jean Thovenot (a.k.a. Louis Bouyer), *Alceste* (Paris: Aubier, 1941); see 132, n. 27.

17. Louis Bouyer, *Introduction à la vie spirituelle* (see 143, n. 67). This work completes Bouyer's trilogy on the three states of life: *Christian Initiation*, trans. J.R. Foster (New York: MacMillan, 1960), on the baptized generally; *The Meaning of Monastic Life*, trans. Kathleen Pond (New York: P.J. Kenedy, 1955), on the religious life; and *Le Sense de la vie sacerdotale* (Tournai: Desclée de Brouwer, 1960), untranslated, on the priesthood.

18. Louis Bouyer, *Dictionnaire theologique* (Tournai: Desclée, 1963), rendered into English as *Dictionary of Theology*, trans. Charles Underhill Quinn (New York: Desclée, 1965). Fr. Michel Birollet (1924–2002) joined the Oratorians in 1947 and was ordained in 1953. He taught philosophy in Strasbourg, 1960–1962, then at the Rocroy-Saint-Léon (see 153, n. 26) at the time this dictionary was being prepared.

19. This was the Commission for Studies and Seminaries, which worked from November 1960 to February 1962; see G. Alberigo and J. Komonchak, eds., *History of Vatican II*, vol. 1, *Announcing and Preparing Vatican Council II. Toward a New Era in Catholicism* (Leuven: Peeters, 1995), 189–92. Bouyer was officially named to it on 24 November 1960; see *Acta Apostolicae Sedis* 52 (1960): 996. John XXIII (Angelo Roncalli, 1881–1963) had been Nuncio to France, 1945–1953, then Patriarch of Venice until his election to the papacy in 1958.

calli,[20] had had me named to it on the recommendation, I think, of Msgr. Blanchet, the rector of the *Institut catholique*.[21]

These years may be called the zenith of my activity at the service of the Church of France. Although what I was teaching did not, or not much, correspond to my actual specialty (or specialties), in Paris, I daresay, I did generally enjoy some esteem and affection on the part of my students. The only drawback, as I was later to notice, was that they may have been too open in stating their feelings. At Strasbourg, too, where my role was only that of formation and spiritual direction, the atmosphere was as encouraging to me as it could be. My relations (in fact our relations as a rule) with the professors of the Theology Department at the University of Strasbourg were excellent. Several of them were more or less old friends of mine, Nédoncelle to begin with, with whom I had undertaken to publish a series of translations of Newman.[22]

Furthermore, I found in Alsace, in a perfectly cordial atmosphere, a good number of my former colleagues in the Lutheran clergy, such as Pastor Bachmann of Saint-Pierre-le-Jeune and his vicar Paul Rigal, who was cousin to my Sancerre friends. This includes even some of my former Protestant theology professors, such as Dean Hauter or Jean Héring, not to forget my colleagues at the Protestant Gymnasium, such as Mugler, now professor of Greek philology at the University.[23]

Above all, though, I was won back by this old medieval town's charm, where the reconciliation of Latin and Germanic culture has found an ideal setting and conditions—although it has to be admitted that we are far from having derived all of its potential benefit. Yet, I wish to underscore all the pleasure and profit I derived in those years

---

20. Roncalli's successor as nuncio in Paris from 1953 to 1959 had been Paolo Marella (1895–1984), to whom Paolo Bertoli (1908–2001) succeeded from 1960 to 1969 before being made cardinal and recalled to Rome as well.

21. Émile Blanchet (1886–1967) was bishop of Saint-Dié in the Vosges region since 1940; he was the rector of the *Institut catholique de Paris*, 1946–1966.

22. Fr. Maurice Nédoncelle (1905–1976), Christian philosopher and professor on the Faculty of Catholic Theology at the University of Strasbourg, where he ultimately became dean and received the title of monsignor. With Bouyer and Henry Tristram, he edited a collection of texts by Newman in translation with commentary; these were published as the *Textes newmaniens* series by Desclée de Brouwer between 1955 and 1961.

23. Fédéric Bachman was born in 1900. Paul Rigal, born in 1913, was about Bouyer's age. For Saint-Pierre-le-Jeune, see 89, n. 27. For Charles Hauter, see 95, n. 62. For Jean Héring, see 97, n. 69. Charles Mugler (1898–1978) was known not only as a Greek specialist but also for his works on Plato: *Platon et la recherché mathématique de son époque* (Strasbourg: P. H. Heitz, 1948) and *La Physique de Platon* (Paris: Klincksiek, 1960). He later taught at the University of Nice.

from my friendship with Msgr. Fischer.[24] He was the archpriest at the cathedral and a personage of signal religious dignity as well as of courteous kindness. He was, for his part, the best example of what such an encounter of the two traditions and cultures ought to produce. It is to his goodwill that I owe a regular ministry of preaching at the cathedral during those three years back in Strasbourg. There were also retreats and recollections at Sainte-Odile, excursions in the Vosges or the Black Forest, and perhaps what I appreciated the most among these escapades out of town: my several stays completely alone in an isolated little country house we had at our disposal just under the crest of the Upper Vosges, very close to the fantastic Hohkoenigsburg castle.[25] From there we overlooked and surveyed the entire Rhine plain, as far as the apocalyptic outline of the hill and town of Altbreisach on the German bank, with its castle and its church's twin towers.[26] Never have I worked and prayed in a more favorable spot, where I would interrupt the hours spent at my desk, which faced that landscape, with walks through the Vosges forest at its most beautiful. All I ever met there were herds of stags and deer that were so unaccustomed to any human presence that they fled from me only at the very moment when I had nearly joined them.

"All this can't last," I would sometimes tell myself. I never did anything to be named, alone of the entire Parisian faculty of theology, on one of the future council's commissions. Nevertheless, I would learn only much later that resentment there had been sharp, among my Jesuit colleagues at least. The first clue of any envy I detected myself was a rather comical incident.

A student had asked to write a dissertation on fourth-century patristic catechesis under my direction; this had been granted to him. Daniélou was to have been its second reader.[27] Since this period was his specialty, I feared that he might be irritated by this and I did everything in my power to convince the candidate to take him as director and me only as reviewer. The student in question persisted, arguing from the well-known fact that Daniélou, whose occupations were even more

---

24. Msgr. Eugène Fischer (1898–1984), archpriest of the Cathedral of Strasbourg, 1941–1966, then vicar-general of the diocese.

25. Hohkoenigsburg castle dates to the twelfth century; Kaiser Wilhelm II (1859–1941) restored it when Alsace was part of Germany (1871–1918). It is perched in the foothills of the Vosges and overlooks the Rhine valley.

26. Altbreisach (in French *Vieux-Brisach*), now simply Breisach, is on the German right bank of the Rhine, as opposed to Neuf-Brisach (in German *Neubreisach*) on the French left bank, which was built by Vauban (1633–1707) as an ideal fortified town.

27. For Daniélou, see 141, n. 62.

diversified than mine, didn't pay much attention to the works he was supposed to oversee.

He produced a dissertation which, without being brilliant, was honorable. Having obtained my approval he submitted it to Daniélou, who straightaway declared that it was absolutely worthless and couldn't even be redrafted. This was so absurd that I smelled a rat. Now, the next year the dear boy who had received this treatment asked me for my advice. I simply told him to change the title and to bring his work back to Daniélou, although this time taking him as director, and to make any modification that he might suggest. Actually, as he told me, Daniélou asked for none and, believing this work to be altogether different from what had been submitted to him the first time around (but which it is difficult to believe that he had been able to read closely), he declared himself completely satisfied by it. Our candidate, whom I had prudently stopped advising in an official capacity, was therefore granted the doctorate—with honors.

Other clues were to follow. Daniélou—again—was in charge of the fifth-year patristic seminars, but he led them only in the vaguest meaning of the term. As a result, a considerable number of students asked me to conduct other seminars in my specialty, the history of spirituality, dealing with the same authors, while they would continue to attend Daniélou's. I accepted only after the faculty, including the Jesuits, accepted without my piping a word or doing a thing to push the project. Yet, when I turned in my grades to the secretary, Father Lecler, SJ,[28] he kindly informed me that since these seminars had been added on top of the regular curriculum, they were not subject to grades. This naturally caused an uproar among the students. I tried to calm them as best I could, having made up my mind to let the matter quietly drop. That is what I could not do, for they insisted on continuing to work with me, even without benefitting from it in terms of grades or honors.

Despite these early warning signs of trouble, I admit that I was surprised when I read in *Études*,[29] shortly after the publication of my *Introduction to Spirituality*,[30] an article by—Daniélou, declaring my book to be absolutely unacceptable.[31] He said that it tended to impose the so-

28. Fr. Joseph Lecler, SJ (1895–1988), Church historian.

29. The French Jesuit scholarly journal, published in Paris.

30. Louis Bouyer, *Introduction to Spirituality* (see 143, n. 67).

31. Jean Daniélou, "À propos d'une introduction à la vie spirituelle," *Études* 308 (1961): 270–75. The same journal published Bouyer's rebuttal in the next issue, ibid., 411–15, to which Daniélou wrote a one-paragraph response stating that he did not wish to *prolonger une polémique*, ibid., 415.

called (by Bremond, actually) "French school" of spirituality, that is to say, as Daniélou specified, that of my congregation. I was all the more flabbergasted that within the Oratory itself I had always insisted that we ought to imitate not the actual achievements of Bérulle, or, especially, Condren, but rather their declared intentions: namely, as Bossuet used to say, to have no spirituality but the Church's.

In fact, my book sought simply to encourage the return to scripture, to the Fathers, to the liturgy and, more generally, to the most traditional sources. Not only were French Oratorian authors barely mentioned in it, but I had given, as we shall soon see, a very positive presentation of Saint Ignatius's spiritual exercises themselves.[32] I had emphasized what is far more broadly and deeply traditional in them than in other spiritualities of the time, which place greater stock on psychological considerations.

In fact, up to that point, not only had all the reviews been exceptionally favorable to me, but I had just received a long letter from my colleague and former teacher, Father Paul Henry, SJ, that was entirely warm and laudatory.[33] Yet, I soon received (as soon, that is, as that issue of *Études* was published) two witnesses that singularly revealed not only the "Good Fathers'" power in general but also the terror that the slightest decision from their authorities could inspire. Father Gautier, PSS,[34] who had just sung my praises more than anyone in the *Semaine religieuse* out of Paris,[35] was literally panic-stricken when he called my superior on the telephone, asking that neither I nor my confreres should make use of his article. And then I received, by the next mail, a second letter from poor Father Henry; it was even more devastated and totally disowned the first one he had sent.

I'll skip further details, except one, because it is particularly revealing. The publishing house Desclée, which had commissioned this volume to

32. The Spiritual Exercises of Saint Ignatius Loyola (1491–1556), founder of the Society of Jesus (the Jesuits), were originally the notes he took down during a retreat at Manresa near Barcelona in 1522. He gave them their final form in 1544. Since then they have been the cornerstone of Jesuit spirituality, which Henri Bremond (see 52–53, n. 25) contrasted to the "French school" of spirituality in his *A Literary History of Religious Thought in France from the Wars of Religion down to Our Times*, trans. K. L. Montgomery (New York: Macmillan, 1928).

33. For Fr. Paul Henry, see 140, n. 61.

34. Fr. Jean Gautier (1896–1974) was ordained as a Sulpician priest; he specialized in the history of his order and in seventeenth-century spirituality. For the Sulpicians, see 129, n. 14.

35. *La Semaine religieuse, revue du culte et des bonnes oeuvres*, a Parisian Catholic weekly running from 1853 to 1966.

replace the manual by M. Tanquerey, SS,[36] that no one wanted any more, was obviously afraid of a severe financial loss. It therefore organized a debate between Daniélou and me in the presence of what is called "The Catholic Press."

I let him vent his grievances. He did so, visibly awkwardly, but insisting that my book was in fact itself an attack on the Jesuits and their influence, and that it obviously called for a defense on their part. At this point I read all that my book said about Saint Ignatius and his *Exercises*, and asked him whether that was what he found unacceptable. He jumped on it and declared that it was nothing more than a wretched caricature.

When he had finished on the subject, I kept to observing that, considering that my book was intended to replace Tanquerey, and since I had found this particular passage of his book difficult to improve on, I had merely kept it as is—especially since I was aware of a review of that manual by Father de Grandmaison, SJ,[37] that was very laudatory in general, but had praised this particular page to the skies. Knowing my business, I had brought the article in question along, and I read it out. It is needless to describe the amusement of the audience—and poor Daniélou's dismay.[38]

Nevertheless, although the journalists in attendance who made a report of this meeting said that I had done well, it is significant that none of them dared to breathe a word on that incident.

After this, with Father Tourde's (my above-mentioned superior general) total agreement, I purely and simply resigned from both my chairs.[39]

At this point there occurred something I had not expected and which very much touched me. My non-Jesuit colleagues on the faculty unanimously became so angry with Daniélou and his confreres that they managed to get the faculty (including the Jesuits!) to vote for a motion that was as humiliating for them as it was honorable for me, asking me

---

36. Adolphe Tanquerey, Sulpician (1854–1932), *Précis de théologie ascétique et mystique* (Paris: Desclée, 1923–1924) was the reference work on mysticism in seminaries until Vatican II. Its English version is *The Spiritual Life: A Treatise on Ascetical and Mystical Theology*, trans. Herman Branderis (Tournai: Desclée, 1930).

37. Fr. Léonce de Grandmaison, SJ (1868–1927), directed *Études* and founded the review *Recherches de sciences religieuses* in 1910.

38. A photograph of Bouyer and Daniélou together, taken on the occasion of this debate, shows the former smiling and the latter bowing to him. See Bouyer, *Métier*, facing p. 112.

39. In 1962.

to withdraw my resignation. I had no desire to do so, but not wishing to be ungrateful, I finally—and regretfully—consented.

Nevertheless, a few months later, now that the first volume of my *History of Christian Spirituality* had been published,[40] it was now the *Revue d'ascétique et mystique* of the Toulouse Jesuits that produced a very long attack. It was far more deeply researched than Daniélou's, and bore the signature of Father Olphe-Gaillard, even though he was blind; it had clearly been written by someone else.[41] No sooner had it been published than a great number of offprints with a special binding were produced and graciously sent to anyone having anything to do with the formation of priests or religious in France.[42]

This time these gentlemen had pulled out all the stops not only with an impudent bad faith, but also with some imprudence, as they were doubtless sure that not one reader in ten would check up on their claims. Among other allegations, I was accused of providing no references, and of ignoring all scholarly works on the topic—even though all one had to do was to open the book and skim through it to be sure of the opposite. Better yet, the better to condemn me, they once again brought up my other book, *Introduction*, to declare that the pure intellectualism of my conception of spirituality allegedly was clearly to be seen when one read what I said there about prayer, whereas I ought to have started from its being essentially "a conversation with God"—as if that very phrase had not been precisely the definition I had given myself! These gentlemen had given themselves so little trouble that they thought they could overwhelm me by writing that the strengths and weaknesses of my various works in this field were explained when one recalled that I was the author of that other book, which was as superficial as it was brilliant: *Bible et Liturgie*. They had forgotten, doubtless in

40. See 143, n. 67.

41. Michel Olphe-Gaillard, SJ (1900–1985), and J. Kirchmeyer, SJ, "Une nouvelle Histoire de la spiritualité chrétienne," *Revue d'ascétique et mystique* 37 (1961): 213–35. The authors admit, in their conclusion (p. 234), that their judgment may seem severe. Their journal published Bouyer's response (ibid., 528–30), and his letter responding to their invitation to express himself further (ibid., 531). The review's authors ended the exchange by writing that "the tone of these two letters takes us beyond the outlook of a scholarly journal and it would be fruitless to refute their content" (ibid). For a more impartial review of Bouyer's book, see H. Crouzel, "Spiritualité patristique," *Bulletin de littérature ecclésiastique*, 3rd series, 62, no. 1 (January–March, 1961): 12–15.

42. Although the editors of the *Revue d'ascétique et mystique* had mentioned these off-prints to allege that they were destined only to the journal's subscribers (who, as Bouyer caustically retorted in his letter back to them, would already have had the review in their own issue of the journal), Olphe-Gaillard and Kirchmeyer claimed that "the dissemination of our article is merely a product of Father Bouyer's imagination" (ibid.).

their haste, that not only was this book not by me, but that its author was Daniélou himself, their honorable confrere and the first one to have attacked me![43]

After this I was content with finishing up the current academic year, then renewing my resignation in terms that excluded any possibility of withdrawing it. My student, Father Marchasson,[44] *agrégé* in history,[45] was elected to succeed to me in the chair of history. Father Cognet applied for the chair of spirituality, along with the Institut's direction since it was bound to it. With that Port-Royal apologist,[46] the good fathers, of course, fell from the frying pan right into the fire! At first they hollered. But all of my other colleagues (except one: Father Jarry,[47] who was as flat as he was enormous, as Bishop Andrieu-Guitrancourt once observed)[48] let them understand that they could take it or leave it: they would vote for no one else. So they had to come to that. Alas! the poor and dear father, elected dean on top of it when Daniélou obtained the cardinalship after the Council, died of overwork![49]

It was only then, amid the chaos that was now beginning to spread, that the Jesuits finally got for themselves the chair and the Institute of Spirituality that their superiors had evidently never stopped coveting. They ran them so badly, what with those they had delegated to this responsibility defrocking one after the other, that within a few years nothing was left of their conquest.

As for me, this is the point when I started teaching at Notre Dame. I have already mentioned what circumstances led me to withdraw from it—along with all the serious instructors who had also allowed themselves to be drawn there. But the lectures I had to give here and there

---

43. Jean Daniélou, *Bible et liturgie, la théologie biblique des sacrements et des fêtes d'après les Pères de l'Église* (Paris: Cerf, 1951); in English *The Bible and the Liturgy*, Liturgical Studies 3 (Notre Dame: University of Notre Dame Press, 1956). The Toulouse Jesuits probably had in mind Bouyer's *La Bible et l'Évangile* (Paris: Cerf, 1952), which also promoted a spirituality rooted in scripture and the liturgy. Actually Olphe-Gaillard committed this error in his (also negative) review of Bouyer's *Introduction to the Spiritual Life* (ibid., 371–75), a review that takes up many of Daniélou's criticisms.

44. Yves Marchasson (1920–1992), who had just obtained a doctorate from the Angelicum in 1961. He would become dean of the *Institut catholique*, 1970–1983, made monsignor, and then vicar general for Oriental Catholics living in France.

45. *Agrégé* means that he successfully passed a State competitive examination in the field, allowing him to teach it.

46. Cognet was a specialist on Jansenism, which the Jesuits had so fiercely combatted in its day; see 149, n. 9.

47. Canon Eugène Jarry (1900–1974), Professor of Church History.

48. For Bishop Andrieu-Guitrancourt, see 138, n. 54.

49. Cognet was elected to that chair in June 1962. He died in 1969.

throughout the United States had obtained for me a notoriety to which I have never had, or ever will have, the equivalent in France. I received invitations for elsewhere yet: Mainz, in Germany, at the Institute für Europäische Studien, directed by Lortz, the famous Reformation historian; Lovanium (in the former Belgian Congo); Bristol, England. In the following years, during which I was decidedly faithful to the United States, I devoted a few semesters to a pleasant women's college run by Dominican Sisters until, like so many others, they fell victim to a superior who had fallen on her head. I then twice accepted a visiting professorship at one of the oldest universities in New England: Brown University, in Providence, Rhode Island.[50] This allowed me to discover that lovely city, as well as all her sisters: Portland, Newport, Concord.[51] I was the only Catholic professor on an excellent Protestant faculty and was given the most attentive and pleasant reception there. I also met, among others, another visiting professor, a supremely distinguished Brahmin. He was married to a Frenchwoman and spoke our language, and English, without accent: Batacharia Kamelashwara.[52] At the height of a fad for all sorts of bargain-basement Hinduism, he was able to protect his students from it far better than any Christian minister or priest! It is notably there that I made a first outline of what was to become my book *Cosmos*,[53] and I had the surprise of finding out that the physics and chemistry students were the easiest to convince that modern science is far from being able to provide us with the last word on the mystery of the supposedly material universe.

A little later, General Rodney Smith (last commander of the SHAPE, and former Brown student) was to present me with a ravishing engraving of its oldest buildings.[54] They are so characteristic of what one of my most charming colleagues in Providence, a Lutheran theologian who was far more Catholic than many post-conciliar Catholics, called the

50. Brown University was founded in 1764. It was the first college in British America to admit students regardless of their Christian denomination.

51. Portland, Maine; Newport, Rhode Island; Concord, Massachusetts.

52. Batacharia Kamelashwara (or Kamaleswar Bhattacharya) was born in 1928 in present-day Bangladesh. He went to France in 1955 as specialist in Sanskrit (the historical language of the cultivated élite in India) and Buddhism. He stayed in France as researcher at the *Centre National de la recherche scientifique*, while teaching in many universities elsewhere as visiting professor, including Brown in 1967–1969.

53. See 55, n. 36.

54. Rodney Smith (1902–1997), military engineer and telecommunications specialist. He ran Radio Free Europe during the Cold War. SHAPE (Supreme Headquarters Allied Powers Europe) is NATO's headquarters, located at Rocquencourt (thirteen miles west of Paris) from 1944 until 1966 when French President Charles de Gaulle (1890-1970) withdrew France from NATO. SHAPE then moved to Belgium.

Greco-Baptist style! More generally, I must say that until then I had never encountered in a Catholic faculty so trusting and kind a welcome as that of these representatives of the most varied Reformation churches, even though I was a Protestant convert to Catholicism. This is an experience I was to renew more than once since. It was the case at Oxford when F. L. Cross, mentioned above,[55] the founder of the International Conference on Patristic Studies,[56] invited me to give a series of lectures in his capacity as Lady Margaret Professor of Divinity.[57] Likewise, as I have already mentioned, this happened when I was chosen by the Glasgow faculty, which is in principle Calvinist, for the Alexander Robertson Lecture. (This invitation must have made its ultra-rich Protestant namesake, who had endowed it in the seventeenth century, turn over in his grave, as he probably never imagined that an agent of the Great Babylon might someday draw on the interest of his sumptuous gift!)[58]

I cannot, however, leave Providence without recounting the joy I had in meeting Austin Warren there.[59] He is an admirable analyst both of the "Caroline Divines" and of the Puritans of old in New England, their contemporaries. I shall never forget the evenings I spent with him and his wife in his exquisite old house, on the edge of the forest along the Narragansett River, amid his library's wealth of all these "worthies," first editions from either side of the Atlantic.

Later I was called to the Catholic University of America in Washington.[60] There I taught three years in a row. This provided me with the excellent friendship of the French parish's rector, Father Réginald de Rocquois, OP,[61] one of the most apostolic priests I have ever met.

---

55. See 173, n. 63.

56. These convene every four years; the first one took place in 1951.

57. Lady Margaret Beaufort (1443–1509), the mother of Henry VIII (1457–1509), founded the chairs of divinity at Oxford and Cambridge.

58. Alexander Robertson is a rather common name in Scotland; this one is the benefactor who endowed this chair for theological lectures in 1640.

59. Austin Warren (1899–1986); his wife was named Antonia. After a distinguished career he had retired from the University of Michigan in 1968 and lived in Providence, Rhode Island, from 1970. He was a literary critic and his *Theory of Literature* (New York: Harcourt, Brace & World, 1956) was the reference for the New Criticism. His principal works on the Puritans are *New England Saints* (Ann Arbor: University of Michigan Press, 1956) and *New England Consciousness* (Ann Arbor: University of Michigan Press, 1966).

60. This university was founded by the US bishops in 1887 with the support of Leo XIII (1810–1893).

61. Réginald de Rocquois, OP (1922–1992), pastor of Saint-Louis-de-France, the French-speaking parish in Washington, 1968–1986. An eminently literary man, he had directed the short-lived review *L'Esprit des lettres*, 1954–1957.

Beyond that, he had a peerless culture and distinction. French overseas parishes are, generally speaking, pitiful. This one, on the other hand, had become exemplary thanks to him. Furthermore he had been able to turn his delightful residence into a gathering place for all French-speaking foreigners (without forgetting a number of African embassies, which were generally kept at arm's length), and also for the elite of the upper echelons in the federal government: the army, the navy, and all the great international institutions. This was in the quiet Friendship Heights neighborhood, near the beautiful Episcopal cathedral[62] just above the old city of Georgetown, which is so picturesque.[63] I was his constant guest during those Washington years, and found him to be an incomparable friend. Thanks to him, I was able make the most precious friendships, be they French or American.

Add to this that in neighboring Maryland, at a short distance, I had reconnected with my former student John Quinn, whom I have mentioned above.[64] He was now on the administration of Mount Saint Mary's Seminary, which is surely one of the best, not only in the USA but in the whole Catholic world.[65]

My best colleagues at the university, such as the famous German patrologist Johannes Quasten,[66] were leaving as they reached retirement age. Likewise the Archbishop, Cardinal Baum, with whom I had become friends, was called back to Rome.[67] And so I gave up the idea of continuing any further my teaching at "Catholic U.," as they say. Before accepting a new call, this time from California, I agreed to teach a semester in that seminary. The opportunity of finding John Quinn there appealed to me, not to mention the charming setting of the Catoctin Mountains and their forests. The whole place is marked with French remembrances, since the founder of Mount Saint Mary's was Bruté, from Brittany, a close friend of Lamennais's and one of the first bishops of the United States.[68]

---

62. The National Cathedral at 3101 Wisconsin Avenue in Washington, DC.

63. Georgetown was founded in 1751 as a small port town on the Potomac River. It was eventually incorporated into the District of Columbia. Its charm is due to its brick buildings and cobblestone streets.

64. For John Quinn see 166.

65. For Mount Saint Mary's Seminary, see 166, n. 22.

66. Johannes Quasten (1900–1987) taught at the Catholic University of America, 1938–1970. He is best known for his *Patrology* (Westminster, MD: Newman Press, 1950).

67. Cardinal Archbishop William Baum (born 1926) was Archbishop of Washington, 1973–1980.

68. Simon Gabriel Bruté de Rémur, SS (1779–1839), left for the USA as a missionary in 1810, worked at Mount St. Mary's from 1812, was sent farther west and was consecrated

Now, however, I need to go back in time, to explain how back in France I left the theology faculty of Paris shortly before leaving the International Seminary of Strasbourg as well.

This was not the only place where my colleagues and I had encountered some local difficulty. Quite on the contrary: after three years our success among both the students and the university and clergy of Strasbourg became so obvious that our colleagues teaching at Mounsoult suspected that we wanted to make them redundant. In their view, the international seminary's newfound appeal threatened them with suppression, and, naturally, they predicted the inevitable extinction of the congregation itself.

This absurd business came on the heels of my recent experience in Paris, as I was nearing fifty years of age and had been most strenuously overworking myself for the Oratory. As if it hadn't been enough for me to dedicate myself to all that had been imposed on me, I had also worn myself thin to provide it with rather considerable sums.[69] All the while the majority of my confreres, those at Montsoult to begin with, lived a life of ease with very little work and without lifting a finger to earn a penny. I admit that all of this suddenly snapped my good will, which, until then, might have seemed inexhaustible.

I told Father Tourde that under these conditions I now wished finally to devote the rest of my time and of my energies to producing the theological work I had projected for so long and had only barely put a hand to. This would be on the basis of what I was making in America in a few months of teaching, which I found more congenial than all of the other responsibilities I had accepted up until then and where, unlike in France, I found only encouragement.

In any event, providential circumstances seemed to be falling into place for me to do so under the best possible conditions. One of my former Paris students, Father Marcel Lelégard, a great archeologist, was in the process of restoring the old Norbertine Abbey of La Lucerne, at a stone's throw from Avranches and Mont Saint-Michel.[70] He wanted to turn it into a spiritual and liturgical center. At the same time, the little

---

Bishop of Vincennes, Indiana, in 1834. At the time this newly erected diocese covered much of the northeastern portion of the immense territory that had been French in the eighteenth century. Lamennais (118, n. 18) took a great interest in the missions of America and encouraged his friend and fellow Breton Bruté to write to him; they kept up their correspondence even after Lamennais's apostasy.

69. These considerable sums may be supposed to be the remainder after expenses of Bouyer's royalties on his books (including their foreign-language versions) and of his salaries in his various teaching positions.

parish of Anctoville, a dependency of Notre-Dame de Granville[71] that our former superior general Father Duprey had accepted for his retirement, was now vacant as a result of his death.[72] The Dean of Granville was offering it to me. I settled in La Lucerne with my books, and at the same time was responsible for the weekly Mass in the little church of Anctoville and had the use of the rectory. Here, during the time when I was not teaching in America, I finally would be able to combine a life of meditation and theological studies with a truly pastoral ministry as I had always desired. Furthermore, this would be in a rural setting, which I increasingly felt I needed for my spiritual life and, simply, for my life. So far it had been broken up into multiple occupations, each of them more absorbing than tiring. Father Tourde and his counsel raised no objection to this project, so long as it was understood that I would keep my ties to the congregation and the pied-à-terre I had kept at Villa Montmorency while my regular residence had been in Strasbourg.

When all these arrangements had been made, in a brief length of time, I may again say: *laqueus contritus est et nos liberati sumus.*[73]

I was finally going to live in peace and quiet in a humane conjunction of pastoral activity, meditative solitude, and theological work, which until then had been "the beautiful dream with which one enchants oneself." Mind you, it had taken only half a century's worth of patience to get there! Of course, I had enough life-experience to suspect that difficulties would not thereby miraculously come to an end. But it is one thing to lead the life to which one feels called and for which one feels equipped, along with inevitable difficulties; it is quite another to have, along with the very same difficulties, an existence at sixes and sevens in which the only thing one cannot get around to undertaking is precisely the one which one has always felt especially made to do.

When in June 1963 I moved into the Abbey at La Lucerne, I had few illusions about the chances its owner's grandiose projects had of reaching completion. He was Father Marcel Lelégard, my former student and

70. R. Marcel Lelégard (1925–1994) had studied at the *Institut catholique*, 1947–1949, where he befriended both Bouyer and Daniélou (see 141, n. 62). He was conservator of antiquities and artwork for the *département* of the Manche (Normandy) from 1963. He had created an association for the preservation of this abbey in 1954 and acquired it in 1959. Its restoration was awarded the *Chefs-d'œuvre en péril* ("Endangered Masterpieces") prize in 1966.

71. Anctoville-sur-Boscq is immediately east of Granville and about eight miles northwest of La Lucerne.

72. Fr. Maurice Duprey (1893–1963) had founded the Oratorian school Saint-Martin de Pontoise (see 121, n. 38).

73. This quotation of Ps 124:7 picks up the titles of chapters seven and eight above.

kind friend. I had trouble seeing him as a restorer of Canons Regular adapted to the needs of a Church that was about to undergo a renovation, be it conciliar or otherwise. Indeed, I knew that, besides his all-encompassing passion for archeology, he also was the most perfect individualist there ever was. For the time being, the use of the Anctoville rectory and the responsibility of Parish services ensured the independence that allowed me to reside at La Lucerne on a regular basis, and especially to have a place conducive to pursuing my work. I did not, therefore, have to depend on the completion of that imaginative man's projects; his dreams were too wondrous ever to go beyond the draft stage.[74]

Above all this was a stop-gap measure for me, before finding a house available nearby or even having one built as I had been considering for a while.

In fact, once I was living in La Lucerne, I soon was quite certain that even making my dwelling merely fit to be lived in was the least concern of my amusing and fanciful but not very reliable friend, however great a scholar and excellent a priest he was—in his own way, of course!

Nevertheless, I was able to have one of the old monastery's rooms converted into a splendid and convenient office-cum-library at my own expense. The monastery dated to the twelfth century, except for the seventeenth-century transom windows. I also made my bedroom out of a tiny, but very pleasant, and above all very easy to heat, room at the end of the same building. The rest of the building, despite a few half-hearted attempts at restoration, remained (and to this day remains) in a state of dilapidation and of indescribable disorder. The only thing to have progressed since then is the abbey church's restoration. As soon as its choir was ready, we had some rather beautiful services there, and before that in a little chapel that had been preserved more or less intact. The people of that district were quite assiduous in their attendance.

I saw, on the one hand, that Father Lelégard did nothing to help me find a house of my own (fearing, wrongly, that I might leave him), while on the other hand the bishop (Bishop Guyot)[75] explained to me that I was providing a counter-witness by keeping up a parish such as Anctoville (where everyone went to Mass). Since I wished to keep an independent home to retire to as I pleased and entertain whomever I wished, I had to seek that last refuge elsewhere.

---

74. In fact restoration was completed in 2003, nine years after Lelégard's death and a year before Bouyer's.

75. Louis-Jean-Frédéric Cardinal Guyot (1905–1988), priest of the diocese of Bordeaux, then Bishop of Coutances (Avranches), 1950–1966. He then became Bishop of Toulouse and was named Cardinal in 1973.

A few years earlier I had been invited to preach the Quimper priests' retreat. I had found a fascinating beauty in that Breton place, towards the end of the Brest harbor on an outcropping of the Crozon peninsula: Landévennec.[76] When the Abbot of Kergonan invited me to give his monks a few lectures on the reform of the Eucharistic liturgy, I found my chance to push on again as far as that *Ultima Thule*[77] and to chat with the monks of the other monastery that live out there.

I soon became friends with the abbot, and even more so with his prior, Dom Laurent Gougay.[78] Thanks to him, I discovered a house for sale at the very top of the cliff overlooking the monastery. It was very simple, but in an incomparable location. It looked over the confluence of the Aulne River and the bay. I could have the island of Térénez right across me, or rather beneath me, and, in the distance, the Menez Hom[79] emerging from the surrounding forest.

I didn't hesitate much to buy it. From that point on for the next ten-odd years I would alternate between these two retreats: La Lucerne in the Anvranches area and Landévennec in deepest Brittany.

When not in America, in England, in Africa, or in Spain as a visiting professor, be it at Notre Dame, Indiana, or Brown University in Providence, Rhode Island, or Lovanium, Zaïre, or Bristol, or Oxford, or later the Catholic University of America, Washington D.C., or even in Salamanca, I lived with one foot in Lower Normandy and the other in Finistère. As a general rule, I stayed in La Lucerne to prepare my books,

76. Landévennec is at the end of a small curved and craggy peninsula at the northern entrance of the Crozon peninsula separating the Brest harbor to the north from Douarnenez to the south at the western extremity of Brittany. On its southern side Landévennec is bounded by a bend in the Aulne River downstream from Châteaulin, which creates the island of Térénez at high tide; after Landévennec the Aulne flows into the Faou estuary at the eastern end of the Brest harbor. Bouyer would buy a cottage nearby named Gwel Kaër ("Beautiful outlook" in the Breton language) with a view over the isle of Térénez with the 1,000-foot-high Menez Hom hill in the distance to the south. The ruins of a fifth-century abbey remain, and a new abbey of the Subiaco congregation was built a little higher up after World War II.

77. Two Benedictine abbeys of the Solesmes congregation (see 153, n. 25) were Kergonan: the men's in 1897 and the women's in 1898. They are now in Plouharnel in the *département* of Morbihan on the south coast of Brittany. *Ultima Thule* is the name medieval mapmakers would give to what lay beyond the known world to the north and west of Europe, following Virgil (see 80, n. 98), *Georgics* 1.30. Bouyer here takes up this term as an equivalent to *finis terrarum*, "the end of the world," which became *Finisterre* in Spanish and *Finistère* in French.

78. Laurent Gougay (1912–1969), ordained priest for the diocese of Quimper et Léon in 1938, joined the abbey of Kerbénéat (founded in 1844 in northern Finistère) in 1944. Its monks rebuilt Landévennec in 1950. He was prior, 1962–1969.

79. For Menez Hom see n. 76.

since that is where I had the more technical books in my library, which covered the walls of my grandiose office in the shadow of an enormous cedar (one of the first to have been shipped to France, probably). On the beautiful days at the end of the spring or in the summer, I would also spend whole afternoons with a book at the end of the long lawn between the abbey and the forest. Raising my eyes once and again upon the serene composition of this harmonious house, between the tall oaks and chestnut trees from which the abbey's lantern-tower jutted out, I had meadows to my left, watered by one of the Thar's tributaries and, on my right, the aqueduct. It was capped with a long wooded crest ending in a stream; Father proudly called it "our river." It then gave out into the Channel at Kairon, just a few kilometers away.

But whenever I reached the final draft of one or the other of my two dogmatic trilogies,[80] or simply whenever I wished to relax or make a retreat, I headed for my perch in Brittany.

There I would be, at the top of my cliff. It plummeted down into the Aulne River valley, with woods as far as the eye can see and, in the distance, the Breton mountain where, they say, King Mark of Cornwall is buried.[81] At first, I was so captivated by the beauty of the place that I had trouble tearing myself away from it. Soon enough, however, it

---

80. The first of these two trilogies is on Creation and Salvation: *The Seat of Wisdom: An Essay on the Place of the Virgin Mary in Christian Theology*, trans. A.V. Littledale (New York: Pantheon Books, 1962); *The Church of God* (see 207, n. 2); and *Cosmos* (see 55, n. 36). The second is *Knowledge of God*: *The Eternal Son: A Theology of the Word of God and Christology*, trans. Simone Inkel and John F. Laughlin (Huntington, IN: Our Sunday Visitor, 1978); *The Invisible Father: Approaches to the Mystery of the Divinity*, trans. Hugh Gilbert (Petersham, MA: St. Bede's Publications, 1999); *Le consolateur: Esprit-Saint et vie de grâce* (Paris: Les Éditions du Cerf, 1980), untranslated. For a third trilogy (Mystery, Knowledge, Wisdom), a fourth (Monasticism, Priesthood, Baptism), and an unfinished fifth (Spirituality), see Jean Duchesne, *Louis Bouyer* (Perpignan: Artège, 2011), 18–22.

81. King Mark (*Marc'h* in Breton) is a mythological hero of both British Cornwall and Cornouaille in southern Brittany. His remains are on the slopes of the Menez Hom (see 201, n. 76), the "Breton mountain." Tristan and Ysolde, the famous legendary lovers, were his nephew and wife respectively. He had a horse's ears (as did King Midas in Greek myth), of which Merlin rid him in an episode of the Arthurian legend. He had acquired these equine appendages when a doe he was hunting turned out to be Dahut the magician and daughter of King Gradlon of Ys, a city that was protected by seawalls in the bay of Douarnenez, south of the Crozon peninsula (see ibid.). The devil seduced Dahut and obtained from her the keys to the levees, which he used to flood the town of Ys. Dahut's father King Gradlon fled with her on horseback, but Saint Winwaloe (see 203, n. 84) warned him that he must abandon his daughter for his own safety. Gradlon ended his days at the abbey of Landévennec and, according to legend, is buried there. Bouyer never failed to regale his guests with all these stories, as well as with the legends of Arthur and the Holy Grail, up at his cottage, Gwel Kaër (see 201, n. 76).

became the best stimulant to my reflections, for its preternatural serenity seemed to clarify them. If I was ever able to come out with some works that helped a certain number of minds to think over anew the central truths of the faith within the context of our time's difficulties and opportunities, it is above all to these two beneficial and complementary refuges that I owe it.

As deeply as I regretted losing my little Anctoville parish, at Landévenec I did get to preach and celebrate one of the two Sunday Masses. This was in the parish church which, along with its enclosure, was located on a spit of land jutting into the bay, like a tiny Mont Saint Michel at the mercy of the sea.[82] The rector there, an old sailor late come to the priesthood, gave me a welcome as only the Bretons know how. At the abbey I found, besides the friendship of the prior—an excellent religious, musician, and poet—an equally fraternal hospitality. Furthermore, I soon had one of my most enriching experiences as a priest. By this I mean that a very simple monk turned to my ministry as a confessor, Dom Jean Abalea, in whom I soon discovered a saint of old.[83] He was to die of cancer, nearly under my very eyes. He was fully lucid and perfectly given over to the divine will. His funeral, in the monks' cemetery that looked over the sea under a canopy of trees hundreds of years old, was the equivalent of what popular canonizations must have been in the days of Saint Winwaloe, the abbey's founder,[84] with all the village singing the *gwerz*[85] for the dead.

My comings and goings between my two stays, most often in one or another kind friend's car, also afforded me many a visit to Arthurian legend-places, such as the forest of Brocéliande[86] with its Barenton fountain[87] and Merlin's steps,[88] Diana's manor and Lancelot's

---

82. The parish church of Notre-Dame-de-Landévennec dates to the seventeenth century and is near the former abbey on the waterfront deep in the bay of Brest. It has an enclosed cemetery.

83. Dom Jean Abaléa (1908–1969) had entered Kerbénéat in 1936.

84. St. Winwaloe, son of Fragan of Dumnonia (modern Devon and Wales) and of Gwen the Three-Breasted, founded the Abbey of Landévennec in the early sixth century; he died there in 532.

85. A *gwerz* is a Breton song relating in mournful couplets mythological and tragic legends.

86. The forest of Paimpont, about twenty-four miles west of Rennes in Brittany.

87. This fountain is where Merlin the sorcerer and adviser to King Arthur met the "Lady of the Lake" (she lived in a "crystal palace" in a pool), the fairy Vivian, who would ultimately be his undoing.

88. Merlin's tomb, actually the remnants of a Neolithic covered alley.

lake.[89] Upon leaving its Vale of No Return,[90] I met the excellent rector of the church that he had turned into a shrine to the Grail.[91] Closer to my Breton cubbyhole, I often also walked through the desert of Anaon, between Saint-Michel de Braspart, the Signal of Toussaines, and the Roc'h Trevezel where some have located the vanishing castle that Percival visited.[92]

All the enchantments of Brittany kept me there for only too few years, alas! As a consequence of accidents to my retinas which threatened a retinal detachment, specialists forbad me to live any longer in that retreat over fifty kilometers away from the nearest hospital. They said that I might need an operation at the drop of a hat, and that it would be pointless after so long a trip.

Happily, Father Lelégard, who, I think, was biting his fingers for not having spent more energy to detain me within his exclusive sphere of influence, discovered at precisely this moment a little Louis XVI-era house at a stone's throw from La Lucerne, tucked away in the woods. I was able to acquire it for a low price, given its dilapidation. I sold my

---

89. Vivian's underwater palace was reputed to have once belonged to Diana, the pagan goddess of the hunt. There she raised a foundling, Lancelot, who was to become the most fervent of the knights that King Arthur gathered around the Round Table.

90. Where the fairy Morgan, King Arthur's half-sister, having herself been disappointed in love would keep all unfaithful knights prisoner. Sir Lancelot would put an end to her spells.

91. The Grail is a cup with magical (or miraculous) powers. All knights, starting with Percival (according to the troubadour Christian of Troyes in the late twelfth century), are on a quest to find it. In a blend of pagan and Christian story-telling, it became the chalice used to catch some of the blood poured out of Christ's side during the crucifixion (Jn 19:34). The legends relate that his passion for King Arthur's wife Guinevere distracted Lancelot from his quest for the Grail. It was left for Galahad the Pure, the son of Lancelot's (mistaken) union with Elaine the daughter of the mysterious Fisher King Pelles who possessed the Grail, to behold it—and die from the sight.

92. This would be the Wounded King's castle where Percival saw the bloody lance and the Holy Grail. In his pseudonymous novel *Prélude à l'Apocalpyse* (see 150, n. 11), Bouyer speaks of "the most impressive desert in all of Brittany, where the ancient Cimmerian peoples [Bouyer means the ancient Celts] located Anaon, in other words their Hell, a hollow dug out between the Roc'h Trevezel, the Signal of Toussaines, and Brasparts on one side, and the massive rocks of Huelgoat on the other." All of these places are roughly forty miles to the east of Brest, in the Arrée Mountains in the middle of western Brittany. Roc'h Trevezel, the Signal of Toussaines, and Mont Saint Michel all reach roughly 1,260 feet. Along with Huelgoat and its chaos of rocks, they surround the plain of the Anaon. Besides several episodes of the quest for the Holy Grail, they also are the setting for other Breton and Celtic legends.

Breton house to some friends[93] and the proceeds allowed me not only to repair my new home, but also to transform a crumbling barn in my garden into a chapel I was delighted with. Father Lelégard provided me with a set of windows from a little medieval shrine that had been demolished to make way for a road. The icon writer Georges Morozoff had made a beautiful *Deësis* that was an ideal fit for my altar.[94] Meanwhile, Corinne Marion[95] painted the walls with Arthurian frescoes: to the south, the Grail procession and to the north the barge taking King Arthur to Avalon, *Rex quondam, rexque futurus*, under the protection of the three queens.[96] On the Gospel side was the Archangel Gabriel presenting the crown of thorns (the Oratory of France's coat of arms), facing Joseph of Arimathea (patron of the chapel) bringing the cruets filled with the Savior's water and blood. Naturally, on the western wall Saint Michael with his scales was separating little children destined to heaven, which children had a strong resemblance to those of the editors of the review *Communio*, regarding which more later,[97] and on the other side a clutch of diversely colored ecclesiastics and religious of all stripes abandoned to a perfectly horrid dragon.[98]

This is where I was to spend what I may call the last years of my mature age, and where I would at last bring to completion the theological *oeuvre* that had for so long remained half-done.

Yet, just as I was reaching an age where I was to start looking for a retirement to break me out of this quasi-solitude, though without diving back into the hurly-burly of modern cities, providential burglars did me the favor of emptying my house of all the most useful and most precious

93. These friends were Jean Duchesne, editor of the French version of these Memoirs, and his wife Marie-José.

94. The *Deësis* (Greek for "prayer" or "intercession") is the representation, on an icon, of the Blessed Virgin and Saint John the Evangelist on either side of Christ and imploring Him for mercy. Georges Mozoroff (1900–1993) gave up banking to write icons. Bouyer's interest in icons led him to write a book on the topic, *Vérité des icônes* (Limoges: Critérion, 1984).

95. Corinne Marion (née Nicolas), wife of French Catholic philosopher Jean-Luc Marion (see 246, n. 16).

96. This phrase forms part of the epitaph on King Arthur's tomb: *Hic jacet Arturus, rex quondam, rexque futurus* ("Here lies Arthur, once and future king"), in Thomas Malory's *Le Morte d'Arthur* 21:5–7.

97. For the founding of *Communio* France, see 236, n. 16.

98. Among these "diversely colored ecclesiastics and religious" are a Jesuit (in black), a Dominican (in white), and a cardinal (in red).

things in it. They had taken advantage of one of the retreats I regularly made at the Isle of Wight, in Quarr Abbey, in those years.[99]

Thereupon, the monks of Saint-Wandrille, my oldest friends in the Church, offered me the retirement I desired for my last years here below, and that in unhoped-for conditions.

99. Quarr Abbey, on the Isle of Wight off the southern coast of England, was founded by Cistercians in the twelfth century. The Benedictines of Solesmes, exiled from France in 1901 along with all religious congregations, settled nearby and built a new abbey, which was consecrated in 1912. After World War I they returned to Solesmes and Quarr Abbey became nearly exclusively English again.

12

About a Council

MY NOMINATION to a Council preparatory commission[1] brought about, as I have said, the end of my teaching duties at the *Institut catholique de Paris*. This nomination would play an equally important role in determining a fundamental evolution in my very concept of the life of the Church. It is very much a characteristic of mine to be slow in drawing conclusions from experience. This explains why my book on the Church,[2] though written towards the end of the Council, was still written in rose-colored ink for all that touches upon "conciliarity" and more specifically upon the "collegiality" about which there had been so much talk at the Council itself, not to mention on its sidelines. I had not yet been cured, at the time, of the illusions that Möhler's[3] and especially

1. This was the Commission for Studies and Seminaries, which worked from November 1960 to February 1962; see G. Alberigo and J. Komonchak ed., *History of Vatican II*, vol. 1, *Announcing and Preparing Vatican Council II. Toward a New Era in Catholicism* (Leuven: Peeters, 1995), 189–92. Archbishop Paolo Bertoli, Apostolic Nuncio to France (1960–1969), had arranged for Bouyer's nomination on the recommendation of Msgr. Blanchet, Rector of the *Institut catholique*; see above, n. 691.

2. *L'Église de Dieu, corps du Christ et temple de l'Esprit* (Paris: Cerf, 1970). English version: *The Church of God: Body of Christ and Temple of the Spirit*, trans. Ch. Underhill Quinn (Chicago: Franciscan Herald Press, 1982).

3. Johann Adam Möhler (1796–1838), German Catholic historian and theologian, author of *Unity in the Church or the Principle of Catholicism: Presented in the Spirit of the Church Fathers of the First Three Centuries*, trans. Peter C. Erb (Washington, D.C.: Catholic University of America Press, 1996), first published in 1825. Bouyer summarizes his ecclesiology in *The Church*, 91–104. Möhler's ecclesiology played a great role at Vatican II, as Bouyer writes in *The Church*, 104: "It was only in the twentieth century, with the Second Vatican Council, that Möhler's ideas received the attention they deserved." Congar (see 106, n. 20) gave a copy of the French version of Möhler's *Einheit* to Paul VI at the latter's pressing insistence on Saturday 14 November 1964; see Y. Congar, *Mon Journal du Concile*, ed. É. Mahieu, vol. 2 (Paris: Cerf, 2002), 222, 267, 269. Congar had had it published in French in 1938 as the second volume of his *Unam Sanctam* series.

Khomyakov's[4] theories on the Church had given me well before my adhesion to the Catholic Church.[5]

To be sure, I have never stopped believing that the Church is, in her ultimate term, "unanimity in love." The most recent Council, however, has cured me of my illusions that the royal path to achieve it might be this "conciliarity." Although my full recovery was therefore quite slow in coming, there is no doubt that its seed was planted when I was first invited to participate in a farce that was indecent from start to finish: the labors of the first commission to which I was called.[6]

Its presidency by Cardinal Pizzardo,[7] whose well-advanced state of senility clearly couldn't much worsen his radical unfitness for the job, was not the worst of it. In point of fact, the delicacy, tact, and superior feel for the issues that characterized its secretary, Msgr. Mayer, a Germanic Benedictine and since Cardinal, acted as a corrective to a situation which, without him, would have been grotesque.[8] The worst of it

---

4. Aleksey Stepanovich Khomyakov (1804–1860), Russian Slavophile poet and thinker who foresaw an ecumenical role for Orthodoxy. He expanded on Möhler's work. Bouyer's term "unity in love" is an expression of Khomyakov's *Sobornost*. According to Khomyakov, the Orthodox Slavic peoples give a living testimony to this unanimity; see Bouyer, *The Church*, 135. Bouyer develops the notion of the Church as "unanimity in love," ibid., 257–64. For both Möhler and Khomyakov:

> the basic intuition is the Christian truth as the truth of the divine love, not only revealed to us through the Gospel but actually communicated among us in the Church. Conversely, it goes without saying that the only guardian and witness of such a truth can be love, effectively lived and exercised in this human (but supernatural) community. (Ibid., 136)

Unlike Möhler, however, Khomyakov saw bishops as those entrusted with merely expressing the spontaneous, as it were, "sense of the faithful"; see ibid. On the other hand, both men approached the Church from a Pneumatological, rather than from a Christological, point of view.

5. The following lines will give some idea of Bouyer's adhesion to these two men's teaching, ibid., 263:

> We can now grasp the sense of the equation between truth and love and therefore between Church and truth, and, finally, the sense of the unity and unicity of the Church so strongly stated by Möhler and Khomyakov, which is assuredly the deepest and most basic teaching on the Church that can be drawn from the New Testament and the Fathers.

6. The Commission for Studies and Seminaries; see 207, n. 1.

7. Giuseppe Pizzardo (1877–1970) was ordained to the priesthood in 1903 and consecrated archbishop in 1930 at the hands of then Cardinal Pacelli. He was Prefect of the Congregation for Seminaries and Universities, 1939–1968, and Secretary of the Holy Office, 1951–1959.

8. Paul Augustin Mayer (1911–2010) entered the Benedictine Abbey of Saint Michael of Metten in 1931 and was ordained to the priesthood in 1935. He was the rector of San Anselmo, 1949–1966. He was secretary of the preparatory commission, 1960–1962. Pope John Paul II created him cardinal on 25 May 1985.

was that the same Pizzardo would remain, for an entire generation, at the head of a Roman congregation that was supposed to run all ecclesiastical studies. As a colleague once said: had the KGB undertaken to undermine the Catholic Church from within, it could hardly have picked a better man!

As for the rest of the commission, although it included a fair number of superior intellects and of deeply sensible and experienced men, they were submerged in a mass of worthless idiots and of those self-confident sorts who, in the Church as in government, so often show themselves to be mere blockheads obstinately clinging to their own limitations.[9]

There were interminable discussions on absurd themes, often sheer verbalism, such as a project of a declaration on the "public" character of Catholic schools and of Catholic schools alone, whatever the local civil legislation might be on the issue. That, along with the refusal to even simply take a look at the already ongoing collapse of ecclesiastical culture in the seminaries, sapped my overly naïve conviction that it would be enough, in the Church, to bring together the "responsible parties" for her to continue her existence in a "better being" arising from their spontaneous harmony.

Among other more peculiar discoveries I made while there, I must mention the crass ignorance as well as the lack of the most elementary judgment of one French bishop. He was destined to become, after the Council, not only archbishop of Paris but also the first president of the conference of bishops.[10]

The highlight of these absurd discussions was a dialog between the Most Eminent *praeses*[11] and Hubert Jedin, the admirable historian of the Council of Trent.[12] The latter maintained, in pure Ciceronian Latin, that it was absurd to prescribe the exclusive use of Latin even in the modern teaching of history, while the former claimed that nothing

---

9. For the full composition of this commission, see *Acta Apostolicae Sedis* 52 (Rome: Typis Polyglottis Vaticanis, 1960), 848–49, 931, 995–96, 1027–28. Bouyer was named to it on 24 November 1960; ibid., 996.

10. François Marty (1904–1994), Bishop of Saint-Flour in 1952; Archbishop of Reims in 1960; Archbishop of Paris, 1968–1981; Cardinal from 1969; president of the Conference of French Bishops, 1966–1975.

11. The official Latin term for the president of a commission, here Cardinal Pizzardo.

12. Hubert Jedin (1900–1980), author of the monumental *Geschichte des Konzils von Trient* (Freiburg: Verlag Herder, 1949–); in English, *A History of the Council of Trent*, trans. Ernest Graf (London: T. Nelson, 1957–1961).

could be easier—but showed himself, for his part, unable to express his point of view otherwise than in Italian![13]

Thank God the inept or incoherent proposals which were all that could emerge from our interminable palavers would not even be examined later on by the Fathers of the Holy Council!

More comforting, though still a mixed bag, would be my experiences in ecumenical matters before, during, and after the Council.

As soon as I had come into the Catholic Church, and even before that, it had been easy for me to notice that as far as the Catholic pioneers of ecumenism were concerned (except for Dom Lambert Beauduin,[14] Dom Clément Lialine,[15] or Father Christophe Dumont, OP[16]), and also as far as its most tenacious enemies were concerned, such as, at the time, the future Cardinals Bea,[17] Journet,[18] or Paul Philippe,[19] simply being a convert disqualified one from being involved in these issues. For the former, this stemmed from the idea of ecumenism, creeping at the time, triumphant today, that Eric Mascall[20] has quite accurately

13. Cardinal Pizzardo was a tireless champion of Latin in the Church. On 15 February 1961 he had written to the Sulpicians to forbid the publication of a history manual on the grounds that it was in the vernacular; see Congar, *Journal*, vol. 1, 51, n. 1. Bouyer had alerted Congar (see 106, n. 20) to Pizzardo's campaign in favor of Latin at about the same time, ibid., 50 (12 March 1961, reporting a conversation of two or three weeks earlier). Three months later, in a June 1961 meeting of the Central Preparatory Commission, he was one of the most vocal advocates of Latin as the language of the upcoming council. See *Acta et documenta Concilio oecumenico Vaticano II apparando; Series secunda (praeparatoria)* (Vatican: Typis Polyglottis, 1969), vol. 2/1, 219–20. Some of the remarks he made there were taken up verbatim in *Veterum Sapientia*; see Étienne Fouilloux, "The Antepreparatory Phase: The Slow Emergence from Inertia (January, 1959–October, 1962)," in Alberigo-Komonchak, *History of Vatican II*, vol. 1, 212, n. 179.

14. For Dom Beauduin and his commitment to ecumenism, see 105, n. 15.

15. For Dom Lialine see 105, n. 16.

16. Christophe-Jean Dumont, OP (1897–1991). He was active in the Russian apostolate and directed *Istina* (Russian for "truth"), the ecumenical center in Paris, for forty years starting in 1927.

17. Augustin Bea, SJ (1881–1968). Made cardinal by John XXIII in 1959, he was the first president of the Secretariat for Promoting Christian Unity from 1960. He played a major role in the document *Nostra Aetate*.

18. Charles Journet (1891–1975), professor at the diocesan seminary of Fribourg (Switzerland), 1924–1965. Paul VI made him cardinal in 1965. He was a strong supporter of *Nostra Aetate* and *Dignitatis Humanae*.

19. Paul-Pierre Philippe (1905–1984), Secretary of the Sacred Congregation for Religious, 1959–1967, Secretary of the CDF, 1967–1973, Cardinal in 1973, and prefect of the Congregation for Eastern Churches, 1973–1980.

20. Eric Lionel Mascall (1905–1993), Anglo-Catholic priest active in ecumenism with the Orthodox Churches; see 173, n. 67.

dubbed "Alice in Wonderland Ecumenism": "Everybody has won, and all must have prizes!" In other words: it is out of the question that anything should change on either side, the important thing being to agree that one may behave or believe as he pleases, as long as all end up thinking that the whole business is unimportant, "yes" and "no" being equivalent answers to every question.

As for the latter group, their suspicion obviously consisted in the possible temptation for converts that all was not false in their original Protestantism after all, and that it might be well to bring something of it into the Catholic Church.

I hasten to point out that this would never cease to afford me incidents, or accidents, of the highest comedic value.

When I had arrived in Strasbourg to take charge of the international seminary there, regular encounters between a certain number of ministers and priests had been established. All of the former, old friends of mine for the most part, whom I was meeting personally in the same atmosphere of cordial understanding that had effortlessly survived from our youthful student days together, naturally wished to see me there. Yet, I was obliged to abstain from seeing them, Father Congar,[21] also at Strasbourg, having decided *motu proprio*[22] and despite whatever they might say for themselves, that it would be an intolerable insult for them. The same thing came a little later, in Lyons, from his confrere Father Dupuy,[23] for a larger and public encounter of this kind. This time it provoked an indignant reaction on the part of several ministers, who wrote to tell me their disgust at the ostracism of which I was the victim, thinking, in their innocence, that it was the Jesuits' doing (for once it was the Dominicans! But obviously, for this kind of foolishness, all the "great orders," as they are called, can shake each other's hand!).

In England, however, I never stopped seeing my old or new Anglican friends—at the price of what snubs on the part of the Catholic clergy! Before John XXIII,[24] it was because I was accused of consorting with heresy; later—and often coming from the same people!—because I was deemed a stumbling block for these "separated brethren."

21. Congar, O.P. (see 106, n. 20), had written on ecumenism: *Chrétiens désunis, principes d'un "œcuménisme" catholique* (Paris: Éditions du Cerf, 1937).

22. *Motu proprio* is the ecclesiastical Latin phrase meaning "by his own initiative." It is reserved for Apostolic Letters by the pope; Bouyer here ironically applies it to Congar.

23. Bernard Dupuy, OP (1925–2014), worked in ecumenism and relations with the Jews.

24. Angelo Giuseppe Roncalli (1881–1963), Pope John XXIII from 1958.

Paradoxically, I was happier in Italy, particularly in Milan and Bergamo. His Excellency Montini,[25] when he was Archbishop of the Great Lombardic See, and the seminaries of Gallarate and of Bergamo invited me to the Weeks for Unity.[26] With the same prelate's full agreement, I was received there—no less cordially—by the Waldensian Church as well.[27]

When the Council resumed after the death of John XXIII, his successor[28] would have liked to call me to it as expert at the Secretariat for Unity. But I had broken with the *Institut catholique de Paris* too recently to run the risk of renewing the good Fathers' bitterness; furthermore, the turn that some interventions were taking, on the part of certain personalities from among those who were hogging the limelight at that Council, did not make me wish to follow any more closely debates whose confusion was daily increasing.

Yet, Father Duprey,[29] of the White Fathers, at this point one of the kingpins of the Secretariat for the Unity of Christians, had made note of what I had written on the subject and very early on wished me to be involved in the work to come. Above all, as well informed as he was about the life of the Orthodox Churches, he knew that many of their bishops and theologians had some regard for what I dare not call my thinking—certainly far higher regard than the Catholic Church did. He considered it an asset to have me in the now-multiplying meetings with them.

And so, leaving aside lesser things, shortly after the end of the Council he had me invited to the first serious working meeting we had with the Russians, at Bari.[30] A whole series of encounters were to follow for me, particularly in Trent.[31] I thus began to become familiar with such

---

25. Giovanni Battista Montini (1897–1978), Archbishop of Milan, 1954–1963, Pope Paul VI from 1963.

26. Lombardy, a northern region of Italy, boasts Milan, the ancient See of Saint Ambrose. Gallarte is to the northwest of Milan while Bergamo is to the northeast.

27. The Waldensian communion, founded by Petro Waldes (1130–1217) in Lyons, France, emphasized apostolic poverty and soon lapsed into heresy. It survives to this day in northern Italy and North America, often merging with Protestant denominations.

28. Paul VI (Giovanni Battisti Montini) succeeded John XXIII in 1963; see 187, n. 19.

29. Pierre Duprey, M. Afr. (1922–2007), Undersecretary in the Secretariat for Christian Unity, 1963–1983, Secretary of Pontifical Council for Promoting Christian Unity, 1983–1999. He was consecrated bishop in 1990. At the Council he was an interpreter for the Eastern Orthodox in attendance.

30. Bari is in southern Italy, on the Adriatic coast.

31. Trent is in northern Italy near the Austrian border. It had been the setting of the famous council there (1545–1563).

personalities as Metropolitan Nikodim of Leningrad and Novgorod,[32] or with the man who was to become Bishop Kyril of Viborg, the superior of the Leningrad Theological Academy before being transferred to Smolensk.[33] And, finally, there was this trip to Russia I was invited to with half a dozen other members of the Secretariat and which I have described in my little book *En quête de la Sagesse*.[34]

This would later bring me, under John Paul II, to belong to the mixed commission for the rapprochement between the Catholic Church and the Orthodox Churches.[35] I would thus participate in the first plenary meetings at Patmos[36] and then at Rhodes, and later yet in Munich and Crete, not to mention all the work in sub-commission under the excellent co-presidency of Metropolitan Georges Khodr[37] (from Lebanon) and of the archbishop of Bari, the Benedictine Magrassi,[38] a great specialist on Rupert of Deutz,[39] before succeeding the other Nicodemus,[40] who had welcomed us with such tact and cordiality during our initial encounter with the Russians at the tomb of St. Nicolas at the express request of the Patriarchate of Moscow's representatives.[41]

---

32. Boris Georgievich Rotov (1929–1978), Nikodim in religion, Metropolitan of Leningrad and Minsk from 1963, Eparch of Novgorod from 1967.

33. This was Vladimir Gundyaev (1946–); Kyril is his religious name. He directed the Theological Academy of Leningrad, 1974–1984. He was Bishop, then Archbishop, of Vyborg (about 85 miles west of Leningrad near the Finnish border) in 1976, after which he was transferred to Smolensk in 1984 (300 miles west of Moscow), thereby acquiring jurisdiction over Kaliningrad in 1989. He was elected Patriarch of Moscow in 2009.

34. *En quête de la sagesse: du Parthénon à l'apocalypse en passant par la nouvelle et la troisième Rome* (Jouques, Bouches-du-Rhône: Éditions du Cloître, 1980).

35. John Paul II nominated Bouyer to this commission on 30 November 1979; see *Acta Apostolicae Sedis* 71 (1979): 1606.

36. Patmos is the small Greek island off the western coast of Turkey where Saint John the Evangelist saw the vision of the end times he describes in the Apocalypse.

37. George Khodr (1923–), Archbishop of Mount Lebanon since 1970, coauthor of *La Parole de Dieu: approche catholique, protestante, orthodoxe* (Tours: Mame, 1966) and, most recently, of *L'appel de l'Esprit: Église et société* (Paris: Cerf, 2001).

38. Mariano Magrassi, OSB (1930–2004), author of *Teologia e storia nel pensiero di Ruperto di Deutz* (Rome: Urbanianum, 1959); Archbishop of Bari, 1977–1982; Archbishop of Bari-Bitonto, 1982–1999.

39. Rupert of Deutz (c. 1075–1129), a Benedictine monk at the Abbey of Saint Maurice in Liège, is famous for his writings on the Real Presence, the problem of evil, the causes of the Incarnation, and the veneration of Our Lady.

40. This Nikodim is probably Metropolitan Nikodim, for whom see n. 32.

41. The relics of Saint Nicolas (c. 270–343), Bishop of Myra in present-day Turkey, were translated to Bari in the eleventh century to avoid their destruction at the hands of the encroaching Muslim armies. This saint enjoys great veneration among the Russians, and the church built in his honor in Bari from 1913 to 1917 was handed over to the Patriarchate of Moscow in 2009.

I would also be one of the participants of the preparatory commission for the first official meeting with the Anglicans, at Malta; I was named to it conjointly, as one of my Anglican friends would say, by the Pope and the Archbishop of Canterbury, Michael Ramsey![42]

But, knowing the English episcopate's persistent grudge against me, except of course for Cardinal Heenan[43] and also for the excellent Bishop Holland,[44] in turn bishop of Portsmouth and then archbishop of Salford after having been Commodore of the Royal Navy, I refused to take any part in the dealings that followed. I do not regret it when I see the equivocal documents they produced, which belie a common ignorance that still subsists between these two worlds, even if a recently better willingness for understanding can be found in them of late.

What these diverse experiences, to which were added that in the International Commission of Theologians founded by Paul VI,[45] after the Council, and above all that in the Consilium for the reform of the liturgical books,[46] have most firmly impressed upon me is the truth of Newman's quip on the inability of committees in general to produce anything of value.[47]

Before embarking upon a few particularly instructive memories of these two latter commissions to which I belonged, I shall return to Councils themselves.

What distinguishes them from such commissions is that in principle they issue from a Eucharistic concelebration[48] in which the bishops belonging to them anticipate sacramentally the "unanimity in love" that is to be achieved in the Church after the *Parousia*.

42. For Ramsey see 109, n. 39. The Malta meeting took place 31 December 1967–3 January 1968 at Mount St. Joseph. It resulted in the "Malta Report," to which is attached a list of the commission's members; see http://www.prounione.urbe.it/dia-int/arcic/doc/e_arcic_malta.html#txt2 [accessed 7 March 2011].

43. For their friendship, see 15 above and 235 below.

44. The Right Reverend Thomas Holland (1908–1999), chaplain in the Royal Navy, 1943–1946; Port Chaplain in Bombay, 1946–1948; member of the Vatican Secretariat for Promoting Christian Unity, 1961–1974; member of the Vatican Secretariat for Unbelievers, 1965–1973; coadjutor bishop of Portsmouth, 1960–1964; Bishop of Salford, 1964–1983.

45. For a look at the ITC's procedures and atmosphere, see William May, "Church Institutions: The International Theological Commission," in *Teaching the Catholic Faith: Central Questions for the 90s*, ed. by Eugene V. Clark, Thirteenth Convention of the Fellowship of Catholic Scholars, Philadelphia, Pennsylvania, 1990 (New York: St. John's University Edition, 1991), 161–72.

46. Chartered by Pope Paul VI on 29 February 1964.

47. See John Henry Newman, *Apologia Pro Vita Sua* (New York: Random House, 1950), 67: "Living movements do not come of committees."

48. For Bouyer's explanation of episcopal concelebration, see his *L'Église*, 366–67.

Yet, even when this very concelebration is not reduced to a mere formality from which no one seriously considers drawing its consequences, in the ensuing discussions incompetence, intrigue, the smoke and mirrors thrust in each other's way as Saint Gregory Nazianzen showed regarding the Council of Constantinople, over which he presided, and as Ratzinger[49] has recalled in his book *Principles of Catholic Theology*[50] (and which the deplorable publicity of the last council could not but push to the extreme), all of these things slowly sap any effect that such a concelebration, even if it is accomplished with the best of living faiths, could have or might have initially had upon the participants. In the best-case scenario, that of a truly ecumenical council in the traditional meaning of the term, i.e. actually representative of an undivided Christendom, the most that divine assistance can ensure for the Apostles' successors is the absence of any possible error in the doctrinal definitions such assemblies venture to produce. But, short of this extreme case, any dosage of approximation, insufficiency, or simple superficiality are to be expected from even so sacrosanct an assembly.[51]

What then is to be expected from simple local councils, not to say anything of episcopal conferences regularly manipulated by more or less irresponsible offices, or of assemblies of so-called "experts," or of any other such commission!

If the Church derives anything of value from them, it is only that which the highest "responsible" persons (as they are called these days) in the apostolic succession, popes or influential bishops, will sift out, be

---

49. Joseph Ratzinger (1927–), ordained 1951; Vatican II peritus (for Cardinal Frings); named to the International Theological Commission by Paul VI. He would be consecrated archbishop and created cardinal in 1977, and Pope from 2005 to his resignation in 2013.

50. Joseph Ratzinger, *Principles of Catholic Theology: Building Stones for a Fundamental Theology* (San Francisco: Ignatius, 1987), 368, quoting Gregory Nazianzen, *Epistle 163 Ad Procopium*: "I am convinced that every assembly of bishops is to be avoided, for I have never experienced a happy ending to any council; not even in the abolition of abuses . . . , but only ambition or wrangling about what was taking place."

51. Contrast this paragraph with the following, written some twenty years earlier in "rose-colored ink" in *L'Église*, 367:

It is in concelebration that their [the bishops'] respective Churches discover each other mutually and conjointly in their gathering together, as a single Church. Following this principle, the deliberations they are then to undertake and the decisions flowing from them, to be considered valid, can never appear as the simple result of a political compromise or of a majority's victory over a minority. Rather, they will be the fruit of their unanimity based on Eucharistic faith and charity.

See also ibid., 532–33.

it by the importance of their sees or by their recognized merits, from its more or less adequate chaff and asides.

Still, it is up to the *sensus communis fidelium*[52]—understood of those who truly are such ["the faithful"]—in the final analysis, to make it its own and, at that level, to make it positive and effective by the benefit they will derive from it in the sphere of the only spiritual progress that counts: that towards Gospel holiness.

And, while we're at it, to finish with this question of what is called "ecumenism" today, if one is willing to leave to the term any connection with the sense in which "ecumenism" applies first to the living unity of the Church, I shall say in the same breath that its only possible meaning is to lead each individual to distinguish, for his own side as for the other, what is truly essential and, therefore, positive from what is only adventitious and always more or less consciously opposed to this gold-bearing vein. On the other hand, the claim that one might reach any kind of a reunion without any change on either side makes no sense. The claim that one might achieve it by reducing oneself to the smallest common denominator doesn't make much more sense. The only reunion that is not a chimera or a simple fig-leaf can only occur through the common rediscovery of a living fullness, unencumbered by anything negative, with the mutual acknowledgement of complementarity or quite simply harmony (this latter point applying especially to the rapprochement between Catholic and Orthodox) of the positive that is held on either side, and which seems to be in opposition only because the rest, unfortunately tacked on, masks or chokes its authentic reality.

But it is not through discussions, and even less through more or less political compromises, that one may hope to mend the tears in the fabric. It is through a common effort of purification, of understanding, and especially of humble faithfulness to what is authentic. Encounters only have value to the extent that they provide the occasion for such discoveries or rediscoveries to those who are disposed to them.

It is, I believe, thanks to such personalities as John XXIII, Paul VI, Athenagoras I,[53] and Metropolitan Nikodim,[54] whose concern for integral truth went hand in hand with authentic charity, that the current

---

52. The *sensus communis fidelium* (the "common sense of the faithful") is the perception of what is essential to the faith among the faithful as a group.

53. Aristokles Spyrou (1886–1972), Athenagoras in religion, Greek Orthodox Patriarch of Constantinople from 1948. He met Paul VI in Jerusalem in 1964 and again in Istanbul (Constantinople) and the Vatican in 1967. These meetings culminated in the lifting of the excommunications connected with the 1054 schism.

54. For Metropolitan Nikodim see 213, n. 32 above.

conversations between Catholics and Orthodox seem actually to progress.

It was the same factors, the same personalities in whom generosity went hand in hand with clear-sightedness, that made the greatness of the first ecumenism contemporary with Stockholm and Lausanne[55] and of the response it then found among too few Catholics, like Cardinal Mercier,[56] Metropolitan Andrey Sheptytsky,[57] or Dom Lambert Beauduin.[58] Just yesterday such men as Anglican Archbishop Michael Ramsey[59] gave admirable examples of this. With few exceptions, they seem to have nearly vanished from Catholic circles, where they never were very numerous . . . just as, these last few years, theologians worthy of the name, as well as authentic spiritual masters, have become very scarce.

Among non-Catholics, too, such men seem more and more to leave behind the circles specialized in ecumenism that the World Council of Churches claims to oversee.[60] The only interest over there now is the progress of a socialism that is more Marxist than Christian in its inspiration—at the very moment when Marxism is falling to pieces!

On the other hand, however, such men are more numerous than ever among those Anglicans or Protestants whose primary concern is faithfulness to the biblical Word of God and to the Gospel in particular. They are therefore just as critical of the school positions of the old Catholic-Protestant controversy as they are of so-called "liberal" Protestantism's proportionately faithless neo-Christianity buttressed by an exegetical pseudoscience, which is itself merely a reasoning of justification for rationalist prejudices erected as axioms. Such Methodists as Outler,[61] Wainwright,[62] or Neville Ward;[63] Lutherans like Cull-

55. Stockholm here refers to the Life and Work Conference; Lausanne refers to Faith and Order. See 58, n. 6 and 59, n. 7.

56. For Désiré-Joseph Mercier see 59, n. 11.

57. From 1900 to his death, Metropolitan Andrey Sheptytsky (1865–1944) was the Archbishop of Byzantine-Rite Ukrainians in union with Rome

58. For Bouyer's first meeting with Beauduin, see 105–06.

59. For Michael Ramsey see 109, n. 39.

60. For the World Council of Churches, see 59, n. 7.

61. Albert Outler (1908–1989), professor of theology at Southern Methodist University, Dallas; sent to the council as observer by the Methodist World Council.

62. Geoffrey Wainwright (1939–), British Methodist theologian, noted for dialogue with Roman Catholics since 1966; co-chairman of the Joint Commission between the World Methodist Council and the Roman Catholic Church since 1986; professor at Duke University since 1983.

63. Neville Ward (1915–1992), author of *Five for Sorrow, Ten for Joy: A Consideration of the Rosary* (London: Epworth, 1971). See John A. Newton, "The Revd. Neville Ward: 'A Methodist Mariologist,'" *Ecumenical Society of the Blessed Virgin Mary* (January 2003).

mann,[64] Lindbeck,[65] Riesenfeld,[66] Gerhardsson,[67] Gärtner,[68] or Jeremias;[69] Anglicans like Macquarrie,[70] Rowan Williams[71] or Louth;[72] and Reformed Protestants like Childs[73] in my opinion still have, in this matter, everything to teach to those whom the Catholic press presents as prophets of the Catholicism of the future (which, if it were to follow their lead, would only vanish into smoke!).

What shall I say, after this, of my collaboration in the Consilium for the reform of liturgical books[74] from which, after the publication of my *Eucharistie*[75] and the call from Paul VI, I could not demur?

I should not like to be too harsh on this commission's labors. It numbered a certain number of genuine scholars and more than one experienced and judicious pastor. Under different circumstances, they might

64. Oscar Cullmann (1902–1999), Lutheran theologian; observer at Vatican II; professor at the Sorbonne in Paris from 1948 and at the University of Basel, 1938–1973; author of *Vatican Council II: The New Direction* (New York: Harper and Row, 1968). Bouyer had had him as a professor during his Protestant seminary days in Strasbourg; see 93, n. 56.

65. George Lindbeck (1923–), History of Theology professor at Yale University, sent to the Council as an observer by the World Lutheran Federation; author of *The Future of Roman Catholic Theology: Vatican II—Catalyst for Change* (Philadelphia: Fortress Press, 1970).

66. Harald Riesenfeld (1913–2008), professor at the University of Uppsala, 1953–1979, and at Tübingen from 1979; collaborator with Daniélou (see 141, n. 62) on *Studia Evangelica* in 1959; joined the Catholic Church at the end of his life.

67. Birger Gerhardsson (1926–), Swedish Lutheran theologian and professor at the University of Lund. His principal area of study is the reliability of oral traditions concerning Jesus. At the time of Bouyer's writing, he had recently published *The Gospel Tradition* (Malmö: CWK Gleerup, 1986).

68. Bertil Edgar Gärtner (1924–2009), Swedish Lutheran theologian; Bishop of Gothenburg, 1970–1991; Professor of New Testament Exegesis at Princeton Theological Seminary. He was conservative and one of the opponents to the ordination of women.

69. Joachim Jeremias (1900–1979), German Lutheran theologian, professor of New Testament studies at the Georg-August University of Göttingen, 1935–1968.

70. John Macquarrie (1919–2007), Presbyterian minister who was ordained an Episcopalian minister in 1965. He sought to see what truth there is in all traditions.

71. Rowan Williams (1950–), ordained an Anglican priest 1977; appointed Lady Margaret Professor of Divinity at Oxford, 1986; Bishop of Monmouth (Wales), 1992–1999; Archbishop of Wales, 1999–2003; Archbishop of Canterbury, 2002–2012. He wrote his doctoral dissertation on Russian Orthodox theologian Vladimir Lossky (see 76–77, n. 84).

72. Andrew Louth (1945–), who converted to Orthodoxy in 1994 and joined the faculty of Durham University in 1996. Bouyer had favorably reviewed his *The Origins of the Christian Mystical Tradition from Plato to Denys* (Oxford: Clarendon Press, 1981). Thanks are due to Fr. Louth for this precision.

73. Brevard Childs (1923–2007), Presbyterian minister, professor at Yale University, 1958–1999.

have accomplished excellent work. Unfortunately, on the one hand, a deadly error in judgment placed the official leadership of this committee in the hands of a man who, though generous and brave, was not very knowledgeable: Cardinal Lercaro.[76] He was utterly incapable of resisting the maneuvers of the mealy-mouthed scoundrel that the Neapolitan Vincentian, Bugnini,[77] a man as bereft of culture as he was of basic honesty, soon revealed himself to be.

Even besides this, there was no hope of producing anything of greater value than what would actually come out of it, what with this claim of recasting from top to bottom and in a few months an entire liturgy it had taken twenty centuries to develop.

Having been expressly called to the sub-commission in charge of the Missal, I was petrified to discover a preparatory sub-commission's projects when I arrived. It was inspired principally by Dom Cipriano Vagaggini[78] from the Bruges Abbey and by the excellent Msgr. Wagner,[79] from Trier. The idea was to obviate the Holland-born fashion of Eucharists being improvised in complete ignorance of the liturgical tradition going back to Christian origins. I still cannot understand by what aberration these excellent people, who were rather good historians and generally reasonable intellects, could suggest that the Roman Canon

74. Pope Paul VI appointed him to the Consilium for the Implementation of the Constitution on the Liturgy (hereafter, "Consilium") on 16 March 1966. See Annibale Bugnini, *The Reform of the Liturgy: 1948–1975* (Collegeville, MN: The Liturgical Press, 1990), 945.

75. See 181, n. 123.

76. Giacomo Lercaro (1891–1976), Archbishop of Ravenna, 1947–1952; Archbishop of Bologna, 1952–1968; cardinal from 1953; president of the Consilium, 1966–1968.

77. Annibale Bugnini (1912–1982), an Italian Vincentian (for this congregation see 123, n. 50), had been the architect of liturgical change in the Roman rite since 1948 and principal author of the Vatican II document on the liturgy, *Sacrosanctum Concilium*. Paul VI appointed him as Secretary of the Consilium on 3 January 1964. See Bugnini, *Reform of the Liturgy*, 13–28, 49–50. He first attended a CPL conference in Le Thieulin (a few miles from Chartres), 16–22 September 1946, having asked its organizer, Pie Duployé, to invite him. He listened attentively without comment, and on the train back to Paris he told Duployé: "I admire what you are doing, but the greatest favor I can do you is never to say a word in Rome of what I have just been hearing"; see P. Duployé, *Les Origines du Centre de Pastorale Liturgique, 1943–1949* (Mulhouse: Salvator, 1968), 320, n. 7.

78. His views on the liturgy will be found in Cipriano Vagaggini, *Theological Dimensions of the Liturgy*, trans. Leonard Doyle (Collegeville, MN: Liturgical Press, 1959); see also 152, n. 20.

79. Johann Wagner (1908–1999), first director of the German Liturgical Institute (roughly the German equivalent of the French CPL, see 154, n. 27) in Trier in 1947, one of the architects of *Sacrosanctum Concilium*, consultor of the Consilium.

should be so disconcertingly carved up and put together again, as well as other projects claiming to be "inspired" by Hippolytus of Rome,[80] but which were no less harebrained.

For my part I was ready to resign on the spot and go home. But Dom Botte[81] convinced me to stay on, if only to obtain some lesser evil.

At the end of the day, the Roman Canon was more or less respected and we managed to produce three Eucharistic Prayers which, despite rather wordy intercessions, reclaimed pieces of great antiquity and unequalled theological and euchological richness, long since out of use since the disappearance of the ancient Gallican rites.[82] I have in mind the anamnesis of the third Eucharistic prayer, and also what we were able to salvage of a rather successful attempt to adapt a series of formulas from the ancient so-called "Saint James's" prayer to the Roman scheme, thanks to Father Gelineau's work,[83] who was not always so well advised.

But what can I say, at a time when the talk was of simplifying the liturgy and of bringing it back to primitive models, about this *actus poenitentialis* inspired by Father Jungmann (an excellent historian of the

80. Bouyer's hesitancy regarding Hippolytus can be explained: at the time of these *Memoirs'* composition, sometime in the late 1980s, the authorship by Hippolytus of the *Apostolic Tradition* with its famous Anaphora had come into question; see for example A. Faivre, "La documentation canonico-liturgique de l'Église ancienne: II. Les unités littéraires et leurs relectures," *Revue de sciences religieuses* 54.4 (1980): 273–97. This was causing some unease among the liturgists who had worked on the Eucharistic prayers of the new Mass; see, e.g., A.-G. Martimort, "Nouvel examen de la 'Tradition Apostolique' d'Hippolyte," *Bulletin de littérature ecclésiastique* 88 (1987): 5–25, especially p. 7. For a good overview of the issues, see B. Steimer, *Vertex Traditionis: Die Gattung der altchristlichen Kirchenordnungen* (Berlin: Walter de Gruyter, 1992), 28–48. Bouyer had already doubted the value of the *Apostolic Tradition* as a witness to third-century Roman practice; see *Eucharist: Theology and Spirituality of the Eucharistic Prayer*, trans. C.U. Quinn (Notre Dame: University of Notre Dame Press, 1968), 158–82, esp. 168: "It probably tells us very little about what had become of the eucharistic liturgy at Rome and even elsewhere in the middle of the third century."

81. Bernard Botte (see 164–65, n. 12) prepared the standard edition of Hippolytus's (?) "Apostolic Tradition": *La Tradition apostolique* (Münster: Aschendorff, 1963).

82. See Louis Bouyer, "The Different Forms of Eucharistic Prayer and Their Genealogy," *Studia Patristica* 8 (1966): 156–70.

83. Joseph Gelineau, SJ (1920–2008), best known for his Psalm settings for congregational use. His *Voices and Instruments in Christian Worship: Principles, Laws, Applications* (Collegeville, MN: Liturgical Press, 1964) influenced the insertion of the Responsorial Psalm into the missal of Paul VI. As a member of the Consilium's group on the revision of the Order of Mass, he was responsible for the Eucharistic Prayers and introduced the acclamation after the Consecration. He gives the detail of his liturgical principles in his *Liturgical Assembly, Liturgical Song*, trans. Paul Innwood (Portland, OR: Pastoral Press, 2002).

Roman Missal—but who, in his entire life, had never celebrated a Solemn Mass!)?[84] The worst of it was an impossible offertory, in a Catholic Action, sentimental "workerist"[85] style, the handiwork of Father Cellier,[86] who with tailor-made arguments manipulated the despicable Bugnini in such a way that his production went through despite nearly unanimous opposition.

You'll have some idea of the deplorable conditions in which this hasty reform was expedited when I recount how the second Eucharistic prayer was cobbled together.[87] Between the indiscriminately archeologizing[88] fanatics who wanted to banish the *Sanctus* and the intercessions from the Eucharistic prayer by taking Hippolytus's Eucharist as is,[89] and those others who couldn't have cared less about his alleged *Apostolic Tradition* and wanted a slapdash Mass, Dom Botte and I were commissioned to patch up its text with a view to inserting these elements, which are certainly quite ancient—by the next morning! Luckily, I discovered, if not in a text by Hippolytus himself certainly in one in his style, a felicitous formula on the Holy Ghost that could provide a transition of the *Vere Sanctus* type to the short epiclesis. For his part Botte produced an

---

84. Josef Jungmann, SJ (1889–1975), author of *The Mass of the Roman Rite: Its Origins and Development* (*Missarum sollemnia*) (New York: Benziger, 1951–1955). Bouyer calls this book "the greatest scholarly work of our times on the history of the Roman Mass," *Liturgical Piety*, 16.

85. Bouyer uses the term "workerist," in French *ouvriériste*, to denounce efforts at reconquering the laboring masses in a Marxist framework. The term entered the English language in a translation from J. Daniélou (see 141, n. 62), "Blessed Are the Poor," trans. William Birmingham, *Cross Currents* 9.4 (Autumn 1959): 381.

86. Father Jacques Cellier (1922–1999), named first director of the *Centre National de Pastorale Liturgique* (see 154, n. 29) on 11 February 1965, a post he would hold until 1973. See L. Mougeot, "Le Père Jacques Cellier (21 janvier 1922–10 janvier 1999)," *La Maison-Dieu* 223 (2000): 113–17.

87. For Dom Botte's recollections, see Bernard Botte, *From Silence to Participation*, trans. John Sullivan (Washington: The Pastoral Press, 1988), 149–52.

88. Archeologism, a tendency that Pius XII had reproved, consists in returning to the very earliest centuries of the liturgy with no regard for the intervening development. See "Mediator Dei," *Acta Apostolicae Sedis* 39 (1947): 546–47, repeating the condemnation made by Pius VI in the 1794 Bull "Auctorem fidei," and Louis Bouyer, "Retour aux sources et archéologisme," in *Le Message des moines à notre temps: Mélanges offerts à dom Alexis, abbé de Boquen* (Paris: Arthème-Fayard, 1958), 169–72. For the temptation to archeologism among the Missal's revisers, see Lauren Pristas, "The Orations of the Vatican II Missal: Policies for Revision," *Communio* 30.4 (2003): 650–51.

89. The English version of "Anaphora of Hippolytus" will be found in Vagaggini, *Canon*, 25–27. The elimination of the intercessions had been proposed by several theologians during and after the council: Hans Küng, K. Amon, and P. Borella; see ibid., 111, n. 8. Vagaggini rebuts their arguments, ibid., 112–14.

intercession worthier of Paul Reboux's "In the manner of..."[90] than of his actual scholarship. Still, I cannot reread that improbable composition without recalling the Trastevere café terrace where we had to put the finishing touches to our assignment in order to show up with it at the Bronze Gate by the time our masters had set![91]

I prefer to say nothing, or little, about the new calendar,[92] the handiwork of a trio of maniacs who suppressed, with no good reason, Septuagesima[93] and the Octave of Pentecost[94] and who scattered three quarters of the Saints higgledy-piggledy,[95] all based on notions of their own devising!

Because these three hotheads obstinately refused to change anything in their work and because the pope wanted to finish up quickly to avoid

90. Bouyer's contribution, which immediately follows the *Sanctus* in Eucharistic Prayer II, is: *Vere sanctus es Domine, fons omnis sanctitatis. Haec ergo dona, quaesumus, Spiritus tui rore sanctifica, ut nobis Corpus et Sanguis fiant Domini nostri Iesu Christi* (*Roman Missal* 2010 version: "You are indeed Holy, O Lord, the fount of all holiness. Make holy, therefore, these gifts, we pray, by sending down your Spirit upon them like the dewfall, so that they may become for us the Body and Blood of our Lord, Jesus Christ"). He found *fons omnis sanctitatis* in the *Liber mozarabicus sacramentorum*; the *Spiritus tui rore sanctifica* is from the *Missale Gothicum*, n. 271, as reported in Consilium ad Exsequendam Consitutionem de Sacra Liturgia, *Schemata, n. 218, De Missali*, 34*bis*, 19 *martii 1967: Coetus X. De Ordine Missae*, typescript, 49; see John Pepino, "Cassandra's Curse: Louis Bouyer, the Liturgical Movement, and the Post-Conciliar Reform of the Mass," *Antiphon* 18.3 (2014) 254–300. Bouyer compares Dom Botte's efforts to the work of Paul Reboux (1877– 1963), a prolific author best known for his pastiches, collected in a series entitled *À la manière de.* . . .

91. Trastevere is a charming working-class neighborhood on the right bank of the Tiber River in Rome. The Bronze Gate on the right side of Saint Peter's basilica leads to the papal apartments overlooking St. Peter's square. By the term "masters" Bouyer means the Consilium authorities; his French term is *régents*, which means both "authorities" and "schoolmasters."

92. The Consilium's study group for the revision of the calendar comprised: Annibale Bugnini, relator (until 1967); A. Dirks, secretary; R. van Doren; J. Wagner; A.-G. Martimort; P. Jounel (relator from 1967); A. Amore; H. Schmidt, members. The principles this group adopted and presented at their first meeting on 23 January 1965 are outlined in "*Principia seu criteria ad Calendarium instaurandum*," *Notitia* 1 (1965): 150–52. For greater detail see Pierre Jounel, "L'Organisation de l'année liturgique," *La Maison-Dieu* 100 (1969): 139–56.

93. Regarding Septuagesima, Bugnini, after summarizing Paul VI's beautiful explanation of the fittingness of three weeks of preparation for Lent, reports in his *Reform*, 307, n. 6: "Then, however, the view prevailed that there should be a simplification: it was not possible to restore Lent to its full importance without sacrificing Septuagesima, which is an extension of Lent." See also Jounel, "L'Organisation," 147–48, where one reads that the Consilium also wished to scrap Ash Wednesday and have Lent begin on its first Sunday.

letting the chaos get out of hand, their project, however insane, was accepted!⁹⁶

The only element undeserving of criticism in this new missal was the enrichment it received, thanks particularly to the restoration of a good number of splendid prefaces taken over from ancient sacramentaries and thanks to the wider biblical readings (although, on this latter point, there was too much haste to produce anything satisfactory). I shall pass over any number of ancient Collects for penitential seasons—that we were forced to mutilate so as to void them, to the extent possible, of—

94. On this octave, Bugnini writes, *Reform*, 307, n. 9: "Here again there was disagreement. The suppression was accepted with the expectation that the formularies of the octave would be used during the nine days of preparation for Pentecost. On this point again there were changes of mind, but the decision of the Fathers finally prevailed." He returns to this suppression, which, as he reports, "subsequently caused confusion and second thoughts," in a lengthy note giving his reasons for it (ibid., 319, n. 38). Bouyer regretted this suppression as this octave focused on the action of the Holy Spirit.

95. P. Jounel, to whom the Temporal had been entrusted, and A. Amore, in charge of the Sanctoral, presented the general structure of the revised calendar to the Consilium's seventh general meeting in October 1966. The draft was definitively approved at the eighth general meeting, 10–19 April 1967. See ibid., 308–9. Jounel was "the principal author of the work," ibid., 315. For an early overview of the principles guiding the Sanctoral, see Jacques Dubois, "Les Saints du nouveau calendrier," *La Maison-Dieu* 100 (1969): 157–78. Jounel had expressed his notion that the feasts of the Saints "must be rare, since rarity is one of the conditions of festive joy" (*doivent être rares, puisque la rareté est une des conditions de l'allégresse festive*), P. Jounel, "Le Culte des Saints," in A.-G. Martimort et al. eds., *L'Église en prière. Introduction à la liturgie* (Paris: Desclée, 1961), 784. See also id., "The Veneration of the Saints," II, "The Roman Calendar," in A.-G. Martimort ed., *The Church at Prayer*, IV, *The Liturgy and Time* (Collegeville, MN: Liturgical Press, 1986), 123–27.

96. Cardinal Lercaro presented this schema to Paul VI on 18 April 1967; the pope decided that it should be submitted to the Congregation for the Doctrine of the Faith and to the Congregation of Rites; see Bugnini, 309, n. 11 for the chronology. Bugnini's assessment of the CDF's study and of its effectiveness is that "it was tinged to some extent with nostalgia for the past ... agreement was quickly reached (even though in the process many requests of the Congregation were effectively denied)," ibid., 311. In a later revision, however, the Congregation rescued Saint Nicolas's day, among other feasts (including Polish saints, all of whom had been dropped, e.g.), from demotion at the hands of the Consilium, ibid., 317. Paul VI announced the publication of the new calendar on 28 April 1969; it was to go into effect on 1 January 1970 (Bugnini mistakenly writes "1969," ibid., 314). Not surprisingly, "the publication of the calendar elicited rather negative reactions among the lay journalists and in the Catholic press generally.... Those of the clergy and faithful whose view of worship and religion generally had been devotion-oriented were disconcerted, although the confusion was also due in part to surprise and a lack of preparation," ibid., 315.

penance, precisely![97] On the flipside, though, there is a noteworthy new composition which is not only irreproachable but even admirably opportune: the new common preface I. For this, homage is due to its author, a monk of Hautecombe,[98] who kept to combining, with an uncommonly sure hand, the most meaningful sentences of Saint Paul, all the while respecting the *cursus*.[99]

After all of this, it's not much surprise if, because of its unbelievable weaknesses, the pathetic creature we produced[100] was to provoke laughter or indignation—so much so that it makes one forget any number of excellent elements it nevertheless contains, and that it would be a shame not to salvage as so many scattered pearls in the revision that will inevitably be called for.

To finish with this sad tale, I shall point out what subterfuge Bugnini used to obtain what was closest to his heart, or, I should say, what the men who have to be called his handlers managed to pass through him.[101]

On several occasions, whether the scuttling of the liturgy of the dead or even that incredible enterprise to expurgate the Psalms for use in the Divine Office,[102] Bugnini ran into an opposition that was not only massive but also, one might say, close to unanimous. In such cases, he didn't hesitate to say: "But the Pope wills it!" After that, of course, there was no question of discussing the matter any further.

Yet, one day when he had made use of that argument I had a lunch

---

97. For the principles guiding the changes in the penitential collects, see Lauren Pristas, "Post-Vatican II Revision of the Lenten Collects," in *Ever Directed to the Lord: The Love of God in the Liturgy of the Eucharist Past, Present, and Hoped For*, ed. Uwe Michael Lang (London: T&T Clark, 2007), 62–89. Louis Bouyer expressed himself on some of these aspects of the liturgical reforms in *Métier*, 81–95.

98. This monk was Dom Antoine Dumas (1915–1999, see Botte, *From Silence*, 151). Hautecombe in Savoie boasts a twelfth-century Cistercian abbey. Some Benedictines of the Solesmes congregation, returning from exile in Italy, took it over in 1922 and stayed there until 1999.

99. The "cursus" is the prose rhythm that brings a Latin sentence to a pleasing close. The *Praefatio Communis I* has a *cursus velox* (/ - - . / - / -): (*ac*)*ípere tribuísti*; then a *cursus trispondaicus* (/ - . - - / -): (*pacifi*)*cávit univérsa*; finally a *cursus planus* (/ - . - / -): (*sa*)*lútis aetérnae*. On *cursus* in the Latin euchological tradition, see Uwe Michael Lang, *The Voice of the Church at Prayer: Reflections on Liturgy and Language* (San Francisco: Ignatius Press, 2012), 86–89 and 114–115.

100. Bouyer writes *l'avorton que nous produisîmes*, which might be more starkly rendered: "the abortus we brought forth."

101. Who were these men whom Bouyer calls Bugnini's *commanditaires*? They do not appear to be members of the Consilium since it unanimously opposed some of the reforms Bugnini pushed through. Bugnini denied allegations that he belonged to Freemasonry in a letter to the Editor, *Homiletic and Pastoral Review* 80 (May 1980): 4–6, quoted in his *Reform*, 92–93.

appointment with my friend Msgr. Del Gallo, who as privy Chamberlain had a flat right above the papal apartments at the time.[103] As I was coming back down—after the siesta, of course—and came out of the lift onto the Cortile San Damaso,[104] Bugnini in person was emerging from the staircase on his way in from the Bronze Gate. At the sight of me, he didn't just turn pale: he was visibly aghast. I straightaway understood that, knowing me to be *notus pontifici*,[105] he supposed I had just been with the pope. But in my innocence I simply could not guess why he would be so terrorized at the idea that I might have had an interview with the pope regarding our affairs.

I would be given the answer, though weeks later, by Paul VI himself. As he was discussing our famous work with me, work which he had finally ratified without being much more satisfied with it than I was, he said to me: "Now why did you do [x] in the reform?" At this point, I must confess that I no longer recall specifically which of the details I have already mentioned was bothering him.[106] Naturally, I answered: "Why, simply because Bugnini had assured us that you absolutely wished it." His reaction was instantaneous: "Can this be? He told me himself that you were unanimous on this!"[107]

102. The following psalms were eventually expurgated from the Divine Office: 57/58; 82/83; 108/109. Other Psalms were censored by a verse or two: 62/63:10–12; 109/110:6; 136/137:7–9. Several council Fathers had asked for the imprecatory, or cursing, psalms to be expurgated during the November 1962 debates on the text that would become *Sacrosanctum Concilium*: E. Ruffini led the charge (see AS I/II, 329), followed by: A. Bacci; J. Corboy; F. Melendro (advocating jettisoning half the Psalms); Garcia Martinez; Vielmo (in a written addition after the speeches); Fernandez, OP; Capozi (in writing); Descuffi (in writing); Molin (in writing); Reiterer (ibid., 409–561). Cardinal Wyszinski gave an impassioned and eloquent defense of the integral Psalter to a storm of applause (ibid., 394); those Fathers representing the canonical and monastic congregations defended the integrity of the Psalter (J. Prou, OSB, ibid., 446; J. Androver of the Canons regular, ibid., 496; B. Reetz, OSB [Beuron], ibid., 559); A. Guano also defended it (ibid., 458).

103. Luigi Del Gallo, Marquis of Roccagiovine (1922–2011), ordained a priest in 1950; Domestic Prelate of His Holiness, 1960–1983; Bishop of Camplum from 1983.

104. The Cortile San Damaso is a courtyard in the middle of the papal palace.

105. This phrase, from John 18:15, describes the disciple who was known to the high priest and went into his court, leaving St. Peter outside to deny knowing Christ. It can also be translated as "someone known to the pope," its first meaning here, though Bouyer intends the reader to make the biblical connection as well.

106. According to students of Bouyer's, who heard the anecdote from him, the expurgated cursing Psalms were the issue.

107. Msgr. Jacques Masson, who had occasion to hear this anecdote from Louis Bouyer in Rome, gives it in a fuller form in his own Memoirs. The chronology does not seem to match but the gist is the same. Jacques Masson, "Monseigneur Lefebvre? On le poussera au schisme!" 8: "La messe, 'puntum dolens'," Hermas, entry posted 1 October 2009, http://www.hermas.info/article-36681786.html (accessed 8 February 2010).

Let's now move on to my experience of the International Theological Commission.[108] Early on, my impression was quite favorable. But it ended in an even worse disappointment.

With few exceptions, the selection of members truly represented this field's strongest minds and the best workers that the Church then had in her service.[109]

From the outset, the organization of work was beyond comparison with that (if any) of the other commissions I had sat on until then.

The pope asked us to reflect upon certain current issues, such as priestly ministry[110] or theological pluralism in the Church.[111] We produced a few "digests,"[112] at the very least, of the most serious contemporary research on such topics. Joseph Ratzinger's clearness of views, his wide knowledge, and his intellectual courage as well as his penetrating judgment distinguished themselves especially—as well as his humor, which was so full of kindness; he was, however, nobody's fool.

During our meetings I would generally sit between him and Hans Urs von Balthasar.[113] I must admit that our asides singularly helped me to put up with the immoderate speeches of some of our colleagues and the quarrels over pinheads of some others. I shall only quote a bon mot Ratzinger whispered to me after three quarters of an hour of Karl Rahner[114] making himself hoarse with a diatribe he had evidently composed for what Americans call "televidiots": "Another monologue on dialogue!" Ratzinger finally sighed with a smile in my direction.[115]

108. Paul VI had announced the forthcoming foundation of such a commission during an allocution ending the consistory on 28 April 1969; *Acta Apostolicae Sedis* 61 (1969): 431–32. Its thirty members were appointed for the first five years on 1 May 1969; Michael Sharkey, *The International Theological Commission: Texts and Documents, 1969–1985* (San Francisco: Ignatius Press, 1989), 327. It was instituted on 12 July 1969 within the Sacred Congregation for the Doctrine of the Faith; its principal task is, as its statutes declare, to "give assistance to the Holy See, and in a special way to the Sacred Congregation, in weighing doctrinal questions of greater importance"; *Acta Apostolicae Sedis* 61 (1969): 540–41. Its first plenary session was held 6–8 October of that year; see ibid., 713. There was an excellent atmosphere with a climate "of liberty and fraternal confidence"; Sharkey, 1.

109. For the list of first appointments see Sharkey, 327.

110. Priestly ministry was the topic of the second plenary session of the International Theological Commission, held 5–7 October 1970. It led to a working document on the topic approved by the Commission on 10 October 1970; an English translation by James Dupuis, SJ, is in Sharkey, 3–87.

111. Theological pluralism was the topic of the fourth plenary session, held 10–11 October 1972; *Acta Apostolicae Sedis* 64 (1972): 682–83. The document it produced is in Sharkey, 89–92.

112. Bouyer uses the English term "digest," which is closer to the original Latin *digesta* than is the French *résumé*.

Nevertheless, our commission—naturally a born object of resentment from the Holy Office's entire staff—had no Secretariat but that of that Congregation. The result was soon made manifest: all the documents we ever produced were simply filed in padlocked cabinets, from which it was out of the question that they should ever be taken out.

For this situation to come to light, Balthasar had to have an audience with Paul VI on the eve of the Episcopal Synod that had been assembled to discuss the priesthood.[116] The pope complained that our Commission hadn't yet provided him with the slightest report on the question. "How so?" answered Balthasar; "I was entrusted with the final version of the text myself; once it was fine-tuned and adopted by a plenary meeting, it was entrusted to the Holy Office months ago!"

Paul VI, indignant, named Balthasar and his main collaborators as Synod secretaries. Still, the report was not, for all that, placed in the pope's hands until it was the bishops' turn to work on the issue.[117] The same, or worse yet, applied to the report on the justification and limits of theological pluralism, which was so important in the post-conciliar situation and which was principally Ratzinger's work with help notably from Balthasar, Sagi-Bunič (a congenial Yugoslavian Capuchin), and myself.[118] It had

113. Hans Urs von Balthasar (1905–1988), Jesuit, 1929–1950; recipient of the Paul VI award for theology in 1984; created cardinal by John Paul II in 1988; see Bouyer, *Métier*, 102, 144, 147, 202. He was a friend of Fathers de Lubac (see 185, n. 8), Daniélou (see 141, n. 62), Ratzinger (future Benedict XVI, see 215, n. 49), and Bouyer. He helped guide the conversion of the mystic visionary Adrienne von Speyr (1902–1967; see Bouyer, *Métier* 144). He produced an abundant literature and sought to introduce aesthetics back into Christian thinking by developing the notion of "drama" and ultimately arriving at a meditation on the three persons of the Trinity. Bouyer described him under the character of Hans von Kasper in his novel *Les Hespérides* (see 132, n. 27). At his funeral that year, Fr. de Lubac said that he was the "most cultured [man] of his time," with which assessment Joseph Ratzinger concurred.

114. German Jesuit Karl Rahner (1904–1984) was a *peritus* at Vatican II. His efforts at reconciling Catholic tradition with secular philosophy (i.e., that of Kant and Heidegger), his thesis of "Anonymous Christians," and his explanation of the Eucharist never did win Bouyer over.

115. Congar reports that Rahner tended to hog the floor; see "Rahner, une fois de plus, accapare la parole," *Journal*, vol. 1, 496 (Thursday 24 October 1963). This event may have occurred during the 5–7 October 1970 session on the priesthood; the document it produced quotes Rahner twice and mentions ecumenical dialogue a couple of times.

116. This Synod, the second general assembly of the Synod of Bishops, met 30 September–6 November 1971 to discuss the ministerial priesthood and international justice; *Acta Apostolicae Sedis* 63 (1971): 775–76, 831–37. Balthasar's audience with the pope, therefore, took place on 29 September 1971, nearly a year after the International Theological Commission had ironed out its document on the ministerial priesthood; see 226, n. 110.

117. The bishops' work resulted in a text *De Sacerdotio Ministeriali*, made public on 30 November 1971; *Acta Apostolicae Sedis* 63 (1971): 898–922.

involved considerable work on our part and had been unanimously approved by our colleagues after the final revisions. Yet, it would never have seen the light of day unless, years later, Cardinal Ratzinger had taken it upon himself to publish it under his personal responsibility.[119]

When I realized the situation, I resigned and gave the pope the reasons why.

I received a touching letter from Cardinal Seper[120] (an excellent but weak man) begging me in the pope's name and in his own to retract my resignation. I knew that our report had been put on ice by the concurrence of future Cardinal Paul Philippe, Holy Office undersecretary,[121] who judged it to be dangerously novel, and of the commissary, the kind and somewhat dopey Charles Moeller,[122] who thought it too conservative. I also knew that there was then no question of freeing ourselves from their two-headed oversight. I, therefore, maintained my resignation. Sometime later, when the commission was being renewed, the pope named me again.[123] Despite the insistence of Msgr. Philippe Delhaye, finally named our secretary (but carefully deprived of the means of exercising his functions effectively),[124] who was infuriated by this farce, I again resigned on the spot.[125] Ever since then, I have had nothing to do with the International Theological Commission. They say it continues its work unperturbed—*bombycinans in vacuo!*[126] Much good may it do!

---

118. The Commission had worked on the topic during its fourth plenary session in 1972. Tomislav Janko Sagi-Bunić (1923–1999), a Croatian Capuchin (i.e. belonging to a branch of the Franciscan family) was Cardinal Seper's secretary and saw to it that such Catholic publications as *Communio* circulated in Communist Yugoslavia. For Seper see n. 120 below.

119. Commissio Theologica Internationalis, *Quinze thèses sur l'unité de la foi et le pluralisme théologique*, J. Ratzinger, P. Delhaye, P. Nemescheggi ed., *Esprit et Vie* 2 (Chambray-les-Tours: CLD, 1978).

120. Cardinal Franjo Seper (1905–1981) succeeded to the Martyr-Cardinal Aloysius Stepinac (1898–1960), the Archbishop of Zagreb (Croatia) who was framed by the Communists for allegedly supporting Nazi sympathizers during the German occupation in World War II. Seper was Prefect of the Congregation for the Doctrine of the Faith, 1968–1981.

121. For Fr. Paul-Pierre Philippe see 210, n. 19.

122. Charles Moeller (1912–1986), one of the contributors to Vatican II document *Gaudium et Spes*, was Secretary of the Secretariat for Christian Unity and rector of the Jerusalem Ecumenical Institute. He taught at Louvain and published a six-volume work, *Littérature du XXe siècle et christianisme*.

123. On 1 August 1974; *Acta Apostolicae Sedis* 66 (1974): 520. Of the 30 original members, 13 were nominated for a second five-year term, including Bouyer; Sharkey, 328.

124. See *Acta Apostolicae Sedis* 66 (1974): 521. Philippe Delhaye (1902–1990), a professor of philosophy at Louvain, was secretary of the International Theological Commission, 1972–1989.

One last word on this Commission: during one of its meetings, Father de Lubac[127] submitted to all of its French-speaking members a letter addressed to the pope. It listed all the obviously deliberate mistranslations in the French version of the new liturgical books, which Bugnini had nevertheless declared in conformity with the authentic Latin text. He had done this no less obviously because of the extra-theological arguments of the current boss of the *Centre National de Pastorale Liturgique*.[128] Everyone, struck by the scandalous character of this tinkering—including Father Congar, usually so anxious not to oppose what he called "Renewal in the Church"—signed this damning document without hesitation.[129] Eight days later, Bugnini got the sack from

125. This resignation took place in the winter of 1974–75 or the spring of 1975. It was after 16 December 1974, when Paul VI in his address to the Commission's sixth session expressed his satisfaction that of the original thirty members the thirteen he had renamed were still on the commission, therefore still counting Bouyer; *Acta Apostolicae Sedis* 67 (1975): 39–40. It took place before 24 April 1975, when the pope nominated Édouard Dhanis, SJ, who thus took Bouyer's place; see *Acta Apostolicae Sedis* 67 (1975): 286 and Sharkey, 328, n. 1: "Father Bouyer did not accept the appointment for personal reasons."

126. Bouyer is here drawing on Anglican controversialist William Chillingworth, *The Religion of Protestants: A Safe Way to Salvation*, published in response to Jesuit Matthias Wilson, alias Edward Knott, in 1637. The Latin phrase translates as "spinning silk in a vacuum."

127. Fr. Henri de Lubac, SJ (1896–1991), named professor of theology at the Catholic Faculty of Lyon in 1929; cofounder with J. Daniélou of the Patristic series *Sources Chrétiennes* in 1941; published his *Surnaturel: Études historiques* in 1946, which led him to lose his teaching position. John XXIII named him consultor to the Pontifical Theological Commission for the preparation of Vatican II in 1960; see *Acta Apostolicae Sedis* 52 (1960), 841. Paul VI named him consultor to the Sacred Congregation for Catholic Education in 1968; see *Acta Apostolicae Sedis* 60 (1968), 365. John Paul II made him Cardinal on 2 February 1983.

128. Father Jacques Cellier (see 154, n. 29) was the director of the CNPL from its foundation in 1966 until July 1973; he was succeeded by Fr. Philippe Béguerie. On this topic Bouyer elsewhere says, after bemoaning the distortions, omissions, "adaptations," and willful mistranslations ("L'Église catholique en crise," 21): "Yet it must be admitted that there was enough blame to go around at Rome itself. In the first place it is inconceivable that the authorities to whom the pope had entrusted the responsibility of checking and authorizing the translations would grant their approval to such textual travesties. It is doubtless better not to go searching for the reasons, or motivations, of this laxity, if one does not wish to lose his last illusions—not so much about the competence as about the probity of certain 'laterales Pontificis' [members of the pope's entourage]."

129. The ITC meeting during which this rebellion of the French-speaking theologians against Bugnini took place must have been its sixth, on 16 December 1974. Indeed the official French version of the Latin *editio typica* of the Novus Ordo Missae was promulgated on 7 October 1974 and the Commission's 16 December 1974 meeting was the first one to include the recently appointed member Fr. Congar. It was the last meeting that Bouyer attended; see n. 125 above. Fr. de Lubac came especially for this purpose, since

the Pope.[130] But, characteristically of Paul VI's kindness veering on weakness in those last years, he consecrated him as bishop a month later[131]—still, only to send him as Nuncio to Khomeiny![132] Along with his exquisite tact, there was in this pontiff a mean streak that very few people seem to have suspected.

After these several experiences, it is understandable that I haven't kept much of my youthful enthusiasm for "conciliarity" in general, and less yet for that pocketsize conciliarity now abusively dubbed "collegiality" where, in fact, a few clever devils regularly pull the strings behind the backs of simple gulls who after all that imagine they've taken decisions others took for them, though under their responsibility.

---

he no longer belonged to the commission at this date. Already Bouyer, Lubac, and Congar along with Frs. Le Guillou and Feuillet had written an open letter to the Bishops of France protesting the replacement of "One, Holy, Catholic and Apostolic" by "One, Holy, Universal and Apostolic" in the new French version of the Creed in October 1970; see "Cinq théologiens demandent le maintien du mot 'catholique' dans la traduction française du 'Credo,'" La Croix, 17 December 1970. The switch to "Universal" had been the CNPL's (see 154–55 above) brainchild; see Bouyer, Métier, 79.

130. Bugnini's fall from grace took place seven months after the December 1974 CTI meeting; Bouyer has telescoped the chronology (he is writing at least ten years after the fact). Other factors played a role in it. Fr. Pierre-Marie Gy (1922–2004; director of the Institut Supérieur de Liturgie, 1956–1986; consultor of the Consilium, 1964–1969 and of the Congregation for Divine Worship from 1969) told French Church historian Luc Perrin that Bugnini's sacking was due to his underhanded encouragement of new Eucharistic prayers (particularly in Belgium and the Netherlands) against Paul VI's wishes (electronic letter from Luc Perrin, 14 November 2010). Bugnini alludes to difficulties in this respect in his Reform, 467–76, including a strongly worded letter from Secretary of State Cardinal Benelli who, still according to Fr. Gy, denounced these maneuvers to Paul VI. Certainly these two reasons render unnecessary the file a cardinal delivered to Paul VI that allegedly convinced him of Bugnini's freemasonic affiliation, which, again allegedly, would explain his dismissal and exile to Iran. Bugnini knew of this file's delivery (and indicates that he strongly suspected who this cardinal was) and wrote to Paul VI on 22 October 1975 to tell the Pope that he did "not know what [Freemasonry] is, what it does, or what its purposes are"; see his Reform, 91–92.

131. Bugnini had in fact been ordained Titular Archbishop of Diocletiana on 13 February 1972, before the rift between him and Paul VI.

132. Bugnini was named Pro-Nuncio to Iran on 4 January 1976. This act of kicking Bugnini upstairs illustrates the Vatican expression promoveatur ut amoveatur ("promote him to remove him"). The interim between his two assignments allowed Bugnini to compose the first draft of his Memoirs, as he says, "between the end of my 'service' as secretary of the Congregation for Divine Worship and the beginning of my 'service' as a diplomat, that is, between July 15, 1975, and January 5, 1976 ... (... they were dies amaritudinis)," Reform, xxiv.

13

Friendships and Favorite Places

THE LAST FEW chapters have essentially mingled a more or less pathetic comedy with seriousness.

The same note is found throughout, whether in my mixed experiences at the Oratory, in my *Institut catholique* misadventures, or in my involvement in the Council's tragi-comic preparations and extensions. Regarding the Council particularly, Ratzinger made the correct observation that Gregory of Nazianzen's disenchanted reflections on the Council of Constantinople applied to it.[1]

And, yet, I never took any of this too seriously, thanks to two factors which, as you will have already sensed, mightily helped me. On the one hand, there are the friendships I have made and that developed through even the most ambiguous of misadventures. On the other hand, despite the sometimes unpleasant stories in which I was involved, certain places were able to help me restore the inner peace my adventure might well have shattered. Thanks be to God, however, none of this did ever deeply trouble it.

I have already said what my three friends from my student days[2] and then my two confreres at Juilly[3] meant to me. Along the way, I have also mentioned many intermittent friendships which were nonetheless often just as meaningful to me. I might mention many others besides; I should rather, however, dwell on two among them. One accompanied me from the first days after my conversion, whereas the other, which had been prepared far earlier yet but was born a little later, did so and came to an end only through death. Both of these, like those I developed with Eliot and then with Tolkien, were writers' friendships born of

---

1. See 215, n. 50.
2. These were Bouyer's friends from his Protestant seminary days, Jacques Deransart, Jean Malbert, and André Hardy (see 64–65).
3. For Fathers Cognet and Joseph see 150.

enthusiastic readings. They came about thanks to encounters, one of which was precipitated by external events, whereas the other was long postponed, but both of which were deep from the very outset and have not since ceased to grow deeper.

The first of these friendships was with Julien Green;[4] the second was with Elizabeth Goudge.[5] These two names alone imply how different these friendships were. Yet, for my part, I find many connections between the two, who are far closer than they appear at first glance.

I have already brought up how precocious my interest—or rather my passion!—was for fantasy literature, starting with my reading certain of Jules Verne's works, but especially with my equally youthful plunge into Poe's works.[6]

It is undeniably a connection with the latter that immediately grabbed me when I launched into *The Dreamer*[7] and then *Midnight*[8] as soon as they came out. But nearly immediately I was sensitive to the more subtle extravaganza implied by the apparent (and how brilliant!) realism of *The Closed Garden* [*Adrienne Mesurat*],[9] that younger, so much simpler and, therefore, more astounding sister of Madame Bovary.[10]

After that the incomparable translator and critic, Pierre Leyris,[11] arranged a meeting that was to spark an uninterrupted series of conversations. Some came in rapid succession, others were more spaced out, but they haven't stopped since the end of World War II.

Green's journal has given our exchanges an unexpected fate, which dispenses me from having to dwell on them much.[12] I shall only point out, not without forthright amusement, that all the more or less serious conversions he has mentioned between us are to be completed by those with a certain Father B. One has to think that the relative mystery in

4. Julien Green (1900–1998), American French-language writer who spent most of his life in France from 1916 on. He was the first foreigner elected to the Académie française, in 1971. For the influence of Bouyer's friendship on Green, see Anthony H. Newbury, *Julien Green: Religion and Sensuality* (Amsterdam: Rodopi, 1986), 71–73.

5. See 173, n. 66.

6. For Bouyer's childhood interest in Edgar Allen Poe, see 42, n. 23.

7. Julien Green, *The Dreamer*, trans. Vyvyan Holland (London: William Heinemann, 1934).

8. Id., *Midnight*, trans. Vyvyan Holland (New York and London, Harper & Brothers, 1936).

9. Id., *The Closed Garden*, trans. Henry Longan Stuart (New York: Harper & Brothers, 1928).

10. Gustave Flaubert published *Madame Bovary* in 1857.

11. For Pierre Leyris see 77, n. 86.

which he has shrouded them is due to the particularly unedifying nature of his speech. Some of the preceding chapters will by now have made my own readers only too familiar with this habit, or rather foible, of mine.

Despite our many differences there are three factors that have contributed to this friendship's importance for both Green and me in our declining years. The first is this shared sense of the mystery of existence, of the world where it plays itself out; I shall underscore that it is a mystery felt just as keenly in the nearly "naturalist" story of *The Closed Garden* as in the diurnal or nocturnal mirages of *The Dreamer* and *Midnight*. In addition to this there is, I should say, the particular religious sensibility of two converts from Protestantism who, though firmly persuaded of the unique authenticity of the Catholic tradition, never had the slightest temptation to cast doubt on the permanent value of elements of their Protestant formation, which modern Catholics, despite praiseworthy efforts, manage to reclaim only awkwardly. By this I mean both a passionate interest in the Bible and the deeply personal nature of the life of faith as the consciousness of a grace that is effectively gratuitous to the highest degree. Hence a personalism which, in fact, postulates the Church's communion, though not any manner of collectivism. This is what the famous Dean Inge[13] expressed quite well in the phrase "one cannot be religious by proxy," a phrase that seems totally incomprehensible to a number of Catholics, be they Lefebvre-style traditionalists, Marxists, or more prosaically "Modernists."

To these two fundamental elements of our friendship must of course be added the fact of a double, French and English, culture. Furthermore, it is one in which an America that is as little "Americanist" as possible, in the ordinary meaning of that term, brings us together, even if it

---

12. For this journal, see Louis Bouyer, "Le Journal de Julien Green," *La Vie spirituelle* 101 (1959): 63–67. Bouyer, under his actual name, first appears in Julien Green's journal on 18 March 1948 when the latter approves of Bouyer's article on Swiss psychoanalysis; *Journal* 1928–1958 (Paris: Plon, 1961), 707. Julien Green's esteem for Bouyer comes out in the following entries: 15 October 1948 (ibid., 735): "I always have the greatest pleasure speaking with Fr. B." (*J'ai toujours un extrême plaisir à parler avec le P.B...*) and 28 January 1951 (ibid., 852): "Father B., who is one of the most knowledge men I know" (*Père B..., qui est un des hommes les plus savants que je connaisse*). Their affinity was such that Bouyer pierced the (homosexual) secret of Green's play *Sud*, as he records on 7 December 1956 (ibid., 1125–26): "Father B. read this play and immediately guessed its secret, as was to be expected of him. . . . When a reader is intuitive, he is in a better position to get it" (*Le Père B . . . a lu cette pièce et en a aussitôt deviné le secret, comme il fallait s'y attendre de sa part. . . . Un lecteur est plus à même de saisir, s'il est intuitif*).

13. William Ralph Inge (1860–1954), the "Gloomy Dean" of St. Paul's Cathedral in London, 1911–1934. He also taught divinity at Cambridge.

is in fact in the seventh *arrondissement* that we have been meeting for the past so many years.

For her part Elizabeth Goudge attracted me with *Green Dolphin Country.*[14] As one of the first translations in the *Feux croisés* collection,[15] which, if I am not mistaken, was founded by Gabriel Marcel,[16] it suddenly became as popular over here as it had been in America, not to mention England. For once England, unlike in the case of those "fakes" mentioned in my conversations with Eliot,[17] had little or no hesitation in acknowledging as her own an author that foreigners, this time correctly, had been the first to distinguish for them.

Afterwards, I became attached to many of her other stories. First it was through their evocation of the countryside, so typically English, and of the bordering sea on the south coast or simply around Guernsey, home of her mother's side of the family. It was above all, however, what I consider to be perhaps her most characteristic masterpiece that got me, *The Scent of Water*,[18] with its evocation of a child's soul opening up to life inseparably from a house and countryside that reveal it to him. This would extend, on the one hand, to that other delightful story in *The Little White Horse*,[19] and even more to the two symphonies that are the *Cathedral Cities* trilogy[20] and, better yet, *The Eliot Family*.[21] The first of these is so delightfully Anglican whereas the second is less specific in its Christianity, but more deeply human.

Yet, I should never have taken it upon myself to enter into a personal relationship with Elizabeth were it not for that exceptional book, *The Castle on the Hill*.[22] In it she so touchingly evokes how the war crushed all that she so rightly held to, even when it may have seemed to be the past in a dream, or even a dream of the past. I then could not help

---

14. Elizabeth Goudge, *Green Dolphin Country* (London: Hodder and Stoughton, 1944), published in the USA as *Green Dolphin Street: A Novel* (New York: Coward-McCann, 1944).

15. Elizabeth Goudge, *Le Pays du Dauphin vert*, trans. Maxime Ouvrard, Collection "Feux croisés, âmes et terres étrangères" (Paris: Plon, 1946).

16. Gabriel Marcel (see 132, n. 26) founded the "Feux croisés" collection, intended to give a French readership to international literature, in 1926.

17. See 178–79.

18. Elizabeth Goudge, *The Scent of Water* (New York: Coward-McCann, 1963).

19. Elizabeth Goudge, *The Little White Horse* (New York: Coward-McCann, 1946).

20. These are: *A City of Bells* (London: Duckworth, 1936); *Towers In the Mist* (ibid., 1938); *The Dean's Watch* (London: Hodder and Stoughton, 1960).

21. *The Bird In the Tree* (London: Duckworth, 1940); *The Herb of Grace* (London: Hodder and Stoughton, 1948), a.k.a. *Pilgrim's Inn* (New York: Coward-McCann, 1948); *The Heart of the Family* (London: Hodder & Stoughton, 1953).

22. *The Castle on the Hill* (London: Duckworth, 1942).

writing to her, both to tell her how much her distress touched me and to assert that the certainties embedded in all the rest of her work could resist even such an attack, or even such an apparent defeat, all the same.

Her extraordinarily confident response brought about a regular correspondence. It was even more enriching than my brief yet regular visits, even as death was nearing. Someday, perhaps, this correspondence will be published. I should be wasting my time if I tried to bring to life here what is contained in it, with the freshness of the moment when thought discovers itself in its own expression.

To these two Anglo-Saxon friendships I should add a third, which a sudden death kept from growing. Yet, it would give rise, I think, to my two best books, though also my shortest. Here I am thinking of Cardinal Heenan, who already had had the only positive reaction to my *Newman*,[23] and also to those two incendiary pamphlets that garnered so much hatred (and so much friendliness too) for me: *The Decomposition of Catholicism*[24] and *Religieux et clercs contre Dieu*.[25] I should never have written them without Heenan's initiative, for after a few of our conversations he proposed that we should collaborate on writing up a dialogue—since ours had begun so well—between a bishop and a theologian on the Council's aftermath. Alas! a cancer that developed with lightning-speed made our common project unachievable. Still, these two little books are its outcome, among others. I agree with a fair number of wits in preferring them to my weightier volumes; they owe it to that friend I lost too soon.

Allow me to bring up a little fact, here again on the same topic, that goes a long way to explain one of this century's most discussed, but generally least understood, personalities: Pope Paul VI. After reading my *Decomposition* he told me, during an audience: "I absolutely have to give you a testimony of the pleasure I had in reading you!" And with that he opened a drawer in his desk and took out . . . an admirable pectoral cross! I have already had another occasion to point out the unexpected mischie-

---

23. *Newman. Sa vie, sa spiritualité* (Paris: Cerf, 1952). English version: *Newman: His Life and Spirituality*, trans. J. Lewis May (London: Burns & Oates, 1958). For Heenan's positive, and everyone else's negative, reviews of this book see 169.

24. Bouyer, *La Décomposition du catholicisme* (Paris: Aubier-Montaigne, 1968); English version, *The Decomposition of Catholicism*, trans. Charles Underhill Quinn (Chicago: Franciscan Herald Press, 1969).

25. Louis Bouyer, *Religieux et clercs contre Dieu* (Paris: Aubier Montaigne, 1975), untranslated into English. Bouyer privately told some intimate friends that this book had allowed him to publish criticisms he had preferred not to include in his book on the same subject, *The Invisible Father* (see 202, n. 80), whose original French edition came out the following year.

vousness of which he was capable,[26] and which very few people have suspected (among these happy few, I am glad to mention Vittorio Peri, the Vatican's *scrittore greco*, an excellent Christian husband and father and, at the same time, an incomparable patrologist and byzantinologist!).[27]

Among these pages dedicated to the memory of friendships that have left their mark on me, I am inclined to say more about that pope. He was so misunderstood, or, rather, so little known. He publicly mentioned his friendship for me on a number of occasions. But I'll admit that I am too afraid to look like a certain show-off regarding whom Bremond[28] used to say "he stinks of ego!" and who has wanted to pose for all history as Paul VI's *kath'exochen* friend![29]

At any rate, since I am not in too bad a position to speak of him, I shall only say that just as John XXIII was far from being the revolutionary he has so often been described as, his successor has never at all been the frightened reactionary some have stupidly invented. As a matter of fact, he was the true liberal. He succeeded an undeniable though intelligent conservative, but could not allow a proper freedom to degenerate into pure (or rather impure!) license.

For the time being I shall leave aside other, more intimate, friendships such as those which, I hope, will accompany my last days here below. I shall first come to some of those particularly beloved places associated with my best friendships. I daresay that my very fascination with the *genius loci* of each has something by way of friendship in it.[30]

Is there not in certain places something personal derived from those whose presence has molded them? Or is it not the case that they have, in an extraordinary manner, contributed to producing those very personalities?

Allow me then to dwell on Brittany and Spain, in parallel with what I may have said in the first pages on Paris in 1914 and later, on Saint-Ger-

---

26. The other act of "unsuspected mischievousness" was appointing Bugnini to Tehran; see 230, n. 132.

27. Vittorio Peri (1932–2006) was named *scrittore greco* (curator of Greek holdings at the Vatican libraries) in 1961.

28. For Henri Bremond see 52–53, n. 25.

29. Bouyer uses a New Testament phrase, κατ' ἐξοχήν, more properly rendered *kat'exochēn* ("preeminent," "principal"), describing dignitaries in King Agrippa's court (Acts 25:23). It here doubtless refers to French philosopher Jean Guitton (1901–1999), member of the Académie française and friend of Cardinal Montini (future Pope Paul VI), on whom he wrote: *Dialogues avec Paul VI* (Paris: Fayard, 1967); *Paul VI et l'Année sainte* (Paris: Fayard, 1974); *Paul VI Secret* (Paris: Desclée De Brouwer, 1979). Guitton was the first layman invited to attend Vatican II.

30. The *genius loci*, Latin for "genius of a given place," i.e., its local spirit.

main-en-Laye after the war, on Asnières between the wars, on Sancerre up to my conversion, then on Juilly, not to mention Alsace and Lower Normandy.[31]

These two countries doubtless had such an attraction for me as soon as I discovered them because of a deferred resurgence of my unconscious or preconscious roots, or at least because of the undeniable kinship deriving from my ancestry.

I may say that around my mother—and especially my grandfather or my aunt Jeanne[32]—I breathed in a sufficiently Hispanic atmosphere that, despite certain reservations in other lines of my pedigree, I felt perfectly attuned to Spanish language and literature, above all in Cervantes, as soon as their study moved me, or rather took hold of my whole being.[33] Yet, it was only right after the Second World War that a scholarly conference held in Barcelona, followed by trips to Montserrat and Vich, immersed me in it once again.[34] Later, two Eucharistic Congresses, one in Zaragoza and the next in Valencia, brought me back to it, not to mention a too-short tourist walk with my confreres back in Barcelona after Madrid, the Escorial and again Toledo following the discovery of Burgos.[35] What was to leave a permanent mark on me, however, was the academic semester I spent in Salamanca in 1972, with occasional trips to Alba de Tormes and Ávila, and another visit to Toledo.[36]

31. For Saint-Germain-en-Laye see chapter 1 above; for Asnières see chapter 2; for Sancerre see chapter 3; for Juilly see chapters 7–9; for Alsace see chapters 5 and 11; for Lower Normandy see chapters 8 and 11.

32. For Bouyer's maternal grandfather, the musician who emigrated from Catalonia, and his mother's younger sister Jeanne, see chapter 1 above.

33. Miguel de Cervantes (1547–1616) wrote *Don Quixote de la Mancha* between 1605 and 1615.

34. Barcelona, on the northeastern shore of Spain, is the capital of Catalonia. Montserrat is a mountain range about twenty-five miles west of Barcelona and reaches 3925 feet; there is a Benedictine abbey there of the Subiaco congregation (see 153, n. 25). Vich (or Vic) is a small episcopal town fifty-five miles north of Barcelona.

35. Zaragoza, the Caesaraugusta of the Romans, is the capital of Aragon in northeastern Spain. It was a stronghold of the Reconquista from the eleventh century on. Valencia is on the eastern shore of Spain, 300 miles south of Barcelona. Madrid, in the middle of Spain, became the Spanish capital in the late Middle Ages. The Escorial is a monastery, palace, and library built between 1563 and 1584 for King Philip II of Spain (1527–1598), about thirty-five miles northwest of Madrid. Toledo, the ancient capital of Visigothic Spain, is fifty-two miles south of Madrid. Burgos, in the center of northern Spain, is the capital of Castille-and-León and another Reconquista stronghold.

36. Salamanca, 170 miles west of Madrid, has a university founded in 1218. Alba de Tormes, seventeen miles southwest of Salamanca, is where the incorrupt body of St. Teresa of Ávila (1515–1582) is kept at the Carmelite convent she founded there. Her birth town, Ávila, is midway between Madrid and Salamanca.

I can still see myself the last time I was there, sipping my chinchon (the excellent local anise spirit) at a café terrace in the Zocodover.[37] Meanwhile, some of those Frenchmen who speak out loud in their own language in another Latin country without being able to imagine that nearly everyone understands them said to each other, pointing at me: "Look at that old priest: what a Spanish head he has, really!" Rarely have I been so flattered—or so involuntarily! The fact of the matter is that both physically and mentally I must look more and more like my mother's father. I have mentioned what he meant to me as a child.

Nothing in me is more deeply ingrained than the lucid passion of the Spanish character, its religious sense as well as the realism with which it approaches life and death. The Spanish landscape alone, whether in its desert-like countryside or in its so familiar, yet so unreal, cities (I am thinking especially of Toledo and Salamanca), brings to life in me that *alegría* before the world and existence.[38] It is both vertigo and exultation.

That other part of my ancestry, which on my paternal grandmother's side goes back to Brittany, overcomes me with just as much happiness when I'm there. And to be sure there is good reason why the novel attributed to Louis Lambert goes so effortlessly from Castille to Brocéliande forest![39] At least for me these are beyond doubt two different yet closely related forms of the mystery of things. The blinding light of Iberian summers and the liquid brightness of the Celtic shores and shades evoke it equally well.

It is, therefore, no surprise that I have become so strongly attached to California these last few years, particularly to San Francisco. Hispanic culture easily transplanted itself there and took root in this other maritime land with woods and hills that, at the western end of America, strangely calls to mind the western end of Europe.

Indeed, recently the friendship of a young Californian Jesuit Father of Italian ancestry, Joseph Fessio, who had studied in Lyon, so to speak in the shadow of Henri de Lubac and Hans Urs von Balthasar, had drawn me there to the Institute of Christian civilization he had founded.[40] This is how I came to know that university. From the top of what is called the Lone Mountain it overlooks on one side the Golden Gate Park as far as

37. The Zodocover (from the Arabic word for a cattle market) is the most popular square in Toledo.

38. *Alegría* means "mirth" or "joyfulness."

39. In the novel Bouyer wrote under the pseudonym Louis Lambert, *Prélude à l'Apocalypse* (see 132, n. 27), the protagonists travel through Castille several times before going to the forest of Brocéliande and the desert of Anaon (see 203–4).

the ocean and on the other side that other park, the Presidio, which skirts the bay. To bring this place's charm to perfection, particularly for me, there is across from the university a convent of Mexican Carmelite nuns. They live in a cloister attached to a delightful church whose style is Hispano-Indian baroque and, though modern, an exceptional success.

Behind us downtown stretches along the bay's inner rim. It mingles particularly whimsical skyscrapers with the sudden change of scene of Chinatown as well as with the survival of the Dolores Mission and its whole neighborhood: there again, super-Hispanic.[41]

I wouldn't dream of giving a detailed description of the walks I take again and again in that city. It is doubly admirable: in itself and in its surrounding landscape. On one side there is the Pacific Ocean and its bay, linked by a canal that winds so much that Drake, Elizabeth's great admiral, could sail to and fro before its entrance without suspecting that it led to an inlet where the whole Spanish fleet was gathered.[42] On the other side of the canal, Mount Tamalpais rises.[43] Muir Woods stretches out on its foothills; it is one of the most fabulously old Sequoia forests.[44] Meanwhile, far to the east and south, there is the Nevada mountain range, and more particularly the extraordinary Yosemite Valley where its own Sequoias frame waterfalls more fantastical than Niagara.[45]

The city itself, with its dizzyingly steep hills, has an astonishing vari-

40. Joseph Fessio, SJ (1941–) did in fact know Fr. Henri de Lubac (see 185, n. 8) in Lyon, where he defended his dissertation on von Balthasar (see 227, n. 113) in 1975; his dissertation director was Fr. Joseph Ratzinger. Fr. Fessio and others founded the Saint Ignatius Institute at the Jesuit University of San Francisco in 1976. It was a Great Books program. Fr. Fessio also founded Ignatius Press in San Francisco in 1978, which has republished several of Bouyer's works: *The Church of God: Body of Christ and Temple of the Spirit* (see 207, n. 2); *The Word: Church and Sacrament in Protestantism and Catholicism*; *Newman's Vision of Faith: A Theology for Times of General Apostasy*; and *Newman: His Life and Spirituality* (see 35, n. 11).

41. The Dolores Mission is the oldest building in San Francisco; the Franciscans founded it in 1776 and its church was consecrated in 1791.

42. Francis Drake (1542–1596), the English freebooter during the reign of Elizabeth I (1533–1603), crossed the Straits of Magellan at the tip of South America and sailed north along the coast as far, perhaps, as Canada. He missed the Golden Gate but founded a colony, New Albion, farther north (location unknown).

43. Mount Tamalpais, at 2,574 feet, has the highest peak in the northern California Coast Ranges.

44. Muir Woods is a few miles west of the northern end of the Golden Gate Bridge. The sequoia there are over 1,000 years old and reach 300 feet in height. The woods are named for Scottish naturalist John Muir (1838–1914).

45. The same John Muir participated in creating Yosemite Valley as a protected area, in the foothills of the Rocky Mountains. Its redwoods are less tall but squatter than the Muir Woods sequoias.

ety of prospects. Its crowded houses are either frankly Spanish or in a local, overelaborate style quite typical of the end of the nineteenth century, with fussy and often multicolored façades.

Yet San Francisco's charm is due, along with the bodies of water on three sides, to its parks. I have already mentioned the Golden Gate Park. In fact in the direction of the Golden Gate itself it has been reduced to a double tree-lined boulevard with elegant houses on either side, while from the Lone Mountain where I live it extends over about ten kilometers all the way to the Pacific. There it spreads north and south over three or four kilometers.

Most weeks I walk its entire length at least once along winding walkways among trees of all the kinds that grow all over the world, along lakes, streams, and waterfalls. The whole thing is dotted with gardens. Some are rose gardens, others have tulips in all possible varieties, while yet others have the immense arum, one of California's specialties.[46]

The other park, the Presidio, is the army's and the navy's domain. It borders the bay's access and has some of the most grandiose vistas of mountain and sea. In places, it is a forest dotted with golf courses; elsewhere it is reduced to the sumptuous gardens of the beautiful Seacliff and Camino del Mar residences.[47] When I am not there, for a change from the inexhaustible variety of Golden Gate Park or wandering about among the entertaining shops in Chinatown, I will go up Marina Avenue farther along the bay, though closer in town, between more very beautiful homes and the marina. Beyond that, glistening in the distance day and night, is the lighthouse on Alcatraz, where for a long time there was a penitentiary, unexpectedly for such a decor.

This city is indeed the gem of our farthest west. It always brings to my mind Constantinople and Leningrad, in the farthest east of our Europe. They are the two marvels on our side of the Atlantic to which I devoted a few pages laden with personal memories in my *En quête de la sagesse*. That little book, to tell the truth, is more like the heart of these memoirs than some appendix to them.[48]

Just as I often go from Hispanic countries to Celtic regions in memory even as I renew my enchantment with San Francisco, so too it is not rare for me to recall my fondest memories of that other spit of land

---

46. The arum can reach a height of three feet and produces a flower with a single, cone-shaped white petal.

47. Seacliff and Camino del Mar are posh neighborhoods west of the Golden Gate Bridge.

48. For "that little book," see 213, n. 34. In it Bouyer discusses his visits to Istanbul (Constantinople) and Leningrad (Saint Petersburg) for ecumenical encounters.

between sea and canal: Landévennec.[49] I have lived unforgettable years there. Its Celtic faerie remains just as present to me as what is left of Brocéliande.[50] Such is its gripping charm; such is its mysterious and constant combination of endlessly interlacing woods and water.

And now it is a monastic site that shelters the years that I hope to be the last of my life, after it had attracted me as few others have when I was a teenager. It is at the heart of the Brotonne forest,[51] where the enclosed valley of the Fonetenelle meets those meanders through which, amid woods and hills, the Seine reaches its estuary. Such is the setting of Saint Wandrille monastery. In our lands it is perhaps the most recollected and sublime place where cloistered life, at the very place where it began a good twelve centuries ago, continues. But this brings me to what ought to be this book's—and my life's—conclusion.

49. For Landévennec see 201, n. 76.
50. For the Breton forest of Brocéliande, see 203, n. 86.
51. The Brotonne forest is across the Seine River to the north of Saint Wandrille (see 71, n. 59). A great bridge crosses the river between the two.

14

Finita jam sunt praelia[1]

THE VERY YEAR my mother was to die in December, the last excursion my father and I made with her was to Rouen and Le Havre.[2] There was at the time a boat that turned that trip on the lower Seine into an unforgettable outing. Nowhere had it yet been spoiled by those hideous warts of so-called "progress": the petroleum works that have transformed one of France's most beautiful riverside landscapes from Nez de Tancarville on into a horror.[3]

I remember very clearly that one time, when we were passing by the opening of the wooded dale that goes up to Saint-Wandrille near the waters of the Fontenelle River, I heard mention of the ancient monastery. It was abandoned at the time, but its beauty was an object of praise. I regretted not being able to glimpse its more or less ruined outline as I had done at Jumièges and I would always keep the nostalgia of it.[4]

Of course, when the "monk of the Eastern Church"[5] suggested that I make a first contact with the Benedictine monks who had just returned to it, this memory was rekindled. A little later on, I found just a handful of monks there. They were laboring under the task of breathing life back into buildings that were as beautiful as the land that had seen them issue forth from the earth. They had been miraculously preserved, except for the church, which had been so beautiful. It was torn down, like so many

1. Opening lines of the Easter hymn, which dates to the twelfth century. Giovanni da Palestrina (1525–1594) set it to music. It is best known to English-speaking audiences as "The Strife is O'er," set to music in 1861 by William Henry Monk (1823–1889).

2. See the beginning of chapter 3 above.

3. These petroleum works are upstream from Saint Wandrille (see 71, n. 59) in the penultimate bend of the Seine; the Tancarville Bridge, erected in 1955–1959, crosses it about sixteen miles upstream.

4. The ruins of the Abbey of Jumièges are nestled in the next meander of the Seine, upstream of that where Saint Wandrille is.

5. Father Lev Gillet (1893–1980); see 66, n. 40.

others, at the very period when the Romantics were endlessly singing the praises of the Gothic!

Yet the monks' discreet warmth and the courage and good spirits they put into bringing back to life that splendid ghost immediately won me over. I shan't once again go over the role these very monks would play in the last preambles to my conversion. Recall only that, once I was Catholic, I could foresee nothing better than to become a monk at Saint-Wandrille.[6]

I wouldn't say now that I regret having been set on another track. Not only could I have done much worse in the Holy Church than the French Oratory, despite its weaknesses; but, when all is said and done, I think that those who directed me towards a more active life and priestly ministry did not mislead me, even if their reasons were not among the best. Please believe me when I say that I am not particularly proud of my life as a whole, or any more especially of what some people (such as my excellent young colleague at the University of San Francisco, Erasmo Leiva) call my "*oeuvre*."[7] Regarding it, I am quite unable, for my part, to discern any of the traces of genius (and even less of holiness) that such kind souls imagine they discover in it. I do, however, believe that I was born to teach, and to teach the Christian religion as the only possible inspiration for a humanism that is not a pipe-dream.

My books strike me as no more than the fruit of a lifetime of work. They remain, simply, the output of an honest and competent professor.

My priestly ministry contributed to their elaboration far more than the other way around. Though its fruits were limited, it was the most effective motivation for my own spiritual and intellectual development. That said, however, I am in the best position to discern its undeniable weaknesses, insufficiencies, or even mistakes.

Having said all of that, it is nonetheless with a profound joy and an ineffable gratitude to God and also to the men He put on my path that I find myself back in this beautiful, and to me so meaningful, place. I am here to end my earthly days, in all likelihood.

There is in this wooded dale a discreet charm, a serene beauty. Its remaining buildings, the Maurists' best, around a cloister dating to the

---

6. See chapter 3 above.

7. Born to a Cuban father and a Greek mother, Erasmo Leiva-Merikakis fled Fidel Castro's communist regime and moved to the USA. He taught literature and theology at the Jesuit University of San Francisco, where he came to know Bouyer. He also works with Ignatius Press as German translator and author, for instance of *Fire of Mercy, Heart of The Word: Meditations on the Gospel According to Saint Matthew*, vol. 1 (San Francisco: Ignatius Press, 1996), for which Bouyer wrote the preface. For his appreciation of Bouyer, see his "Louis Bouyer the Theologian," *Communio* (USA edition) 16.2 (1989): 257–82.

last centuries of the Middle Ages give it light and life without in any way lessening or subduing nature around it.[8] Though it is perhaps less charming than the Sancerre region I have loved so, it is yet a witness to that implicit art with which the Benedictines have humanized it even as they were sanctifying themselves in it.

I confess that I still prefer the Romanesque refectory's austere harmony to those buildings; it is at the bottom of the vale. Likewise, I prefer the exquisite, yet so crude, Saint-Saturnin chapel, which is pre-Romanesque.[9]

Yet, I do very much like the felicitous contrast between the old church's ruins that erupt up to the sky and the rustic and joyful bareness of the fifteenth-century barn that an impeccably tactful architect-monk transformed into an oratory. He did so simply by adding an altar and a sanctuary whose precise sobriety one could not hope for today!

Still, I wonder: perhaps I prefer that other barn nearby, from an earlier century. He was able to split it into two stories. The ground level houses meeting rooms while the second floor has a few cells that look out onto the beautiful tall trees. These act as a curtain at the edge of the property as it is today, before the meadows stretching between the two sections of the forest where the valley continues.

One of these cells is my bedroom. Right next to it is my study, where I am now writing these lines.[10] I don't attend the night service, and I only go to Lauds in the morning on days when they are sung from beginning to end (recited psalmody is monotonous and inevitably puts me to sleep). Yet, whether I am in choir or not, I unite myself to liturgical prayer at its appointed times. Never have I felt the pacifying, refreshing effect of the Church's traditional prayer as I do in this solitude and silence—*sicut lilia in transitu aquae*, as the motto goes.[11]

---

8. The Benedictine congregation of the Maurists was founded in France in 1620 and suppressed during the revolution. Their patron is Saint Maurus (c. 512–c. 584), disciple of Saint Benedict; he is said to have introduced the Benedictine rule in Gaul. The Maurists reformed, renewed, and founded abbeys, but are best known for their historical and patristic scholarship. Their most famous members are Dom Jean Mabillon (1632–1707) and Dom Bernard de Montfaucon (1655–1741), founders of the sciences of diplomatics (the study of ancient documents) and paleography (the study of ancient handwriting).

9. Saint Wandrille (see 71, n. 59) is said to have built this chapel himself in the seventh century; work was done on it in the eleventh century.

10. Other cells in the loft of this ancient and repurposed barn housed Henri Groüès, the famous French humanitarian Capuchin monk known as *l'Abbé Pierre* (1912–2007). Bouyer and he got on quite well.

11. The motto *quasi lilia quae sunt in transitu aquae* ("as the lilies that are on the brink of the water," Ecclesiasticus 50:8) was added to the monastery's coat of arms in 1894.

When I came here, I gave away all of my books that had an equivalent in the monks' library, along with my liturgical vestments and the great icon of the Deësis that was above my chapel's altar.[12] All of that is now in the women's Abbey of Notre Dame de la Fidélité, regarding which I shall speak presently. The books that I have kept, aside from those that are in Paris, line the walls of my bedroom and of this office. The spaces between them are principally filled with icons, particularly of the twelve great feasts, though I still prefer the admirable composition of the life of Saint Elijah; it is probably from Novgorod. Among them there are also pictures of the places I have been to and loved the most, from Delphi to San Francisco, from La Lucerne to Washington, and from Oxford to Salamanca.[13]

I am too rarely and too briefly in Paris anymore to occupy a room in the Villa Montmorency, which belongs to the community on which I still depend.[14] My friends the Duchesnes have had the kindness to provide me with a place to stay for short visits,[15] as they have done for other members of the Communio group.[16] It, too, is filled with books and

---

12. For this Deësis icon, see 205, n. 94.

13. Delphi, northwest of Athens, was famous in antiquity for its shrine to the god Apollo. Bouyer narrates his visit there in *En quête de la sagesse* (see 213, n. 34).

14. For the Villa Montmorency, see 133, n. 32.

15. 30 rue d'Auteuil, in the sixteenth *arrondissement* of Paris. This apartment was made available to Bouyer in 1977 by the parents of Marie-José Roussel (1947–), wife of Jean Duchesne (1944–), Professor of English at the Lycée Condorcet and editor of the French original of these memoirs.

16. Starting in 1966 a group of literature students who would soon enter the *École Normale Supérieure* indulged in amateur theology with Msgr. Maxime Charles, founder of the Centre Richelieu (the Catholic chaplaincy at the Sorbonne) and at the time exiled to the Sacré-Cœur in Montmartre. At the time they published a review, *Résurrection*, including contributions by theologians they admired, such as Bouyer, Daniélou, de Lubac, Le Guillou, Balthasar, and Ratzinger. These bright young men were: Jean-Robert Armogathe (1947–), ordained a priest in 1976 and now Professor and *Directeur de Recherches* at the prestigious *École Pratique des Hautes Études* in the "Religious Sciences" section; Rémi Brague (1947–), now Professor of Medieval and Arab philosophy at Paris I and titular professor of Christian Anthropology at Ludwig-Maximilian University in Munich (succeeding Romano Guardini and Karl Rahner); Jean Duchesne (1944–, see foregoing note); Jean-Luc Marion (1946–), Professor of Philosophy at the Sorbonne (Chair of Metaphysics) and at the University of Chicago and member of the Académie Française (succeeding to Cardinal Lustiger); Jean Congourdeau (1948–), tax inspector whose administrative expertise was a great help for *Résurrection* and, from its foundation in 1975, for the French editions of *Communio*. The four latter's wives played a great role too: Françoise Brague, Corinne Marion, Marie-José Duchesne, and Marie-Hélène Congourdeau, who is a researcher on Byzantium at the *Institut National de la Recherche Scientifique*. Along with Jean-Robert Armogathe (1947–), a priest and university professor, these

memories, and gives me a marvelous view onto the Seine riverfront from the Eiffel Tower to the heights of Meudon.[17]

These young academics, who have taken me on as counselor (a counselor who is more often heard than listened to), surround me with a friendship that is precious to me every time I come around.[18] This friendship is youthful, warm and, which doesn't spoil anything, somewhat *khanularesque*, as these graduates of the *École Normale* would say![19]

But I have to say that the greatest grace of my latter years is the affection of a family and its three children: two sisters and their slightly older cousin. They have adopted me as grandfather *honoris causa*, since their own male ancestors inopportunely left this life just as they entered it.

four couples became friends starting in 1967 at the Parisian church called Sacré-Cœur de Montmartre in *Résurrection*, a student organization. They published a review by the same name whose sponsor was Msgr. Maxime Charles (1908–1993), who in 1945 had founded the Richelieu Center as the Catholic chaplaincy of the Sorbonne. Msgr. Charles encouraged them to respond to the urging of some theologians he had introduced to them (Bouyer, Daniélou [see 141, n. 62], von Balthasar [227, n. 113], and de Lubac [see 185, n. 8]) to found the French edition of *Communio*, a federation of journals originally founded in 1972 by Joseph Ratzinger (see 215, n. 49), de Lubac, von Balthasar, and others; active contributors included Tomislav Janko Sagi-Bunić (see 228, n. 118) and future cardinals Karl Lehmann (1936–) and Angelo Scola (1941–). Bouyer had taken part in *Résurrection* meetings in Paris and welcomed and presided over such meetings at La Lucerne (see 198–99). These helped form other churchmen in their younger years, among whom were future Cardinals Christoph Schönborn (1945–) and Philippe Barbarin (1950–, current Archbishop of Lyon and Primate of the Gauls), Jean-Pierre Batut (1954–, currently auxiliary bishop in Lyon), Fr. Michel Gitton (1945–, founder of the apostolic community Aïn Karem), Fr. Jacques Benoist (1946–), Friar Nicolas-Jean Séd, OP (former director of the Éditions du Cerf), and many others too numerous to mention. All consider themselves to be in Bouyer's debt. Bouyer, however, declined the invitation to join the editorial board of *Communio* in any formal capacity because of the time his "dogmatic trilogies" (see 202, n. 80) demanded and because of the enmity he had incurred in the Church of France with his *Decomposition of Catholicism* (see 235, n. 24). Bouyer was a regular contributor from the start for the following fifteen years, which is as long as he was able to write.

17. Bouyer's studio was on the seventh floor facing east and enabled him to see, from left to right on the left bank of the Seine, the top of the Eiffel Tower, the tall modern buildings on the riverfront, and the slopes of Meudon.

18. The four couples mentioned above were all neighbors at 28 and 30 Rue d'Auteuil, the building belonging to Marie-José Duchesne's parents. Thanks are due to Jean Duchesne for kindly providing the details on the group.

19. The untranslatable *khanularesque* is a play on the words *canular*, meaning a prank or a hoax (here simply humor), and the term *khâgneux*, which describes students preparing the entrance examination for the *École Normale Supérieure* (see 113, n. 51). This group would often spend its evenings discussing graphic novels such as *The Adventures of Tintin*, which everybody, including Bouyer, enjoyed reading.

And so here I am: I who spent so much time taking care either of teen-agers or youngsters of the male sex now find myself at the end of my life brought back to what had been my first beginnings: a markedly feminine environment. I need only dwell on what these three little women, whom I am not the only one to find extraordinary, have given me in these years that are to me the dusk and to them the dawn. The novel *Les Hespérides*, by a certain Prospero Catella,[20] has said just about all that I might say about it. I shall simply add that the girl who is called Miranda in it, now aged twenty-four, has just got engaged, closely following in the footsteps of Oriana, three years her junior. As for the Sibyl, she has just reached eighteen years of age and I cannot yet say what she will make of herself. One can, however, count on her precocious shrewdness not to lose her way.[21]

I hold them inseparably in an equal affection, each one with her own gifts as the novel has not failed to point out. Nevertheless, I have to say that I owe Oriana a singular illumination of my old age. Not only is she interested in all that interests me, but, as different as this exquisitely beautiful youth may be from me, if I ever had had a granddaughter by heredity, I could not have found in her such a similarity of likes and dis-likes and more generally of reactions to things, to persons, to life, as I have found in this surprising little wisp of a woman. I usually express this by saying that though I love the other two for their qualities, I love this one just as much for her flaws—for the very reason that they are mine, too! I hasten to add that in her case, a mother's care, something I was too soon deprived of, has more or less managed to bring out some qualities: that consolation is beyond hope in my case!

On this topic I shall say that if the religious vocation, or simply a priestly vocation, may legitimize or even demand giving up marriage and conjugal love, in the final analysis it can only be to associate us lim-itlessly to the divine paternity.

My long experience has taught me, however, that it is not always espe-cially with those who are most to our liking that this paternity turns out to be fruitful and lasting. Yet, the far better understanding of male psy-chology that women have as compared to men seems to help to correct, without seeming to, the well-intentioned blunders that are not so easily avoided or overcome between men: which boils down to saying that

20. Prospero Catella (a.k.a. Louis Bouyer), *Les Hespérides* (Paris: SOS, 1985).

21. Because Bouyer did not lift the veil of privacy from the pseudonyms "Miranda," "Oriana," and "the Sibyl," in these Memoirs, which he intended to be published eventu-ally, the editors have opted not to reveal these young ladies' identities. Since "the Sibyl" was born in 1972, Bouyer finished his Memoirs in 1990.

women end up behaving in a far more maternal than filial fashion with men who are (or think they are!) their fathers or grandfathers—and quite effectively too! I once wrote about Saint Jerome and the young Paula whose education he took pride in having more or less perfected. I said that it was rather she who had done him the favor, and I confess that I did not suspect that such a thing would happen to me![22] As long as I am on the topic of feminine affections or friendships that have unexpectedly given light to my last days, I ought at least to bring up the monastery of Notre Dame de Fidélité, in Jouques in the foothills of the Alps halfway between Aix-en-Provence and Manosque.[23] By the greatest of coincidences, the first time I went there on the advice of Dom Gontard[24] I noticed that its abbess was none other than the aunt of my Hesperides! This abbey seems, in fact, to be the liveliest offshoot of the Benedictines of the rue Monsieur where, after many others, I discovered Gregorian chant. It is the nuns of Jouques, however, who in my humble opinion are more faithful to it in the youthful freshness of their cantillation than those Venerable Dames whose vocal liquescences, having once brought such a hardboiled sort as Huysmans to the brink of fainting,[25] dissolved the more soluble Du Bos into streams of his own tears.[26]

They have successfully combined their *labor improbus*,[27] which supports them up in their aerie where they climb up onto tractors after the Divine Office, with an uncommon quality of intellectual culture. This has kept them from falling into that overly ecstatic style. On the other

22. St. Jerome (see 80, n. 98) oversaw the religious instruction of young Paula; he founded a convent in Bethlehem with her mother Eustochium and her grandmother, also called Paula, in the late 380s. Bouyer's words on St. Jerome are worth quoting, as they shed light on Bouyer himself: "The truth seems to be that this intractable and fantastic old man [Jerome] was to find in this little wisp of womanhood someone to complete his own education." See *A History of Christian Spirituality*, vol. 1, *The Spirituality Of the New Testament and the Fathers*, trans. Mary Ryan (New York: Seabury, 1963), 466.

23. This abbey of Benedictine nuns was founded in 1967 by nuns issuing from the Saint-Louis-du-Temple Abbey (see 65, n. 37). It became an independent priory in 1970 and was elevated to the rank of Abbey in 1981. For its liturgy it returned to the pre-conciliar form as soon as possible (1984), in conformity with Pope John Paul II's Letter *Quattuor abhinc annos*, though it remains open to the celebration of the ordinary form.

24. Dom Gabriel Gontard was then Abbot of Saint-Wandrille at the time; see 71, n. 59.

25. Joris-Karl Huysmans (see 53, n. 26) describes his reaction to the chant sung by the Benedictine nuns of the rue Monsieur in *En Route*, trans. C. Kegan Paul (New York, E.P. Dutton, 1920), 137–40.

26. For Charles du Bos, see 81, n. 106.

27. The phrase refers to farm work. It is from Virgil (see 80, n. 98), *Georgic* I, 145–46: *labor omnia vicit / improbus* ("toil conquered all, / Remorseless toil" in J.B. Greenough's translation).

hand, the jubilant health of their ascetic discipline—as well as of their mysticism—has earned them recruits not only from all over France but also from the world over. For many years now, I have been returning to their mountainous solitude, which reminds me of Ávila, both for Christmas and around Assumptiontide.[28] It was no surprise to me when my dear Oriana, in order to make a friend brought up without religion decide to prepare herself for baptism, found nothing better than simply to bring her up to spend a few days with her in that elevated place that is as solitary as its air is divine! Of course, since she hides her best deeds as well as others do their failings, the naughty girl hadn't informed me of this and I had to find out by chance!

Now back from that Provençal and feminine cloister, I am in my Norman and masculine abbey where I usually live when I am not on the Pacific Rim. I shall say that finding myself here at the end of the race renews the sympathy I had for Paul VI. He, too, was perpetually more attracted to the Benedictine tradition than to any other, but was also kept in the secular clergy by a spiritual director (who happened to be an Oratorian: Father, later Cardinal, Bevilacqua,[29] whom I knew well, too, and admired). One of the last times we were comparing our curiously parallel trajectories, as different as they may be, he told me with the mischievousness I have already mentioned twice[30] (but on which, in my opinion, one could not insist enough): "When all is said and done, the two of us are just failed Benedictines!"

I was the more fortunate one. I have some chance of ending things in this monastic cell where I already am, while he had to abandon all hope of reaching the end in the cell he had reserved for himself at Monte Cassino.[31]

And since I am again speaking of this figure who has been so little understood, I wish to reveal two little things that concern me personally. The depth of his humanity, his exquisite delicacy, come out in them. This is all the more the case that, in each instance, I was unable to profit from them, if that word can be used.

28. The Benedictine nuns of Joucques keep a very good memory of Fr. Bouyer, who started going there in 1975.

29. Giulio Bevilacqua (1881–1965), ordained a priest of the Oratory in 1908. Paul VI elevated him to the purple in 1965.

30. Bouyer mentions Paul VI's mischievousness in connection with the removal of Archbishop Bugnini to Tehran (see 230, nn. 130–32) and his proposal to make Bouyer a bishop (see 235).

31. Monte Cassino is a hill between Rome and Naples in Italy on top of which St. Benedict of Nursia (c. 480–543/547) founded an abbey that became the cradle of the Benedictine order.

The year that Paul VI died,[32] he had invited me to spend a few weeks'
vacation with him at Castel Gandolfo.[33] I declined the honor and the
pleasure he wished to give me: at the time I was overburdened with
occupations and, I confess especially, some of the recent episcopal nominations in France seemed deplorable to me.[34] I feared that a conversation between us on that theme, which would be difficult to avoid, might
become rather unpleasant to say the least. If I had not got out of it, I
would have had the heartbreak, and the consolation, of seeing him die
before my very eyes.

This brings me to conclude these remarks, which if they are not from
beyond the grave are at least on my tomb's edge,[35] with what can no
longer be an indiscretion.

At the most critical point of the post-conciliar period, he had wanted
to make me one of his closest collaborators by elevating me, as one says,
to the cardinalate. He gave up, realizing the uproar such a nomination
would have produced at the French conference of bishops, at least
among its president's entourage at the time.[36]

When I think of poor Daniélou, who did receive that honor (and
what a crushing responsibility!), of the death he was sent to, of the vile

32. Paul VI died on 6 August 1978.

33. Castel Gandolfo is the summer residence of the Popes. It overlooks Lake Albano,
to the southeast of Rome.

34. Here are the episcopal nominations in France for Paul VI's last years: André
Quélen, Coadjutor of Moulins (17 September 1974, succeeded 2 December 1975); Michel
Marie Saudreau, Bishop of Le Havre (22 September 1974); Robert Sarrabère, Coadjutor
of Aire and Dax (7 November 1974); Jean Cuminal, Auxiliary Bishop of Besançon (2 Jan-
uary 1975); Pierre Chagué, Bishop of Gap (18 January 1975); Jean Rémond, Auxiliary
Bishop of the Mission de France (6 May 1975); Gilbert-Antoine Duchêne, Bishop of
Saint-Claude (10 June 1975); Paul Bertrand, Auxiliary Bishop of Lyon (-Vienne) (12 June
1975); Louis Boffet, Coadjutor of Montpellier (21 June 1975); Lucien Daloz, Bishop of
Langres (5 August 1975, consecrated 19 October); Jacques de Saint-Blanquat, Bishop of
Montauban (5 August 1975, consecrated 5 October); Eugène-Marie Ernoult, Coadjutor
of Sens (9 September 1975); Maurice Delorme, Auxiliary of Lyon (2 October 1975);
Jacques Delaporte, Auxiliary of Nancy (22 June 1976); Georges Gilson, Auxiliary of Paris
(13 July 1976); Jean Romary, Auxiliary Bishop-Elect of Paris (13 July 1976); Guy Der-
oubaix, Co-adjutor of Saint-Denis (2 October 1976, consecrated 21 November); Pierre
Kervennic, Bishop of Saint-Brieuc (2 October 1976, consecrated 28 November); Charles
Brand, Auxiliary of Strasbourg (18 November 1976); Maurice-Adolphe Gaidon, Auxil-
iary of Autun (20 May 1977); Jacques Fihey, Auxiliary of Marseilles (31 May 1977);
François-Marie-Christian Favreau, Coadjutor of La Rochelle (7 October 1977); François
Bussini, Auxiliary of Grenoble (12 December 1977).

35. Bouyer here alludes to Chateaubriand's *Mémoires d'outre-tombe,* "Memoirs from
Beyond the Grave," written in 1849–1850.

36. The president of the French conference of bishops at the time was Archbishop
François Marty (see 209, n. 10), president 1969–1975.

calumnies that even his own people employed in an attempt to smear him![37] When I think, too, of the revelation that Cardinal Villot (himself likewise ignobly calumniated)[38] made to me the day before he died, telling me what I had avoided, far from having any regrets I have felt only relief, perhaps selfishly, in my own case. This was accompanied with profound sympathy and also a total absence of resentment for the poor man whose superiors alone had compelled him to attack me and who himself, I am quite sure of it, did so only *perinde ac cadaver*![39]

Even more than such a fate as his, I have happily avoided responsibilities and a lifestyle to which I was not suited. This has kept me free to produce the work, whether it is good or mediocre, of which I was capable by leaving me to the kind of private life of which La Fontaine had said: "A happy life is a hidden life!"—the very La Fontaine who was only ever a novice in the Oratory (at Juilly, no less!), but one can see what must have attracted him to it.[40]

37. Daniélou (see 141, n. 62) died on 20 May 1974 while bringing to a former prostitute funds to pay her jailed husband's lawyer. The cardinal had a heart attack after dashing up to her floor and died on the staircase landing. Seizing on this circumstance, a sensationalist weekly, the *Canard enchaîné*, printed the worst possible interpretation of his death, and his confreres' first official clarifications were not clear enough to dispel this wrong impression.

38. Jean-Marie Villot (1905–1979), named Cardinal in 1965, Archbishop of Lyons 1965–1967, Prefect of the Congregation for the Council 1967–1969, Vatican Secretary of State 1969–1979. He was accused of poisoning John Paul I in such publications as David Yallop, *In God's Name: An Investigation into the Murder of Pope John Paul I* (New York: Bantam, 1984).

39. See chapter 11 above for these attacks. The phrase *perinde ac cadaver*, "like a lifeless body," drawn from the Jesuit constitutions, describes the total obedience owed to one's superior. Indeed Daniélou's own attitude towards Bouyer until then had been quite different. In a letter dated 16 February 1946, he saw Bouyer as an ally in the renewal of Christian thought against the scholastic mode; see Fouilloux, *La Collection "Sources chrétiennes,"* 177, n. 1. Bouyer came to the Jesuits' assistance during their wrangling with the Toulouse Dominicans in his article "Le Renouveau des études patristiques," *La Vie intellectuelle* 15.2 (1947): 6–15. Daniélou, in a letter dated 29 March 1956, was delighted by Bouyer's recent article denouncing Catholic exegetes who were presenting a réchauffé of fifty-year old Protestant theories, "Où en est le mouvement biblique?" *Bible et vie chrétienne* 13 (1956): 7–21; see E. Fouilloux, *Une Église*, 227, n. 75.

40. Actually this sentence, "Pour vivre heureux vivons cachés!," is from the next best fabulist after La Fontaine: Jean-Pierre Claris de Florian (1755–1794). The poem from which Bouyer quotes is *"Le Grillon,"* "The Cricket," in which the cricket initially envies the butterfly, but ends up satisfied with his own lot when he sees "the winged insect [who] shone with the brightest colors" cut to pieces by guileless children who clumsily sought to catch it to have a closer look at it.

Index of Names

(Only names mentioned in Bouyer's text, not the notes, are indexed)

About the Author

LOUIS BOUYER (1913–2004) was born to a Parisian Protestant family on the eve of the First World War. A brilliant intellect, he was ordained as a Lutheran pastor at 23. His reflections on the Church and the liturgy led to his conversion to Catholicism in 1939; he was ordained a priest for the Oratory of France on the Feast of the Annunciation in 1944. He then devoted his life to meditating, teaching on three continents, and writing on the major themes of Christian theology: the Trinity, the Church, spirituality, scripture, etc.; his works have had an enduring impact on Catholic theology to this day. He also participated in the liturgical and ecumenical movements with an enthusiasm that turned into disappointment at the direction both movements soon took. His work and reputation led to his appointment to the preparatory phase of Vatican II as well as to the Consilium for the reform of the liturgical books of the Roman rite, where he collaborated in composing Eucharistic Prayer II.

His literary tastes and talent (he wrote four novels anonymously) allowed him to form deep and lasting friendships with such writers as J.R.R. Tolkien and others, while his clear and courageous theological mind earned him the friendship of Joseph Ratzinger (Benedict XVI), Cardinal Heenan, and Paul VI—who wished to make Bouyer a bishop and later a cardinal.

In retirement he lived in the Benedictine monastery of Saint Wandrille and would spend the feasts of the Assumption and Christmas among the Benedictine nuns in Jouques. He died in 2004, at the age of 89.

About the Translator

JOHN PEPINO holds a doctorate in Greek and Latin from the Catholic University of America and teaches at Our Lady of Guadalupe Seminary in Denton, Nebraska. His interest in continuity and transformation in the life of the Church led him to study Louis Bouyer's analyses of twentieth-century Catholicism, including these *Memoirs*.

Made in the USA
San Bernardino, CA
28 August 2015